Health, medicine and society

Taking as its point of departure recent developments in health and social theory, *Health, Medicine and Society* brings together twenty eminent, international scholars to debate the key issues at the turn of the century.

Contributors draw upon a range of contemporary theories, both modernist and postmodernist, in order to illustrate these issues and provide a fresh critical analysis. The four main themes of the book are health and social structure, the contested nature of the body, the salience of consumption and risk, and the challenge of emotions both inside and outside the formal health care arena.

Health, Medicine and Society provides a 'state-of-the-art' assessment of health-related issues at the millennium and a cogent set of arguments for the centrality of health to contemporary social theory. Written in a clear, accessible style it will be ideal reading for students and researchers in medical sociology, health studies, public health, medicine and nursing.

Simon J. Williams is Senior Lecturer in Sociology at the University of Warwick; **Jonathan Gabe** is Senior Research Fellow at Royal Holloway, University of London; **Michael Calnan** is Professor of Sociology of Health Studies, University of Kent.

The book contains contributions from Ellen Annandale, Mildred Blaxter, Michael Bury, Helen Busby, Michael Calnan, Simon Carter, Judith Clark, Robert Crawford, Nick Crossley, Nick Fox, Jonathan Gabe, Graham Hart, Deborah Lupton, Emily Martin, Virginia Olesen, Lindsay Prior, Alan Prout, Chris Smaje, Deborah Lynn Steinberg, Gareth Williams, and Simon Williams.

LIBRARY
EDUCATION CENTRE
ROYAL ALEXANDRA HOSPITAL
CORSEBAR ROAD
PAISLEY PA2 9PN

Health, medicine and society

Key theories, future agendas

Edited by Simon J. Williams,
Jonathan Gabe and Michael Calnan

London and New York

UNIVERSITY OF
PAISLEY LIBRARY

306.461
WIL

First published 2000 by Routledge
11 New Fetter Lane, London EC4P 4EE

Simultaneously published in the USA and Canada
by Routledge
29 West 35th Street, New York, NY 10001

Routledge is an imprint of the Taylor & Francis Group

© 2000 Edited by Simon J. Williams, Jonathan Gabe and Michael Calnan

Typeset in Times by Florence Production, Stoodleigh, Devon.
Printed and bound in Great Britain by TJ International Ltd, Padstow, Cornwall

All rights reserved. No part of this book may be reprinted or
reproduced or utilised in any form or by any electronic, mechanical,
or other means, now known or hereafter invented, including
photocopying and recording, or in any information storage or retrieval
system, without permission in writing from the publishers.

British Library Cataloguing in Publication Data
A catalogue record for this book is available from the British Library

Library of Congress Cataloging in Publication Data
Health, medicine, and society: key theories, future agendas / edited by
Simon J. Williams, Jonathan Gabe, and Michael Calnan.
    p. cm.
  Includes bibliographical references and index.
  ISBN 0-415-22135-8 – ISBN 0-415-22136-6
  1. Social medicine. 2. Health—Social aspects. I. Williams, Simon J.
(Simon Johnson), 1961– II. Gabe, Jonathan. III. Calnan, Michael

RA418.H393 2000
306.4′61—dc21   99-045375

ISBN 0-415-22135-8 (hbk)
ISBN 0-415-22136-6 (pbk)

In memory of Winsome Gabe who died while this book was being prepared

Contents

List of Contributors

Ellen Annandale is a Senior Lecturer in Sociology at the University of Leicester. She has been involved in research on issues of gender, health and inequalities for a number of years, and has published widely in these areas, including *The Sociology of Health and Medicine* (Polity Press, 1998), a forthcoming book *Feminist Theory and the Sociology of Health and Illness* (Routledge) and a co-edited volume (with Kate Hunt) *Gender Inequalities in Health* (Open University Press).

Mildred Blaxter is Honorary Professor of Sociology in the School of Health Policy and Practice, University of East Anglia, and Senior Editor of the Journal *Social Science and Medicine*. She has published widely in the fields of inequality in health and lay attitudes to health.

Michael Bury is Professor of Sociology and Head of the Department of Social and Political Science, at Royal Holloway, University of London. His research interests cover social dimensions of chronic illness and disability, ageing, and cultural dimensions of health and medical treatment. He has published widely in all of these fields. His latest book *Health and Illness in a Changing Society* was published by Routledge in 1997. Currently he teaches on the M.Sc. in Medical Sociology at Royal Holloway and is co-editor of the journal *Sociology of Health and Illness*.

Helen Busby is an anthropologist. She is currently a Research Fellow at the National Primary Care R & D Centre at Salford University. In addition to her current work about musculoskeletal disorders and primary care, her research interests include the relationship between paid work and illness; the place of labour in contemporary sociological theory; and the social and policy responses to health needs.

Michael Calnan is Professor of the Sociology of Health Studies and Director of the Centre for Health Services Studies (CHSS) at the University of Kent. His current research interests focus on the sociology of dentistry and general practice, and the sociology of comparative health care systems.

Simon Carter is a Research Fellow at the MRC Social and Public Health Sciences Unit, University of Glasgow, where he has been studying the ways in which risk and danger are understood. He is currently examining lay and expert understandings of the biomedical sciences.

Judith Clark teaches in the Department of Sociology, University of Warwick, with a long-standing involvement in the development of the MA Sociological Research in Health Care. Her research interests include the sociology of human reproduction, women's health and literature, and recently the division of labour in medicine and nursing.

Robert Crawford is on faculty at the University of Washington, Tacoma, USA, where he teaches an interdisciplinary arts and science programme. In 1996, he received the University's Distinguished Teaching Award. He has written in the area of health, culture and ideology since the late 1970s.

Nick Crossley is a lecturer in sociology at the University of Manchester. He has published two books, *The Politics of Subjectivity: between Foucault and Merleau-Ponty* (Averbury, 1994) and *Intersubjectivity: the Fabric of Social Becoming* (Sage, 1997), in addition to a number of papers. He is currently working on an ESRC funded project concerning social movements in mental health in postwar Britain, and a book on 'embodied sociology'.

Nick Fox is Senior Lecturer in Sociology at the University of Sheffield, and is author of *The Social Meaning of Surgery* (Open University Press, 1992), *Postmodernism, Sociology and Health* (Open University Press, 1993) and *Beyond Health* (Free Association Books, 1999). His research interests include postmodern social theory, perceptions of care and the use of the Internet in education.

Jonathan Gabe is Senior Research Fellow in the Department of Social and Political Science at Royal Holloway, University of London. He has published widely in the areas of mental health, health care professions, health policy, the mass media and health and health risks. He is the editor or author of a number of books, including Sociological Perspectives on the New Genetics (edited with Peter Conrad), (Basil Blackwell, 1999). He is co-editor of the journal *Sociology of Health and Illness*.

Graham Hart is a Professor and Associate Director of the MRC Social and Public Health Sciences Unit at the University of Glasgow. He heads the Unit's programme of research on sexual and reproductive health, and has published widely on sexual and drug related risk behaviour. He is joint editor of *AIDS Care* (Carfax), co-editor of *The Social Aspects of AIDS* series (Taylor and Francis) and General Editor of the book series *Health, Risk and Society* (UCL Press).

Deborah Lupton is Professor of Sociology and Cultural Studies and Associate Director of the Centre for Cultural Risk Research at Charles Sturt University, Bathurst, Australia. Her recent books include *Food, the Body and the Self* (Sage, 1996), *The New Public Health: Health and the Self in the Age of Risk* (with A. Petersen, Sage, 1996), *Television, AIDS and Risk: a Cultural Studies Approach to Health Communication* (with J. Tulloch, Sage, 1997), *Constructing Fatherhood: Discourses and Experiences* (with L. Barclay, Sage, 1997) and *The Emotional Self* (Sage, 1998).

Emily Martin is Professor of Anthropology at Princeton University. Her research over the years has led her in many different directions, including the shaping of medical language through gender stereotypes, and the interplay between scientific and popular conceptions of the immune system. These studies yielded two major books, *The Woman in the Body: a Cultural Analysis of Reproduction* (Beacon Press, 1987) – which won the Eileen Basker Memorial Prize of the Society for Medical Anthropology – and *Flexible Bodies: Tracking Immunity in American Culture from the Days of Polio to the Age of AIDS* (Beacon Press, 1994). Her present work is on theories of normalisation and the evolving constitution of self-hood in contemporary society.

Virginia Olesen, Professor Emerita of Sociology at the University of California, San Francisco, teaches feminism and qualitative research and seminars on the body and emotions. She is co-author with S. Ruzek and A. Clarke of *Women's Health: Complexities and Differences*, (Ohio State University Press, 1997), and with A. Clarke of *Re/Visioning Women's Health: Perspectives from Science Studies, Cultural Studies and Feminist Theory*, (Routledge, 1998). She continues to pursue her interests in emotions in rationalising health care contexts.

Lindsay Prior holds a joint Cardiff University/University of Wales College of Medicine post as Research Director for a Health and Risk programme. His previous published work has focused on the sociology of death and the sociology of mental illness.

Alan Prout is Director of the ESRC Children 5–16 Programme and Professor of Sociology at the University of Stirling. He previously held posts at the Universities of Hull, Keele and Cambridge. He has worked on interdisciplinary research projects concerning children's health beliefs, parenthood education, children and medicine use and childhood asthma. A sociologist of childhood, he is co-author of *Theorizing Childhood* (Polity Press, 1998) and co-editor of *Constructing and Reconstructing Childhood* published as a second, revised edition, by Falmer Press in 1997. He is currently editing a book *Childhood and the Body* for Macmillan.

Chris Smaje is a lecturer in the Department of Sociology at the University of Surrey. He has published widely on issues relating to the health and health care of minority ethnic groups, including a book – *Health, Race and Ethnicity: Making Sense of the Evidence* (King's Fund, 1995). He has also written on sociological theories of race and ethnicity, and is currently working on issues in the historical sociology of race and colonialism, the topic of a forthcoming book *Natural Hierarchies: The Historical Sociology of Race and Caste* (Blackwell, 2000).

Deborah Lynn Steinberg is a senior lecturer teaching feminist and cultural theory at Warwick University. She has written widely on the topics of science, popular culture, narrative and embodiment. Recent publications include: *Bodies in Glass: Genetics, Eugenics, Embryo Ethics* (Manchester University Press, 1997) and *Border Patrols: Policing the Boundaries of Heterosexuality* (Cassell, 1997), co-edited with Debbie Epstein and Richard Johnson.

Gareth Williams is Professorial Fellow in the School of Social Sciences, Cardiff University. He has published widely in academic and professional journals, and is co-author of: *Markets and Networks: Contracting in Community Health Services* (Open University Press, 1996), and *Understanding Rheumatoid Arthritis* (Routledge, 1996). He is currently one of the principal researchers on an ESRC-funded study of health inequalities.

Simon J. Williams is a Senior Lecturer/Warwick Research Fellow in the Department of Sociology, University of Warwick, and co-Director of the new Centre for Research in Health, Medicine and Society. He has published widely in the fields of chronic illness and disability, class, health and lifestyles, health promotion, and the lay evaluation of modern medicine. His current research interests centre on the relationship between social theory and the sociology of health and illness, with particular reference to issues of emotions, embodiment and the need to re-think the 'biological' in non-reductionist terms. Recent books include *Modern Medicine: Lay Perspectives and Experiences* (with M. Calnan, UCL Press, 1996), *Emotions in Social Life: Critical Themes and Contemporary Issues* (with G. Bendelow, Routledge, 1998), The Lived Body: Sociological Themes, Embodied Issues (with G. Bendelow, Routledge, 1998), *Emotions and Social Theory* (Sage), and a forthcoming text, *Medicine, Emotions and the Body* (Sage).

Introduction – Health, medicine and society: Key theories, future agendas

Simon J. Williams, Jonathan Gabe and Michael Calnan

What is the relationship between sociological theory and medical sociology? How are we to theorise recent developments in health, medicine and society? And what does this tell us about the nature of the sociological enterprise and the future development of medical sociology at the turn of the century? These are some of the issues which this volume seeks to address.

Debates as to the nature and status of medical sociology have been an abiding theme since its inception. It is not, however, our intention to rehearse them again here.[1] Suffice it to say that the charge of an atheoretical, policy-driven discipline, in-the-service-of medicine, has now been largely dispensed with. Ideas about health and illness, as Gerhardt (1989) notes, have played a central role in the development of general sociological theory since the Second World War, including issues of order and control, 'deviance' and 'normality'.[2] Contemporary work encompasses a variety of perspectives, from phenomenology to constructionism, and despite various 'border skirmishes' and 'internal disputes' (Strong 1979; Bury 1986), the sociology of health and illness remains a flourishing sub-discipline, both theoretically and empirically.[3]

Not only is qualitative sociological research – formerly the 'poor relation' of social epidemiology – increasingly valued in medical circles (Green 1998; Blaxter 1996; Pope and Mays 1995; Black 1994), but debates as to the relevance of theory itself, including the advent of so-called 'narrative based medicine' (Greenhalgh and Hurwitz 1998), are now appearing in such hallowed places as the *British Medical Journal* (Alderson 1998). Tensions nonetheless remain, not simply concerning this eclectic theoretical base, but also regarding various funding crises, institutional dilemmas and the push towards more evaluative health service research (HSR), including 'evidence based' medicine and 'quality assurance' initiatives. Should medical sociologists, given these pressures, remain true to their trade, both theoretically and empirically (i.e. the autonomous, 'outsider' solution); or should they 'toil' instead under the banner of public health, HSR or some other such title in the hope of promoting 'change from within' (i.e. the 'pragmatic', insider solution)? These, to be sure, are familiar concerns, including the dilemma of 'sociological imperialism' itself (Strong 1979). We are all, moreover, given the vicissitudes of funding and institutional constraints, called upon to be 'double-agents' at times. What has changed, however, both inside and outside the academy, are the reflexive parameters within which these and other debates are currently taking place: a dynamism in which the 'limits' of expertise, whatever its source, are increasingly exposed.

A key question here concerns whether or not we are living in a post-modern society? For some theorists the modern project – linked as it is to processes of rationality, discipline and control – is all but over (Lyotard 1984; Baudrillard 1988). Modernist notions of causality, identity, the subject and truth should, it is claimed, be abandoned in favour of a more destabilised, desedimented position which celebrates indeterminacy, contingency and flux: a postmodern carnival in which surface substitutes for depth, time dissipates into a series of ephemeral presents, the subject becomes de-centred and reality itself becomes 'hyper-real'.

Others, however, dismiss these claims as rash and hasty, preferring instead to reconsider the nature of modernity itself. Giddens (1990, 1991), for example, sees reflexivity as a constant (i.e. chronic) feature in the history of modernity; a trend which he claims has been exacerbated in contemporary Western society through the disembedding mechanisms of globalisation and the internally referential nature of contemporary social life. Seen in these terms, we are not living in a postmodern era, but one in which the consequences of modernity are only now becoming fully realised (see also Habermas 1992; Gellner 1992). Despite tying itself to the 'certainties' of science and rationality, modernity has always been an ambivalent, ambiguous order, involving both liberty and discipline (Wagner 1994), certainty and doubt, the Apollonian (i.e. control) and the Dionysian (i.e. chaos) (Rojek 1994). The Renaissance and the Enlighten-ment, as Durkheim reminds us, were both periods of excessive anomie, the latter involving both science and irrationality, higher rights and brutal oppression, cosmopolitanism and nationalism. Seen from this angle, the Enlightenment 'project', like the civilising process, has a certain 'counter-feit' quality or feel to it; one which displays an 'irrational passion for dispassionate rationality' and a betrayal – from witch-hunts, colonialism and slavery to the Holocaust and beyond – of its bloody roots and barbaric foundations (Mestrovic 1993, 1997).

In a similar vein, Bauman has suggested that postmodernity, properly interpreted, is really 'modernity looking at itself at a distance rather than from inside, making a full inventory of its gains and issues, psycho-analysing itself' (1991: 272). (See also Berman 1982 and Touraine 1995). Taken together, these critiques, alongside the emergence of critical realism as a dominant new force and promising alternative in contemporary social theory (Archer *et al.* 1998; Bhaskar 1989a, 1989b), suggest that the notion of 'postmodernity' is highly problematic, thereby encouraging the alternative view, endorsed by many contributors to this particular volume, that 'contemporary social changes are best understood as *the increased dominance of certain aspects of modernity over others*, rather than as indicators of a radical break with modernity as such' (Mellor and Shilling 1997: 188). To the extent that so-called 'postmodern' perspectives have shaken the foundations of rational thought, destabilised seemingly ossified conceptual forms, and opened up new (ethical) questions and ways of being and caring for each other, they are to be welcomed. To see this as the 'death of modernity' however, to say the very least, is premature.[4] Rather, processes of rationality, including ongoing advances in science and technology and a resurgence of biological explanations (Benton 1991), continue to hold sway over large tracts of society, at one and the same time as new forms of sociality, emotionality and communality begin to emerge (Maffesoli 1995, 1996).

It is within this context that the rationale for the present volume is located, the central aim of which is to address explicitly the relationship between mainstream sociological theory and medical sociology in the light of a number of key issues within the field of health at the turn of the century. Whilst, as we have argued, medical sociology has never been an atheoretical discipline, it nonetheless remains the case, particularly in the current economic and political climate with its emphasis on evaluation and cost-effectiveness, that bridges between mainstream theory and the sociology of health and illness need to be continually built if an instructive and *mutually informing dialogue* is to occur. Four key themes, we suggest, are central here both to current mainstream theorising and contemporary research within the sociology of health and illness. *Re-thinking of social structure*, the first of these, raises a series of issues, from debates over the future of class, to the blurring of traditional categories and distinctions concerning gender, 'race' and 'ageing' in the late/postmodern era. The *body*, our second theme, is also becoming increasingly 'contested' and 'uncertain' at the turn of the century, both inside and outside the academy. What sense are we to make of these corporeal developments, and in what ways do the embodied dilemmas of health and medicine help clarify the issues at stake? *Consumption and risk*, our third key theme, mesh closely with these arguments, from the 'rituals' of health promotion in the 'epidemiological clinic' of late modernity (Bunton and Burrows 1995), to the commodification of health care in the 'marketised' state. *Emotions* are equally central here, partly through this upsurge of interest in the body, consumption and risk, and partly through the broader debates, postmodern or otherwise, they engender concerning the project of rationality itself. How should we see emotions in this context, and what role do they play in the health arena? These and other issues, as we shall see, are as central to health as they are to mainstream theory. The lines of influence, in other words – from the sick role to the clinical gaze and beyond – flow both ways. Medical sociology, in short, for the first time in its history perhaps, may become a 'leading edge' of contemporary social theory (Turner 1992). It is to a fuller exposition of these themes, and the chapters which follow, that we now turn.

Rethinking social structure and health

Within medical sociology the debate about the relationship between social structure and health has focused, at least until recently, on the inverse relationship between social class position, health status and longevity – the so-called 'inequality in health' debate. Social class position, in this respect, has tended to be conceptualised 'atheoretically', measured as it is through occupational class. Much of this research has been empirical in nature (mainly from a social epidemiological perspective), including the identification and description of more or less 'patterned' statistical relationships between indicators of occupational class, indicators of ill health and mortality and factors that might mediate between the two.

A central issue here has been the extent to which the relationship between occupational social class and ill health can be explained by social selection or by structural (material) factors. The catalyst for this debate was the Black Report of 1980. As MacIntyre (1997) points out in her review of developments since the report's publication, the debate has tended to become polarised, confusing what she sees as the 'hard' and 'soft' versions of the four different explanations proposed: artefact, natural/social selection, cultural/behavioural and materialist/structuralist. The Black Report accepted the hard version of a materialist/structuralist explanation (i.e. material, physical conditions of life associated with the class structure are the complete explanation for class gradients in health), but rejected the explanatory power of hard versions of the other three. It did not, however, reject the soft versions of these three explanations, and there now appears to be some consensus that these explanations are not necessarily alternatives. As MacIntyre states:

> The 'selection versus causation', 'artefact versus real differences' and 'behaviour versus material circumstances' distinctions can thus be seen to be politically and conceptually important but are becoming false antitheses if treated as being mutually exclusive: the same applies to new distinctions, such as those between material and psychosocial factors, and between early life and adult life influences on inequalities.
> (1997: 740)

One of the newer (and perhaps more sociological) explanations that MacIntyre refers to is that proposed by Wilkinson (1996). He argues

that it is income inequality rather than low income which is the key determinant of poor health, in that relative income is more important than
absolute income in rich, developed countries. For Wilkinson income
inequalities influence national mortality rates primarily by determining the
strength of impact of relative deprivation on health. Narrowing health
inequalities give rise to faster improvements in national mortality rates.
Thus a nation's health reflects the way resources are distributed and not
simply the existence of different levels of income between socio-economic
groups. Relative differences in income are said to undermine social cohesion in different societies by increasing the stress of the disadvantaged
and damaging their self-esteem. Thus emphasis is placed on the role of
psychosocial factors rather than the physical effects of poverty (see Chapter
15 by Williams).

However, this overall approach has been criticised, at least from a sociological point of view, as being atheoretical and divorced from mainstream
sociological debates about class. As Mildred Blaxter points out in Chapter
1, not only have critics focused on the sociological limitations of the oper-
ationalisation of the concepts of social class and health used in these
debates, they have also pointed out the neglect of broader questions about
changes in the meaning of class and in the significance of occupation,
suggesting that the notion of occupational social class depicted in these
debates is now outmoded.

Medical sociology, Blaxter suggests, has responded positively to such
criticisms, taking cognisance of contemporary debates about class and
responding creatively to them. The key explanatory concept for Blaxter is
time (social, calendar and personal). Her analysis begins by showing how
current debates about the concept of class manifest themselves in medical
sociological research. She shows, for example, how new sociological forms
of occupational classification have begun to be used to explore class as an
explanatory (as opposed to a descriptive) factor in health. This has manifested itself in research exploring the relations between social structure and
health and the way resources associated with different social positions
enable differential management and control of risks to health and ontological insecurity. The approach builds on the work of Beck (1992) who claims
that we are no longer primarily divided by access to wealth, but by our
relative vulnerability to risk. This argument is illustrated by research on
stress, control and the social distribution of risk which is found in studies
examining job insecurity, unemployment and health.

For Blaxter, however, time is the key to explaining the relationship
between the development of social capital over an individual's lifecourse
(or even in the generation before) and the link with health. A distinction
is drawn here between social time, calendar time and personal time; the
latter being of central relevance to *biography*. Individuals have their own
definitions of biotemporal orderliness which provide structure to life and

death. For example, one of the features for those living in deprivation is that time accelerates the perceived ageing process and makes those in such circumstances feel they are deprived of time. More importantly Blaxter suggests that the process of individualisation which has undermined hierarchial models of social class stratification has led to biographies tending to be private and ahistorical, with people no longer being aware of their parents' life circumstances.

In these and many other ways, Blaxter moves these class related debates on, both theoretically and empirically, relating the 'private' realm of personal troubles, *qua* biography, to broader 'public' issues of social structure and temporality, itself the defining hallmark of the 'sociological imagination (Mills 1959). Moreover, it also suggests some promising new linkages between traditional concerns within the sociology of chronic illness centred on notions of 'biographical disruption' (Bury 1982) and ongoing inequalities and life-events research.

Social class also features in Ellen Annandale and Judith Clark's chapter on gender, postmodernism and health. They consider the changing nature of class and gender and argue that the contemporary debate about class allows for the conceptualisation of gender as part of and integrated within the restructuring of the 'economic base' of society. However, they claim that the effects of the mutuality of class and gender have been neglected by mainstream medical sociology.

Drawing on Ebert's (1996) 'resistance' postmodern feminism, they analyse contemporary relationships between gender and health focusing specifically on health-related behaviours. They note that postmodern feminists reject the grounding of 'modernist' feminism in terms of a difference between men and women and agree with Ebert 'that the fragmentation of gender is a "reality" of late twentieth century society, itself thrown up by the metamorphosis of capital'.

Annandale and Clark then go on to explore these ideas in the context of gender, health and illness, taking health related behaviour, and more specifically tobacco consumption, to illustrate their analytical approach. They argue that changes in health related behaviour have accompanied the 'loosening of gender prescriptions' and that products that were once marketed as 'male' activities are now also marketed at women and vice versa. The authors argue that gender and health related practices reflect both the 'opening up' of gender, in terms of marketing fitness products, and the maintenance of gender differences, but in reverse form, as illustrated by patterns of cigarette smoking. Anorexia nervosa is also used to illustrate the point that the 'dual demands' of gender (i.e. the dual demands of 'female domesticity' and 'male mastery' that are placed on women) affect women more than men.

Turning to race and health, Chris Smaje, in his chapter on the way medical sociology has engaged with sociological arguments about race and ethnicity, suggests that while the latter's influence is evident in medical sociology there is a tension between these two fields. On the one hand medical sociology has examined aspects of the health of groups in the population defined according to some notion of their race or ethnicity. In doing so, it has produced a diverse and intriguing body of empirical findings. On the other, medical sociology has used sociological arguments to criticise the basis upon which categories like race and ethnicity have come to be defined. Smaje, however, is critical of what he sees as a negative critique of racial categories and argues that it is both necessary and possible to theorise race in such a way that it is neither a secondary extension of some other analytical category, or constructed as a 'natural' fact.

Smaje's theoretical perspective on race and health draws on the writings of Bourdieu and, in particular, his 'theory of practice' and the concepts of 'habitus' and 'capital'. Smaje sets out a research programme in two areas: the racial patterning of health status, and health service use by people from racialised minority groups. For example, he suggests that Bourdieu's approach to the genesis of social groups and their embodied practices might provide a useful basis for understanding evidence of a relationship between the structure and organisation of a community and health. He also draws on Bourdieu's approach to capital (social/cultural) to explain the 'over-utilisation' of GP services but relatively low use of hospital outpatient services by several racialised minority groups. In doing so, he suggests that the ability to mobilise the social capital required to conduct a consultation with 'apparent' competence may vary according to racialised identity.

In the final chapter in this part (Chapter 4) Michael Bury focuses on health and ageing. Like Blaxter, he emphasises the importance of locating sociological analysis in the context of the concept of the 'lifecourse'. His analysis focuses on two main contemporary perspectives, one of which identifies a more 'optimistic' approach and the other a more traditional 'negative' or pessimistic approach to ageing.

The 'optimistic' approach draws on Laslett's (1989) 'Theory of the Third Age' and 'postmodern' forms of sociological writing on ageing. The basic idea is that ill health and disability will be prevalent over a shorter period (the fourth one) in later life, thus allowing for a more positive and successful form of ageing to occur. The shifting position of the elderly is in part due to the changing meaning of work and the increasing importance of consumerism and leisure. Also age related boundaries have become more permeable and modes of behaviour and experience are less tied to chronological stages of a 'lifecycle'.

In parallel with this 'celebratory' perspective on ageing is a more pessimistic perspective which emphasises inequalities around the lifecourse and particularly the impact of maternal deprivation and the consequences of dependency. For example, Bury notes that there is an increasing body of evidence suggesting that disadvantages in early life shape experiences in later life. In conclusion, Bury suggests that these two perspectives have tended to operate in isolation. He argues for a more integrated perspective which requires a closer and more realistic understanding of problem oriented research by the 'optimists' and a greater recognition of social discontinuity and change among the 'pessimists'.

The body

Recent years have witnessed a veritable explosion of body-centred sociological discourse. Indeed, currently the body is both everywhere and nowhere: an elusive victim of its own success (Williams and Bendelow 1998). Fortunately, however, this deafening chorus of cries to 'bring the body back in' is now being replaced by a new, more critical call; one which seeks to 'question' the body, re-open debates about the role of biology, and move towards a more 'integrative' phase of social theorising. Here the emphasis is not simply on re-reading old sociological themes in a new corporeal light, but on mapping out new ways of thinking and research agendas which challenge previous dualistic positions; positions which have sought to divorce mind from body, biology from society and reason from emotion. To this, we may add the growing body of empirical research on the body in everyday life, research which is providing a much needed counterweight to the predominantly theoretical nature of these corporeal debates to date (Nettleton and Watson 1998).

The body, as Frank (1991a) suggests, is 'constituted', sociologically speaking, at the intersection of an equilateral triangle composed of institutions, discourses and corporeality (i.e. the flesh as an 'obdurate fact'). From this perspective, bodies are the foundation of both discourse and institutions as well as being their products. Discourses, in other words, are embodied, and social institutions cannot be understood apart from the real, lived experiences and actions of bodies; including the embodied actions of sociological practitioners themselves. What is required, therefore, is not so much a sociology *of* the body as an *embodied* sociology (Williams and Bendelow 1998): a position which mirrors recent debates over a sociology of postmodernity versus a postmodern sociology (Bauman 1992). The basis of social theory must, in short, be the body's consciousness of itself (Frank 1991a: 91). Only on this basis can theory put the mind back in the body, the body back in society and society back in the body (Williams and Bendelow 1998).

Certainly, the sociology of health and illness – dealing as it does with issues of pain and sickness, disability and death – provides a fertile terrain upon which to fashion some of these evolving debates on human embodiment, including the need to work at the 'interface' between materialism and constructionism, experience and representation, culture and the flesh.

Indeed, underlying questions of human embodiment constitute what is perhaps one of *the* core problematics of medical sociology: the contingencies of the flesh and the search for meaning and identity in an ambivalent, health-conscious, age.

These issues are taken up in Chapter 5 by Alan Prout. He adopts Turner's (1992) analytical distinction between foundationalist and anti-foundationalist accounts of the body – i.e. the body as founded *beyond* or *within* the social – to illustrate these different positions with examples drawn from the literature on childhood. Shilling's (1993) notion of the body as a biologically and socially 'unfinished' entity is seen as a useful way forward in this respect, but one which overemphasises children's passivity in social life and underemphasises their specificity as social actors. What is missing here, as Prout rightly argues, is a sense of childhood as a *being* as well as a *becoming*; childhood as staged and children as active, creative performers. Within this formulation the possibility arises that childhood itself is created through, perhaps even requires, certain kinds of bodily performance; performances which themselves exhibit difference at the level of bodily conduct. More generally, it suggests that bodies, as resource and constraint, both shape and are shaped, at one and the same time, by social relations.

These issues are taken further by Prout through his advocacy of the sociology of *translation* as an alternative framework for discussing children's bodies. Such an approach not only draws into play bodies as a constituent of sociality conceived in heterogeneous terms, but also the part played by artefacts, those other materialised hybrids of nature and culture. Seen in these terms, childhoods and bodies, like all other phenomena, are constituted not only from human minds and their interactions; not only from human bodies and their interactions; but also through an 'unending mutually constituting set of interactions of a vast array of material and non-material resources'. The upshot of these arguments is clear. Attention to childhoods and children's bodies serves as a litmus paper test of the broader claims which currently circulate both in sociological discourse on the body in general, and the sociology of health and illness in particular.

In Chapter 6, Emily Martin discusses a new, emerging conception of the body in the US which, she suggests, has the potential to lead to new forms of discipline and control. From this perspective the body is seen not as a collection of mechanical parts, but as a complex, fluid, non-linear system in constant motion. As Martin notes, this has, in part, occurred through an ever increasing cultural emphasis on the body's immune system, something which is central to organising the ways in which people think about health and work, life and leisure. This new, ever changing body, exists in a delicate relationship to its environment, including late capitalist imperatives for a flexible, post-Fordist workforce. For Martin, this cultural shift signifies the emergence of a new post-Darwinian conception of 'fitness' in which some will 'survive' and others will 'perish'. Such flex-ibility, on closer inspection, turns out to be both highly constrained and morally suspect.

If immunological discourse is one site in which bodies are (rapidly) being transformed in contemporary Western society, then the new genetics is another. In Chapter 7, Deborah Lynn Steinberg takes up these issues through the cultural analysis of a selection of 'genetics advocacy' literature located within the wider genre of 'high culture', popular science. Taking as her point of departure Sontag's (1978) early work on illness as metaphor, together with other more recent writings on scientific narratives and narra-tive theory more generally, Steinberg examines three texts, all of which, in their different ways, make a case for a widening practice of 'recombi-nant genetics' (i.e. genetic engineering). In the first, Stephanie Yanchinski's (1985) *Setting Genes to Work*, Steinberg identifies what she terms a 'liber-tarian, free market, individual utopian' discourse in which capitalist metaphors and narratives dominate the text. In contrast, Steve Jones and Borin Van Loon's (1993) *Genetics for Beginners* presents what might be termed an 'imperialist liberal utopia' characterised by colonial metaphors and narratives. Finally, in Philip Kitcher's (1996) text, *The Lives to Come*, a quintessentially 'American social conscience, liberal utopia' of genetics is presented; one involving narratives of quests and journeys of the Bunyan variety. Within this latter discourse, Kitcher, at one and the same time, locates science within/disaggregates it from social hierarchy and practice. For Steinberg, it is this narrative frame of reference which makes it possible for 'dystopian' dimensions of the new genetics revolution to be acknowl-edged, embattled and ultimately 'saved'.

Discussion of genetics and the human genome project, in turn raises a broader set of issues about the biological and social constitution of so-called 'disabled' bodies. As Williams and Busby note in Chapter 8, disability has become a 'hotly contested' issue in recent years. Indeed, the language of disability itself has become the object of political analysis and dispute. Finding terms to describe chronic illness and disability in an 'innocent way' therefore becomes increasingly difficult. On the one hand, it is argued – both inside and outside the disability movement – that too close a focus on impairment deflects attention from the systematic way in which the environment excludes people from participation in civil society (i.e. disability as 'social oppression'). On the other hand, focusing too closely on subjective experience is said to lead the investigator into a 'bottomless pit' of phenomenological analysis where the structures which underpin or destroy identities and the disabling barriers which deny access and participation in society are lost sight of.

The question therefore becomes how impairment can be 'brought back in' without re-entering the embrace of biomedicine? More generally, it concerns how we are to reconcile the 'politics of exclusion' with the real effects of different impairments and the complex, 'negotiated' aspects of everyday life. It is with these thorny questions in mind that Williams and Busby's chapter proceeds. In many ways, as they note, disability is fundamentally a 'representational' problem: there is no 'untainted' language within which adequately to discuss it. The language and categories we use influence both its definition and measurement, and there is a continuing dispute as to who are the legitimate representatives of the experience and reality of disability in contemporary Western society. Whilst some may find this situation itself 'disabling', Williams and Busby stress instead that it is still possible to be politically committed without being sociologically one-dimensional. They also suggest that a multi-dimensional understanding of disability is required if ways are to be found of making disability less oppressive for people with many different bodies, experiences and circumstances.

Moving from disability to death, Lindsay Prior, in the final chapter (Chapter 9) of Part 2, offers a series of reflections on the 'mortal' body in late modernity. In doing so, he draws a useful distinction between the *sociology of mortality* as an examination of structures, patterns and causes of death in populations, and the *sociology of death* as an examination of the meanings and experiences of death for individuals. Prior then proceeds to explore more fully the calculability and predictability of death in the modern world, including the sequestration and deconstruction of death itself (i.e. the privatisation of death and the reduction of death to its diseases). Central issues here concern the 'risks' of dying, risks for collectivities and for individuals alike. This, in turn, enables Prior to conclude with a broader set of reflections on the relationship between death, risk and the everyday world, including narratives of disaster and consumer oriented death in late/postmodernity. Again we glimpse, through this insightful chapter, how arguments within the sociology of health and illness mesh, more or less closely, with ongoing debates, corporeally focused or otherwise, within mainstream theory itself.

Risk and consumption

Sociologists have come relatively late to issues of risk and consumption. As regards risk, they only really started to make a mark during the 1980s, by focusing on environmental risks such as hazardous nuclear waste, landfill sites or the use of herbicides, the differing risk assessments of regulatory authorities and public distrust in risk experts (Jasanoff 1987; Wynne 1980, 1982, 1989). This in turn has become part and parcel of a wider analysis of the problems of calculating risk in a 'risk society' faced with ecological mega hazards (Beck 1992; Giddens 1990, 1991). From this perspective risk has become a defining feature of late modern societies as a result of these societies' growing vulnerability to major socio-technical dislocations and their ever-increasing interdependence in a global marketplace. In the face of such risks old class-based inequalities collapse to be replaced by new ones based on differences in ability to deal with insecurity and risk (Beck 1992).

It is against this background that the sociology of health and illness has started to make its own distinctive contribution. Taking as its starting point that risks are socially constructed or framed and collectively perceived, medical sociologists have concentrated on the cultural factors shaping risk perceptions of hazards to health and their management, and the role of material factors and social interests in shaping responses to health risks. Consideration has thus been given to the ways in which perception of health risks and risk behaviour are contextually dependent or socially situated and may also be influenced by social interaction, behavioural norms, habit and the distribution of power (Rhodes 1997). In addition a distinction has been drawn between risks from the environment and from an individual's lifestyle and embodied or corporeal risks. While environmental risks happen to people and lifestyle risks stem from what people do or do not do, embodied risks are located within the bodies of individuals and say something about what a person is (Kavanagh and Broom 1998).

Consumption has also only been a source of interest for sociologists in recent times (Campbell 1995). Two broad approaches have been taken (Warde 1990). The first has focused on consumption sector cleavages and the extent to which they have replaced production-based cleavages as the major fault line in social relations. Much of the work in this area has concentrated on public sector services such as housing and water and whether increasing private ownership has altered political alignments (e.g. Saunders and Harris 1990, Savage et al. 1990). In the health field such arguments have been taken up by Busfield (1990) and Calnan et al. (1993) who have considered the consequences of the increased consumption of private medicine for sectoral divisions.

The second approach has focused on the growth of a consumer culture in late modernity and the consequences of the construction of divergent lifestyles for the self (Featherstone 1991). In the health field this focus has been taken up by those interested in studying health promotion, with attention being paid to the way in which the consumption of goods and services such as alcohol, fashion, fitness, food and leisure activities contribute to an individual's body image and sense of health (Bunton and Burrows 1995; Lupton 1994).

Chapter 10 takes up some of these issues in relation to the risks associated with food consumption as they are represented and perceived, negotiated and experienced in contemporary western society. As Deborah Lupton notes, hardly a day goes by without a report in the news media either on the linking of a food substance with illness, or a claim that a particular food is protective against disease. The link between health status and food consumption is, in other words, constantly made across the commercial advertising/health promotion divide. As a consequence, food has become 'profoundly medicalised' in its association with health, illness and disease. Risks associated with food consumption also involve challenges to the self, including the maintenance of self-autonomy and control, the shape and size of the body, as well as broader issues of social group membership.

In discussing these dimensions of risk and food consumption, Lupton examines three major theoretical perspectives. In the first, 'risk society' perspective (e.g. Giddens 1991 and Beck 1992), attention is drawn to macro issues and political aspects of risk discourse, locating the major cause of current anxiety within broader concerns about the negative outcomes of modernisation and industrialisation. Concern about risk, from this perspective, is a rational (i.e. cognitive) response to individuals' perceptions of the uncertainties and growing hazards of life in late (i.e. reflexive) modernity. The 'cultural' approach, in contrast, directs attention to more latent meanings underpinning concerns about food. Exponents of this perspective (e.g. Douglas 1966/1980 and Kristeva 1982), highlight the symbolic role that food plays in passing across (i.e. 'transgressing') cultural boundaries, and the risks that are integral to this act of incorporation of 'other' into 'self'. Finally, within the third, 'civility' perspective (e.g. Elias 1978), the consumption of food is seen as being surrounded by the 'social' risks of embarrassment, shame or humiliation through 'inappropriate' (i.e. 'uncivilised') eating practices or in demonstrating to oneself and others one's lack of discipline and self-control (i.e. the 'grotesque' body).

Whilst these perspectives address the topic of food consumption and risk at differing levels of analysis, and with more or less conceptual depth, they are nonetheless, as Lupton notes, insightful in underlining that notions of risk are integral to notions of the body, selfhood and social relations. Seen in these terms, the risks associated with eating extend far beyond the biological effects of poisonous, indigestible or carcinogenic food substances. Rather, their 'danger' is founded far more on the social norms and cultural conventions associated with the need for individuals or social groups to 'maintain some sense of certainty and order, preserve self-integrity, present themselves as "civilised" and defend their bodily and symbolic boundaries against transgression'. Risk, in short, is a socio-cultural issue through and through.

The relationship between transgression, risk and taboo is also taken up and elegantly addressed by Robert Crawford in Chapter 11. Building on his previous work on the cultural contradictions of health in contemporary (American) society, Crawford considers health promotion – both popular and professional – as a 'ritual': one which opens a 'window' on the symbolic practices undertaken in its name. Health promotion, in other words, is both a professionally mediated and popular ritual which provides a symbolic repertoire for making sense of and morally managing 'matter out of place' – i.e. the contradictory demands and internalised mandates for 'control' and 'release' as they are meaningfully experienced in the current era.

Metaphorically homologous with economic experience, health promotion serves as an 'emotionally resonant' expression and commentary on the 'conflict-generating' logic of economic restructuring. Seen in these terms, health promotion can profitably be understood as a 'displacement onto the medicalised body' of the middle classes' ambivalence about discipline and pleasure; a highly stylised blend of discursive practices for managing and moralising this very ambivalence. In adopting this stance, Crawford deepens Martin's analysis of 'flexible' bodies (Chapter 6) within contemporary American society, noting how the current emphasis on balance and flexibility will not, in all likelihood, be easily achieved. Some 'matter', in short, will always remain 'out of place', for better or worse.

These issues, in turn, raise a broader series of questions, currently under debate, concerning the relationship between health and illness, transgression and taboo. Previously thought of, in Parsonian (1951) terms, as 'conformity' to the 'norm', could it be that health itself, particularly through its 'release' modality, harbours these 'deviant' qualities: attributes previously seen as the sole province of illness (Williams 1998; Frank 1991b; Pflanz and Rohde 1970)?

In the next chapter, Graham Hart and Simon Carter discuss the differing social perspectives which have been used to understand the risks associated with intravenous (IV) drug use and HIV, and the extent to which there exists a sufficiently cohesive body of literature to review present progress within these areas and inform future research. The chapter begins with an example of how a recent drug scare raises a range of issues which are important for an understanding of drug use. Having done so, Hart and Carter then proceed to develop a sociological analysis of drug culture at three interrelated levels, namely: the macro or supra-structural; the mid or meso-structural; and, finally, the micro-social level. Previously used to understand sexual risk behaviour and HIV infection, they suggest this approach can also contribute to our understanding of the relationship between drug use and risk.

From this more sociological perspective, it is the links shared by and connecting social actors, and the contexts within which actions occur, which are significant (i.e. risk as situated *between* people rather than residing within their individual cognition). Within this context, issues of pleasure associated with bodies, risk and consumption come to the fore. More generally, in contrast to previous epidemiological and (social) psychological models, the sociology of HIV risk behaviours demonstrates that broader socio-structural factors should be the *starting point* rather than end point of any adequate study of the social dynamics of risk.

In the final chapter of Part 3 (Chapter 13), Jonathan Gabe and Michael Calnan consider the relevance of sociological debates about consumption for understanding the changing experience of health care by users of the British National Health Service (NHS). Starting with the observation that sociologists have generally employed a rather loose consumerist perspective to frame their discussions, they turn to Warde's (1990) model of production/consumption cycles to see what light it can throw on the consumption of health care. The model represents a rare attempt to link production with consumption and identifies four modes of provision – market, state, household and communal – which are said to have potential consequences for social relations governing access, the manner of delivery and the experience of consumption.

Gabe and Calnan focus on market and state modes of provision as they relate to the NHS and ask whether this distinction can be sustained in the 1990s. They also assess the consequences of the changing mode of provision for the users of health care and for citizenship rights, enquiring whether users have been empowered by the changes or whether social divisions have been enhanced. These questions are addressed as they assess the impact of three changes to the structure of NHS provision during the 1980s and 1990s, namely: the implementation of the internal market, the introduction of new managerialism and the development of welfare pluralism. They suggest that Warde's model never adequately portrayed the complex nature of the production and consumption of health care in the NHS, but that since the 1980s the distinction has been harder to maintain. Indeed, they argue that it would be more accurate to describe the current mode of provision as that of the 'marketised state'. This new set of arrangements has in turn helped to an extent to undermine social rights to equity and justice while social divisions have, if anything, worsened as a result of these changes.

Emotions

In the final part of the volume, we take up the problem of emotions in social life through the lens of health. Like the body to which they are so closely tied, emotions, historically speaking, have tended to enjoy a rather 'ethereal existence', lurking in the shadows or banished to the margins of (malestream) sociological thought and practice. Certainly, it is possible to trace implicit if not explicit emotional themes in the work of classical sociological thinkers, from Marx's writings on alienation to Durkheim's discussion of collective effervescence, and from Weber's analysis of asceticism and the charismatic leader to Simmel's observations on the sociological significance of the senses and the vicissitudes of mental life in the metropolis. Nonetheless, it is really only since the 1980s that a distinct 'corpus' of work, mostly American in origin, has begun to emerge on the sociology of emotions.[5]

Emotions lie at the juncture of a number of fundamental dualisms in western thought such as mind/body, nature/culture, public/private. A major strength of the sociological study of emotion lies, therefore, in its ability to transcend many of these former dichotomous ways of thinking; divisions which serve to limit social thought and scientific investigation in unnecessary, self-perpetuating ways. Certainly many of those in the field of emotions are actively engaged with or contesting divisions such as the biological versus the social, the micro versus the macro, quantitative versus qualitative, positivism versus naturalism, managing versus accounting for emotions, prediction versus description, and so on (see, for example, Kemper 1990, and more recently, Bendelow and Williams 1998). Again, work within the sociology of health and illness is proving central to this enterprise.

Whilst debates continue to rage as to what, precisely, emotions are,[6] it is perhaps most profitable to view them as multi-faceted, embodied phenomena which are irreducible to any one domain or discourse. Emotions, in other words, are thinking, moving, feeling 'complexes' which, sociologically speaking, are relational in nature; i.e. communicative, inter-corporeal and intersubjective. This, in turn, offers us a way of moving beyond more micro-oriented sociological concerns with issues of emotional experience and expression, to broader, more macro-oriented concerns such as the commercialisation/commodification of human feeling, and the relationship between the private realm of 'personal troubles' and broader 'public issues' of social structure, conflict and control (Bendelow and Williams 1998; Mills 1959).

At first glance, the work of Habermas (1986, 1988, 1992) may seem to offer little to sociologists interested in emotions and health. In a critical reworking of the Habermasian programme, however, Nick Crossley (Chapter 14) provides us with a paradigmatic example of the insights which can be gained from a return to his *Theory of Communicative Action* (1986, 1988) and deliberations on the rationalisation of society/colonisation of the lifeworld. Taking as his point of departure a re-thinking of the very notion of reason – one which comprises mutual understandability, accountability and the possibility for critical, argumentative discourse – Crossley shows how emotions can themselves be seen as communicatively rational in this re-worked sense of the word. Having done so, he then proceeds to consider the emotion–psychiatry–order nexus from both a systems and a lifeworld perspective, charting the growth during the postwar era of the 'emotion industry' – from pharmaceutical companies to public sector psychiatry, and from psychotherapy to the booming sales of psychologically oriented self-help manuals. Not only does this enable us to question the dividing line drawn, by psychiatry and other disciplines, between 'reasonable' and 'irrational' emotions. It also allows us to cast the technology of emotions offered by the emotion industry more generally in a new Habermasian light, contrasting it with a viable alternative; namely, the rational regulation of emotion in the lifeworld. The Habermasian programme, therefore, as Crossley rightly argues, provides us with some interesting new hypotheses for future sociological work within these and related domains.

Complementing this Habermasian focus on the relationship between system and lifeworld, Simon Williams, in Chapter 15, takes up the related problem of micro–macro linkages in health through a critical analysis of the role of emotions in bridging this traditional sociological divide. Taking as his point of departure the 'epidemiological transition' and the shift from *direct* material to *indirect* psychosocial pathways to disease in the western world, Williams explores the centrality of emotions to the relationship between class, health and society. In doing so, he brings the health inequalities and the life-events literature into a new theoretical alignment through a focus on 'emotional capital' and the links this provides between 'distressful' feelings and the emotionally expressive body. Following Gerhardt (1979), a key analytical distinction is drawn here between 'psycho-neuro-immunological *adaptation*', 'psycho-social *coping*' and 'socio-political *praxis*': responses linked to different types of life-events and difficulties. These issues are then related, in the final section of Williams's chapter, to a broader set of reflections on emotions, health and 'distributive justice', and a reconsideration of the role of the 'biological' in social explanation (i.e. the need for a non-reductionist, socially 'pliable' biology and a critical realist ontology of the body).

Building on these emotional themes and micro–macro linkages, Virginia Olesen, in the next chapter (Chapter 16), considers the relationship between emotions and gender in contemporary US health care contexts. In particular, she argues that changes currently taking place within this field serve as a microcosm for the interplay between gender, emotions and rationalisation. In many other contexts too, such as the law, education, business and the church, gendered differences in emotion – interactive and being done – are crucially and obdurately embedded in the occupational and gender stratification systems, with potential for insuring stability or change.

Looking at differences in health care contexts and their relation to wider institutional change therefore provides fruitful leads as to how these changes may 'play out' differentially in other areas unrelated to health. More generally, Olesen argues, the analysis of gender, emotions and changing health care contexts integrates the sociology of health and the discipline of sociology in ways which enlarge and expand each one's theoretical possibilities. In doing so, one is able to attend to the enduring problems of a sociology of 'humane health care': one which demands that the theoretical and empirical enterprise does not founder in the 'thicket of abstractions' or 'waves of objectified data', thereby losing sight of the *interactive, affective, subjective and relational* elements in organisations.

This notion of a new, more 'humane', approach to health is also taken up and critically explored by Nick Fox in the last chapter (Chapter 17) of the volume. In addressing these issues Fox wishes to consider, in a more explicitly postmodern vein than previous chapters, what recent social theories can contribute to the understanding of human engagements in 'caring' relationships. His exploration starts, therefore, from the post-structuralist feminist position of Hélène Cixous and others, and their notion of a 'gift' relationship – as opposed to the masculine 'proper'. Unlike Maussian 'gifts' (which assume reciprocity), the 'true gift' is one which the giver is unaware of giving. This postmodern reading of gift relations, in turn, leads Fox onto an exploration of the connection with Deleuze and Guattari's (1984) ideas of 'nomadic subjectivity' (i.e. the 'becoming other' of the subject). Relating these philosophical explorations to certain concrete episodes of caring, Fox is able to engage in a series of postmodern reflec-tions on difference and diversity as a starting point for ethical and political engagement with those with whom we interact, including those for whom we care. In taking this line, Fox returns to and deepens his earlier insights concerning the pursuit of so-called 'arche-health' (i.e. a 'becoming different which is potentially emancipatory'). For Fox, the celebration of 'difference' entails the abandonment of tried and trusted formulae – any such formula would simply offer yet another new discourse on 'how to do caring'. The message, in short, is that resistance is always possible, that anything we do is potentially a 'gift', and that things can and should be different: a new ethics of existence in a supposedly pluralised, 'postmodern' world.

This, in turn, keys in to broader claims by writers such as Michel Maffesoli (1996), that we are now living at a decisive moment in the history of moder-nity: one in which the 'rationalization of the world' is being displaced if not replaced by a parallel 're-enchantment of the world' and a resurgence of more emotional forms of sociality – i.e. Durkheimian 'collective effervescence' and the rise of 'neo-tribalism', a shift captured in the move from Promethean to Dionysian values. From astrology to macrobiotic food, ecological move-ments to alternative therapies, the 'keep your distance' mentality, common to western epistemologies and social practices alike, is, Maffesoli claims, giving way to more 'participatory' modes of being: a 'fusional realm' or 'commu-nalized empathy', constituting all those forms of 'being together' which, for the past few decades, have been steadily transforming society.

Here we return to some of the debates discussed above concerning the modernity/postmodernity question. Modernity, as we have argued, is a com-plex network of *mixed possibilities* involving a constant *dialectic* between order and chaos, the subject and reason, (scientific) instrumentality and (emotional) expressivity. Seen in this light, whilst writers such as Fox and Maffesoli may be somewhat over-optimistic, they nonetheless point to the central role which health is playing, on the one hand, in the resurgence of the emotions and, on the other hand, in the re-evaluation of morality, ethics and what it is to be 'human' at the start of the new millennium. Things could indeed, as Foucault rightly suggests, 'be otherwise', and health, in all probability, is a central currency within which these potential changes and transformations are likely to be forged (Williams 1998; Frank 1991b).

Taken together, the chapters contained in this volume suggest a promising future, both theoretically and empirically, for the sociology of health and illness. To be sure, there are pressures, both inside and outside the academy, which point towards a fragmentation of the discipline and its dispersal within a variety of other fields such as epidemiology, public health and community medicine. To this we may add the weight of research funding priorities – what Turner (1992) refers to as the commercialisation or 'McDonaldization' (cf. Ritzer 1993; Smart 1999) of social science research alongside the commercialisation of medicine itself – whereby only those projects which contribute directly or indirectly to economic productivity, or the evaluation of service provision, are likely to be funded, whilst other less applied, more theory driven, types of research are starved of economic support. Whatever its future prospects, one thing remains clear; without an adequate theoretical base, the identity and disciplinary integrity of medical sociology will surely suffer. A theoretically informed defence of medical sociology is therefore both timely and necessary. The very fact that bridge building exercises of this nature are possible, and that a volume of this nature has been compiled, offers us more than a glimmer of theoretical hope for the future. The lines of influence between mainstream theory and the sociology of health and illness, in short, are mutually reinforcing: a ritual point of contact in an 'ambivalent' age?

References

Alderson, P. (1998) 'The importance of theories in health care', *British Medical Journal* 317: 1,007–10.

Annandale, E. (1998) *The Sociology of Health and Medicine: a Critical Introduction*, Cambridge: Polity Press.

Archer, M., Bhaskar, R., Collier, A., Lawson, A. and Norrie, A. (eds) (1998) *Critical Realism: Essential Readings*, London: Routledge.

Baudrillard, J. (1988) *Selected Writings* in M. Poster (ed.), Cambridge: Polity Press.

Bauman, Z. (1991) *Modernity and Ambivalence*, Cambridge: Polity Press.

—— (1992) *Intimations of Postmodernity*, London: Routledge.

Beck, U. (1992) *Risk Society: Towards a New Modernity*, London: Sage.

Bendelow, G. and Williams S. J. (eds) (1998) *Emotions in Social Life: Critical Themes and Contemporary Issues*, London: Routledge.

Benton, T. (1991) 'Biology and social science: why the return of the repressed should be given a (cautious) welcome', *Sociology* 25(1): 1–29.

Berman, M. (1982) *All That is Solid Melts into Air: the Experience of Modernity*, London: Verso.

Bhaskar, R. (1989a) *Reclaiming Reality*, London: Verso.

—— (1989b) *The Possibility of Naturalism*, Hemel Hempstead: Harvester Wheatsheaf.

Black, N. (1994) 'Why we need qualitative research', *Journal of Epidemiology and Community Health* 48: 425–6.

Blaxter, M. (1996) 'Criteria for the evaluation of qualitative research methods', *Medical Sociology News* 22: 68–71.

Bunton, R. and Burrows, R. (1995) 'Consumption and health in the "epidemiological" clinic of late modern medicine', in R. Bunton, S. Nettleton and R. Burrows (eds) *The Sociology of Health Promotion*, London: Routledge.

Bury, M. (1982) 'Chronic illness as biographical disruption', *Sociology of Health and Illness* 4: 167–82.

—— (1986) 'Social constructionism and the development of medical sociology', *Sociology of Health and Illness* 8: 137–69.

—— (1991) 'The sociology of chronic illness: a review of research and prospects', *Sociology of Health and Illness* 13(4): 451–68.

Busfield, J. (1990) 'Sectoral divisions in consumption: the case of medical care', *Sociology* 24(1): 77–98.

Calnan, M., Cant, S. and Gabe, J. (1993) *Going Private: Why People Pay for their Health Care*, Buckingham: Open University Press.

Campbell, C. (1995) 'The sociology of consumption', in D. Miller (ed.) *Acknowledging Consumption: A Review of New Studies*, London: Routledge.

Clarke, J. (1981) 'A multiple paradigm approach to the sociology of medicine, health and illness', *Sociology of Health and Illness* 3(1): 89–103.

Claus, L. (1983) 'The development of medical sociology in Europe', *Social Science and Medicine* 17(1): 591–7.

Deleuze, G. and Guattari, F. (1984) *Anti-Oedipus: Capitalism and Schizophrenia*, London: Athlone.

Denzin, N. K. (1984) *On Understanding Emotion*, San Francisco: Jossey-Bass.

Douglas, M. (1966/1980) *Purity and Danger: an Analysis of Concepts of Pollution and Taboo*, London: Routledge and Kegan Paul.

Ebert, T. (1996) *Ludic Feminism and After: Postmodernism, Desire and Labor in Late Capitalism*, Ann Arbor: University of Michigan.

Elias, N. (1978) *The History of Manners: the Civilizing Process*, volume 1, Oxford: Blackwell.

Featherstone, M. (1991) 'The body in consumer culture', in M. Featherstone, M. Hepworth and B.S. Turner (eds) *The Body: Social Processes and Cultural Theory*, London: Sage.

Fineman, S. (1993) *Emotion in Organizations*, London: Sage.

Foucault, M. (1973) *The Birth of the Clinic: an Archaeology of Medical Perception*, London: Tavistock.

—— (1977) *Discipline and Punish: the Birth of the Prison*, London: Tavistock.

Fox, N. (1993) *Postmodernism, Sociology and Health*, Milton Keynes: Open University Press.

Frank, A. W. (1991a) 'For a sociology of the body: an analytical review', in M. Featherstone, M. Hepworth and B.S. Turner (eds) *The Body: Social Process and Cultural Theory*, London: Sage.

—— (1991b) 'From sick role to health role: deconstructing Parsons', in R. Robertson and B. S. Turner (eds) *Parsons: Theorist of Modernity*, London: Sage.

Franks, D. D. and McCarthy, E. Doyle. (eds) (1989) *The Sociology of Emotions: Original Essays and Research Papers*, Greenwich, CT: JAI Press.

Gellner, E. (1992) *Reason and Culture*, Oxford: Blackwell.

Gerhardt, U. (1979) 'Coping as social action: theoretical reconstruction of the life-events approach', *Sociology of Health and Illness* 1: 195–225.

—— (1989) *Ideas About Illness: an Intellectual and Political History of Medical Sociology*, London: Macmillan.

Giddens, A. (1990) *The Consequences of Modernity*, Cambridge: Polity Press.

—— (1991) *Modernity and Self-Identity: Self and Society in the Late Modern Age*, Cambridge: Polity Press.

Gold, M. (1977) 'A crisis of identity: the case of medical sociology', *Journal of Health and Social Behaviour* 18: 160–8.

Goleman, D. (1996) *Emotional Intelligence: Why it can Matter more than IQ*, London: Bloomsbury.

Green, J. (1998) 'Commentary: grounded theory and constant comparison', *British Medical Journal* 316: 1,064–5.

Greenhalgh, T. and Hurwitz, B. (eds) (1998) *Narrative Based Medicine: Dialogue and Discourse in Clinical Practice*, London: BMJ.

Habermas, J. (1986) *Theory of Communicative Action*, Vol. I, Cambridge: Polity Press.

—— (1988) *Theory of Communicative Action*, Vol. II, Cambridge: Polity Press.

—— (1992) *Knowledge and Human Interests*, Cambridge: Polity Press.

Hochschild, A. R. (1983) *The Managed Heart: the Commercialisation of Human Feeling*, Berkeley, CA: University of California Press.

—— (with Machung, A.) (1990) *The Second Shift: Working Parents and the Revolution at Home*, London: Piatkus.

James, V. and Gabe, J. (eds) (1996) *Health and the Sociology of Emotions*, Oxford: Blackwell.

Jasanoff, S. (1987) 'Cultural aspects of risk assessment in Britain and the United States', in B.B. Johnson and V.T. Covello (eds) *The Social and Cultural Construction of Risk*, Dordrecht: Reidel Publishing Company.

Jones, S. and Van Loon, B. (1993) *Genetics for Beginners*, Cambridge: Icon Books.

Kavanagh, A. and Broom, D. (1998) 'Embodied risk: my body, myself', *Social Science and Medicine* 46(3): 437–44.

Kemper, T. (1990) *Research Agendas in the Sociology of Emotions*, New York: State University of New York Press.

Kitcher, P. (1996) *The Lives to Come: the Genetics Revolution and Human Possibilities*, Harmondsworth: Penguin.

Kristeva, J. (1982) *Powers of Horror: an Essay on Abjection*, New York: Columbia University Press.

Laslett, P. (1989) *A Fresh Map of Life: the Emergence of the Third Age*, London: Weidenfeld and Nicolson.

Lupton, D. (1994) *Medicine as Culture*, London: Sage.

Lyotard, J.-F. (1984) *The Postmodern Condition*, Manchester: Manchester University Press.

MacIntyre, S. (1997) 'The Black Report and beyond: what are the issues'? *Social Science and Medicine* 6(44): 723–46.

Maffesoli, M. (1995) *The Time of the Tribes: the Decline of Individualism*, London: Sage.

—— (1996) *Ordinary Knowledge*, Cambridge: Polity Press.

Mellor, P. and Shilling, C. (1997) *Re-forming the Body: Religion, Community and Modernity*, London: Sage.

Mestrovic, S. G. (1993) *The Barbarian Temperament*, London: Routledge.

—— (1997) *Postemotional Society*, London: Sage.

Mills, C. Wright (1959) *The Sociological Imagination*, New York: Oxford University Press.

Nettleton, S. and Watson, J. (eds) (1998) *The Body in Everyday Life*, London: Routledge.

Parsons, T. (1951) *The Social System*, London: Routledge and Kegan Paul.

Pflanz, M. and Rohde J. J. (1970) 'Illness: deviant behaviour or conformity', *Social Science and Medicine* 4: 645–53.

Pope, C. and Mays, N. (1995) 'Qualitative research: Researching the parts other methods cannot reach', *British Medical Journal* 311: 42–5.

Rhodes, T. (1997) 'Risk theory in epidemic times: sex, drugs and the organisation of risk', *Sociology of Health and Illness* 19(2): 208–27.

Ritzer, G. (1993) *The McDonaldization of Society: An Investigation into the Changing Character of Contemporary Social Life*, Thousand Oaks, CA: Pine Forge Press.

Rojek, C. (1994) *Ways of Escape: Modern Transformations in Leisure and Travel*, Lanham MD: Rowman and Littlefield.

Saunders, P. and Harris, C. (1990) 'Privatization and the consumer', *Sociology* 24(1): 57–75.

Savage, M., Watt, P. and Arber, S. (1990) 'The consumption sector debate and housing mobility', *Sociology* 24(1): 97–117.

Scambler, G. (ed.) (1987) *Sociological Theory and Medical Sociology*, London: Tavistock.

Scambler, G. and Higgs, P. (eds) (1998) *Modernity, Medicine and Health*, London: Routledge.

Shilling, C. (1993) *The Body and Social Theory*, London: Sage.

—— (1997) 'Embodiment, emotions and the sensation of society', *The Sociological Review* 45(2): 195–219.

Smart, B. (eds) (1999) *Resisting McDonaldization*, London: Sage.

Sontag, S. (1978) *Illness as Metaphor*, Harmondsworth: Penguin.

Stacey, M. and Homans, H. (1978) 'The sociology of health and illness: its present state, futures and potential for health research', *Sociology* 12: 281–307.

Straus, R. (1957) 'The nature and status of medical sociology', *American Sociological Review* 22: 200.

Strong, P. (1979) 'Sociological imperialism and the profession of medicine: a critical examination of the thesis of medical imperialism', *Social Science and Medicine* 13A: 199–215.

Touraine, A. (1995) *Critique of Modernity*, Oxford: Blackwell.

Turner, B. S. (1992) *Regulating Bodies: Essays in Medical Sociology*, London: Tavistock.

—— (1996) *The Body and Society*, 2nd edn, London: Sage.

Wagner, P. (1994) *A Sociology of Modernity: Liberty and Discipline*, London: Routledge.

Warde, A. (1990) 'Introduction to the sociology of consumption', *Sociology* 24(1): 1–4.

Wilkinson, R. (1996) *Unhealthy Societies: from Inequality to Well-being*, London: Routledge.

Williams, S. J. (1998) 'Health as moral performance: ritual, transgression and taboo', *Health* 2(4): 435–57.

Williams, S. J. and Bendelow, G. A. (1998) *The Lived Body: Sociological Themes, Embodied Issues*, London: Routledge.

Williams, S. J., Annandale, E. and Tritter, J. (1998) 'The sociology of health and illness at the turn of the century: back to the future'? *Sociological Research Online* 3. 4:1.html>

Wynne, B. (1980) 'Technology, risk and participation: on the social treatment of uncertainty', in J. Conrad (ed.) *Society, Technology and Risk*, London and New York: Academic Press.

—— (1982) *Rationality and Ritual: The Windscale Inquiry and Nuclear Decisions in Britain*, Chalfont St Giles: British Society for the History of Science.

—— (1989) 'Frameworks of rationality in risk management: towards the testing of naive sociology', in J. Brown (ed.) *Environmental Threats: Perception, Analysis and Management*, London: Bellhaven Press.

Yanchinski, S. (1985) *Setting Genes to Work: the Industrial Era of Biotechnology*, Harmondsworth: Penguin.

Part I

Rethinking social structure and health

Chapter 1

Class, time and biography

Mildred Blaxter

Social class has always been a fundamental concept in medical sociology, demonstrating its empirical value for the understanding of 'health chances' for the individual ever since the early years of this century when Stevenson constructed a classification based on father's occupation for the purpose of analysing infant mortality in England and Wales (Stevenson 1925). In the past, however, medical sociologists have been criticised for an atheoretical use of class. Registrar General's Social Class (RGSC) was undoubtedly useful. In many decades of national statistics, and in countless studies of health outcomes, experiences, behaviour and attitudes, linear trends by RGSC have been the norm. But, increasingly, not only is this time-honoured instrument beginning to falter in certain circumstances, but the processes which lie behind such a classification are coming under scrutiny.

Medical sociology, and especially the 'inequality in health' debate, have thus been criticised as being isolated from developments in wider sociology. The theme of this chapter, however, is to document how this is changing. It is argued that, currently, medical sociology is both taking note of contemporary theory of class and contributing to it.

This is occurring largely through an attempt to incorporate the concept of time. Health is a characteristic where time cannot be ignored: the sociology of health is concerned with birth and death, ageing and the lifecourse, becoming ill and getting better, moving through both personal and historical trajectories. Health is neither simply a characteristic of the individual nor an event, but their meeting as they come together in biography. Thus health is a topic which adds in a special way to both structure and action as they are conceived of in the theory of class.

The questions addressed here (and illustrated in an inevitably selected way by reference to a variety of bodies of research) are:

- in what ways has medical sociology articulated with contemporary debates about the concept of *class*?
- how is *time* being incorporated, both theoretically and empirically?
- in what ways does *biography* represent the synthesis of class and time?

The journey is in part from 'class and health' to 'biography and health'. This is a journey from an area which is stereotypically, though not invariably, quantitative, cross-sectional, static, depending on measures of health and of class which are as precise as possible, to a field of work which is probably, though not necessarily, qualitative, encompassing change and the constructed nature of both health and social structure. This journey is mapped in more detail throughout this volume.

Class

In 'inequality' studies particularly, social class has always been a key concept. For most of this century RG Social Class has played a major role in the monitoring of trends in mortality and morbidity. The principal question of recent decades has been how to explain the observed linear relationship between health and occupational class. This general pattern is seen throughout industrialised societies and across most measures of health, and remains relatively unaffected by social policies and by generally improving health and lengthening expectation of life. Specific diseases may have specific causes, but cutting across these there is a vulnerability which is clearly related to social structure. Thus the importance of 'class' remains, and RG Social Class is still commonly used in analysis on the grounds that it permits comparison with data over a long period of the past, and that it is still a useful predictor of ill health.

In the wider sociological arena, however, the way in which medical sociology has used the system has been criticised for an unclear theoretical basis, and it is argued that contemporary discussion of the meaning of class has been ignored. What Holton and Turner (1994) called the 'debate and pseudo-debate' about the 'future' of class analysis (Goldthorpe and Marshall 1992), or its 'death' (Clark and Lipset 1991), 'attenuation' (Morris and Scott 1996) and 'fragmentation' (Compton 1996), cannot be rehearsed here. In the practical empirical terms which were perhaps first seen as relevant in medical sociology, the basis of the mounting criticism of class analysis was that large and growing numbers of any population are routinely omitted from the standard classification: the retired, welfare recipients, women engaged in household duties, those who have never been employed. In particular, the use of a system designed for male occupations and lifestyles was increasingly found to be inappropriate for women.

The wider debate on class involved more than simply pointing to the problems of detail in a system which might be outmoded, however. Though changes in the social standing of particular occupations and shifts in the occupational structure have led to modifications in the Registrar General system at successive censuses, there are more fundamental criticisms. Among these is that the class structure of modern industrialised societies, and indeed the very meaning of class, have changed: this is not simply historical change in the relative positions of occupations, but fundamental changes in the significance of occupation. There have been extensive changes in the world of production, with the decline in manufacturing industry. The middle classes have not only increased in size, in both absolute and relative terms, but have also become more differentiated. There has been a shrinkage of the wage labour society, through extended education, earlier retirement, shorter hours, and the development of part-time, shared, and contract work. The boundaries between work and non-work become more fluid, with flexible forms of employment and domestic and wage labour less clearly separated. There is a shortening of the proportion of the lifespan spent in work. Rising living standards, a decline in the influence of traditional institutions, and the erosion of traditional status orders, have all been implicated in the changing meaning of class.

These practical problems of applying RG Social Class, and doubts about the continuing validity of the system, have caused increasing unease about using class as an explanatory variable in health. In the field of inequality of health, for instance, class continues, despite all the problems noted above, to be a useful descriptive variable, but it offers little to *explanation*, to the identification of the factors which cause social variation. There is no clarity about what RG Social Class actually measures, or with what accuracy. The basis is officially described as level of occupational skill, implicitly presumed to be associated with both a material, economic dimension and a status dimension. The conflation has been criticised by Weberians and Marxists alike. In fact, rather little attention has been paid by theoretical sociologists to mapping either changing rewards or shifting prestige in RG classes over time, since in the wider sociological arena it is preferred to dismiss the simple RGSC I–V altogether. It is only medical sociology which has remained to some extent tied to the system because of its use for census and mortality data.

The elaboration of class in medical sociology

Thus it is in medical sociology, particularly, that a large body of work has developed in the elaboration of RG Social Class, seeking associations and explanations for socially patterned health in terms of the possible components of class – education, income, occupation, work conditions, lifestyles. This work was, certainly at its beginning, empirically rather than theoretically driven. It does, however, feed back into the concept of class by trying to 'unpack' its dimensions.

The use of, for instance, house tenure or car ownership can be seen as an early approach to the replacement of occupational categories by consumption patterns (see e.g. Goldblatt 1990; Davey Smith *et al.* 1990). Again, recognising that income and living conditions vary widely within social class groupings, research workers have constructed indicators which combine social class with living conditions or financial difficulties (Carstairs and Morris 1989; Bartley *et al.* 1994; Power *et al.* 1996). Whilst the UK has continued to emphasise occupationally-based concepts of class, other European countries have tended to use educational qualifications either together with, or in place of, occupation (Rahkonen and Lahelma 1992; Lahelma *et al.* 1994; Kunst and Mackenbach 1994). Dahl (1994) looked at the joint effects of income, occupation, and education in Norway, concluding that in this study, as in others, occupational class remained the most consistent and important predictor of health. Other work sees class as predicting other measures, such as income or education, but something which ought to be kept separate. Townsend, for instance, has argued for the importance of keeping social class out of his area-based deprivation measure, on the grounds that to include it would confuse the measure of deprivation with its causes (Townsend *et al.* 1987).

The particular study of groups to which RG Social Class is less easily applicable has made special contributions. Various elaborated measures have been used to analyse health and class in adolescence (Macintyre and West 1991), for older people (Arber and Ginn 1991, 1993; Martelin 1994), or to test alternative classifications for women (Moser *et al.* 1988; Pugh *et al.* 1991).

The work on women can be instanced as a particular example of this. Just as, in the past, comparison of the health of men in certain occupations with that of their wives was a central tactic of classical epidemiology, so the 'new' social epidemiology is illuminated by considering the meaning of social class for women and for men. Traditionally, the individualistic approach to socio-economic variation in women's health, using married women's own occupations rather than their husband's class, produces narrower class differentials for women than for men, seeming to show that, for married women, 'own' occupation is not so clearly an indicator of the household's material position. For many years alternative ways of classifying have used a combined husband and wife class measure, or have used both the partner's occupation and own occupation separately as indicators for women's health (Britten and Heath 1983; Martikainen 1995) Arber (1997) suggests that the increase in employment rates among married women and the greater fluidity in marital status may mean that in future the individualistic approach may be favoured. In an analysis of a large sample from the British General Household Survey, she demonstrated that the usefulness of different approaches may depend on what outcome measures are being used. Women's 'limiting long-standing illness' was associated with their own labour market characteristics, whereas self-assessed health was better predicted by a range of variables including husband's class and the material conditions of the household. It was concluded that several indicators of social class, each depicting distinct aspects of socio-economic status, should be used.

Class, as a dimension, cross cuts with other social statuses. Arber (1991) pointed out that while women entered into the British debate on class differences in health somewhat belatedly, an American tradition had long been dominated by role analysis, with women's health considered primarily in terms of marital, parental and employment roles. Using, again, the General Household Survey, she demonstrates how both traditions can be reformulated and integrated. The ways in which women's roles are associated with health status is determined by material circumstances, but these cannot be captured by occupational class alone. Much other research has similarly explored the ways in which women's roles and health have to be seen within a structural context, and the interactions between employment status and other variables. Except for those with young children, exclusion from the labour market is clearly associated, for women, with poorer health.

New occupation-based classifications

Another important trend is the work which is beginning to make comparisons of different ways in which occupational class might be defined in explicitly theoretical terms, seeking not just to 'unpack' RG Social Class but to explore other systems. Occupation-based classifications used for other areas in sociology such as mobility studies have, for instance, been associated with the names of Goldthorpe and colleagues (Goldthorpe and Hope 1974). The Erikson-Goldthorpe schema, an eleven-category validated measure based on an explicit theory of occupational groupings (Erikson and Goldthorpe 1992) is currently being used for health studies. 'Classes' are distinguished in terms of such dimensions of the work setting as conditions of employment, occupational security and promotion prospects. This system has been adopted for a large international comparative study (Kunst and Mackenbach 1994) and has been used in Britain by Bartley et al. (1996a). Using a 1971 and a 1981 cohort from the OPCS Longitudinal Study, these authors found similar magnitudes of class difference to those represented by RGSC, and they comment

> It is of considerable significance that substantial and persistent differences in mortality between social groups . . . have been identified by a schema designed explicitly to group occupations with similar employment relations and with no reference to health data.
>
> (p. 467)

Another example, this time considering morbidity rather than mortality, is the analysis of Wolfarth (1997), who compared classification systems using both conventional measures of socio-economic status (education, occupational prestige) and operationalisations of what was called a neo-Marxist concept of class in terms of control of production (ownership of the means of production, control over labour and investment and control over own work). The latter classification distinguished eight classes, such as bourgeosie, decision-makers, workers, semi-autonomous employees, etc. It was suggested that socio-economic status describes a gradual, quantitative difference between strata, while these neo-Marxist classes are clear entities qualitatively different from one another. In the empirical test, which was of various measures of psychiatric morbidity in a large Israeli sample, both classifications provided predictors for morbidity, but the overlap between them was small. Each appeared to have a unique relationship to psychiatric outcome variables, with 'class' adding significantly to the prediction provided by 'socio-economic status'. The conclusion is that they are distinguishable both theoretically and empirically, and conceptualising social inequality in different ways can enhance the understanding of – in this case – psychiatric morbidity.

Elaborated and differentiated measures of class position were also used by Pierret (1993), but in this case for the study of health-related concepts and discourses rather than health outcomes. In a sample of 'residents of an old quarter of Paris', 'residents of a new city', and 'farmers from a rural commune', the traditional occupational classification proved inadequate in the search for correlates of discourses about health. A classification based on 'positions in the production system' proved more illuminating. Five groups were formed:

- small farmers
- unskilled or semiskilled workers and persons with unstable jobs
- middle-level employees in the public sector
- middle-level employees in the private sector
- school teachers.

Pierret asked 'Might discourses about health (and illness) be organised . . . on the basis of "constants" such as a person's sense of time, relations to the state, or feelings of security?' These groups did indeed provide distinct discourses. For instance, for the groups with manual occupations, bodies were tools, or instruments for work. There were, however, differences between farmers and workers: for farmers, health fitted into a relatively homogenous world view based on a cycle of life, while workers felt socially vulnerable. What distinguished the three non-manual groups was whether they were in the public or private sectors. Public employees referred to concepts of social order; those in the private sector had individualistic models. Pierret concluded: 'In France, persons' relations to the state, and in particular whether they work in the public or private sectors, seem to be as important as social origin' (p. 22).

The risk society

These new types of occupational classification begin to explore class as an explanatory factor in health, rather than simply a descriptive category. Concepts of risk, resources and social control become relevant. Risk, in the form of risk factors for disease, relative risks of mortality, or predictors of ill health, has always been one of the basic concepts of social epidemiology. After a long period when the focus appeared to be on individual risk factors, the concept of the 'risk society' (Beck 1992) is now being found particularly fruitful. In part, this is a consequence of the limitations for epidemiology of the conventional individualised approach: even in one of the best cases, for instance, when all known risk factors for coronary heart disease are considered together, they account for only about 40 per cent of the incidence of the disease (Marmot and Winkelstein 1975).

In the conventional model, risk factors tended to be defined largely in terms of behavioural characteristics, and at one time factors such as smoking were offered as the most important part of social class differentials. Without denying that of course lifestyles and behaviours are socially distributed, it is now seen as less simple: in the longitudinal study of British civil servants of different grades known as the Whitehall study, for instance, the social gradient in coronary heart disease mortality was clearly not explained away by smoking, since gradients were similar among smokers and non-smokers (Marmot 1986). There is also a strong suggestion that such behavioural factors have different significance for different social groups: in the large-scale Health and Lifestyle Surveys in England, Wales and Scotland, for instance, 'healthy' behaviour was found to be more protective against ill health in better environments and more favourably placed social groups (Blaxter 1990). Measured lung function, among those who gave up smoking, was found to improve more over seven years in non-manual men than in manual, and among those who continued to smoke was found to deteriorate to a greater extent in manual men than in non-manual (Cox et al. 1993).

If this conventional individualised risk factor approach is found to be limited, attention has to turn to the characteristics of societies which foster or correct inequalities in health. The work of Wilkinson and others feeds into this, pointing to factors relating to social organisation (Wilkinson 1994, 1996a, 1996b). Improvement or deterioration in national health is, it is suggested, not simply related to economic growth, but also to the distribution of resources within societies.

Thus attention turns back to social class, but in a new form. What are the precise pathways by which social structure affects health? How is health affected by features of the social order? Wilkinson associates the extent of material inequality with social cohesion, and its effect on psychosocial health. Other forms of explanation turn back to risk. Sooner or later, Beck (1992) suggested, in modernising societies,

> the social positions and conflicts of a 'wealth-distributing society' become joined by those of a 'risk-distributing society'; social risk positions spring up, which are not exactly class positions, but which are associated with them because the ability to deal with risk is unequally distributed in occupational and educational groups.
>
> (p. 20)

Heirarchies are self-created by internal differentiation within classes, by new forms of residential patterns and family structures:

> The reflexive conduct of life, the planning of one's own biography and social relations, gives rise to a new inequality, the inequality of dealing with insecurity and reflexivity.
>
> (p. 98)

What develops is what Beck calls 'a society of employees', defined in terms of socio-political categories, a form of 'class' which neither Marx nor Weber saw. In a current transitional stage, traditional inequalities coincide with an individualised post-class society which is no longer traditional. Inequalities do not disappear but become redefined in terms of an individualisation of social risks. In terms of health, research in medical sociology is relevant which explores the relationship between individual crisis and sickness.

The empirical work which is relevant here is that which has focused on concepts such as stress, 'sense of coherence', insecurity and lack of control. If specific occupational risks are no longer the main cause of ill health related to work, and thus provide only a small part of the explanation for differentials between occupational classes, other explanations must be sought. The possible pathways by which social situations affect health – not only in the context of work, but especially there because of the association of occupational social class with health inequality – have long been thought to be associated with psychological mechanisms to do with stress. A sense of hopelessness, depression, and a lack of sense of control, have all been associated with higher mortality rates (Berkman and Syme 1979; Alfredsson et al. 1982). In the specific context of work, Karasek and Theorell (1990) developed a two-factor model along the dimensions of demand and control. High demands in the presence of high control are not health-harming, but high demands with low control are associated, it is suggested, with increased risk. Siegrist et al. (1990) similarly have a model which takes into account personal coping and adaptation to work demands. High effort and low reward (in the form of money, esteem or security) produce a sustained distress which is a health risk. Bartley et al. (1996a) note that the clear differentials in health produced by the Erikson-Goldthorpe schema, designed and validated as a measure of employment security and control over the work situation, support the hypothesised mechanism by which the psychosocial characteristics of work affect health.

The question of control has also been particularly addressed in the Whitehall studies, where the distribution of feelings of control and decision-making responsibility have been examined in the context of inequality in health between civil service grades (Marmot et al. 1978). These longitudinal studies, beginning in the 1960s, led Marmot and colleagues to suggest that the use of conventional social class underestimated the association of social factors with mortality. Twenty years later, though a flattening of pay differences between grades suggested that health differentials might reduce, they had in fact widened for a number of measures. It was suggested that this perhaps reflected organisational change and insecurity: the lower the occupational status, the greater the frequency of reported financial problems, stressful life events, and low control and satisfaction at work (Marmot et al. 1991).

One obvious meeting place of this research on stress, control, and the social distribution of risk within the structural approach is in the fields of unemployment or work insecurity. For instance, Bartley et al. (1996b) used the National Child Development Study, the cohort of children born in 1958 and studied longitudinally, to compare men aged 23–33 with more and less secure employment histories. At 23, previous work insecurity rather than economic position was associated with poor self-rated health, independent of the relationship between class background and the risk of unemployment. Work insecurity also had an independent relationship with poor psychological health at 33. Bartley (1994), considering the observed general relationship between ill health and unemployment, suggests that – though of course selection may be operating, in that those with poorer health become unemployed – this may be an indicator of a more general insecurity. In a study of one department in the Whitehall studies, those civil servants who were facing restructuring of their employment into the private sector showed a deterioration in mental and physical health, compared with those whose departments were remaining within the civil service (Ferrie et al. 1995). In a further study, of the whole Whitehall II cohort of over 10,000, adverse changes not only in self-assessed health but also in clinical measures were associated both with anticipation of restructuring and with actual organisational change, with the possibility of selection excluded by controlling for baseline health status (Ferrie et al. 1998).

Consumption, lifestyle and class structuring

A rather different approach to the changing meaning of class is the contemporary emphasis on individualism, lifestyle and consumption: social class not in terms of life chances but as a source of social identity. Much of the work in this area is directed not simply at producing occupational classifications, but at tracing the 'real lines of social division to which life chances, cultural outlooks and household living standards can be related' (Compton 1993: p. 166). Warde (1990) identified two aspects of consumption: economic 'consumption sector cleavages', and an emphasis on social and cultural consumption. If the approaches to the understanding of class which have been described so far relate mainly to the first, there are others within medical sociology which are beginning to take up the second.

In attempts to theorise the structure/agency problem in relation to health-related behaviour, medical sociology has particularly used the work of Bourdieu, concerned with the active process of class structuring, the construction and consolidation of class position or 'habitus': habitus, formed in the context of objective conditions and social positions, generates schemes of perception which in turn produce lifestyle practices (Williams 1995). This implies the mapping of cultural or consumption patterns, rather than orthodox occupational class analysis. Health becomes an expression of the interpretation of the world, and class and health become interacting 'cultural performances'. This may best be captured by qualitative work.

An empirical example of this is the writing of Prout (1996), who demonstrated how families and households are sites for the enactment of these performances, suggesting that 'the dynamic and processual aspects of households' class trajectory may be more important in shaping the views and practices of its members around health than static notions (or measurements) of class position'. Prout demonstrates by case studies of contrasting middle-class and working-class families that though class position might determine a range of social indicators, health attitudes and behaviours were also enmeshed in different 'habituses', and the distribution of these, not straightforwardly related to class position, was explicable if household histories were taken into account:

> Instead of looking at each as statically middle or working class this involved asking: what sort of class origins did the adults have, what were their expectations for the future, what aspirations did they have for their children, what forms of capital were being transmitted to the children, and how were these expressed in the lifestyle constructed for each household?
>
> (p. 16)

Differences between the families were linked to positioning in the private or service sectors in the case of the middle class, and to the families' past, present and future anticipation of their position, their aspirations, social networks, and perceptions of their economic, physical, social and cultural capital.

Time

Though it has not been explicitly discussed, it is obvious that the question of time is already becoming relevant. One of the problems of occupational classifications at a cross-sectional level is that increasingly a current (or a 'last') occupation may not represent a lifecourse or even a life position in any real way. Such things as education, relationship to the labour market, or class 'trajectories', may be better indicators of the accumulation of social capital which can be linked to health. These relationships exist in historical time: generations following one another, social and occupational structures changing, individuals, families and groups perceiving, creating and consolidating class positions. The very meaning of class changes with time, and so also do the variables which are used to represent the phenomenon of 'health'. The mortality of past historic periods is not the same as today's, for the distribution of its causes changes. Illsley and Baker (1997) have noted how all-cause mortality rates conceal historical changes in the prevalence of different diseases, particularly those which are associated with health-related behaviours which are strongly 'mobile' within gender, or age groups, or classes. Even in one lifetime the clinical meanings and social correlates of disease are continuously changing, and these relationships at any one point of time have to be regarded as a 'historical moment', to be viewed in the context of time.

There are, of course, several different sorts of time. There is this social time, with change taking place at irregular rates in society; there is 'real' calendar or clock time, where years go by at a regular pace in the lives of individuals, child following parent and adulthood following childhood; and there is personal time, time as the individual experiences and perceives it.

Calendar time

All these sorts of time, but especially 'real' calendar time, imply longitudinal research. Here, the birth cohorts and other longitudinal data-banks, in Britain and elsewhere, have been of crucial importance. The topics have been health as cumulative within a lifetime, health-related mobility and selection into social classes, 'sleeper' effects and childhood influences on health and on health-related lifestyles, and the patterns over the lifecourse of all those components of class which affect health – material resources, occupations, risks and security and the cultural and behavioural environment. The concept is of class trajectories rather than static class positions.

One of the major thrusts towards the understanding of class has been the immense research effort devoted to intergenerational and intragenerational health. This can be no more than glanced at, but it can perhaps be argued that it began through the attempt to deal with the problems of class which have been described.

For instance, the old question of whether observed class differences in health are due simply to selective social mobility has, to a large extent, been answered. In particular, the Longitudinal Study of 1 per cent of the population of England and Wales, and the British birth cohort studies following individuals born in 1946 (the National Survey of Health and Development) and 1958 (the National Child Development Study), have been used. These have shown that though, obviously, poor health is likely to have an adverse effect on life chances and movement through the social scale, mobility seems to make only a minor contribution to class differences in mortality and ill health (see e.g. Fox *et al.* 1985; Wadsworth 1986; Power and Peckham 1990). In the National Child Development Study (Power *et al.* 1991), for instance, intergenerational mobility either up or down the social class scale when the young people entered the labour market was, at age 23, certainly found to be associated with differences in their health. However, Power *et al.* noted that mobility was not the only, nor indeed the major, influence on social class variation in health at this stage of life. At each stage of youthful life there appeared to be both direct and indirect effects of factors associated with social class. In a later analysis at the age of 33, for instance, birthweight was still related to achieved social class (Bartley *et al.* 1994). It was argued that the relationship was not necessarily causal, however, but rather that birthweight acted as a marker for circumstances later in life.

A debate about the importance of the earliest stages of life – events occurring in infancy and in the womb – has re-emerged in Britain. From the 1950s it had been shown that a woman's reproductive performance reflected her social and health history from birth, and that there was a dynamic relationship between health and the environment at birth and later (Illsley 1955). The renewed focus on the first stages of life, associated particularly with the names of Barker and colleagues, emphasises the possibility of biological programming at these early stages which has long-term consequences: contemporary social class (and geographical) variation can be explained by the social conditions experienced by the mothers of the previous generation. Events during gestation (for instance, indicated by birthweight) and in infancy (for instance, indicated by growth in the first year) have been shown to be associated with cardiovascular disease, obstructive lung disease, hypertension, and diabetes, in later life (Barker 1991, 1992, 1994). In the 1946 birth cohort, Wadsworth *et al.* have similarly shown, for instance, the association of high blood pressure at 36 with low social class of origin and with birthweight (Wadsworth 1991) through, it is suggested, specific mechanisms in the intrauterine environment. In this lifecourse perspective on health, follow-up, 'catch-up' or 'follow-back' designs of research have made particular contributions. Time has to be accommodated.

As Power *et al.* (1996) point out, an alternative to the idea of biological programming is that parental social circumstances, and their effect on outcomes such as birthweight, are simply an indicator of life chances: these processes are not mutually exclusive, but are probably additive or interactive. Wadsworth (1996) similarly suggests that though family circumstances in childhood provide the basis for health in later life, throughout life opportunities exist to augment or deplete the capital present at birth, through education, occupation and later family life. Wadsworth offers a summary of how the childhood cohorts have shown in particular detail how social capital and the associated health capital accumulate or are dispersed throughout childhood. A poor start in life, associated with poorer parental circumstances and vulnerability to illness, can be reinforced by lower levels of parental concern about education, poorer achievement, and thus lower socio-economic class and poorer health. On the other hand, the stock of health can be augmented: higher parental socio-economic status and education are associated with greater educational achievement in the child and a higher occupational status for the young adult.

The associations between social class and health are thus shown to depend strongly on time patterns: some are long-term, some short; some are 'sleeper' effects; some attenuate over the lifecourse; different mechanisms of association are salient at different parts of the lifecourse. Several studies have shown that social class differences are less marked in adolescence than they are in infancy or later adulthood for most health measures (West *et al.* 1990; Glendenning *et al.* 1992; Rahkonen and Lahelma 1992). It has been suggested that perhaps social class, as conventionally defined, is becoming less salient for young people (Chisholm *et al.* 1990).

What is certainly generally agreed, however, is that social class effects on health press most heavily in middle age. It is here that mortality rate differentials are at their widest. The depletion of health capital is most obvious at the ages when chronic or degenerative diseases are beginning to strike. In the Health and Lifestyle Surveys, there were not only clear differences by social class in the proportions of people in middle age groups who said, re-interviewed after seven years, that their health had deteriorated during this period, but there were also class differences in deterioration in some measured health characteristics such as lung function (Cox *et al.* 1993).

The sense of coherence and coping ability already discussed may be part of this accumulated capital, beginning in childhood. Lundberg (1997) using large samples of both panel and cross-sectional data from the Swedish Level of Living Surveys found that family conflict in childhood had some direct effect on sense of coherence in later life, though family size or the experience of a broken home were not so related. Childhood conditions and adult sense of coherence were, it was suggested, complementary and additive factors affecting adult health.

Questions are now being asked about the meaning of social class in older age. Arber and Ginn (1991), for instance, suggested that the health of the elderly has to be seen in terms of biography: elderly women have fewer resources and experience greater constraints than elderly men, and their health-related capital is profoundly affected by their labour market position in earlier life. Dahl and Birkelund (1997) similarly asked to what extent socio-economic conditions, as measured by social class when people were economically active, have an independent effect in post-retirement age. The social and economic conditions that elderly people experienced fifty or more years before still seem to exert an influence on current health. Work such as this is beginning to discuss the theoretical appropriateness of using occupational class, whether defined as 'last' occupation or that followed for the greater part of the lifecourse, when considering older people. No significant relationship was found between health in old age and *father's* social class, which seems to demonstrate the effect of the changing meaning of specific occupational classes over a relatively long period already discussed: class of origin is too crude a proxy, for an elderly population, for social conditions in childhood.

Socio-historical time

This is at the level of the progression through time of the individual life, or the regular replacement of the generations. Calendar time is not the same, however, as social time. As the work with the elderly suggested, generations are not only distanced differently by numbers of years, but are also cohorts which move continuously through a structure of occupations and social classes which is itself in constant flux. Historical change takes place over generations at varying rates. If a society is relatively static, it may be possible to regard the succession of age-cohorts as simply the repetition of previous generations. If the social environment is changing rapidly, each cohort has a unique history. As Frankenberg (1987) has pointed out, the concept of the lifecycle has its dangers. Life is not in fact cyclical for the individual or for society. Generations have the 'imprint of time' (Wadsworth 1991).

Class-related vulnerability may be associated with economic conditions in particular historical periods, or with changing behavioural patterns (dietary changes, smoking prevalence). Wadsworth (1996) notes that the interpretation of how social factors operate has to be undertaken in the light of these wider social factors, which condition what is possible for the individual, and so leave their mark on each generation. For instance:

> Those who live their childhood in times of sharply gender differenti- ated opportunity, as happened to the generation now in their 50s, carry the imprint of that effect in later life . . . Similarly, those who were children in times of serious economic depression carry the effects in their thinking and behaviour in later life.
>
> (p. 158)

Changing prevalence of smoking provides one example. Wadsworth (1997) notes that those who were children at the time when smoking was less common among women will have been less exposed to risk than those who were *in utero* or in infancy when smoking was at its peak, and the effects of gender differences in the time of the first popularity of smoking are seen now in gender differences in lung cancer rates. The life of those aged 50 now has seen periods of great change in smoking, as in other factors such as diet; those born into a period of high parental smoking now live in a time of much reduced smoking. One life history study (Mann *et al.* 1992) showed that the risk to health from smoking was greatest among those born into manual classes when parental smoking was very prevalent, who then became smokers. The long-term consequences of other general changes in social conditions and lifestyles, such as those concerned with diet, are equally complex: as early as 1978, for instance, Forsdahl noted the raised risk of arteriosclerotic heart disease mortality in popula- tions born into poor circumstances but shifting as adults into relative affluence.

The opportunity to establish social and health capital is affected by the social environment, both through individual attitudes and behaviour and by social (and medical) policy. There are period effects of living through epidemics. The effects of the American Depression upon parents were associated with their children's behaviour in their own marriages and employment (Elder 1974). As Wadsworth points out, the effects of change are particularly complex since it is early experiences which may affect reactions throughout life, whether behavioural, psychological or biological.

Biography

The movement from calendar time to social time thus leads eventually to personal time, to biography. It is obvious to note both that biography and health are always intertwined, and that subjective time is not the same as either calendar or socio-historical time. A real lifetime is measured subjectively in social periods – infancy, schooldays, family formation, work, retirement – rather than calendar years: periods of life which may be determined by social roles, but are particular to individuals. These temporal profiles are crucial to our perceptions and expectations: they are part of what Garfinkel called 'background expectancies'. Few people spend much time calculating the probability of the year of their death, but a lot of time is spent considering temporal regularities which are not usually defined very precisely in years. In creating and recounting their biographies, all research demonstrates that people add up periods of time which may not even be juxtaposed in calendar time: the genesis of this problem was this, then something else contributed, then this outcome followed – though the events recounted may be many years apart (Blaxter 1993). These definitions of biotemporal orderliness provide structure to life and health. To suffer physical events outside their proper time is disconcerting: to develop chronic illness in relative youth is, in Bury's (1982) terms, biographical disruption. This 'proper' time is personally and socially constructed, and is not incorporated into the sort of structural regularities represented by Standardised Mortality Ratios analysed according to RG social class. To a considerable extent, it is constructed by family and inter-generational biographies as well as personal ones.

It is a trivial and obvious truth that time goes by at different rates in different circumstances and at different ages. One of the disadvantages of troubled lives is that time accelerates. So, using the example of the women studied by Blaxter and Paterson (1982) in Scotland, for a woman who leaves school at the earliest possible moment, has children in her teens, becomes a grandmother before 40, and is widowed in her 50s, all the stages of life have become compressed. Thus these women spoke of their lives being over, of having, in their 50s, to expect the deterioration of old age. Their daughters, whose lives were following much the same pattern, spoke as if they were middle-aged: as one said, at the age of 23, 'After three children you're past it, it doesn't matter if you lose your figure.' One of the deprivations of disadvantaged lives was to be robbed of time (Blaxter 1985).

People themselves perceive health as biography. Research such as that of Williams (1993), for instance, demonstrates how they recount this, how 'in articulating the experience of illness in relation to their social milieux, individuals elaborate moral discourses based on their own biographical experiences' (p. 92). Individualistic ideology, Williams suggests, may prevent people from seeing the (class) relationships between them and society: nevertheless biographical experience and the accounts of illness which rest on it can be understood only in relation to the wider social and historical settings through which the individual has passed. Health biographies take place in, and are interpreted through, 'the situated pragmatism of everyday life'. So, in the case-history Williams uses, the 'pursuit of virtue' in terms of independence and the issues of control over life, exhibited by a sufferer from arthritis, can be seen as the product of a social biography. These socially imposed constraints are not, Williams notes, to be viewed in some unidirectional way as determined by class position, but they are certainly related to the structure of society and the individual's perception of her place within it.

Personal time is the way individuals perceive their own lives in the context of historical time, in the light of class situations of the past and class rhetorics of the present. A return to Beck (1992) and the 'risk society' is relevant: Beck suggests that the hierarchical models of social class stratification have increasingly been subverted by the process of individualisation. While patterns of class variation in such characteristics as health have in fact remained relatively stable, their perceived social meaning has changed: 'the experience of historical continuity has been disrupted' (p. 92). Beck suggests that class thus loses its subcultural basis: 'forms of perception become private and ahistorical. Children no longer know their parents' life context, much less that of their grandparents' (p. 235). Instead of being socially prescribed, biography becomes self-produced, with each person's in their own hands. What Beck calls 'the temporal horizons of perception' narrow, until everything revolves around the axis of the individual's own personal life. Thus biographies become reflexive. People choose their own different lifestyles and subcultures, and are no longer so dependent on historical class patterns. What Beck terms 'secondary agencies and institutions' (economic markets, fashion, social policy) take the place of traditional social forms.

This resonates with the idea of class discussed earlier, derived from Bourdieu, as 'performed trajectory', and of class and health as 'interpenetrating performances'. Prout (1996), for instance, showed from his contrasting family case histories, that families who were 'middle class' by occupation could differ fundamentally by a 'habitus' defined in terms of Crawford's (1984) dichotomy of health seen as control/health seen as release, and so could working-class families. Differences in health as a cultural value (and differences in health-related behaviour) could be explained by class trajectories – by family and personal histories over time – rather than simply by class positions.

This and other research shows that it is not necessarily true that family history is now unimportant in people's creation of the story of their lives. Beck's thesis that children no longer know their parents' life context may be an over-statement, or may refer to groups of people with particular biographies: that is, may actually represent part of the process of class stratification. Accounts of people talking of their health can show that intergenerational patterns seemed, at least in the 1970s and 1980s, to be important to them (Herzlich 1973; Blaxter 1983). Those whose family history was within the poorest families were still conscious of the social and health deprivations of their youth or of past generations. They might well have experienced considerable historical change. Wadsworth (1996) notes that when the members of the 1946 birth cohort were two years old, almost half lived in houses without running hot water. The stories of the childhood living conditions of the sample of middle-aged, social class IV–V Scottish women in the late 1970s were vivid and horrifying (Blaxter and Paterson 1982). Of course, these women were conscious of an improvement in social conditions: the historical perception of which Beck speaks had not disappeared.

However, there is a finding which seems at first sight to be anomalous: that it is people such as this, most exposed to structural inequalities, who are least likely – at least in the interview situation, where they are being asked to talk about the causes of health and illness – to stress social and environmental causes. The idea that there are structured class differences in health (as distinct from the obvious and specific effects of, say, damp houses or dangerous jobs) appears to be an unwelcome suggestion which poorer people may flatly deny. Of course, life chances are unfair in many ways, but health is one area of life where we are all equal. In a study by Calnan (1987) of the health-related beliefs of women in England in different social classes, a working-class woman said: 'No, I couldn't think it makes any difference myself. I mean, it's like people with money, they get the same illnesses as we get. So I shouldn't think it would make any difference whether you are skilled or unskilled' (p. 79). Statements such as this were echoed by the Scottish women, who roundly rejected any idea of class inequalities.

At the level of a large-scale survey, similar evidence emerged from the Health and Lifestyle Surveys (Cox *et al.* 1987; Blaxter 1990) when answers to open-ended questions about the causes of ill health were analysed by social class. Considering not simply answers to single questions, but replies to a large range of questions in different contexts, it was those with higher incomes, better environments, non-manual rather than manual jobs, who were more likely to mention the fact that socio-economic factors might have an influence on health. And work, as a particular element of the social environment, was more likely to be seen as a source of ill health by professional and managerial classes (largely on grounds of stress) and of *good* health by those with the unhealthiest jobs (largely on grounds of physical activity).

There is a variety of possible reasons why 'the victims blame themselves', stressing behavioural factors rather than those outside their control, including features of the research methods themselves (Blaxter 1993, 1997). However, people's perception of the course of historical time seems relevant. The Scottish women were very conscious of improvement in social conditions. They were therefore naturally reluctant to admit inequality in health *now*: everyone was healthier, partly because of what they saw as relative prosperity but even more, in their eyes, because of the advances of medicine. Children no longer died of diphtheria, mothers no longer died in childbirth. Since it was their families which, they recognised, had suffered disproportionately in the past, then surely they were less 'unequal' now. From this perspective they did not stress the necessity for change in the environment of their social group, or the lives of their children, now.

When elderly people think about – and report – economic hardship during their upbringing, do they have absolute material poverty in mind? Dahl and Birkelund (1997) asked this question, and pointed out that if this is so then future generations, less likely to experience such absolute deprivation, may react in different ways to a present generation. Health effects of childhood conditions may be perceived differently. If, however, there is an element of relative deprivation in the experience and memories of the elderly, the same long-term health effects may apply for those whose childhoods are more recently relatively deprived.

At the individual level the effects on health of the acquisition or deprivation of health capital, of relative deprivation, of lack of social integration, or low levels of perceived control over life, are beginning to be unravelled. As Wadsworth (1996) has pointed out, what is needed now is a greater emphasis on the broader societal level, and the changing effects of historical time. The processes of class-related change in the individual life intersect with broader social change, with health consequences which must always be seen as a process in time.

Conclusion

It would of course be overweening to suggest that medical sociology has offered solutions to any of the problems of contemporary class analysis. What has been described here is no more than a beginning. But what is being added, it is suggested, piece by piece, is the empirical base. Beginning with a practical problem – that those doing health surveys, or analysing health statistics, or investigating risk factors for disease, were increasingly aware of the theoretical problems of the categories they were using, but were still faced with the fact that some concept of 'social class' seemed to remain an indispensable tool – the detailed exploration which has been sketched was begun.

'Class' is elaborated rather than dismissed: in many ways the concept grows in importance, even if the old certainties of Registrar General I–V have to be relinquished. Sociologists have not, of course, been the only discipline involved: much of the work described has been done by social epidemiologists, social psychologists, and others.

The contribution of specific causal factors to health is seen as not necessarily stable over time, and influences are shown to have different relative importance at different historical periods. Successive cohorts experience them differently. All these issues represent new problems for research design and methodology, and for statistics (Dean 1993). It can be suggested that – in some crude sense – this is a synthesis of quantitative and qualitative approaches: statistical method has to take account of the real complexities of time.

The simultaneous movement through individual lives and through historical time, and the additional complication that perceptions expressed by the people who take part in research represent their personal time, mean that this is never going to be easy. However, this chapter has argued that medical sociology is currently attempting to provide some of the most precise and the most extensive evidence to contribute to theories of class. It may at last be beginning to be more truly theoretically based.

Acknowledgement

Some of the ideas which have been developed in this chapter were first explored in a Plenary Address to the British Sociological Association Medical Sociology Group Annual Conference, Edinburgh, 1992. Thanks are due to Raymond Illsley for helpful comments on an earlier draft.

References

Alfredsson, L., Karasek, R. and Theorell, T. (1982) 'Myocardial infarction risk and psychosocial work environment', *Social Science and Medicine* 16(4): 463–7.

Arber, S. (1991) 'Class, paid employment and family roles: making sense of structural disadvantage, gender and health status', *Social Science and Medicine* 32(4): 425–36.

—— (1997) 'Comparing inequalities in women's and men's health: Britain in the 1990s', *Social Science and Medicine* 44(6): 773–88.

Arber, S. and Ginn, J. (1991) *Gender and Later Life: a Sociological Analysis of Resources and Constraints*, London: Sage.

—— (1993) 'Gender and inequalities in health in later life', *Social Science and Medicine* 36(1): 33–46.

Barker, D. J. P. (1991) 'The foetal and infant origins of inequalities in health in Britain', *Journal of Public Health Medicine* 13: 64–8.

—— (1992) *The Foetal and Infant Origins of Adult Disease*, London: BMJ Publications.

—— (1994) *Mothers, Babies and Disease in Later Life*, London: BMJ Publications.

Bartley, M. (1994) 'Unemployment and health: understanding the relationship', *Journal of Epidemiology and Community Health* 48(4): 333–7.

Bartley, M., Carpenter, L., Dunnell, K. and Fitzpatrick, R. (1996a) 'Measuring inequalities in health: an analysis of mortality patterns using two social classifications', *Sociology of Health and Illness* 18(4): 455–74.

Bartley, M., Montgomery, S., Cook, D. and Wadsworth, M. (1996b) 'Health and work insecurity in young men', in D. Blane *et al.* (eds) *Health and Social Organisation*, London: Routledge, 255–71.

Bartley, M., Power, C., Blane, D. and Davey Smith, G. (1994) 'Birthweight and later socioeconomic disadvantage', *British Medical Journal* 309: 1475–8.

Beck, U. (1992) *Risk Society: Towards a New Modernity*, London: Sage.

Berkman, L. F. and Syme, S. L. (1979) 'Social networks, host resistance and mortality: a nine-year follow-up study of Alameda County residents', *American Journal of Epidemiology* 109: 186–204.

Blaxter, M. (1983) 'The causes of disease: women talking', *Social Science and Medicine* 1(2): 59–67.

—— (1985) 'Le temps qu'on leur vole', *Penelope, pour Histoire des Femmes* 13: 60–6.

—— (1990) *Health and Lifestyles*, London: Routledge.

—— (1993) 'Why do the victims blame themselves?', in A. Radley (ed.) *Worlds of Illness: Biographical and Cultural Perspectives on Health and Disease*, London: Routledge.

—— (1997) 'Whose fault is it? People's own conceptions of the reasons for health inequalities', *Social Science and Medicine* 44(6): 747–56.

Blaxter, M. and Paterson, E. (1982) *Mothers and Daughters*, London: Heinemann.

Britten, N. and Heath, A. (1983) 'Women, men and social class', in E. Gamarnikov *et al.* (eds) *Gender Class and Work*, London: Heinemann.

Bury, M. (1982) 'Chronic illness as biographical disruption', *Sociology of Health and Illness* 4: 167–82

Calnan, M. (1987) *Health and Illness: the Lay Perspective*, London: Tavistock.

Carstairs, V. and Morris, R. (1989) *Deprivation and Health in Scotland*, Aberdeen: Aberdeen University Press.

Chisholm, L., Buchner, P., Kruger, H. and Brown, P. (eds) (1990) *Childhood, Youth and Social Change: a Comparative Perspective*, London: Falmer Press.

Clark, T. N. and Lipset, S. M. (1991) 'Are social classes dying?', *International Sociology* 6: 397–410.

Compton, R. (1993) *Class and Stratification*, Cambridge: Polity Press.

—— (1996) 'The fragmentation of class analysis', *British Journal of Sociology* 47: 56.

Cox, B. D., Blaxter, M., Buckle, A. L. J., Fenner, F., Golding, J. F., Gore, M., Huppert, F. A., Nickson, J., Roth, Sir M., Wadsworth, M. E. J. and Whichelow, M. (1987) *The Health and Lifestyle Survey*, Cambridge: The Health Promotion Research Trust.

Cox, D. B., Huppert, F. A. and Whichelow, M. J. (1993) *The Health and Lifestyle Survey: Seven Years On*, Aldershot: Dartmouth.

Crawford, R. (1984) 'A cultural account of health: control, release and the social body', in J. B. McKinlay (ed.) *Issues in the Political Economy of Health Care*, New York: Tavistock, 60–103.

Dahl, E. (1994) 'Social inequality in health: the significance of occupational status, education and income: results from a Norwegian survey', *Sociology of Health and Illness* 16: 664–7.

Dahl, E. and Birkelund, G. E. (1997) 'Health inequalities in later life in a social democratic welfare state', *Social Science and Medicine*, 44(6): 871–82.

Davey Smith, G., Shipley, M. J. and Rose, G. (1990) 'The magnitude and causes of socio-economic differentials in mortality: further evidence from the Whitehall study', *Journal of Epidemiology and Community Health* 44: 265–70.

Dean, K. (1993) (ed.) *Population Health Research: Linking Theory and Methods*. London: Sage.

Elder, G. H. (1974) *Children of the Great Depression*, Chicago: Chicago University Press.

Erikson, R. and Goldthorpe, J. H. (1992) *The Constant Flux*, Oxford: Oxford University Press.

Ferrie, J. E., Shipley, M. J., Marmot, M. G., Stansfield, S. and Davey Smith, G. (1995) 'Health effects of anticipation of job change and non-employment: longitudinal data from the Whitehall II study', *British Medical Journal* 311: 1,264–9.

Ferrie, J. E., Shipley, M. J., Marmot, M., Stansfield, S. and Davey Smith, G. (1998) 'The health effects of major organisational change and job insecurity', *Social Science and Medicine* 46(2): 243–54.

Forsdahl, A. (1978) 'Living conditions in childhood and subsequent development of risk factors for arterio-sclerotic heart disease', *Journal of Epidemiology and Community Health* 32: 34.

Fox, A. J., Goldblatt, P. O. and Jones, D. R. (1985) 'Social class mortality differentials: artefact, selection or life circumstances?', *Journal of Epidemiology and Community Health* 39: 1–8.

Frankenberg, R. (1987) 'Lifestyle trajectory or pilgrimage? A social production approach to Marxism, metaphor and mortality', in A. Bryman *et al.* (eds) *Rethinking the Lifecycle*, London: Macmillan.

Glendenning, A., Love, J., Hendry, L. B. and Shucksmith, J. (1992) 'Adolescence and health inequalities', *Social Science and Medicine* 35: 679–87.

Goldblatt, P. (1990) 'Mortality and alternative social classifications', in P. Goldblatt (ed.) *Longitudinal Study: Mortality and Social Organisation*, London: HMSO, 163–92.

Goldthorpe, J. H. and Hope, K. (1974) *The Social Grading of Occupations*, Oxford: Clarendon Press.

Goldthorpe, J. H. and Marshall, G. (1992) 'The promising future of class analysis', *Sociology* 26(3): 381–400.

Herzlich, C. (1973) *Health and Illness*, London: Academic Press.

Holton, R. and Turner, B. (1994) 'The debate and pseudo-debate in class analysis', *Sociology* 28(3): 799–804.

Illsley, R. (1955) 'Social class selection and class differences in relation to still-births and infant deaths', *British Medical Journal* 2: 1,520–4.

Illsley, R. and Baker, D. (1997) *Inequalities in Health: Adapting the Theory to Fit the Facts*, Bath Social Policy Papers, no. 26, Bath University.

Karasek, R. and Theorell, T. (1990) *Healthy Work: Stress, Productivity and the Reconstruction of Working Life*, New York: Basic Books.

Kunst, A. E. and Mackenbach, J. P. (1994) 'International variations in the size of mortality differences associated with occupational status', *International Journal of Epidemiology* 23: 742–50.

Kunst, A. E. and Mackenbach, J. P. (1994) *Measuring Socioeconomic Inequalities in Health*, Copenhagen: WHO Europe.

Lahelma, E., Manderbacka, K., Rahkonen, O. and Karisto, A. (1994) 'Comparison of inequality in health: evidence from national surveys in Finland, Norway and Sweden', *Social Science and Medicine* 38: 517–24.

Lundberg, O. (1997) 'Childhood conditions, sense of coherence, social class and adult health: exploring their theoretical and empirical relations', *Social Science and Medicine* 44(6): 821–32.

Machenbach, J. P. and Kunst, A. E. (1996) 'Measuring the magnitude of socioeconomic inequalities in health: an overview of available measures illustrated
with two examples from Europe', *Social Science and Medicine* 44(6): 757–72.

Macintyre, S. and West, P. (1991) 'Lack of class variation in health at adolescence: an artefact of an occupational measure of social class', *Social Science
and Medicine* 32: 395–402.

Mann, S. L., Wadsworth, E. J. and Colley, J. R. T. (1992) 'Accumulation of
factors influencing respiratory illness in members of a national birth cohort
and their offspring', *Journal of Epidemiology and Community Health* 46:
286–92.

Manor, O., Matthews, S. and Power, C. (1997) 'Comparing measures of health
and inequality', *Social Science and Medicine* 45(5): 76–7.

Marmot, M. G. (1986) 'Social inequalities in morbidity: the social environment',
in R. G. Wilkinson (ed.) *Class and Health: Research and Longitudinal Data*,
London: Tavistock, 21–33.

Marmot, M. and Feeney, A. (1996) 'Work and health: implications for individuals and society', in D. Blanc *et al.* (eds) *Health and Social Organisation*,
London: Routledge, 235–54.

Marmot, M. G. and Winkelstein, W. (1975) 'Epidemiologic observations on intervention trials for prevention of CHD', *American Journal of Epidemiology* 101:
177–81.

Marmot, M. G., Davey Smith, G., Stansfield, S., Patel, C., North, F., Head, J.,
White, I., Brunner, E. and Feeney, A. (1991) 'Health inequalities among British
Civil Servants: the Whitehall II study', *Lancet* 337: 1,387 93.

Marmot, M. G., Rose, G., Shipley, M. J. and Hamilton, P. J. S. (1978)
'Employment grade and coronary heart disease in British Civil Servants',
Journal of Epidemiology and Community Health 32: 244–9.

Martelin, T. (1994) 'Mortality by indicators of socioeconomic status among the
Finnish elderly', *Social Science and Medicine* 38: 1,257–78.

Martikainen, P. (1995) 'Women's and men's socioeconomic differentials according
to own and spouse's characteristics in Finland', *Sociology of Health and Illness*
17: 353–75.

Montgomery, S. M., Bartley, M. J., Cook, D. G. and Wadsworth, M. E. J. (1996)
'Health and social precursors of unemployment in young men', *Journal of
Epidemiology and Community Health* 50(4): 415–22.

Morris, L. and Scott, J. (1996) 'The attenuation of class analysis', *British Journal
of Sociology* 47: 1 45–55.

Moser, K., Pugh, H. S. and Goldblatt, P. (1988) 'Inequalities in women's health:
looking at mortality differentials using an alternative approach', *British Medical
Journal* 296: 1,221–4.

Pierret, J. (1993) 'Constructing discourses about health and their social determinants', in A. Radley (ed.) *Worlds of Illness: Biographical and Cultural
Perspectives on Health and Disease*, London: Routledge.

Power, C. and Peckham, C. (1990) 'Childhood morbidity and adulthood ill health',
Journal of Epidemiology and Community Health 44: 69–74.

Power, C., Bartley, M., Davey Smith, G. and Blane, D. (1996) 'Transmission of
social and biological risks across the lifecourse', in D. Blane *et al.* (eds) *Health
and Social Organisation*, London: Routledge.

Power, C., Manor, O. and Fox, J. (1991) *Health and Class, the Early Years*, London: Chapman and Hall.

Prout, A. (1996) 'Performance, habitus and trajectory: new directions in the study of class and health', mimeo, Keele University.

Pugh, H., Power, C., Goldblatt, P. and Arber, S. (1991) 'Women's lung cancer mortality, socioeconomic status and changing smoking patterns', *Social Science and Medicine* 32: 1,105–10.

Rahkonen, O. and Lahelma, E. (1992) 'Gender, social class and illness among young people', *Social Science and Medicine* 34: 649–56.

Siegrist, J., Peter, R., Junge, A., Cremer, P. and Seidel, D. (1990) 'Low status control, high effort at work and ischaemic heart disease: prospective evidence from blue-collar men', *Social Science and Medicine* 31: 1,127–34.

Stevenson, T. H. C. (1925) 'The social distribution of mortality from different causes in England and Wales 1910–12', *Biometrika XV*.

Townsend, P., Philimore, P. and Beattie, A. (1987) *Health and Deprivation: Inequality in the North*, London: Croom Helm.

Valkonen, T. (1993) 'Problems in the measurement and international comparisons of socio-economic differences in mortality', *Social Science and Medicine* 36: 409–18.

Wadsworth, M. E. J. (1986) 'Serious illness in childhood at its association with later life achievment', in R.G. Wilkinson (ed.) *Class and Health: Research and Longitudinal Data*, London: Tavistock.

—— (1991) *The Imprint of Time: Childhood History and Adult Life*, Oxford: Oxford University Press.

—— (1996) 'Family and education as determinants of health', in D. Blane *et al.* (eds) *Health and Social Organisation*, London: Routledge, 152–70.

—— (1997) 'Health inequalities in the life course perspective', *Social Science and Medicine* 44: 859–70.

Warde, A. (1990) 'Introduction to the sociology of consumption', *Sociology* 24: 1–4.

West, P., Macintyre, S., Annandale, E. and Hunt, K. (1990) 'Social class and health in youth: findings from the west of Scotland 20–07 study', *Social Science and Medicine* 30: 665–73.

Wilkinson, R. (1994) 'The epidemiological transition: from material scarcity to social disadvantage?', *Daedalus* 123: 61–77.

Wilkinson, R. (1996a) 'How can secular improvements in life expectancy be explained', in D. Blane *et al.* (eds) *Health and Social Organisation*, London: Routledge, 109–24.

Wilkinson, R. (1996b) *Unhealthy Societies: the Afflictions of Inequality*, London: Routledge.

Williams, G. (1993) 'Chronic illness and the pursuit of virtue in everyday life', in A. Radley (ed.) *Worlds of Illness: Biographical and Cultural Perspectives on Health and Disease*, London: Routledge, 92–108.

Williams, S. J. (1995) 'Theorising class, health and lifestyles: can Bourdieu help?', *Sociology of Health and Illness* 17: 577–604.

Wolfarth, T. (1997) 'Socioeconomic inequality and psychopathology: are socioeconomic status and social class interchangeable', *Social Science and Medicine* 45: 399–410.

Chapter 2

Gender, postmodernism and health

Ellen Annandale and Judith Clark

Introduction

'Challenging orthodoxies, and questioning the taken for granted – stirring it', as Gabriele Griffin *et al.* (1994: 1) put it – has long been the 'business of feminists'. Yet feminism's critical acuity is under significant challenge. This comes in the first place from critiques *external* to feminism witnessed in the current backlash literature which blames women's new found 'equality' for all kinds of social ills, such as the so-called breakdown of the family (see Fauldi 1991; Oakley 1997). The second challenge comes from the *internal* fragmentation of feminism, evident in the often bitter disputes that have emerged between competing perspectives. While, of course, internal debates have historically driven feminist thought, the contemporary period is marked by a vituperative stand-off between post-modern and modernist perspectives. The fundamental issue at the heart of this debate is the *nature of feminist politics* in a social world which no longer readily lends itself to being understood through the relatively stable categories of class and gender divisions and their intersection, and the implications that this has for an understanding of the relationships between gender and health. Any contemporary consideration of this topic must therefore grapple with the substantial theoretical task of how to at once appreciate diversity and its radical implications, while also recognising the powerful hegemonic discourses that simultaneously construct simi-larity and facilitate difference. In this chapter we take up Teresa Ebert's attempt to develop such a position, conceptualised as *resistance post-modern feminism*, as a framework within which to explore the issue of gender and health.

Above all, Ebert is concerned to show that postmodern feminism is not a unitary perspective. Thus her own 'resistance' position is developed in distinction to what she terms 'ludic' (i.e. playful) postmodern feminism (for her, typified by the work of Judith Butler (see 1993) and Drucilla Cornell (see 1991)). Together, both the 'resistance' and the 'ludic' position reject the grounding of 'modernist' feminism[1] in a notion of what Ebert

(1996a) conceptualises as *difference-between* (i.e. difference between men and women). That is, both 'ludic' and 'resistance' feminism contest the certainty, or decidability, of a modernist epistemology where difference is produced in terms of difference-between relatively stable categories (e.g. women, men). Within 'ludic' postmodern feminism, difference-between is replaced by a concern for *difference-within*. That is, gender difference is conceived as 'self-divided, as always split by its other' (p. 157). The political intention of 'ludic' feminism is therefore to disrupt the 'clarity and certainty of meaning' about gender, thereby 'dehierarchizing binary oppositions, inscribing the *difference-within*, [and] celebrating undecidability' (p. 167). Thus in the context of health, this radically decentred approach to gender would put diversity in the place of universalising assumptions about men and women, thus undermining the dualities (such as male/female, healthy/unhealthy) that sustain patriarchy. When the binaristic conceptualisations which underlie the connections between 'male = health' and 'female = illness', for example, are opened-up (or deconstructed), it is theoretically possible to see that things could be otherwise (Annandale 1998a).

For Ebert, this form of feminism is on decidedly shaky ground. She questions how 'ludic' postmodern feminism can 'build a transformative politics on a postmodern difference that throws out certainty and destabilizes identity' (1996a: 158). This point of criticism is, of course, one that has been made by feminists of various theoretical persuasions. Susan Bordo (1993), for example, has pointed out that the protean standpoint of multiple axes of identity can end up as a 'view from nowhere'. However, what makes Ebert's approach particularly compelling for our own discussion of gender and health, is her insistence that *undecidability is itself imbricated within new sites of exploitation which actually rely upon a deconstruction of gender as part of a wider critical reflexivity*. This reflexivity implicates health and the body in important ways, including a mandate of consumption which cross-cuts and restructures gender – for example, in changes in health-related behaviours such as diet, exercise and cigarette and alcohol consumption. With its insistence that postmodernism's stress upon differences-within gender and similarities-across gender are conceived as material effects of changing contradictions in the divisions of labour of late capitalism (conceptualised as *differences-in-relation* to the system of exploitation), Ebert's 'resistance' postmodern feminism provides a foundation from which to explore aspects of contemporary relationships between gender and health.

We begin the chapter by revisiting the class and gender debate that drove materialist feminism during the 1970s and early 1980s, and the critical challenges that it faced in response to the social structural changes of the late twentieth century and feminism's turn away from Marxism. Subsequently, in the main body of the chapter, we consider the potential of 'ludic' and 'resistance' postmodern feminism to draw our attention to new sites of health-related exploitation (focusing on health-related behaviours) to which the politics of gender are crucial.

Beginnings: the class and gender debate

The relationship between Marxism and feminism marked the heartland of feminist theory during the 1970s and into the early 1980s (Leonard and Adkins 1996). At the centre of debate lay the subsumption of gender under the economic relation of capital and labour within Marxism. This laid the foundations for 'more than a decade of debate around the relative priority of capital versus patriarchy and class versus gender' within feminism (Marshall 1994: 76). So-called 'dual systems' theorists sought to identify the separate but intersecting operation of patriarchy and capital. In the context of inequalities in health status, for example, it could be pointed out that when women report higher rates of illness within the common class positions which men and women occupy (recognising that common experience is not easily determined) (see Popay et al. 1993), this suggests that there is an 'added effect' of patriarchy over and above capitalism, or gender over class. At the end of the day, these attempts to recuperate Marxism in the name of feminism moved towards the conclusion offered by Zalewski (1990: 238) who, writing about health care, remarks that 'the realities of patriarchy and capitalism mesh together to create a society in which men as well as women suffer oppression, but women suffer the double oppression of both patriarchy and capitalism'. 'Unified systems' theorists (see Young 1981) cast aside any attempt to determine the separate effects of capitalism and patriarchy and argued instead that capitalism is effectively *founded upon* gender hierarchy. This might be illustrated through the example of health care which relies *both* upon cheap paid female labour in the formal sector and unpaid care work in the home, *and* a supply of 'defective' female bodies ripe for surgical and other interventions. Together these assure higher incomes for male workers and substantial profits for hospital and other health care industries worldwide. Unified systems theory then was the precursor to the increasing recognition by the late 1980s that class and gender are, as Johnson (1996: 194) puts it, 'indissolubly intertwined'.

On the face of it, recognition of the mutual imbrication of class and gender seems an expedient development and, moreover, it is one that feminists of all persuasions now claim to appreciate. For radical feminists it rebuts taunts of gender essentialism, while for materialist feminists it displaces criticisms of economic determinism, while still leaving open the possibility that the category 'woman' (for radical feminists) and 'the economic' (for materialist feminists) may have primacy under certain conditions. This would seem to deal with 'multiple subject positions' while also permitting the narratives of class and gender to exist in largely unre-constituted form (i.e. in grand narratives). To a very large degree medical sociology can be seen to have embraced these developments in its work on gender and health status, which has increasingly begun to argue that we need to avoid assuming blanket differences between men and women; to recognise that individuals are more than bundles of categorical and separate roles and statuses; and to point out that it is crucial to explore the meanings that certain 'statuses' (such as gender, age, 'class' and so on) have for individuals and their health. However, this research – both conceptual and empirical – has tended to occur in isolation from wider sociological debates on the contemporary meanings of class and gender. At this wider level, the mutuality of class and gender has a qualitatively different significance which has been insufficiently realised within the sub-discipline of medical sociology. It is to this issue and its significance for research on gender and health that we now turn, through a consideration of a shift away from class and gender as categorical social divisions which structure experience.

Class and gender in transition

The contentious debate over the primacy of capital and patriarchy as struc-turing principles has entered new terrains in materialist feminism's simultaneous engagement with revisions to Marxism and the challenge of feminist postmodernism. A new vibrancy fanned the flames of debate as feminists began to wrestle with the postmodern rejection of binary divi-sions of gender (i.e. difference-between in Ebert's terms) and the contention of post-Marxists that capitalism has entered a new more resolute phase, as exploitative as any that went before. Together post-Marxism and post-modern feminism contest the modernist theoretical approaches to class and gender as formative social divisions. First, it is evident that the meaning of class as traditionally conceived by sociologists is under significant ques-tion at the current time. Holton and Turner (1989: 161; see also Holton 1996), for example, insist that strong *Gemeinschaft*-based theories of society 'where class idiom operates both as a structural account of relations of power, inequality, and exploitation, and simultaneously as an account of consciousness, group formation, and social movements as emancipatory social change' is now obsolete. For these authors, recent economic and social changes such as the decline in manual work and the manufacturing industry and rise of the service sector, the globalisation of capital, and the conceptualisation of the citizen as a consumer rather than a producer, mean that 'class' is now meaningful only in its weaker *Gesellschaft*-based form where it is but one of several patterns of power and inequality. Lash and Urry (1994) have also emphasised the decline of strong class struc-ture consequent upon the rise of what they call a phase of 'disorganised capitalism'. 'Class' here exists only as a collection of individuals as disorganized capitalism replaces any sense of shared meaning with a process of 'individuation, normalization and atomization' (p. 314). It is crucial to recognise, however, that the loosening of 'group and grid' that Lash and Urry refer to certainly does not mean a decline in inequality, just as Jan Pakulski and Malcolm Waters (1996: 157) put it, a 'decline in *class* inequality and conflict'.

These debates of course take place within the wider assault upon Marxism which is strongly criticised for having engaged in a construction of the world through 'systematic, essentialising, and hierarchical conceptual categories', which evidently all too often 'reduced complex social formations to expressions of articulated modes of production, and subordinated struggles and "resistance" of all sorts to the economistic primacy of the "class struggle"' (Callari *et al.* 1995: 3). The important point for us is that this contemporary debate on class permits a concern for gender in a way that was never the case in theory of the 1970s and early 1980s (discussed above) for the reason that gender itself is recognised as part and parcel of the restructuring of the 'economic base' of society. Notably, the restructuring of the economy is underpinned by a fracturing of the demarcations of production and social production, work and home which were traditional of industrial capitalism, and the arena of cultural consumption (particularly in the youth market) relies upon gender-identities that are open to shifting alignments. These changes have prompted post-Marxists and materialist feminists alike to level criticism at 'traditional Marxism' (the nature of which is of course itself contested) for its narrow interpretation of materialism. Specifically, there is strong recognition that culture, knowledge and ideologies (the superstructure of 'traditional Marxism') are themselves now commodities and the major arenas for profit generation. The economic and the cultural therefore cannot be separated; the production of ideology *is* a material action with material effects (Landry and MacLean 1993). Thus consumption replaces production as the major source of gender distinctions. It is not so much that the economic no longer has primacy, but that it has shifted beyond its traditional 'base': the 'pervasive power of the economic is far from exhausted' as 'the market is "in" everything and nothing is incapable of being commodified' (Landry and MacLean 1993: xii).

The old 'class and gender' debate loses its significance with the restructuring of capital as new contours of gender are not just simply made possible, but virtually mandated. It is in this context that the mutuality of class and gender, referred to in the previous section, takes on a significance which is different from its general understanding within debates on gender and health within mainstream medical sociology. Gender can no longer be conceived readily as a straightforward binary division (be this on social or biological grounds) since, along with class and other hierarchies (such as age) it is no longer a taken-for-granted basis of experience for many. Within mainstream medical sociology the implications of this shift have largely been limited to research on the experience of illness and the body in analyses that give little or no consideration to gender (see, for example, Frank 1995). This means that the effects of the mutuality of class and gender are significantly under-explored within the discipline. We therefore move now to consider the implications of the recombinant nature of class and gender in contemporary society in order to draw out the point that more fluid conceptualisations of class and gender are open to exploitation by capital, before we broadly illustrate just some of the implications that this has for health.

Ludic and resistance postmodern feminism

As has been noted in the introduction to the chapter, Teresa Ebert (1993: 19) contends that 'feminists, by and large, have failed to see that postmodernism is itself divided by a radical difference'. There has been a tendency by many to 'write off' postmodernism for 'deconstructing' gender out of existence with its emphasis on flux, contingency and the death of subjectivity, a position which many see as antithetical to the improvement of women's social and economic circumstances. Ebert (1993, 1996a, 1996b), as we have seen, labels this approach 'ludic' postmodernism, an anti-foundationalist perspective which celebrates the play of difference. The pleasures of 'the local, the popular, and, above all, the body (*jouissance*)' (Ebert 1993: 7, emphasis in the original) are the source of gender-related liberation in the works of feminist authors such as Judith Butler (1990) and Teresa de Lauretis (1987) which locate gender politics at the semiotic level. Here, as discussed earlier, the emphasis is on the deconstruction of gender as a binary opposition, with the aim of preventing categories like male/female being a fixed ground for experience. Ebert (1993: 16) argues that while 'the ['ludic'] postmodern problematisation of signifying practices is a necessary move in that it denaturalises dominant meanings and opens up a space for the disarticulation of established signifiers constituting identities', it is problematic since it is disarticulated from the social relations which *produce* signifying practices. For this reason, 'ludic' postmodern feminism is itself argued to be very much *a product of* the capitalist postmodern; that condition which 'is the ensemble of conflicting discourses produced in late patriarchy in which capital and the sexual division of labour are deployed in new ways' (p. 14). Therefore, 'resistance' postmodern materialist feminism suggests that the seemingly disconnected differences of the 'ludic' position are systematically linked through exploitation within the labour process, legitimating capitalism's mobilisation of fragmented identities in the name of profit generation. Rosemary Hennessy, who shares Ebert's problematic, expresses this point well:

by refiguring the self as a permeable and fragmented subjectivity but then stopping there, some postmodern discourses contribute to the formation of a subject more adequate to a globally-dispersed and state-controlled multinational consumer culture which relies upon increasingly atomized social relations. In the 'age of information', cybernetics, instantaneous global finance, export processing zones, artificial intelligence, and hyper-realities, an atomized socius affords an increasingly fluid and permeable capital its producers, its workforce, and its new markets. To the extent that some postmodern knowledges situate their permeable and fluid subjectivities, their 'new' identities within *noncausal, dehistoricized* frames of intelligibility, these theories can be readily recuperated for capital's rapidly re-forming and diffused horizons.

(Hennessy 1993: 6, emphasis orig.)

Thus gender difference is, as Hennessy relates, entangled in economic and political power structures, not *transgressive* of them, as 'ludic' post-modern feminism often seems to contend. The issue which must now be considered is 'resistance' postmodern feminism's own accommodation to post-Marxist understandings of 'structure'. Specifically, what takes the place of the protean standpoint of the 'ludic' position? For Ebert (1993: 21), patriarchy's sense of unity within the postmodern is an ideological effect, 'continuous on the level of the structure or organisation of oppression and discontinuous, that is, heterogeneous, in its historically specific and conjunctural practices'. It becomes a 'totality in process, a self-divided, multiple arena of struggle' (p. 21). Therefore differences *do arise* – the socially constructed gendered subject of modernism is repudiated – but crucially these are 'differences-in-relation to the system of exploitation and the relations of production that is capitalism' (Ebert 1996b: 344).

In sum, this position is removed from the 'free play' of gender and the lack of an ethical position that is often taken to be typical and problematic of postmodern feminism by sociologists working in the area of health and illness (see Busfield 1996; Doyal 1995). However, it crucially appreciates that the fragmentation of gender is a 'reality' of late twentieth-century society, itself thrown up by the metamorphosis of capital. The overdetermined nature of 'class' and 'gender' is, in Hennessy's (1993) perception, both a site for capital and a site of resistance. The maintenance of the capitalist system through gender fragmentation is bound to guarantee inequity (although at the level of individuals rather than class or gender aggregates) as identical effects (i.e. oppression) are produced differently. We now move on to employ these ideas in a more focused manner than has been possible so far in the context of gender, health and illness.

New order, new problems

Gender relations under capitalist postmodernism have a complex relationship to the production of health and illness. As gender becomes progressively less amenable to containment within a dichotomy (traditional gender roles), it becomes at once more reflexive and conflictual. Reflexivity as emphasised by 'ludic' postmodern feminists implicates the openness of the body to gender investment through 'health and lifestyles', converting the body as a means of labour to a source of pleasure. At the present time, far from being conceived as a fixed property of the biological body, health (and its breakdown) is increasingly marketed as a result of lifestyle choice. This is manifest in a myriad of ways such as the connection between the display of a healthy body and essential virtue pursued through rigid self *control* (in diet, exercise and body size, for example). It is also evident in the mandate to consume market-offered goods in a hedonistic manner (for example, positing immediate *gratification* as a source of well-being) (see Crawford 1984). Mike Savage *et al.* (1992: 114–15) propose that as the world of paid work changes such that people no longer have a 'job for life', and innovation and flexibility become the order of the day, a 'healthy lifestyle' is instrumentally converted into the display of health to increase earning capacity. Mixing Robert Crawford's mandate for control and release, individuals dubbed 'postmodern' in lifestyle combine extravagance and excess (through diet and alcohol consumption, for example) with what Savage *et al.* call a 'culture of the body' which is ascetic in nature. While authors such as Savage *et al.* and Crawford make little or no reference to gender, feminists writing about capitalism's formation of new gendered subjects make no reference to health and illness. They can, however, be brought together because, as Robin Saltonstall (1993: 12) has discussed, 'the doing of health is a form of doing gender'. Since 'health is not a universal fact, but is a constituted social reality, constructed through the medium of social meaning and symbol' (p. 12), we should not be surprised to find that attributes of gender as they concern health are differences in relation to economic production.

It is evident, for example, that commodity asceticism and commodity hedonism as they implicate health can often be more 'productive' if they destabilise traditional gender dichotomies. This is quite simply because the subjects that are produced through these new ideologies are increasingly amenable to products and activities that were traditionally 'gendered', opening up a wider market. This process can be seen to operate most clearly at the level of health-related behaviours. Activities that were once virtually the undisputed province of either men or women, now concern both. For example, female 'keep fit' turns into 'aerobics' open to men; male 'weight lifting' extends into 'fitness training' open to women. Promotional material for one of our local health clubs, for example, carries endorsements from men and women (of a range of ages) in equal numbers, with recovery from illness and sociability emphasised by all. Hygiene and cosmetic products, once the province of women, now target men – some, such as Calvin Klein's No. 1 fragrance, explicitly trade on youth androgeny. Others begin with an expression of gender difference, then enact a counter move which establishes similarity. This is seen, for example, in advertisements for Pampers nappies, which until quite recently sold a specific product for boys and girls emphasising the need for a different design because of physiological differences between female and male infants. Now, Pampers has 'said goodbye to boy/girl' nappies, marketing instead a uniform product. This shift is of course simply a feature of the flexible specialisation of production, as goods of all kinds are 'reinvented' to attract new consumers and recapture old ones with a new and 'different' product. What is of interest to us specifically is the flexible deployment of gender as part of this process, illustrating Ebert's (1996a: 170) point that gender 'difference is explainable only by the system of production that deploys that difference'.

In Hennessy's (1993: 9) terms, the entrepreneurial subject has been replaced by the decentred, fragmented, porous subject who is 'better equipped for the heightened alienation of late capitalism's refined divisions of labour, more readily disciplined by a pandemic corporate state, and more available to a broad nexus of ideological controls'. Counter identities created against male/capitalist definitions, it has been argued (Lowe 1995), are particularly vulnerable to this process since they are easily co-opted through the segmentation of lifestyle consumption. This process has been facilitated by the explosion of new information and communication structures – such as computers and telematics, market research and account planning in advertising (Nixon 1996) – which have contributed to the rescripting of gender relations. At the forefront of this has been a revision of the ideology of separate spheres as more and more women have been recruited into the labour market. In sheer numerical terms there are now as many women as men in paid employment, as men's employment has 'fallen relentlessly' in Britain, while women's has 'risen continually' since the 1960s (Hatt 1997: 19). But, of course, numerical equality does not mean equivalent terms and conditions of work. It is precisely the 'new' service and information industries, referred to above, in which women are concentrated, notably in part-time work. The restructuring of the economy fosters changes in material conditions of life. Here it is instructive to note the changes in health-related behaviours that have accompanied the loosening of gender proscriptions, and the marketing of once male confined activities to women.

Tobacco consumption is one interesting illustration of this process. As we have seen, at the core of resistance postmodern feminism, and evident in the work of both Ebert and Hennessy, is the point that gender difference

– here referring to the range of differences that can be deployed, i.e. differences between men and women as social groups; the similarities between men and women as social groups; and the similarities and differences that exist within men and within women – are the ideological effects of the positioning of men and women within late capitalism. Crucially, in a context where the meanings of male and female, masculinity and femininity are strategically deployed in the name of profit maximisation, the similar effect of oppression is produced differently. Thus if we consider health status specifically, the similar result of ill health (oppression) is produced by a wide variety of means. Tobacco, for example, might be consumed for a variety of reasons including for pleasure/gratification (or *jouissance* in 'ludic' terms), for social reasons, and/or to alleviate stress (and, significantly, it is likely to be marketed in these terms, even though in the British context – but not in many other countries – advertising restrictions have meant that surreal images have replaced overtly gendered messages). Yet, the ultimate, and oppressive end is likely to be the same: ill health.

Counter identities which are created against male/capitalist definitions are particularly vulnerable to this process since they are easily co-opted through the segmentation of lifestyle consumption and the new stresses and strains of the modern economy (i.e. changing gender-related patterns of employment). Here, again, it is instructive to note the changes in health-related behaviours that have accompanied the loosening of gender proscriptions, and the marketing of once male confined activities to women. In the nineteenth century, tobacco consumption was the preserve of men, its use largely confined to pipes, cigars, snuff and tobacco chewing. As Graham (1993) has outlined, women's smoking can be linked to the rise of manufactured cigarettes in the late 1800s, and the loosened prohibitions which accompanied the 1914–18 war. By 1949, over 50 per cent of British women between the ages of 20 and 34 were cigarette smokers (although most smoked on average less than ten per day). Over the next forty years, prevalence rates for all ages remained stable at around 40 per cent, although consumption levels rose. It was not until the 1970s as smoking began to decline in overall popularity, that we saw a shift in the gender profile. In 1948, one and a half times as many men as women smoked cigarettes. By the early 1990s, the gender difference in prevalence had all but disappeared, with 31 per cent of men and 29 per cent of women smoking (Graham 1993). Among young people the gender balance has in fact been reversed, as prevalence rates for women aged between 16 and 19, and between 20 and 24, have overtaken those of men. Hence Graham (p. 13) predicts that as these 'younger cohorts age, the smoking population is likely to become increasingly female'. However, at the present time it is women of middle and late middle age (50s and early 60s), who are of particular interest with respect to the relationships between gender-related social change, smoking and disease.

There has been a gradual decline in the female mortality advantage until male and female rates (for all-ages and all causes of death) reached virtual parity in the early 1990s, and even suggest a reverse trend from 1992 onwards. Male death rates show a very gradual, but continuing decline (i.e. improvement), from 12.4 per 1,000 population in 1966 to under 11 into the early 1990s, while for women there is much less change over the same period: the death rate was 11.2 per 1,000 population in 1966, and despite some fluctuations upwards, was around 11 in the early 1990s.[2] A consideration of age-specific death rates by gender adds weight and explanatory power to this trend by pointing to a declining mortality advantage among women in middle and late middle age (that is, in these official statistics between the ages 45–54 and 55–64). In the latter group, for example, the sex mortality ratio has steadily decreased from 2.05 in the mid-1960s, to around 1.70 during the early 1990s (for more detail, see Annandale 1998b). Thus, although it is certainly still the case that most women live longer than most men today, there is a suggestion of a reversing trend among specific age cohorts. Why might this be? A number of complex factors may be playing a role (including breast cancer deaths), but for England and Wales, male deaths from lung cancer alone nearly halved between 1971 and 1992, while female rates increased by 16 per cent over the same period (CSO 1995). Given the lag between exposure and incidence of disease, it is within these cohorts of middle and late middle age that we would expect to see the effect upon mortality. Although these mortality data are crude they have been presented to reveal what Ebert (1996a: 132) conceptualises as the 'continuity within the ever more innovative forms capitalism' – here multinational tobacco companies – 'takes in its search for profits', through the repositioning of gender-identity in relation to smoking and its relation to health.

In the wider international context, patterns of smoking by gender in relation to mortality are complex. Surveys on smoking vary in both type and quality, in sample size and representativeness of populations, and figures may be distorted through cultural resistance to admission of smoking (Chollat-Tracquet 1992) which makes comparisons difficult and prone to over-generalisations. But bearing in mind the problematic nature of the data, various patterns can be identified. A useful four-stage typology depicting the history of smoking with its related mortality for both males and females has been proposed by Amanda Amos (1996). *Stage one* represents countries in which the rate of smoking for males is generally less than 20 per cent, and that for females, less than 5 per cent. In this stage mortality from smoking-related disease is less than 5 per cent for men and not yet identifiable in women, as seen, for example, in countries of sub-Sahara Africa. In *stage two*, the rates for smoking for men rise rapidly from around 20 per cent to 70 per cent, whilst for women the rise is from

5 per cent to around 40 per cent. Within a period of fifty years of smoking the differential percentage of death rates between men and women is about 9 per cent, compared with 2 per cent at twenty years. Countries represented in this stage include China, Japan and some countries of Latin America (notably Brazil), North Africa and Asia. In *stage three*, smoking for both men and women has reached a peak and has begun to decline, showing a steeper descent for men and more of a plateau for women. The differential mortality rate at the end of stage three, i.e. eighty years, has widened to 27 per cent. Countries demonstrating this pattern include those in Eastern and Southern Europe. *Stage four* is represented by the UK (as discussed above), the USA, and Central and Western Europe. Here smoking rates for men and women are almost identical, and the gap for smoking-related mortality has narrowed on average to about 10 per cent.

The patterns of mortality derived from demographic and epidemiological data collected for the Pacific Islands, show a close correspondence with these four stages of evolution. The countries which have primarily a 'traditional' mortality pattern have a life expectancy of less than 60 years, and include Papua New Guinea, and the Solomon Islands. Here infectious diseases are the main cause of death. Countries identified as at the 'middle stage' of epidemiological and demographic transition have a life expectancy of 60 to 64 years, and include groups like the Fiji Indians who have a mostly 'modernized' pattern of mortality, and Fiji Melanesians who have a primarily 'traditional pattern' (Marshall 1991). Within this group, the Fijian Indians and Fiji Melanesians also show higher percentages of women smokers in rural areas: 50 per cent rural smokers compared with 44 per cent urban smokers among the Melanesians, and 44 per cent rural smokers compared with 22 per cent urban smokers among the Indians (Chollat-Traquet 1992). Smoking as a contributor to mortality is a feature of the 'modernized' pattern of mortality. For example, in Polynesia lung cancer represents 30 per cent of all cancers for men, and 10 to 15 per cent of cancers for women (Marshall 1991). There is evidence, therefore, that the history of smoking has close correspondence with the transition from a 'traditional' to a 'modernized' mortality pattern. Using evidence from Oceania, it has been suggested by Marshall (1991) and Doyal (1995) that the timing of the transition coincides with the production and marketing of cigarettes by multinational tobacco companies. This evidence is supported by data from Eastern Europe (Piha *et al.* 1993) where economic restructuring is taking place. At a time of economic instability and reduction in home produced tobacco and cigarettes, the fear is beginning to be realised that the influx of capital from multinational tobacco companies will exploit existing markets and create new ones furthering already high mortality rates. Lung cancer rates for middle-aged men are among the highest in the world, contributed to by heavy smoking at an early age. Smoking accounts for 41 per cent of the deaths among men, and 14 per cent of the deaths among women in

Hungary, and 43 per cent of the deaths among men, and 10 per cent of the deaths among women in Poland. In the Russian Federation the figures are 42 per cent for men and 6 per cent for women. The lower percentage of women's deaths is attributable to the lag in the women's smoking pattern in evidence across countries, and the within country differences are reflective of the social acceptability of smoking (Piha *et al.* 1993). These are trends which would appear to be set to continue.

At the macro level the figures denoting gender differences in smoking reflect its social acceptability and in the context of 'resistance' postmodern feminism represent the ideological effects of patriarchy. At the micro level, i.e. within countries, social acceptability, furthermore, is not only exhibited in rural and urban difference (as in the Fijian example quoted above, and in India where the average of 3 per cent of women smokers rises to 67 per cent in some rural communities), but also in tobacco use, where, for example, chewing tobacco is more common than smoking. In countries which have a long tradition of smoking, 'reverse smoking' where the lit end of a chutta or cheroot is turned around and kept burning inside the mouth (Doyal, 1995), may be the most acceptable, i.e. most 'feminine', form for women. Such different uses of tobacco and smoking practices bring with them different patterns of morbidity and pathology; for example, ulceration and mouth cancers. Research among Filipino women who indulge in 'reverse smoking' has shown changes in the epithelial cells of the palate, of fissuring, pigmentation and thickening of the palatal mucosa (Ortiz *et al.* 1996). Doyal (1995) cites evidence that pan chewing, combined with smoking, gives a risk of mouth cancer 36 times greater than that of someone who does not use tobacco at all. And, of course, as in the developed world smoking has harmful effects on the reproductive health of women and of their offspring, and has been implicated in infertility, low birthweight and perinatal death.

The spread of capital through the multinational tobacco companies in developing countries interacts with the existing social practices of smoking which in turn are representative of ongoing gender struggles within patriarchy. It is a challenge to patriarchy in areas where, ironically, patriarchy has served to protect women's health; that is, in countries where smoking is socially unacceptable. It colludes with patriarchy where smoking is already an established practice, as for example in reinforcing the already dangerous practice of 'reverse smoking'. It creates new markets particularly in the urban areas, where smoking has become a key part of new lifestyles. In Brazil, for example, the rate of female smoking is rapidly overtaking that of the US and Brazilian women now rank fourteenth in the world in the league table of female lung cancer deaths, and are moving upwards rapidly (Doyal 1995).

Evidently, it is not simply that once largely male-only products and behaviours are aimed at women and vice versa, but that individual men and individual women are increasingly subject to 'dual demands' of gender, something which arguably affects women more than men. Ebert (1988: 36) emphasises that the categorical division between men and women (i.e. difference-between) is the 'site at which the economic order puts patriarchy under pressure, forcing it to allow some shifting of gendered features to meet transformations in the relations of production'. However, there are limitations to full freedom since it would undermine the illusion of 'natural' difference that equally needs to be deployed. Hence, individuals are permitted to 'take on *limited* attributes of the other gender – only to the degree that it is specifically required by the current relations of production and only so far as the primacy of male gender is not substantially threatened' (p. 36).

Bordo (1993) highlights the dual demands of 'female domesticity' and 'male mastery' that are placed on contemporary young women. The anorexic, she writes, pursues slenderness through the conventional feminine practice of attending to appearance and, once engaged in this practice, 'discovers' male values of self-mastery and control. Thus, at the point of anorectic excess 'the conventionally feminine deconstructs, we might say, into its opposite and opens into those values our culture has coded as male' (p. 179). This then is illustrative of Ebert's (1993) insistence that contemporary patriarchal capitalism produces the similar effect of oppression (here eating disorder) differently (a phenomenon which is also experienced by a significant minority of men). Far from disrupting and transforming (the 'ludic' position), gender performativity through the body in this context redoubles women's oppression.

Conclusion

In this chapter our intention within the spirit of previous work (Annandale and Clark 1996) has been to stimulate and extend debate concerning the relations of gender, health and postmodernism, and thus to consider the theoretical issues raised through postmodern feminism. Drawing upon Ebert's distinction between 'ludic' and 'resistance' perspectives, we have argued that the contemporary restructuring of class and gender portends not the supersession of patriarchy, but its continuation in more capricious form as capitalism, in the search for new arenas for profit, actively recuperates the fragmentation (and individuation) of health and gender identities.

In the process of discussion it has been possible to take Hennessy's (1993: 137) insight that postmodern knowledge claims can be appropriated 'in such a way as to make visible the contesting interests at stake in their social analytics and rearticulate them within a theoretical framework that is congruent with feminism's political agenda'. Patriarchy's *unity* is clearly evident at the level of (capitalist) ideology which produces a range of *different effects* at the level of individual experience. It is for this reason that health practices evince *both* the 'opening up' of gender (e.g. in marketing fitness products) *and the entrenchment* of gender dualities, but in 'reverse form' (e.g. in patterns of cigarette smoking; male concern with health and appearance). Gender is restructured, but not self-evidently in ways that reduce inequality. In a discussion that has been self-evidently speculative in tone, we have tried to illustrate that health and illness is embedded in this process through the example of health-related behaviours.

References

Amos, A. (1996) 'Women and smoking: a global issue', *World Health Statistics Quarterly* 49: 127–33.

Annandale, E. (1998a) 'Health, illness and the politics of gender', in D. Field and S. Taylor (eds) *Perspectives in the Sociology of Health and Illness*, Oxford: Blackwell Scientific.

—— (1998b) *The Sociology of Health and Medicine*, Cambridge: Polity Press.

Annandale, E. and Clark, J. (1996) 'What is gender? Feminist theory and the sociology of human reproduction', *Sociology of Health & Illness*, 18(1): 7–44.

Bordo, S. (1993) *Unbearable Weight: Feminism, Western Culture and the Body*, London: University of California Press.

Busfield, J. (1996) *Men, Women and Madness*, London: Macmillan.

Butler, J. (1990) *Gender Trouble: Feminism and the Subversion of Identity*, London: Routledge.

—— (1993) *Bodies That Matter*, New York: Routledge.

CSO (1995) (Central Statistics Office) *Social Trends 1995 Edition*, London: HMSO.

Callari, A., Cullenberg, S. and Biewener, C. (1995) 'Marxism in the new world order', in A. Callari, S. Cullenberg and C. Biewener (eds) *Marxism in the Postmodern Age*, London: Guildford Press, 1–10.

Chollat-Tracquet, C. (1992) *Women and Tobacco*, Geneva: World Health Organization.

Cornell, D. (1991) *Beyond Accommodation*, New York: Routledge.

Crawford, R. (1984) 'A cultural account of "health": control, release, and the social body', in J. McKinlay (ed.) *Issues in the Political Economy of Health*, London: Tavistock Publications, 60–103.

de Lauretis, T. (1987) *Technologies of Gender*, Bloomington, IN: Indiana University Press.

Doyal, L. (1995) *What Makes Women Sick?*, London: Macmillan.

Ebert, T. (1988) 'The romance of patriarchy: ideology, subjectivity, and post-modern feminist cultural theory', *Cultural Critique* (fall): 19–57.

—— (1993) 'Ludic feminism, the body, performance, and labor: Bringing Materialism back into feminist cultural studies', *Cultural Critique* (winter): 5–50.

—— (1996a) *Ludic Feminism and After. Postmodernism, Desire and Labor in Late Capitalism*, Ann Arbor, MI: University of Michigan Press.

—— (1996b) 'The crisis of (ludic) socialist feminism', in C. Siegel and A. Kibbey (eds) *Forming and Reforming Identity*, London: New York University Press, 339–69.

Fauldi, S. (1991) *Backlash*, New York: Crown Publishers.

Frank, A. (1995) *The Wounded Storyteller*, London: Chicago University Press.

Graham, H. (1993) *When Life's a Drag*, London: HMSO.

Griffin, G., Hester, M., Rai, S., and Roseneil, S. (1994) 'Introduction. Stirring it: challenges for feminism', in G. Griffin, M. Hester, S. Rai and S. Roseneil (eds) *Stirring It: challenges for Feminism*, London: Taylor & Francis, 1–7.

Hatt, S. (1997) *Gender, Work and Labour Markets*, London: Macmillan.

Hennessy, R. (1993) *Materialist Feminism and the Politics of Discourse*, London: Routledge.

Holton, R. (1996) 'Has class analysis a future?', in D. Lee and B. Turner (eds) *Conflicts about Class*, London: Longman, 26–41.

Holton, R. and Turner, B. (1989) *Max Weber on Economy and Society*, London: Routledge.

Johnson, C. (1996) 'Does capitalism need patriarchy?', *Women's Studies International Forum* 19(3): 193–202.

Landry, D. and MacLean, G. (1993) *Materialist Feminisms*, Oxford: Blackwell.

Lash, S. and Urry, J. (1994) *Economies of Signs and Space*, London: Sage.

Leonard, D. and Adkins, L. (1996) 'Reconstructing French feminism: commodification, materialism and sex', in D. Leonard and L. Adkins (eds) *Sex in Question: French Materialist Feminism*, London: Taylor & Francis, 1–23.

Lowe, D. (1995) *The Body in Late Capitalist USA*, London: Duke University Press.

Marshall, B. (1994) *Engendering Modernity*, Cambridge: Polity Press.

Marshall, M. (1991) 'The second fatal impact: cigarette smoking, chronic disease, and the epidemiological transition in Oceania', *Social Science and Medicine* 33: 1,327–42.

Nixon, S. (1996) *Hard Looks*, London: UCL Press.

Oakley, A. (1997) 'A brief history of gender', in A. Oakley and J. Mitchell (eds) *Who's Afraid of Feminism?*, London: Hamish Hamilton, 29–54.

Ortiz, G. M., Pierce, A. M., and Wilson, D. F. (1996) 'Palatal changes associated with reverse smoking in Filipino Women', *Oral Diseases* 2: 232–7.

Pakulski, J. and Waters, M. (1996) *The Death of Class*, London: Sage.

Piha, T., Besselink, E., and Lopez, A. D. (1993) 'Tobacco or health', *World Health Statistical Quarterly* 46: 188–94.

Popay, J., Bartley, M. and Owen, C. (1993) 'Gender inequalities in health: social position, affective disorder and minor physical morbidity', *Social Science and Medicine* 36: 21–32.

Saltonstall, R. (1993) 'Healthy Bodies, social bodies: men's and women's concepts and practices of health in everyday life', *Social Science and Medicine* 36: 7–14.

Savage, M., Barlow, J., Dickens, P. and Fielding, T. (1992) *Property, Bureaucracy and Culture*, London: Routledge.

Tickle, L. (1996) 'Mortality trends in the United Kingdom, 1982 to 1992', *Population Trends* 86: 21–8.

Young, I. (1981) 'Beyond the unhappy marriage: a critique of dual-systems theory', in L. Sargent (ed.) *Women and Revolution*, Montreal: Black Rose Books, 43–69.

Zalewski, M. (1990) 'Logical contradictions in feminist health care: a rejoinder to Peggy Foster', *Journal of Social Policy* 19: 235–44.

Chapter 3

A place for race?

Medical sociology and the critique of racial ideology

Chris Smaje

Introduction

This chapter explores a tension in the way that medical sociology has engaged with questions of race and ethnicity. On the one hand, it has studied aspects of the health of groups in the population defined according to some notion of their race or ethnicity and accordingly produced a diverse and intriguing body of empirical findings. On the other, it has drawn upon sociological theory to criticise the very basis upon which categories like race and ethnicity have come to be defined. The result, as I shall argue, is an unfortunate and unproductive divergence between theory and empirical research which urgently needs to be transcended. This is no easy task, and I do not claim to have achieved it here. However, I hope to indicate some directions in which our efforts may usefully proceed. In particular, I shall oppose the essentially negative critique of race and ethnicity as 'ideological' categories, arguing that sociological theory contains more productive ways of addressing the concept of ideology. I draw upon the work of the influential French sociologist Pierre Bourdieu in order to articulate this argument in such a way that a theoretically plausible field of 'race and health' research can be defined, and I conclude with some tentative suggestions for theoretically informed empirical work of this kind.

Before proceeding, an introductory word on the concepts of race and ethnicity is in order. The idea of race is bound up with the historical development of European political institutions, and in particular with colonialism and its associated views of the inherent biological and cultural inferiority of colonised peoples. There are thankfully few academic proponents of this view today, and some scholars prefer to invoke the more recently formulated concept of 'ethnicity' to refer to the construction of collective identities around culturally defined criteria. While sympathetic to this approach, I have retained the term 'race' (or, better, 'racialised') in my discussion for two reasons. First, I think that the reference points of colonialism and racism are still relevant to contemporary experience. For example, in the USA the 'ethnic' designation 'African-American' is increasingly favoured over the 'racial' designation 'black'. Whatever the political merits of this, I concur with Grant and Orr's (1996) argument that if African-Americans constitute only one of several other ethnic groups (Italian-Americans, Irish-Americans etc), nevertheless they have been and remain a uniquely marginalised and stigmatised one. Moreover, the social and political consciousness of African-Americans has differed accordingly. My aim here is not to consign African-Americans to what Paul Gilroy (1990) has called the 'problem-victim' couplet but, on the contrary, to emphasise the way in which a racialised identity is articulated in ways which are not reducible to some universal process of ethnic identity formation. This essentially is the second point: the ethnic concept conflates a huge variety of struggles around class, religion, nation, race and language as if to a universal dynamic, and in this sense becomes theoretically vacuous.[1] As I hope to show in the following section, when shorn of biological and cultural essentialisms the concept of race therefore retains a critical quality which may be germane to the field of medical sociology.

Race, medical sociology and the critique of ideology

Despite the manifold issues upon which it is divided, sociological theory can broadly be characterised as a critique of ideology. Here, as with much of the sociological lexicon, words which resemble ones widely understood in everyday usage mean something slightly different. 'Critique' refers to a systematic exposition of the underlying structure or logic to an idea or practice, a meaning related to, but distinct from the everyday concept of 'criticism' as censure or finding fault. 'Ideology' refers to any more or less coherent body of beliefs, ideas or wisdom through which people articulate their behaviour, and thus refers to something much wider than the pejorative connotations of 'ideology' in everyday language as the dogmatic espousal of an unreasonable point of view. Indeed, the central contribution of sociological theory has been to show that 'reason' itself is a variable property, and that most if not all of what people hold to be 'reasonable', 'natural' or 'self-evident' turns out to be only one among many possible ways of imagining things as they 'really' are.

The concept of race which emerged in the 'scientific racism' of later nineteenth-century biological thought has long been a target of the sociological critique of ideology. Scientific racism refers, broadly speaking, to the notion that biological characteristics exist which are homogenous within a specific human collectivity and heterogeneous across several collectivities such that the human species can be precisely subdivided. Typically, it also involves the view that such characteristics affect people's socio-cultural behaviour and capabilities so that these collectivities can be ranked in a hierarchical order of merit. Such views have been subjected to sustained and compelling critique in the twentieth century. But although there are few proponents of this biological essentialism today, complementary cultural essentialisms persist which sustain the logic of the older argument in suggesting that contrastive socio-cultural characteristics uniquely define human collectivities and may, indeed, be used to evaluate their merit. Again, such essentialism has been the focus of considerable sociological critique.[2]

Medical sociology has made its own – and in a sense parallel – contributions to the critique of ideology. A foundational insight of the sub-discipline was that sickness and health, far from being purely biological states of the human organism, were also ideological categories which were socially defined and variable over and above any strictly biological referent. This insight has proved a richly productive one for empirical research, but the sub-discipline is also associated with a rather different and older empirical tradition, namely the public health or epidemiological concern to investigate the patterning of sickness and health by social characteristics. Thus, the insight that sickness has a socio-cultural as well as a biological referent is supplemented by the insight that its biological referent is socio-culturally mediated, and public health research has long been associated with social criticism and movements for reform of the conditions producing sickness among disadvantaged sections of the population.

In recent years, the sociological critique of race and the critiques of biomedical thinking which have emerged in medical sociology have come together in a concern with the sickness and health of people defined according to the processes of racial or ethnic categorisation described above. However, as I have already suggested, their conjuncture has not always been a happy or productive one. A good deal of the work has been undertaken within the public health tradition; this has generally assumed that familiar racial and/or ethnic categories constitute social distinctions around which empirical investigation into the patterning of health can fruitfully be undertaken.[3] Other writers have invoked elements of the sociological critique of race to oppose the essentialist tendency they see in the assumption that racial or ethnic distinctions can form an appropriate basis for enquiry. Medical sociology's own critique of ideology has necessarily been a subordinate third party to this debate over the 'reality' of racial distinctions. However, to the extent that it has raised questions about the way that the social character of health and illness covaries with the social character of race it can be assimilated to the empirical orientation of the public health tradition in relation to racial categories.

Thus, the critique of ideology in the field of race and health has been an essentially negative one which opposes analytic attention to categories forged within the essentialist traditions of racial thought. For example, in a widely cited paper Sheldon and Parker have argued:

if public health workers continue to use the term 'race' because people act as though race exists they are guilty of conferring analytical status on what is nothing more than an ideological construct.

(1992: 105)

The negative critique of ideology involved in this statement corresponds more closely to the vernacular than to the sociological sense of its two key terms; it criticises or opposes arguments based upon an idea – race – that it sees as an unreasonable dogma. If we accept such an argument, two questions follow. First, given that – as Sheldon and Parker concede – people *do* act as though race exists, how can we account for such behaviour? In other words, if the concept of race is unreasonable, what 'reasonable' grounds can we invoke for its provenance in contemporary thought? Second, given that strong 'racial' patterns emerge when the experience of health and sickness is examined, how can the apparently real effects of this 'unreal' category be explained? A common answer is often given to the two questions. In keeping with its oppressive origins, so the argument runs, the concept of race stems from an ideology (here in the sociological sense) of racism which operates to make the active production of social inequalities appear a legitimate or 'natural' feature of ineluctable human differences. Thus, racism is regarded as a particular form of class conflict which reproduces social inequalities manifested, among other things, in health experience. Sociologists who invoke the concept of race can therefore be accused of substantialising as analytically given a category which is a product of the political processes through which inequalities are reproduced.

The argument has considerable merit. There is no doubt that ideas of racial (or cultural) difference can and have been invoked to justify social inequalities and that such inequalities underlie a good deal of any apparently 'racial' disparity in health. However, the decisive issue from a theoretical perspective, it seems to me, is not that racial ideology *does* operate to justify inequalities but that it *can* operate in this way and, moreover, that such justification appears necessary. In other words, if race 'naturalises' inequality we need to ask what it is in ideas about 'nature' which can so effectively mask the arbitrary and political character of that inequality. More radically, we must recognise that the very concepts of 'nature', 'politics' and, indeed, 'equality' are as fully ideological as that of 'race'. It is commonly pointed out that the concept of race as we know it today is a relatively recent innovation of European thought, with authors pinpointing its gradual emergence from anywhere around the fifteenth century (Hannaford 1996) to, rather more implausibly, the nineteenth century (Malik 1996). Less commonly heard is the argument that a parallel historical trajectory marks many other familiar concepts: the idea that the human world is composed of independent individuals, equal in nature; the idea that political rule stems from the consent of such individuals; the idea that human labour can be abstracted from the context of specific social relationships; the very idea that a 'human world' exists, and that humans have the critical faculty of reason setting them over and against 'nature' and enabling them to define the moral principles of society, all emerged over more or less the same period of time.[4] Thus, while our medieval forebears knew none of the invidious racial distinctions with which we are familiar today, their world was nevertheless not only a profoundly inegalitarian one but also one in which inequality required no justification because it was regarded as a necessary manifestation of the hierarchy of the cosmos.[5] It is, I would argue, theoretically suspect to render one of these emergent categories as simply causal (or epiphenomenal) to another one (in the way that 'race' is often explained via 'class'). It is also anachronistic to argue, as Hannaford (1996) does, that the repudiation of the idea of race warrants a return to pre-racial concepts of political citizenship, because the motivation to oppose the inegalitarian implications of racial ideology with those concepts is predicated upon a view of equality alien to that pre-racial order. Indeed, attempts to undermine the ontological basis of race by pointing to its contingent historical origins – a peculiarly common tactic in critiques of the concept – are undermined by an inability to see the grounding of their own argument within the ideological order of which race is an emergent entity. Foucault makes an effective criticism of this 'search for origins', which 'makes possible a field of knowledge whose function is to recover [truth], but always in a false recognition due to the excesses of its own speech' (1977: 143).

Thus, the argument that racial ideology legitimates social inequality is an over-simplification. A better approach, in my view, would suggest that modern Europe saw the emergence of the concept of the individual person enjoying a formal equality in nature with other persons. This raised in an unprecedented manner the problem of the legitimacy of the state which ruled over them, representing a contradiction within the emergent ideology of modern Europe with which the early political philosophers such as Thomas Hobbes and John Locke wrestled. One resolution is the idea that the state expresses the will of the people, embodying their spirit or essence, an idea which Kapferer describes as 'part of the fury of Western political philosophical discourse from the seventeenth century on' (1988: 166). This philosophical trajectory was matched with political and economic developments, and particularly with the colonising expansion of mercantile capital which engaged people beyond European borders. In these parallel developments, the seeds of nationalist and racist thought become apparent.

None of this, of course, commits sociology to according race the status of a 'real' analytical concept but, as an intellectual heir to the modern European tradition, it behoves the discipline to work through the contradictions of this tradition rather than to rule only part of it as problematic, and thus to 'explain' race in terms of some other category emergent within it such as class. It is legitimate to start this process of internal critique, as many writers have done, with the repudiation of biological or cultural essentialism. Such essentialisms are invariably articulated as political or intellectual doctrine or as rationalisation for belief and, as David Goldberg (1993: 81) has argued, as such can easily be shown to be vacuous and incoherent. However, thereby to conclude that, logically, the concept of race is analytically redundant is to adopt an inappropriate analytical focus. Here, it may be helpful to regard race as a *symbolic* phenomenon and to consider Dan Sperber's engaging metaphor of the light source in his argument concerning the sociological interpretation of symbols:

> Those who try to interpret symbols in and of themselves look at the light source and say 'I don't see anything.' But the light source is there, not to be looked at, but so that one may look at what it illuminates.
>
> (1975: 70)

Analogously, I would argue that to demonstrate the conceptual redundancy of racial meanings – to look at the light source – does not exhaust the concept of race and establish it as extraneous to reality. The sentiments activated in intimations of race are a part of reality. Indeed, there is a strongly reductionist tendency in the negative critique which fails to provide any analytical purchase upon the social meanings, identities and relationships which people construct through the idiom of race in their everyday lives. This failing, common to all functionalist social theory, has been the object of sustained theoretical critique (e.g. Sahlins 1976), but persists in much of the sociological literature on race. Yet if, as Sahlins suggests, we can judge theories as much by what they leave out as by what they explain, then we might conclude that the negative critique actually tells us very little about the ways in which racial meanings may operate as categories of human experience. Moreover, one might even argue that the apparently materialist grounding of the negative critique masks an idealist conceit in its self-effacing claim to establish racial meanings as 'ideological' in contradistinction to the 'truth' of its own position. For as Vološinov points out, 'consciousness' and 'understanding' are acts of reference between signs which are always materially embodied, 'nowhere is there a break in the chain, nowhere does the chain plunge into inner being, nonmaterial in nature and unembodied in signs' (1986: 11). Both race and its negation or critique are as fully 'real' as each other, though no less ideological for all that.

At issue here is the tendency of sociological theory to level all social distinctions to class (or, at least, 'power') and consider this to be an adequate explanatory procedure. Alternatively, I suggest not that race has

some irreducible 'meaning' but that the various social distinctions identified earlier as emergent within modern European thought constitute a
social order which is not reducible to some single explanatory key. Taken
together, these distinctions objectify modes of thinking whose reproduction
is not merely the reproduction of a hegemonic authority structure, but –
to paraphrase an argument of Nancy Munn's (1970) essayed in a very
different context – also the reproduction of the *a priori* grounds upon
which the possibilities of this structure are built. To employ the concept
of race in sociological analysis is certainly an analytic artifice but, I would
argue, when it is conceived syntagmatically as a moment of cultural process
it is a rather more plausible one than the familiar reductionism. Baldly
put, the ideologies of, for example, anti-racist political activism, or of
Rastafarian belief, or of white racial supremacy all motivate concepts of
'race' (which, of course, is not to say that they do so in ways which are
equally valid or appropriate). So too do many other aesthetic, political
and social movements which work upon and transform the meanings of
the concept. As Paul Gilroy (1993) has argued in relation to the 'Black
Atlantic' diaspora, these movements are not simply a reactive mirror to
racist essentialism but actively produce ideological meaning. Thus, to draw
once again upon Vološinov (1986: 102), 'race' should not be accorded
the status of a single, abhorrent meaning; rather, the 'reality' connoted by
race is the dialogic totality of the words and counter-words (or practices
and counter-practices) with which it is associated.[6]

These arguments go rather beyond the usual concerns of medical sociology, but they are relevant insofar as they serve to question the
implications of a common tendency within the sub-discipline for a negative
critique of the concept of race which – as with Sheldon and Parker –
conflates a (sociological) critique of ideology with a (vernacular) criticism
of dogma.[7] This negative critique implicitly takes the view that sociological analysis can effect a simple separation between ideology and
ontology, the former 'false' categories of socio-political dogma the latter
'real' categories of social being. The purpose of my preceding argument
is to question this distinction and the objectivist grounds upon which
arguments of the sort articulated by Sheldon and Parker assert their own
authority. In order to establish this position further and to anticipate its
implications for empirical research in medical sociology, I turn now to a
brief excursus on the work of Pierre Bourdieu.

Pierre Bourdieu: habitus, capital and meta-theory

I do not propose any general summary of Bourdieu's writings here, but
merely select three features of his theoretical enterprise which are salient
for present purposes: the concepts of habitus and capital, which are fundamental aspects of his 'theory of practice', and his meta-theoretical concern

with the 'practice of theory', in other words with the epistemological purview of sociological theory itself.

A central feature of Bourdieu's work is his concern with examining specific practices as emergent from an overall process of patterning or structure in the human world. Bourdieu subordinates the diversity of practices to a generative schema which he calls the *habitus*, 'the durably installed generative principle of regulated improvisations' (1990: 57). This schema, a kind of conceptual map through which individuals orchestrate their behaviour in socially competent ways, is inculcated in them by an 'implicit pedagogy' which operates from birth, often via learning the most mundane and 'obvious' of physical and social distinctions (inside/outside, male/female etc.). In this sense, the principles of social life are embodied via the habitus. In addition, Bourdieu emphasises the temporal dimensions of this process:

> The *habitus*, a product of history, produces individual and collective practices – more history – in accordance with the schemes generated by history. It ensures the active presence of past experiences, which, deposited in each organism in the form of schemes of perception, thought and action, tend to guarantee the 'correctness' of practices and their constancy over time, more reliably than all formal rules and explicit norms.
>
> (1990: 54)

Thus, for Bourdieu, 'practice unfolds in time and it has all the correlative properties, such as irreversibility, that synchronisation destroys. Its temporal structure ... and ... its directionality is constitutive of its meaning' (1990: 81).

With these ideas, Bourdieu is attempting to transcend the limitations of several strands of sociological theory. Against the structuralist tendency to abolish agency he posits an active subject, while refusing to conflate the latter with the individual of rational choice or utilitarian theory, strategically pursuing their self-transparent interests. Yet the incorporation of strategy along with time into his theory enables him to go beyond a view of social life as the mechanical reproduction of a reified system or order, of agents following 'rules'. Taken together, these insights suggest that social structures are actively reproduced, and their reproduction contains a constrained potential for change which establishes a necessary directionality to social life. Thus, against a critique of ideology which detaches unconscious functional purposes from people's self-conception of their actions and which identifies the former as the privileged level of sociological explanation, Bourdieu emphasises the embodied nature of social practice. Although there have been surprisingly few attempts to employ this approach to theorising race or ethnicity,[8] its potential for understanding the embodiment and transformation of historically objectified racial categories is apparent.

Bourdieu's concept of *capital* extends the micro-social level of habitus to the macro-social domain. Against the tendency of some theoretical schools to view structure as merely a product of social interaction, the idea of capital places emphasis upon the cumulative nature of social forms. Although a similar approach is taken in rational choice theory, which locates action within an 'economy of practices' through which agents attempt to maximise their store of wealth, the originality of Bourdieu lies in his recognition that capital can be extra-economic, and his concepts of symbolic, social and cultural capital enable him to build a sophisticated approach to social action, which he has developed most fully in his work on education (Bourdieu 1984, 1986; Bourdieu and Passeron 1977). The argument does not easily lend itself to summary, but in essence Bourdieu suggests that inequalities in educational outcome between children from different social classes do not necessarily stem from greater inputs in *economic* capital from their parents or in the schools they attend, but in the work of inculcation to acquire valued dispositions and knowledges which function as codes of inclusion and exclusion. There are, to be sure, links between cultural and economic capital, as where wealthier parents have more time or more money to invest in status attainment. But the likely 'return' on status investment is valued socially according to class habitus and different contexts will imply different kinds of investments. In view of the *modus operandi* of the habitus, these investments are not those of the rationally calculating subject, but are inculcated implicitly in formal and especially informal pedagogy. As Bourdieu puts it, 'because the social conditions of . . . [the] transmission and acquisition [of cultural capital] are more disguised than those of economic capital, it is predisposed to function as symbolic capital, ie. to be unrecognized as capital and recognized as legitimate competence' (1986: 245). In this way, 'ability' or the 'feel for the game' in given social contexts is reproduced as a correlate of class position.

It is important to note the nature of the distinction Bourdieu draws between economic capital and social or cultural capital; the latter is not the 'superstructure' to the former's 'base', and there may be radical differences in social or cultural capital between different fractions of a given economic 'class'. In this respect, the approach is considerably at odds with the Marxist tradition. Indeed, Bourdieu (1985) proffers powerful criticisms of Marxist class theory for its economism and for the 'ontological promotion' effected in Marx's famous distinction between classes 'in' and 'for' themselves, which fails to provide any account of how common economic or material conditions (what Bourdieu terms a 'class on paper') in themselves generate collective self-consciousness (a 'class in struggle'). Bourdieu's sophistication lies in describing with theoretical economy the ways in which familiar social attributes such as gender, occupational class, age and race, along with less familiar ones such as consumer and aesthetic taste, transform each other's collective meaning. This represents a development of class theory more akin to Weber than to Marx and is an aspect of the sociological critique of ideology which, as I argue below, could be usefully incorporated into the epidemiological traditions of medical sociology by helping to identify the convergences and divergences between 'class' as shared material circumstances and 'class' as collective consciousness.

However, notwithstanding the preceding points, there is something of a tension in Bourdieu's writings in relation to class theory, and at certain points his arguments coincide (or are at least homologous) with the economism he criticises. For example, in his more empirical mode (e.g. 1984) he works with an essentially economic model of class difference as 'working class', 'middle class' etc., upon which other distinctions are superimposed.[9] Perhaps more significantly, Bourdieu's insistence that the forms of capital are inter-convertible, such that symbolic capital effects the 'misrecognition' of class interest, seems ultimately to re-unite his approach with economistic class theory, emptying non-economic forms of capital of substantive meaning. Indeed, the very notion of 'capital' rather occludes the possibility that social status may not be articulated for strategic gain. In this respect, the reformulation of Marxist class theory in Bourdieu's account of the 'genesis of groups', while suggestive in many particulars, seems little less mechanistic than the economism he rightly criticises. At the same time, some critics regard Bourdieu's approach via key concepts such as habitus and capital as a *deus ex machina* which resolves theoretical contradictions only by burying them in elusive dialectics, a charge that Bourdieu's own pronouncements do little to dispel. His clearest statement on the concept of capital (1986) fails wholly to clarify the boundaries of symbolic, cultural and social capital, while he appears actively to celebrate the vagueness of the concept of habitus, arguing that 'habitus itself is in cahoots with the fuzzy and the vague', and against 'excessive logic and . . . the pursuit of anthropological coherence where it does not exist' (Bourdieu and Wacquant 1992: 22–3).

These apparently contradictory tendencies towards both vagueness and scientistic reductionism may have a common root in Bourdieu's attempt to establish sociology as an objective science of social meaning. Brubaker (1985) argues that Bourdieu's conceptual tools are not intended to constitute a theory of social life, but a meta-theory of the epistemological grounds upon which sociological theories are constructed. On this basis, he absolves Bourdieu from the apparent theoretical failings discussed above. This is a debatable move, and more critical approaches such as Dreyfus and Rabinow's (1993) attempt to disentangle the metaphysical claims of Bourdieu's 'science' from the weaker ontology implied in his theory of embodied practice are perhaps more convincing. Nevertheless, Brubaker correctly draws attention to Bourdieu's meta-theory, which recognises not only that social categories are inescapably ideological (in the sociological sense) but that intellectual categories formulated to account for them – albeit thereby breaking with a commitment to the ontological claims implied in those categories – are themselves ideological in the same sense. In this part of his work, he represents along with writers like Vološinov and perhaps the early Foucault a more self-reflective working through of the Marxist tradition – one which refuses to represent its critique of ideology as non-ideological – than that represented by the Althusserian critique of ideology which would appear to inform the position adopted by Sheldon and Parker. Bourdieu thus provides one way of treating categories like race theoretically (i.e. as ideology, in the sociological sense) without either abolishing them via arbitrary reductions or reifying them as given facts of social life, through showing how they can act as implicit models for other categories, while recognising that to accord any particular one a determinant role is merely an analytical conceit. The problem, perhaps, is that the argument operates at a highly abstract level and, although Bourdieu himself is one of the few sociologists to combine theoretically innovative scholarship with an active programme of empirical research, it is not always clear precisely how his meta-theory might inform a research agenda. In my view, his writings warrant an approach to health and race which constructs the health of racialised groups as an empirical problem and which demands testable theoretical constructions of the 'micro-practices' sustaining the reproduction of racialised patterns in health experience. At present, we lack both attempts to formulate the latter with any degree of sophistication or data sufficiently refined to test them.[10] I do not pretend to offer any simple solutions here, but in the final section of the chapter I set out some tentative thoughts on how these metatheoretical considerations may help to generate a programme of empirical research.

A research programme: health status and health care utilisation

In this section, I focus upon two areas of research; the racial patterning of health status and health service use by people from racialised minority groups.

A considerable body of evidence shows that differences exist in rates of illness between populations stratified according to conventional racial or ethnic criteria in Britain and elsewhere.[11] It is also apparent that most – though, I would argue, probably not all – of these differences are explicable in terms of the disadvantaged socio-economic position of racialised minorities. Perhaps through the combined influence of the negative critique and the broader focus of the public health tradition, this often leads to the suggestion that attention should be directed at the relationship between socio-economic status and health, and not at race *per se* (Sheldon and Parker 1992; Nazroo 1997: 144). The point is a salutary reminder to avoid invoking untested and essentialist assumptions about biological or cultural difference, but there is a danger here of conflating an untheorised or 'objective' notion of class as material position with an ontological notion of class as a self-conscious group (Bourdieu's 'classes on paper' and 'classes in struggle'). The health of racialised minorities may indeed be largely explained through socio-economic mechanisms which are not peculiar to those groups. This does not, however, mean that race is a redundant analytical category in health research, because for all the reasons set out earlier (and whatever the actual aetiological mechanisms), no specifically ontological grounds exist in the logic of this finding which can assimilate race to some other category of being. Thus, attention to the health of racialised minority groups remains of valid interest. While attempts to account in absolute terms for the extent of racial variation are undoubtedly best directed at socio-economic mechanisms (though the mediation of socio-economic status by race may usefully be addressed), here I wish to focus on other mechanisms which raise the possibility that race as a self-conscious collective identity may be relevant to health, albeit probably of lesser overall import.

Perhaps the most commonly invoked aetiological mechanism other than socio-economic status to explain racial variations in health is the idea of 'culture', a category inherited from the arguably rather unhelpful distinction made in the influential Black Report between 'materialist' and 'cultural/behavioural' explanations for inequalities in health (Townsend and Davidson 1992). It is not necessary for present purposes to rehearse all the arguments spawned by the distinction and the entrenched political positions about the causes of health inequalities associated with it. Here, it is sufficient to note, in keeping with the epidemiological rather than the critical traditions of medical sociology, that 'culture' has been understood in fairly empiricist – if not necessarily essentialist – fashion as a particular practice or set of practices associated with a given racialised group. However, from a theoretical perspective this conflation of 'culture' with specific practices is of limited utility and a more sophisticated approach is required.

Gantley's (1994) fascinating discussion of Sudden Infant Death Syndrome (SIDS) among Bangladeshis in Cardiff provides one indication of how to proceed in this regard. Gantley argues that the low incidence of SIDS among Bangladeshi infants in comparison to the general population may result from distinctive patterns of family interaction leading to a 'consistently rich sensory environment'. Households often consist of joint multigenerational families. Within a family, adults and infants typically sleep together in the same bed and infants feed regularly throughout the night, a practice facilitated by the fact that the adult men, who work predominantly in the restaurant trade, arrive home in the small hours of the morning, disturbing the other family members' sleep. Here, then, we observe a particular set of 'cultural' practices which may be shaped by a variety of factors: characteristic values – or at least behaviours – concerning family form; residential overcrowding; occupational constraints; feeding practices informed by specific local traditions, and so on. These practices may be the norm statistically, but may or may not be an aspired 'norm' given a difference in any of the circumstances described above. Moreover, when 'cultural practices' are explained in a specific context such as this, they begin to lose some of their mystique and some of their particularity. I am not myself Bangladeshi, nor do I work in a restaurant, yet the family sleeping patterns described by Gantley conform quite closely to those in my own family. My point here is that when a practice is specified, its occurrence can – in theory at least – be described as an empirical distribution which will most likely not be wholly confined to a particular racialised group, although it may be more prevalent in some than others. It may, of course, be a mistake to infer inter-group commonalities on the basis of similar practices with different generative factors and different links with other dimensions of social experience. But, in the context of a concern with health, that is an assertion that can be examined empirically by comparing health outcomes. This seems altogether preferable to the occult procedure which ties the racial patterning of health to given but unspecified 'cultural difference'. The approach, moreover, identifies the potential for change and variability introduced by the complexity of its elements, rather than simply assuming the persistence of difference.

The idea of 'culture' involved here is quite a specific, and specifically structured one. It is unlikely to be exactly the same as that associated with the kind of racialised appropriations of 'culture' invoked in political, aesthetic and other kinds of practice mentioned earlier. It may be that the highly deconstructive forms of theorising identities currently in vogue in mainstream sociological theory have some merit in understanding the transformations of racial meaning worked out in explicit political or aesthetic representations of 'blackness'. However, in the context of health this may be of lesser significance than tracking specific causal pathways which cut across racial identities however they are being defined, though there is clearly scope for psychological research which works on their intersection. Merely to point to the general ways in which cultural identifications are invested with racial significance does not in itself establish the significance of 'cultural factors' for the racial patterning of health.

Another sense in which the term 'culture' has been used within medical sociology which is germane to the present argument is the idea of specific 'cultures of health' within delimited social groups or communities. In the context of race, research in both the USA and Britain has suggested that people from racialised minority populations living in areas where these populations are concentrated residentially may enjoy better health than their counterparts living in areas of lower residential concentration, other things being equal (LaVeist 1993; Smaje 1995b). While requiring further empirical corroboration, this suggests that community-level features may exist which affect health and which are related, but not reducible, to economic or racial 'classes' (in Bourdieu's sense of the term). The US research suggests that these findings cannot easily be explained by simple material or economic mechanisms. Bourdieu's approach to the genesis of social groups and their embodied practice might prove to be a useful basis from which to approach these findings through its ability to theorise the mutually determining intersection of discrete group identities.

The second general area of interest relates to racial patterns in the use of health services. British studies have found a consistent tendency towards excess utilisation of GP services among several racialised minority groups – particularly South Asian ones – in relation to the white population, but low use of acute outpatient services. This finding is not readily explained by differences in demographic profile, socio-economic status, morbidity or GP referral behaviour (Smaje and Le Grand 1997; Smaje 1998), raising the possibility that services for racialised minorities are not delivered as effectively as for the population as a whole. Research in this area has been relatively sparse and several ways of accounting for these findings remain open. Here I raise three possibilities, all of which broadly fit into Bourdieu's 'forms of capital' framework.

First, in keeping with the critique of ideology associated with the traditions of medical sociology, it is possible that patients have different dispositions and motivations for medical consultation and that these at least partially covary with racialised identity. Remarkably little ethnographic 'thick description' exists regarding patient attitudes to using health services, particularly in relation to racialised identity, yet such motivations may affect service use in ways which could either raise or lower consultation rates. For example, Donovan's (1986) ethnographic study describes a characteristic disinclination among young Caribbean men to use GP services, while Thorogood (1992) reports a predilection among Caribbean women for the use of private general practitioners; recent quantitative research supports the former but not the latter finding (Smaje and Le Grand 1997; Smaje 1998). Further detailed qualitative research into the meanings people attach to health care use is certainly warranted. Following Bourdieu, the fact that health care might be socially valued in ways which differ within and between people in given social-structural positions, including racialised identification, is worthy of consideration. Of course, previous experiences of service use may crystallise over time into particular dispositions concerning their role or importance.

Second, it is possible that the ability to mobilise the social capital required to conduct a consultation with apparent 'competence' – as described by Bourdieu in the passage cited earlier – may also covary with racialised identity, such that either or both parties judge its 'quality' relative to a given need as poorer, necessitating further remedial action (including additional consultations). If the consultation constitutes a 'meeting between experts', to use the phrase of Tuckett *et al.* (1985), then perhaps some people have access to resources which make them appear more 'expert' than others. The appropriate conduct of a health care consultation is learned, and depends upon straightforward qualities such as mutual linguistic comprehension as well as more intangible factors such as the expectations in both parties regarding a satisfactory outcome. Again, detailed research is required to corroborate this point. However, it receives some support from an analysis of ethnic patterns in children's use of GP services. According to the government's General Household Surveys of 1992–4, children described by their parents as of Indian, Pakistani or Bangladeshi (henceforth, 'South Asian') ethnicity were, overall, 31 per cent more likely to have consulted a GP in the previous fortnight than children described as 'white', after adjusting statistically for demographic factors, parental occupational status and health status. However, when this figure is broken down by parental place of birth, it is apparent that this excess is associated with non-UK born parents, particularly mothers, while South Asian children with UK-born parents were *less* likely to have consulted a GP in the preceding fortnight (Cooper *et al.* 1999). If British birth proxies for the inculcation of 'legitimate competence' in Bourdieu's terms, then this may account for differences in patterns of utilisation. It should, however, be pointed out that due to problems of sample size these figures are not statistically significant and can therefore only be taken as suggestive. Moreover, when the same analysis is repeated for the Caribbean group, non-UK born parents appear slightly *less* likely to use GP services, indicating that the mechanism suggested above cannot easily be generalised as a monocausal explanation.

Finally, and in a related sense, it may be that particular kinds of behaviours and expectations are motivated in both parties to the encounter by an explicit or implicit consciousness of its racialised context. Most existing research on this point has examined professional rather than patient behaviours. For example, Bowler's (1993) ethnographic study of the way midwives mobilise racial stereotypes in managing their caseload is one example of how this process may operate. Hughes and Griffiths (1996) have also shown how particular stereotypes of social characteristics including race animate clinical decision-making, while I have found in my own research that health professionals sometimes make judgments about patient competence on the basis of social characteristics, including race, a process itself transformed by the racialised identity of the professional. Although taking a slightly different focus, Porter's (1993) ethnographic study shows how senior health professionals from racialised minority groups are able to defuse the racism of colleagues by mobilising the cultural capital accruing from their professional status. He further comments that professional codes curtail racist behaviours which workers may articulate in other social contexts. Thus, while the behaviours described here may be characterised as 'racist', it is important to note the way that racialised differences appear to be actively constructed within particular contexts. In other contexts quite different sensibilities may be motivated. However, following Bourdieu's arguments, it could be suggested that this particular racialised habitus functions as one of the ways in which race (or 'culture') is itself embodied.

It is worth noting finally that the 'forms of capital' framework developed by Bourdieu and employed here has been criticised for its resemblance to the earlier culture of poverty theory, which was widely condemned for its tendency to 'blame the victim' (Jenkins 1992). In my view, this criticism is largely misdirected because, unlike the culture of poverty theory, Bourdieu's approach contains no implication of situational maladaptation. In fact, the power of professionals to normalise their own definitions of competence or appropriate use runs throughout the preceding examples and, despite my earlier criticisms, Bourdieu's account of the convertibility of capital and in particular of the 'misrecognition' of symbolic capital is of some value in this context. However, the broader contribution of this kind of approach is its ability to transcend overdrawn dualities like 'blame the victim/blame the system' or 'part of the problem/part of the solution'. Clearer specification of how the 'victim' and the 'system' interact and are reproduced seems a necessary step for a theoretically-informed medical sociology to understand the relation of agents with structures. It may also help inform various political movements organised around the interests of the 'victim'. Certainly, it brings into focus the tensions between the public health and critical traditions of medical sociology, in which a normative standard for the amount of service people 'ought' to be using is counterposed to a much more ambivalent sense of the role of health services in the structuring of social life.

Conclusion

The suggestions above for the direction that empirical work on racial patterns in health status and in the use of health services are necessarily tentative and will undoubtedly require further conceptual refinement. They are proffered here merely as an attempt to move beyond some of the more entrenched dualities of thinking in this area. More broadly, I hope to have shown in this chapter that the negative critique of racial ideology – which seeks to abolish the concept of race from the analytical project of sociology (including medical sociology) – is theoretically inadequate, and that it is both necessary and possible to theorise race in such a way that it is neither rendered as epiphenomenal to some other analytical category, nor reified as a given fact of nature. This, I suggest, can help to develop a theoretically informed programme of empirical research in medical sociology. It may be over-ambitious to suggest that such a research programme could, in turn, help to refine approaches to the concept of race within broader sociological theory, but it is worth recalling the dictum that in health we find the substrate or remainder of all society's other activities. Attention to the racialised patterning of health experience may help us to see more clearly how race is configured within these activities and this, in turn, may help us to break down overly essentialist views of race or culture. Bhopal, writing critically from within the public health tradition, has argued that:

> to date most research on ethnic minority health has been by researchers whose main interest is in one . . . disorder . . . They seek a new perspective on that disorder; the ethnic minority angle is peripheral. In the future, more research needs to be done by researchers whose main interest is in ethnic minorities and their health; the disorder being peripheral.
>
> (1992: 54)

Medical sociologists are well placed to accept this challenge by beginning to articulate how health experience intersects with racial identification, without arbitrarily subsuming the latter into something else. My 'defence of race' in the context of medical sociology thus rests upon two planks; a *theoretical* argument that race – despite its historically contingent and politically dubious origins – cannot be expunged without cost from the categories of sociological analysis, and an argument warranted by this assertion that, empirically, racialised identifications of various kinds *may* affect health. In my view, this approach enables a more productive inter-meshing of sociology's various critical and empirical traditions than has hitherto proved possible.

Acknowledgements

I am grateful to the editors for comments on an earlier draft of the chapter, and to Helen Cooper for assistance in providing information on children's use of services.

References

Banks, M. (1996) *Ethnicity: Anthropological Constructions*, London: Routledge.
Bentley, G. (1987) 'Ethnicity and practice', *Comparative Studies in Society and History* 29: 24–55.

Bhopal, R. (1992) 'Future research on the health of ethnic minorities: back to basics: a personal view' in W. Ahmad (ed.) *The Politics of 'Race' and Health*, Bradford: Race Relations Research Unit.

Bourdieu, P. (1984) *Distinction: a Social Critique of the Judgement of Taste*, Cambridge, MA: Harvard University Press.

—— (1985) 'The social space and the genesis of groups', *Theory and Society* 14: 723–44.

—— (1986) 'The forms of capital' in J. Richardson (ed.) *Handbook of Theory and Research for the Sociology of Education*, New York: Greenwood Press.

—— (1990) *The Logic of Practice*, Cambridge: Polity Press.

Bourdieu, P. and Passeron, J.-C. (1977) *Reproduction in Education, Society and Culture*, London: Sage.

Bourdieu, P. and Wacquant, L. (1992) *Invitation to Reflexive Sociology*, Cambridge: Polity Press.

Bowler, I. (1993) '"They're not the same as us": midwives' stereotypes of South Asian descent maternity patients', *Sociology of Health and Illness* 15: 157–78.

Brubaker, R. (1985) 'Rethinking classical theory: the sociological vision of Pierre Bourdieu', *Theory and Society* 14: 745–75.

Cooper, H., Smaje, C. and Arber, S. (1999) 'Equity in health service use: examining the ethnic paradox', *Journal of Social Policy* 28: 457–78.

Donovan, J. (1986) *We Don't Buy Sickness: It Just Comes*, Aldershot: Gower.

Dreyfus, H. and Rabinow, P. (1993). 'Can there be a science of existential structure and social meaning' in C. Calhoun, E. LiPuma and M. Postone (eds) *Bourdieu: Critical Perspectives*, Cambridge: Polity Press.

Dumont, L. (1986) *Essays on Individualism: Modern Ideology in Anthropological Perspective*, Chicago: University of Chicago Press.

Foucault, M. (1970) *The Order of Things*, New York: Vintage.

—— (1977) 'Nietzsche, genealogy, history', in D. Bouchard (ed.) *Language, Counter-Memory, Practice*, Ithaca: Cornell University Press.

Gantley, M. (1994) 'Ethnicity and the sudden infant death syndrome: anthropological perspectives', *Early Human Development*, 38: 203–8.

Gilroy, P. (1990) 'The end of anti-racism', *New Community* 17: 71–83.

—— (1993) *The Black Atlantic: Modernity and Double Consciousness*, London: Verso.

Goldberg, D. (1993) *Racist Culture: Philosophy and the Politics of Meaning*, Oxford: Blackwell.

Grant, R. and Orr, M. (1996) 'Language, race and politics: from "black" to "African-American"', *Politics and Society* 24: 137–52.

Habermas, J. (1987) *The Philosophical Discourse of Modernity*, Cambridge: Polity Press.

Hannaford, I. (1996) *Race: the History of an Idea in the West*, Baltimore: Johns Hopkins University Press.

Hughes, D. and Griffiths, L. (1996) '"But if you look at the coronary anatomy . . .": risk and rationing in cardiac surgery', *Sociology of Health and Illness* 18: 172–97.

Jenkins, R. (1992) *Bourdieu*, London: Routledge.

Kapferer, B. (1988) *Legends of People, Myths of State: Violence, Intolerance and Religious Culture in Sri Lanka and Australia*, Washington, DC: Smithsonian Institution Press.

LaVeist, T. (1993) 'Segregation, poverty and empowerment: health consequences for African-Americans', *Milbank Quarterly* 71: 41–64.

Malik, K. (1996) *The Meaning of Race: Race, History and Culture in Western Society*, Basingstoke: Macmillan.

Marmot, M. (1989) 'General approaches to migrant studies: the relation between disease, social class and ethnic origin', in J. Cruickshank and D. Beevers (eds) *Ethnic Factors in Health and Disease*, Sevenoaks: Wright.

Munn, N. (1970) 'The transformation of subjects into objects in Walbiri and Pitjantjatjara myth', in R. Berndt (ed.) *Australian Aboriginal Anthropology*, Nedlands: University of Western Australia Press.

Nazroo, J. (1997) *The Health of Britain's Ethnic Minorities*, London: Policy Studies Institute.

Porter, S. (1993) 'Critical realist ethnography: the case of racism and professionalism in a medical setting', *Sociology* 27: 591–609.

Sahlins, M. (1975) *Culture and Practical Reason*, Chicago: University of Chicago Press.

Sheldon, T. and Parker, H. (1992) 'Race and ethnicity in health research', *Journal of Public Health Medicine* 14: 104–10.

Smaje, C. (1995a) *Health, 'Race' and Ethnicity: Making Sense of the Evidence*, London: King's Fund.

——(1995b) 'Ethnic residential concentration and health: evidence for a positive effect?', *Policy and Politics* 23: 251–69.

——(1997) 'Not just a social construct: theorising race and ethnicity', *Sociology* 31(2): 307–27.

——(1998) 'Equity and the ethnic patterning of GP services in Britain', *Social Policy and Administration* 32: 116–31.

Smaje, C. and Le Grand, J. (1997) 'Ethnicity, equity and the use of health services in the British NHS', *Social Science and Medicine* 45(3): 485–96.

Smith, R. (1996) 'On the disutility of the concept of 'ethnic group' for understanding status struggles in the modern world', in R. Smith, *The Matrifocal Family*, London: Routledge.

Sperber, D. (1975) *Rethinking Symbolism*, Cambridge: Cambridge University Press.

Stocking, G. (1968) *Race, Culture and Evolution: Essays in the History of Anthropology*, Chicago: University of Chicago Press.

Taylor, C. (1989) *Sources of the Self: the Making of Modern Identity*, Cambridge: Cambridge University Press.

Thorogood, N. (1992) 'Private medicine: you pays your money and you gets your treatment', *Sociology of Health and Illness* 14(1): 23–38.

Townsend, P. and Davidson, N. (1992) *Inequalities in Health: the Black Report and the Health Divide*, Harmondsworth: Penguin.

Tuckett, D., Boulton, M., Olson, C. and Williams, A. (1985) *Meetings Between Experts: An Approach to Sharing Ideas in Medical Consultations*, London: Tavistock.

Vološinov, V. (1986) *Marxism and the Philosophy of Language*, Cambridge, MA: Harvard University Press.

Williams, B. (1991) *Stains On My Name, War In My Veins: Guyana and the Politics of Cultural Struggle*, Durham, NC: Duke University Press.

Williams, S. (1995) 'Theorising class, health and lifestyles: can Bourdieu help us?', *Sociology of Health & Illness* 17: 577–604.

Chapter 4

Health, ageing and the lifecourse

Michael Bury

Introduction

The purpose of this chapter is to trace some of the connections between health, ageing and the lifecourse. Since the 1970s, medical sociology has developed a wide range of research on social influences in the occurrence and variations in health status and on the experience of health and health care. Whilst it has been concerned to examine the influences of social class, gender and, more recently, ethnicity on health, it has paid relatively little attention to age (Arber 1994). Yet, it is clear that age and health are related in ways that go beyond the most obvious biological parameters; for example, that sight, hearing or mobility diminish in later life. Certainly, the relationship between disability and ageing has received considerable attention on policy related social research and in social gerontology, but more sociological perspectives in such matters have been noticeable by their absence. It has been relatively rare to find articles on ageing and health published in medical sociology journals (Arber 1994). Though, as will be shown later, work on health inequalities is now making connections with ageing and the lifecourse, most medical sociology research has neglected these topics.

One of the reasons for this situation may be the fact that much of the agenda and funding of medical sociology has been influenced by academic and service based medical practitioners, especially in public health and primary care – for whom, with the obvious exceptions of geriatricians and gerontologists, ageing has not been a priority. However, this is unlikely to have been the only reason. Sociological researchers in health may also have been preoccupied with issues closer to their own circumstances and biographies, for example, the now considerable literatures on reproductive health among younger women, and that on illness experience and health beliefs among the middle aged. Likewise, the preoccupations with medical power and 'medicalisation' processes (with some recent work on the medicalisation of old age, e.g. Katz 1996) have also stemmed from the preoccupations of medical sociology as a fledgling sub-specialty finding its feet and needing to strike out at its powerful 'allies' (Strong 1979).

However, part of the problem here also lies with the concept of ageing. Though aspects of age are often mentioned in the kind of work discussed above, this is rarely done by employing age or ageing as sociological concepts. Rather, age is used as a taken-for-granted social variable that can be employed, commonsensically, when it seems necessary to group aggregate data together for presentational purposes. Thus, for example mortality data on inequalities might be presented in the form of 'male/female', 'aged 16–64', without any clear discussion of what the theoretical rationale for this might be.

'Ageing' remains an ambiguous concept if only because it is used synonymously for the study of old age – just as the term 'gender' is frequently used, wrongly, to mean the study of women. Although the present discussion will focus on a number of aspects of health and its determinants in later life and old age, it is important to identify at the outset the dual meaning of the term 'ageing' when used in a sociological context.

'Ageing' involves two interrelated but analytically separable aspects of change over time: 'biographical' and 'historical' time (cf. Blaxter 1992 for distinctions between 'personal', 'calender' and 'social' time in the context of health research). In the first place, ageing refers to the processes, experiences and events that occur during a person's lifetime – that is, the *experiential* aspects of ageing. These relate to the variable nature of biographical events such as age at leaving school, entering and exiting the workforce (if at all), the onset of illness or disability (Bury 1982, 1991) and the occurrence of 'life events' such as marriage, divorce, bereavement and the like. Whilst some of these experiential aspects of ageing are highly individual, unpredictable and 'emergent' in character, many of them are influenced by the social contexts within which a person lives, as well as the operation of 'age related structures' that stand apart from the individual (Riley *et al.* 1988) and govern events. Age related structures that influence biographical experience, such as the school leaving or retirement age are set by governmental or economic institutions and have a direct impact on the person's biography.

Second, historical time is important to the concept of ageing in a number of important ways. In particular, it directs our attention to the influences of *cohort effects* on the experience of ageing. That is, it suggests the need to see individuals as part of generational groups that are born and age in different historical contexts; as members of age related collectivities, as well as individuals moving in and out of age related structures. Indeed, generational and historical contexts interact in powerful ways, for example in the changing nature of school leaving age and its influence on the educational and occupational achievement of individuals in later life. In a study carried out of the very old in the late 1980s by Bury and Holme (1991) it was found that many people from the cohort born in the final years of the last century left school at age 13 or younger. While upper-class respondents may have stayed in education until their middle or even later teens, others left much earlier. One man reported leaving school at age 9. At school he and his fellow pupils had to pay 'twopence a week and take our pens and pencils with us' (Bury and Holme 1991: 24). Memories of such events stayed with the respondents in this study throughout their long lives. As will be shown, the effects of early experiences of health as well as on matters such as education are no less dramatic. One needs an active historical imagination (as well as good empirical data) to consider the changes in age related structures and social organisation, as well as in the pattern of illness, that have affected the experience and beliefs of different birth cohorts throughout the twentieth century.

In approaching the nature of ageing in biographical and historical terms, and thus as sociological phenomena, the concept of 'lifecourse' has particular attractions. Overarching terms such as 'lifespan' or 'lifecycle', previously used in medical and social gerontology writings, tend to convey an overly static view of ageing, or at best one that suggests a predictable series of stages through which people inevitably pass. While birth, maturation and death may well be constants of most human existence they clearly set only the most general limitations on experience. As Hockey and James argue, in developing a 'discussion of ageing within a lifecourse, rather than a life cycle, perspective it becomes possible to emphasise the variations and continuities in social status and position which people experience as they mature' (Hockey and James, 1993: 14). It is in the spirit of this approach that the current discussion hopes to promote a more sociologically consistent approach to ageing and health.

This chapter develops this argument by exploring two main contemporary perspectives on health, ageing and the lifecourse. First, it examines the way in which the lifecourse has been reconceptualised in recent years, through ideas such as the 'Theory of the Third Age', put forward by the historical sociologist, Peter Laslett (1989) and through 'postmodern' forms of sociological writing on ageing. These attempts to develop new approaches to ageing rest on certain assumptions, not only about changes in the age structure of contemporary populations, but also about the health experience of different birth cohorts. Laslett, in particular, builds his case on the idea that future generations will increasingly experience a 'compression of morbidity' in later life, allowing for a more positive and 'successful' form of ageing to occur. Postmodern arguments, for example those of Featherstone and Hepworth (1989), centre on the idea of an erosion of the boundaries surrounding stages of the lifecourse, and these, too, assume greater health, a capacity to be active and greater material well-being in later life. Both approaches add up to a challenge to adopt a more optimistic perspective on the lifecourse and ageing.

Second, the chapter examines a more pessimistic perspective which draws on arguments and evidence that show the negative impact that age related structures and early experience may have on material well-being and health in later life. Far from seeing more fluid boundaries in the lifecourse, this approach argues that adult occupational structures in particular, continue to have a determining effect on material circumstances and health as the years unfold. The resulting deprivation, poverty and dependency found among significant groups of the elderly are taken to be central here. In assessing the logic of this argument, the chapter also examines more recent evidence from work on health inequalities which suggests that early experiences of poor health, in childhood, as well as adverse circumstance, may significantly influence health status and social position in later life. From this viewpoint early health and social circumstance are central to the development of a sociological view of the lifecourse.

Finally, the chapter attempts to draw the threads of these two perspectives together. It suggests that while the optimistic perspective breaks with negative stereotypes of the lifecourse and ageing, it may risk seriously underestimating the problems associated with ageing in late modern society. On the other hand, while pessimistic approaches may appear to document problems in a realistic manner, they may undermine the need for a greater recognition of change and heterogeneity of experience across the lifecourse. The chapter concludes by arguing for a greater dialogue between the two perspectives in order to produce a more sociologically-coherent approach to ageing, health and the lifecourse.

Changing boundaries across the lifecourse: the optimistic perspective

It is no coincidence that greater attention to the concept of the 'lifecourse' is occurring as rapid changes in the nature of ageing are taking place in late modern societies. As argued above, the adoption of a lifecourse perspective signals a move away from a view of ageing that is based on fixed stages or cycles. And arguments that ageing, in both its social structural and experiential dimensions, is becoming more 'fluid' in character and less constrained by institutional and cultural boundaries are increasingly commonplace (Featherstone and Hepworth 1989, 1991; Hazan 1994). The advent of greater consumer confidence among older people, the extension of youth culture more generally to older cohorts, a fall in the average age of retirement, and developments such as a reduction in age barriers to medical treatments, all signal change in the pattern of ageing, and in social life more generally.

Behaviours that were once confined to a particular phase of the 'lifecycle' may now occur at different times, in a more open ended lifecourse.

The saying 'you are as old as you feel' takes on new salience as people in later life adopt aspects of consumer lifestyles (including health promoting activities, as well as leisure activities) that were once confined to the young. As will be shown below, a decline in the prevalence of ill health in later life is being heralded as a major factor underpinning such cultural change. And it is worth noting that change in this area may be reinforced by frequent reports of bio-medical research which appear to show not only that a healthier and more active old age is possible, but that the biological parameters of the human lifespan themselves may be more open ended than once thought.

One of the most trenchant arguments for a recognition of changes in the ageing of modern populations, especially the need for a new and more positive perspective on the lifecourse, is that of the historical sociologist, Peter Laslett. Laslett's 'Theory of the Third Age', has particular relevance for examining connections between health, ageing and the lifecourse (Laslett 1987,1989). Although few sociologists who are currently writing on changes in the lifecourse have drawn explicitly on Laslett's demographic analysis and social commentary, much of what he has had to say has a direct bearing on the development of sociological approaches to ageing and health.

Laslett's approach is based on an analysis of the 'demographic transition' which has occurred in most Western societies, and is now extending rapidly on a global scale. In essence this process has involved the extension of longevity to an ever greater proportion of the population, to the point where a 'Third Age Structure' is held to be emerging. What Laslett means by this is that where populations reach a point where 'the majority of all males, and thus of all females reaching their 25th birthday will go on to their 70th' then a Third Age structure has emerged (Laslett 1989: 85). The 'Third Age' (essentially a period in middle and early old age) is the pivotal point around which Laslett's call for a redesignation of the 'ages of man' occurs.

In this schema, the two stages before the Third Age are those of dependency in childhood – the First Age – and independence (of 'earning and saving') – the Second Age. What is distinctive about late modern societies, according to Laslett, is the existence of an extensive Third Age for the majority of the population – one that is characterised by individuals being outside the constraints of the labour market, and thus being able to pursue valued goals; in other words, an era of 'personal fulfilment'. Though it is clear that Laslett's definition of the Third Age must mean, following his demographic analysis, that it is located in the years before and after official retirement age, it does not follow that the cultural attributes associated with the Third Age have to be confined to that age group alone. The Third Age may be experienced, variably, across a considerable span of the lifecourse, depending on circumstance and attitude. People may enter the Third Age early, through choice, or through events such as early retirement, and still be in it well beyond retirement. Following the Third age, The Fourth Age – an era of 'dependence, decrepitude and death' – finally occurs. Though the transition from the Third to the Fourth age is at some point inevitable for Laslett, it, again, is not fixed at a specific age – though he clearly has in mind some time around the age of 80 or 85 (Laslett 1989: 41).

Laslett's 'Theory of the Third Age' is based, as has been shown, partly on changing demographic structures. The 'Third Age' in this sense is descriptive of secular changes in age structures of modern populations. However, Laslett also presumes a certain level of material well-being for the Third Age to flourish (as do those postmodernists that speak of the emergence of 'post-scarcity values', Featherstone and Hepworth 1989, see below), and Laslett argues for changes in the value orientation of younger cohorts as they now approach the Third Age, especially women. These value orientations may be expressed in the need for education in later life or in other ways of actively embracing a positive approach to growing old. However, the present discussion focuses on the implications for health that are involved in such an approach to the 'Third Age' (for a more general review see Bury 1992, 1995).

Central to Laslett's optimistic perspective on ageing and the lifecourse (at least in the Third Age) is his argument concerning improved health status in later life. If the Third Age is to represent a progressive step forward in a reconceptualised map of the 'ages of man', it must be based on a presumption that health and quality of life during this period is likely to improve. Without such a presumption, the extension of the average lifespan will simply mean 'living longer and doing worse'. If, however, in Laslett's terms, health problems associated with ageing can be postponed to the end of the lifecourse, i.e. into a short 'Fourth Age', then the potential gains of the Third Age may be realised.

In developing this line of argument, Laslett follows the work of the American physician James Fries (1980, 1989), and his ideas concerning the 'compression of morbidity': the postponement of ill health and disability into an ever later stage of the lifecourse. The 'compression of morbidity' in Fries' formulation rests on an assumption that the maximum lifespan is fixed, at around the age of 80. If increased levels of poor health were to become characteristic in old age, a greater proportion of the lifespan would then be spent in poor health; i.e. an 'extension of morbidity' would occur. Moreover, if the maximum lifespan of humans is not fixed but increasing, as some scientists maintain, then added years of ill health would necessarily increase, short of a dramatic delay in onset. In such circumstances, even a later age of onset might still be accompanied by an 'extension of morbidity'. In 1980 Fries argued, however, that his own assessment led to the conclusion, that 'the number of very old persons will not increase, that the average age of diminished physical vigour will decrease, that chronic illness will occupy a smaller proportion of the typical lifespan, and that the need for medical care in later life will decrease' (Fries 1980: 130). In other words, old age is likely to be accompanied by shorter periods of ill health and that, as a result, the 'compression of morbidity' will occur.

In 1989, despite considerable criticism of this position, especially Fries' erroneous prediction that the number of the very old will not increase (Brody 1985; Bury 1988) Fries was able to maintain that 'emerging data demonstrate a slowing of increases in life expectancy and a delay in the age of onset of major chronic diseases' (Fries 1989: 209). Of course, the fact that average life expectancy may be slowing (doubtful in itself) does not mean that the *number* of the very old will not increase, because this is significantly affected by the size of successive *cohorts* moving into old age. But leaving this on one side, the optimistic picture painted by Fries, in which the task of policy-makers and doctors is to encourage individual choice, and a 'use it or lose it' approach to health and ageing, one in which 'a goal of a vigorous long life might be an attainable one' (Fries 1980: 135) has been enormously attractive to a number of writers on ageing, including Laslett.

Although Laslett acknowledges the difficulties with Fries' position, especially, as noted, the latter's tendency to underestimate the increase in the numbers of the very old (Laslett 1989: 58), Laslett argues that the main line of Fries' argument 'is in harmony with one of the principal precepts of the theory of the Third Age' (Laslett 1989: 61). This is, that people will (indeed 'must') conduct themselves across the lifecourse, especially during the Third Age with 'continued activity of body and mind' in such a way that the Fourth Age 'will come as late and be as brief as possible' (p. 61). Physical exercise, the adoption of a healthy diet and other health promoting activities should thus be engaged in throughout life, not merely in an effort to extend it, but in order to ensure that the 'compression of morbidity' occurs in later years. This is especially relevant to women, who are not only more numerous than men in later life, but who also need to shake off, Laslett argues, the more negative forms of behaviour often associated with old age and women's social position in the past, for example, 'wearing black, looking submissive and regretful, being thankful that no new thing is to be expected from them' (Laslett 1989: 78). 'Activism' will replace 'disengagement' in later life, as people are healthy and motivated enough to emphasise 'planning and doing, up to the very moment when the Fourth Age makes itself manifest' (Laslett 1989: 156).

It is here, though, that this more optimistic view of ageing, runs into some difficulty. As Laslett himself acknowledges, evidence of an increase in the postponement of ill health and disability to the very last years if not months of life, is very difficult to assess. And the idea that the Fourth

Age is, or will become, the repository of serious morbidity and disability problems runs the risk of transferring negative views of ageing in general to the 'oldest old'. This is especially unfortunate given the growing evidence that the very old are themselves more heterogeneous than is often thought (Bury and Holme 1991; Tinker 1996: 70–1) and that some aspects of the 'compression of morbidity argument' are therefore reconcilable with very old age. In a careful review, Suzman *et al.* (1992) have argued that disability may be offset by *improved* functional capacity in the very old, and that it is 'no longer feasible for health and social policy to accept disability as an inevitable, permanent, or residual state *at any age*' (Suzman *et al.* 1992: 10, emphasis in original).

However, whatever one's view of the relationship between the 'Third' and 'Fourth' age is, even these attempts to question the 'inevitable' links between poor health, dependency and later life all speak to a more 'fluid' form of lifecourse, one which is less based on fixed biological assumptions about health in old age, or on cultural assumptions about behaviours that might be deemed 'appropriate' to a specific age group. Laslett and Fries both presume that the adoption of 'healthy lifestyles' across the lifecourse, and not just among the young, is desirable and feasible. Fries' 'use it or lose it' might be the catch-phrase for people at any age, in today's health promoting culture. More importantly, such an approach to health and ageing chimes in with the development of other sociological views of the lifecourse.

For example, sociologists have recently pointed to the ways in which changes in the age structure of modern populations are now interacting with other institutions to bring about major alterations in experience. Just as Laslett saw that the 'Second Age' of productive life may not be fixed within defined chronological boundaries, so Kholi (1988) has argued that the cultural underpinnings of modern society, especially its 'work ethic' may no longer be able to manage the changes underway. He asks: 'Given that social life is structured around work and its organisation, how can we theoretically cope with a situation in which a large (and still growing) part of the population has left the domain of formally organised gainful work, and left it for good?' (Kholi 1988: 371). The answer to his own question lies in the argument that modern culture may be moving away from a reliance of 'work' as a central motif. Although Kholi argues that 'the structure of work is still in place', he also suggests that 'the domain of consumption and leisure is expanding, in terms of available resources, and culturally, in terms of basic values' (p. 372).

The task for sociology in such a context is not simply to reflect on the ageing process, but on the effects of the interaction of demographic and socio-economic change on society as a whole. Boundaries and markers that functioned in a society with a clear work ethic and lines drawn round working life and retirement no longer hold sway. Other commentators such as Featherstone and Hepworth (1989) have emphasised the argument that 'universal stages of life development can be seen to be flawed' (Featherstone and Hepworth 1989: 143). This means that there is 'less emphasis than in the past being placed on age specific role transitions and scheduled identity development' (p. 144). Although, as with Kholi, these changes are seen as 'emergent cultural tendencies', rather than fully developed properties of contemporary cultures, nonetheless Featherstone and Hepworth argue that people will 'continue to deny the need to slow down, to rest, to take a back seat' (Featherstone and Hepworth 1991: 374).

Moreover, not only is the world of work less central, but 'post-scarcity values' – again, of consumerism and leisure – become more important. And, as with Laslett, the position of women and ageing is significant, in that they will be less 'disengaged' and 'hidden from history'; rather, they will be 'valid partners' on the social scene (Featherstone and Hepworth 1991: 145–6) as relations between the sexes becomes less dominated by patriarchy. The impact of consumerism and its impact of changing lifestyles, the media's ability to circulate information and imagery at an increasing pace, together with other 'democratising' cultural developments leads to the possibility of a relative shift in the relationships between men and women, and the emergence of more positive imagery of old age more generally (Featherstone and Hepworth 1993). In turn, later life itself is becoming 'feminised' (Arber and Ginn 1991) both in the sense of the continuing preferential survival of women and of the increasing salience of the interests and values of women across the lifecourse, for example, 'mutual assistance, solidarity, and reciprocal respect' (Arber and Ginn 1991: 49; see Bury 1995, for a fuller discussion of gender and ageing).

Such notions reinforce the adoption of a more optimistic perspective on ageing in the future. Katz (1996) for example, argues that under conditions of rapid cultural change 'disciplinary practices' surrounding old age (social regulation *and* the development of discursive practices such as gerontology) are less stable and sure of themselves than they once were. This may lead to the 'undisciplining' of ageing, in which 'the elderly' as a category may disappear. If age related boundaries are more permeable, and if modes of behaviour and experience are less tied to chronological stages of a 'lifecycle' then the need for the 'dividing practices, that give rise to categories such as 'the elderly' are themselves undermined, especially when we consider the many ways old age is 'crosscut by gender, class and ethnic divisions, religious affiliation, and regional differences' (Katz 1996: 136). Under such circumstances heterogeneity becomes the watchword, and diversity becomes the focus of research: 'current field studies suggest that changes in work, lifestyle, health, demography, politics and lifecourse divisions are making unified concepts of old age untenable' (p. 136). From this optimistic viewpoint sociology needs to analyse the impact of changing experience in the ageing process, in order, specifically, to challenge the assumption that poor health is an inevitable characteristic of growing old.

Inequalities across the lifecourse: the pessimistic perspective

Alongside the development of optimistic, and, in some cases, openly 'celebratory' postmodern views of ageing and the lifecourse, including its health dimensions, lies a perspective which has consistently stressed inequality and dependency across the lifecourse, and especially in old age. Whilst the optimistic perspective is, perhaps, in the ascendant in sociological writing on old age, this more pessimistic perspective continues to exert considerable influence, especially in social policy circles and in social research on health in later life.

This pessimistic view stems in large part from arguments concerning the effects of factors associated with social class and material deprivation on the lifecourse, and on dependency creating structures in old age. The first of these approaches is particularly associated with the work of writers such as Walker in the UK and Estes in the US. In a series of papers these authors have mapped the effects of labour market position among adults on the life chances of the elderly. Not surprisingly, they find that the more favourable individuals' positions are during their working lives, the better off they are in retirement. Occupational pensions, income, housing and other factors in old age reflect social position at earlier stages of the lifecourse. While some older people have benefited from economic development since the end of the Second World War, talk of 'post-scarcity values' is misplaced from this viewpoint, when poverty and deprivation are still significant for many, perhaps the majority, in old age.

Walker, for example, although arguing for a view of later life that moves away from over-emphasising biological differences and psychological adjustment to the ageing process stresses the 'social creation' of dependency (Walker 1981, 1987, 1993; see also Townsend 1981). Central to this process is the impact of the division of labour in modern societies, and especially the operation of the labour market. Although there is 'some reality' behind the myth of affluence among the elderly today (Walker 1993: 287) 'poverty is still the principal financial problem faced by this group' (p. 281). Walker argues that 'while just over one in five (21 per cent) of all persons in Great Britain are over pension age they comprise nearly three out of ten of those living on incomes on or below the income support level, or socially agreed, standard of poverty' (p. 281). Estes has argued a similar case for the US (Estes 1986, 1991) calling for an approach to ageing which stresses the influence of 'one's location in the social structure and the relations generated by the economic mode of production', including the gendered nature of the division of labour (Estes 1991: 21).

Like Walker, this produces a picture of accumulated disadvantage for women in particular across the lifecourse and in old age, reinforced as we shall see, by dependency through poor health and disability.

Recently, attempts have been made to square this view of economic determination of quality of life, with changes in the labour market. Phillipson (1994), for example, noting Kholi's and Featherstone and Hepworth's work amongst others, still argues for a perspective that recognises the nature of a changing 'political economy of the labour market, over the last twenty years, with the vulnerability of certain groups to prolonged unemployment, early exit from work or consignment to low paid employment' (1994: 132), pointing to a largely pessimistic scenario. Increasingly, though life is now being managed 'outside formal occupational roles . . . the financing of diverse routes being taken out of work is only secured by those who combine high status positions within paid employment, with secure pathways out of the workforce' (p. 146). For many, and especially women, 'inequalities will arise from taking the traditional male pattern of work as typical of workers now (and of women in particular) as a basis for organising pensions and other benefits in the future' (p. 144). That is, benefits will still be linked to patterns of continuous, permanent, full time and relatively well paid male employment, which are increasingly less available. If this persists, scarcity rather than 'post-scarcity' will accompany the decline in the 'work society', and will dominate the lives of large sections of older people, as they move into retirement.

Such a picture of changing patterns of work, material well-being and the lifecourse has a powerful bearing on health considerations. The documentation of health problems in later life, from this perspective, far from striking a note of optimism, as the result of a process of the 'compression of morbidity', sets out to demonstrate the extent of health problems in later life, even when heterogeneity is recognised. Again, the focus of those working within this framework is on disadvantages experienced by men and especially women across the lifecourse.

Arber and Ginn (1991) for example, whilst recognising the dangers of creating a 'false impression that old age is primarily a time of health problems' (Arber and Ginn 1991: 107) justify concentrating on poor health, illness and disability among the elderly because of the significance these have for policy-makers. Like Walker and others, their discussion sees poor health and material disadvantage in later life being two sides of the same (class and gendered) coin. Poor health and poor levels of income lead to the creation of poor and dependent pensioners. As a result, data on health in later life are almost entirely concerned with negative issues, with a 'paucity of data on positive health and well being' (p. 107). This negativity stems, in part, Arber and Ginn argue, from the nearness to death which inevitably accompanies later stages of the lifecourse, and which work on the elderly invokes. Though these authors note the arguments of Fries and others concerning prospects for healthier old age, in the future, they go on to document the burden of ill health in the present – especially among women.

Quoting the work of Hall and Channing (1990) they state that 'among those over 75 twice as many women as men were housebound (22 compared to 11 percent) and that 36 percent of men were medically assessed as fit compared to a quarter of women' among the elderly sample in the study (Arber and Ginn 1991: 111). Their own analysis of the General Household Survey shows that moderate and severe disability increases step wise with advancing years, from age 65 upwards (p. 114). Again, women are worse off than men, even taking into account the possibility that women report more ill health that men in this age group. The sex differences in illness that cause restrictions in mobility, most notably arthritis, are likely to be the main cause.

Arber and Ginn suggest that evidence of the 'compression of morbidity' is difficult to assess, with sociologists such as Verbrugge pointing out that fatal conditions are increasingly turned into chronic ones (Arber and Ginn 1991: 119; Verbrugge 1989), whilst others (e.g. Fries) see health promotion and judicious use of health care, together with improved living standards, producing a healthier old age for future cohorts. It seems that in terms of *reported* ill health the more pessimistic perspective of a growing 'burden' of ill health associated with an ageing population may be more justified. Recent evidence from the General Household Survey, appears to show a worsening of self-reported health over a ten year period (CSO 1998). Although it is recognised that changes in reported ill health may reflect methodological artefacts, or the effects of greater expectations about health over time, the fact that such expectations may be changing also means that demands for health services may likewise increase. Though the well documented evidence of the association between ageing and the use of health and personal social services across the lifecourse may sometimes disguise the enormous costs of serious and life threatening illness among *infants and children*, the increase in numbers of the old and especially the very old clearly give policy-makers and politicians cause for concern.

In this context, it is important to consider recent research on health inequalities which has begun to connect data on health in early life with the debates about the lifecourse, health and ageing. Though, as will be evident, there are different emphases in such work, it, too, points to sources of differential experience and the accumulated burden of poor health over biographical time, with little evidence of a reduction of morbidity with the passing of historical time. In the main, such work documents the substitution of diseases associated with greater longevity, especially 'degenerative' diseases such as coronary heart disease, cancer and those causing disability, for those (mainly the infections) that affected younger people in previous generations. Wittingly or otherwise, this adds to the concern with the burden of illness and dependency in an ageing population.

The increase in interest in lifecourse research and health inequalities has been stimulated, in part, from debates surrounding the work of David Barker, in which the pattern of ill health in adult and later life is seen to be strongly influenced, if not determined, by circumstances in infancy, and even *in utero* (the so called 'Barker Thesis'; see the collection of essays in, Barker 1992). Barker's ideas have come to hold considerable sway, especially in public health and other medical circles, as they provide a way of approaching health inequalities in disorders such as cardiovascular disease, bronchitis and hypertension, within a lifecourse perspective. Vagero and Illsley (1995) argue that, in fact, the evidence of the effects of such factors as low birth weight on health in adult and later life, *in the absence of social disadvantage* is less than clear cut and this suggests that 'the theory of adult disease having foetal origins is riddled with problems' (Vagero and Illsley 1995: 231). The notion of 'biological programming' introduced by Barker is particularly singled out for criticism, as it can easily deflect attention from the role of adverse circumstances in the present.

However, these authors go on to argue that the emphasis on the early environment has advantages, if set within a lifecourse perspective. Existing birth cohort studies in Britain, and elsewhere, which are now in a position to examine health in adult and later life, are drawing on, and contributing to such perspectives in their mapping of inequalities. Of importance here, though, is that while the positive effects of social mobility over time are recognised in such work, the data presented tend to reinforce a pessimistic view of those factors producing poor health and persisting inequalities. Indeed, early biological *and* social disadvantage combine, in such an approach, to create a strongly determined and a largely negative picture of outcomes for health in later life. In this sense they connect with social policy research on the influence of occupational structures discussed above.

In a review of a variety of methods used to examine health inequalities across the lifecourse, Wadsworth (1997) for example, suggests that the value of prospective 'follow-up' designs, though often constrained by the need to wait for age to increase, allows for an exploration of the intersection of historical and biological factors. By early adult life the 'imprint of time' (Wadsworth 1991) including the importance of educational attainment, is evident 'in occupational and socio-economic status; and these in turn are strongly associated with health' (Wadsworth 1997: 862). Whilst few of the available cohort studies, such as Wadsworth's own national sample of people born in 1946, have yet produced information on the elderly, it is likely, Wadsworth argues, that such work will reveal important

connections between favourable and unfavourable socio-economic circumstances in early life, occupational status and vulnerability to unemployment
in adult life, and good or ill health in later life (Wadsworth 1997: 863;
also see, Power *et al.* 1996, on the 1958 birth cohort study; and Davey
Smith *et al.* 1997, on socio-economic influences on health in the lifecourse of men in the west of Scotland).

Prospective studies which are following through cohorts already in their
middle age, for example the 20–07 study in Glasgow, are showing a picture
of lifetime inequality affecting health in later life (Ford *et al.* 1994).
Although interventions at the earliest stage of life hold out the best prosect
of prevention, as Wadsworth points out 'it is unlikely that health inequalities can be easily or rapidly reduced, increasingly so as the individual
ages, since individuals carry an accumulation of health potential which is
hard to change' (Wadsworth 1997: 867). The accumulation of structural
and material influences on health through the lifecourse appears to offer
no easy policy solutions to those articulating the pessimistic perspective,
short of major changes in social relations, especially those relating to
persistent class and status differences.

Conclusion

This chapter has provided a brief overview of current approaches to health,
ageing and the lifecourse. Though much of the present discussion has
focused on later life, a sociological approach to 'ageing' does not necessarily mean a preoccupation with old age alone, when approached from
a lifecourse perspective. Social and biological influences on health across
the lifecourse, including those in childhood, adolescence, the adult years
and later life, are now clearly available for study with a variety of data
and from a number of viewpoints (e.g. Hockey and James 1993; Davey
1995). In as much as the concern of policy-makers and researchers lies
with health and dependency in later life, the influences of early and adult
life *and* conditions among older people need to come into the picture. It
is clear that early material circumstances in childhood and adult life not
only have an effect on the standard of living and quality of life in old
age, but also on health, as shown by the fact that mortality ratios still
correlate closely with earlier social class position, even at age 85 (Fox
et al. 1985).

This chapter has grouped together some of the current approaches to
health, ageing and the lifecourse within two broad perspectives, optimistic
and pessimistic. It is likely that readers of this chapter and authors of
some of the work reviewed may object to this division, and it has to be
admitted that this has been more a means of organising the material, that
an attempt to set up rigid boundaries. As noted, sociologists such as Arber
recognise the dangers of operating solely within a 'problems perspective'

in studying old age, even though it may be justified in documenting inequalities in later life. However, the chapter has suggested that, in the main, perspectives used in the field of ageing are adopted uncritically. To this extent the distinction used in this chapter may serve to throw into relief the contours of research on health, ageing and the lifecourse.

As far as the 'optimistic' perspective is concerned the main tension lies in the tendency to regard social change as bringing about a secular trend towards a wealthier and healthier old age. The demographic trends in contemporary societies and the prevailing ideology of health promotion are taken by 'Third Age' advocates to constitute the basis for a radically different view of the lifecourse. The increasing 'compression of morbidity' is presumed to mean that old age in the future, if not the present, will be characterised by a healthy, active lifestyle. Research on 'successful ageing' will become the focus of enquiry (e.g. Baltes and Carstensen 1996) even taking into account the nature of inevitable biological changes and 'decrements' in later life, and the persistence of 'disengagement' as well as 'engagement', especially amongst the 'oldest old' (Johnson and Barer 1992).

From this perspective a 'postmodern' view of ageing and the lifecourse emerges, one which, as we have seen, stresses the waning of the 'work society' and the consequent blurring of boundaries round different stages of the lifecourse. Here, as with 'Third Age' theorising, the possibilities of adopting different lifestyles across the lifecourse are emphasised, rejecting the negative imagery that has hitherto surrounded growing old. Even the process of 'infantilisation' which sociologists have argued characterises popular imagery and some behaviour towards the elderly – treating older people as dependent children (Hockey and James 1993; Bytheway 1995) may be celebrated, if only in a postmodern and ironic fashion, as a means of resisting 'adult' values (Hepworth 1996).

Important though this optimistic perspective may be in striking a counter-intuitive and positive note about ageing, it frequently falls foul of appearing unrealistic and even romantic about old age. The need for a sober analysis of health and the lifecourse, one in which improvements *and* persistent sources of dependency, pain and poor quality of life are recognised, is frequently lost in the optimistic view. The idea of 'post-scarcity values' for example, sits uneasily alongside anecdotal and research evidence of poverty in old age. General references to 'heterogeneity' in old age do not entirely resolve this dilemma.

The 'pessimistic perspective', on the other hand, runs the risk, as has been shown, of conveying a view of health and ageing across the lifecourse as being dominated by persistent inequality, poverty and deprivation. Social and biological circumstances interact in this view, to create a situation that is strongly deterministic of a host of problems. The pessimistic view sees strong elements of continuity between generations in contrast to the optimistic perspective, where discontinuity prevails. The pessimistic perspective is one locked into a view of modern society and its discontents; the optimistic perspective celebrates the advent of change and cultural forms where healthy lifestyle can be adopted with effect at all ages (Bury 1998) whilst the pessimistic view sees little cause for celebration.

It is unfortunate that these perspectives on health, ageing and the life-course have tended to operate with little reference to each other. The optimistic view seems unconcerned with the presence of real problems in the lives of many older people, and the pessimistic view underplays real changes and improvements that have occurred under 'late modern' conditions.

A more integrated perspective requires a closer and more realistic appreciation of problems-oriented research by the 'optimists' and a greater recognition of social discontinuity and change among the 'pessimists'. The pessimists' views of the lifelong deleterious effects of modern society, in particular, all too often fail to recognise the gains in organisational, material and health terms that modern society has brought about. But both perspectives suffer from a tendency to ignore evidence and argument from the opposite camp. Rather, in tackling modern and postmodern conditions, there is a need to explore the possibility that 'knowledge of old age should . . . emerge in the interstices between the two' (Hazan 1994: 97).

In methodological terms medical sociology is well placed to employ a variety of methods to explore the 'interstices' to which Hazan refers. The somewhat 'data free' mode of reasoning in postmodern writings, and the reliance on epidemiological and especially secondary data in the analyses of inequalities, both fall short of a much needed theoretically informed and 'fine grained' approach to health, ageing and the lifecourse. Some years ago Illsley (1980) argued for the need for more closely observed studies of health and illness within specific communities. He pleaded for 'intensive studies of small samples of different population groups' (Illsley 1980: 58) and for their funding, so that basic research could be carried out on the health of people in modern societies. Subsequently, work by Rory Williams (1990), on health beliefs among older people in Aberdeen, has provided much needed evidence on the subjective dimensions of health among the elderly, and the influence of 'generation' on such beliefs. And the now extensive research on health beliefs at earlier ages, including their class, gender and ethnicity dimensions, now makes age related comparisons possible. A lifecourse perspective can therefore focus on the extent to which the experience of health is shaped by current circumstances, the process of ageing and the influence of belonging to a historically and culturally specific birth cohort.

Returning to the argument set out at the beginning of this chapter, sociological concepts of biographical continuity and disruption across the lifecourse, which combine attention to the influence of social and economic hardship, with a recognition of the possibilities of significant positive changes in social relations, hold out the prospect of a fruitful sociological focus. The relays between biography and history, modernity and postmodernity, and continuity and change, constitute a major vantage point for future medical sociological research on health, ageing and the lifecourse.

References

Arber, S. (1994) 'Gender health and ageing', *Medical Sociology News* 20: 14–22.

Arber, S. and Ginn, J. (1991) *Gender and Later Life: a Sociological Analysis of Resources and Constraints*, London: Sage.

Arber, S. and Evandrou, M. (eds) (1993) *Ageing, Independence and the Life Course*, London: Jessica Kingsley Publishers.

Baltes, M. M. and Carstensen, L. L. (1996) 'The process of successful ageing', *Ageing and Society* 16: 397–422.

Barker, D. (ed.) (1992) *The Fetal and Infant Origins of Adult Disease*, London: BMJ Publications.

Blaxter, M. (1992) 'Inequality in health and the problem of time', *Medical Sociology News* 18: 12–24.

Brody, J. A. (1985) 'Prospects for an ageing population', *Nature* 315: 463.

Bury, M. (1982) 'Chronic illness as biographical disruption', *Sociology of Health and Illness* 4(2): 167–82.

—— (1988) 'Arguments about ageing: long life and its consequences', in N. Wells and C. Freer (eds) *The Ageing Population: Burden or Challenge*, Basingstoke: Macmillan, 17–31.

—— (1991) 'The Sociology of chronic illness. a review of research and prospects', *Sociology of Health and Illness* 13(4): 451–68.

—— (1992) 'The future of ageing: changing perceptions and realities', in J. C. Brockelhurst, R. C. Tallis and H. Fillit (eds) *Textbook of Geriatric Medicine and Gerontology*, London: Churchill Livingstone.

—— (1995) 'Ageing, gender and sociological theory', in S. Arber and J. Ginn (eds) *Connecting Ageing and Gender: a Sociological Approach*, Buckingham: Open University Press.

—— (1998) 'Postmodernity and health', in G. Scambler and P. Higgs (eds) *Modernism, Postmodernism and Health*, London: UCL Press.

Bury, M. and Holme, A. (1991) *Life after Ninety*, London: Routledge.

Bury. M., Gabe, J. and Wright, Z. (1994) *Health Promotion and Mental Health*, London: Health Education Authority.

Bytheway, B. (1995) *Ageism*, Buckingham: Open University Press.

CSO (1998) Social Trends, London: HMSO.

Davey, B. (1995) (ed.) *Birth to Old Age: Health in Transition*, Buckingham: Open University Press.

Davey Smith, G., Hart, C. L., Blanc, D., Gillis, C. and Hawthorne, V. M. (1997) 'Lifetime socioeconomic position and mortality: prospective observational study', *British Medical Journal* 314: 547–52.

Estes, C. (1986) 'Politics of ageing in America', *Ageing in Society* 6(2): 121–34.

—— (1991) 'The new political economy of ageing: introduction and critique', in M. Minkler and C. L. Estes (eds) *Critical Perspectives on Ageing: the Moral and Political Economy of Growing Old*, New York: Baywood Publishing Co.

Featherstone, M. and Hepworth, M. (1989) 'Ageing and old age: reflections on the postmodern life course', in B. Bytheway (ed.) *Becoming and Being Old: Sociological Approaches to Later Life*, London: Sage.

—— (1991) 'The mask of ageing and the postmodern life course', in M. Featherstone, M. Hepworth and B.S. Turner (eds) *The Body: Social Process and Cultural Theory*, London: Sage.

—— (1993) 'Images of ageing', in J. Bond and P. Coleman (eds) *Ageing in Society: An Introduction to Social Gerontology*, London: Sage.

Ford, G., Ecob, R., Hunt, K., Macintyre, S. and West, P. (1994) 'Patterns of class inequality throughout the lifespan: class gradients at 15, 35, and 55 in the west of Scotland', *Social Science and Medicine* 39: 1,037–50.

Fox, A. J., Goldblatt, P. O. and Jones, D. R. (1985) 'Social class mortality differentials: artefact, selection or life circumstances', *Journal of Epidemiology and Community Medicine* 31: 1.

Fries, J. F. (1980) 'Aging, natural death and the compression of morbidity', *New England Journal of Medicine* 303: 130–5.

—— (1989) 'The compression of morbidity: near or far?', *The Milbank Quarterly* 67(2): 208–32.

Hall, R. G. P. and Channing, D. M. (1990) 'Age, pattern of consultations, and functional disability in elderly patients in one general practice', *British Medical Journal* 301: 424–7.

Hazan, H. (1994) *Old Age: Constructions and Deconstructions*, Cambridge: Cambridge University Press.

Hepworth, M. (1996) '"William" and the old folks: notes on infantalism', *Ageing and Society* 16: 423–41.

Hockey, J. and James, A. (1993) *Growing Up and Growing Old: Ageing, Dependency and the Life Course*, London: Sage.

Illsley, R. (1980) *Professional or Public Health: Sociology in Health and Medicine*, London: Nuffield Provincial Hospital Trust.

Johnson, C. L. and Barer, B. M. (1992) 'Patterns of engagement and disengagement among the oldest old', *Journal of Aging Studies* 6(4): 351–64.

Katz, S. (1996) *Disciplining Old Age: The Formation of Gerontological Knowledge*, Virginia: University Press of Virginia.

Kohli, M. (1988) 'Ageing as a challenge for sociological theory', *Ageing and Society* 8(4): 368–94.

Kohli, M. and Meyer, J. W. (1986) 'Social structure and the social construction of life stages', *Human Development* 29: 145–80.

Laslett, P. (1987) 'The emergence of the third age', *Ageing and Society* 7: 133–60.

—— (1989) 'The demographic scene: an overview', in, J. Eekelaar, and D. Pearl, *An Ageing World: Dilemmas and Challenges for Law and Social Policy*, Oxford: Clarendon Press.

—— (1989) *A Fresh Map of Life: The Emergence of the Third Age*, London: Weidenfeld and Nicolson.

Phillipson, C. (1994) 'The modernisation of the life course: implications for social security and older people', in S. Baldwin and J. Falkinham (eds) *Social Security and Social Change; New Challenges to the Beveridge Model*, Hemel Hempstead: Harvester Wheatsheaf.

Power, C., Bartley, M., Davey Smith, G. and Blane, D. (1996) 'Transmission of social and biological risk across the life course' in D. Blane, E. Brunner and R. Wilkinson (eds) *Health and Social Organisation: Towards a Health Policy for the 21st Century*, London: Routledge.

Riley, M. W., Foner, A. and Waring, J. (1988) 'Sociology of age' in N. J. Smelser (ed.) *Handbook of Sociology*, London and Newbury Park: Sage.

Strong, P. (1979) 'Sociological imperialism and the profession of medicine', *Social Science and Medicine* 13A: 199–215.

Suzman, R. M., Willis, D. P. and Manton, K. G. (eds) (1992) *The Oldest Old*, New York and Oxford: Oxford University Press.

Tinker, A. (1996) *Older People in Modern Society*, 4th edn, London: Longman.

Townsend, P. (1981) 'The structured dependency of the elderly: a creation of social policy in the twentieth century', *Ageing and Society* 1(1): 5–28.

Vagero, D. and Illsley, R. (1995) 'Explaining health inequalities: beyond Black and Barker', *European Sociological Review* 11(3): 219–41.

Verbrugge, L. M. (1989) 'The dynamics of population ageing and health', in S. Lewis (ed.) *Aging and Health*, Michigan: Lewis, 23–40.

Wadsworth, M. (1991) *The Imprint of Time: Childhood, History and Adult Life*, Oxford: Oxford University Press.

—— (1997) 'Health inequalities in the life course perspective', *Social Science and Medicine* 44(6): 859–69.

Walker, A. (1981) 'Towards a political economy of old age', *Ageing and Society* 1(1): 73–94.

—— (1987) 'The poor relation: poverty among older women', in C. Glendinning and J. Millar (eds) *Women and Poverty in Britain*, Brighton: Wheatsheaf Books, 178–98.

—— (1993) 'Poverty and inequality in old age', in J. Bond and P. Coleman (eds) *Ageing in Society: an Introduction to Social Gerontology*, London: Sage.

Williams, R. (1990) *A Protestant Legacy: Attitudes to Death and Illness Among Older Aberdonians*, Oxford: Clarendon Press.

Part II

The body

Chapter 5

Childhood bodies

Social construction and translation

Alan Prout

Introduction

Since the 1980s both 'childhood' and 'the body' have been reassessed as legitimate topics of social theory and sociological investigation.[1] In general, however, these developments have occurred on separate tracks with remarkably little contact between the two fields and only occasional cross-reference. Remarkable because, whatever their other differences, there is an important parallel: in both cases social constructionism has exercised a powerful effect on their theoretical imaginations and analytical intents. In this chapter I will suggest that whilst social constructionism undoubtedly provided a necessary and useful, perhaps even essential, counterpoint to biological reductionism, helping to create a conceptual space within which to think about the non-biological correlates of both the body and childhood, the time has come to undertake a re-examination.

As a sociologist of childhood I am most concerned with the one side of this childhood/body correspondence. This chapter, however, suggests that objects of sociological enquiry (such as the body or childhood) can be apprehended as both material and representational entities when placed in a theoretical perspective which renders the character of the social (as in 'social constructionism') problematic. For this purpose I draw on Latour's notion that social life takes place in and through networks of (that is mediated or translated connections between) heterogeneous elements. These networks are, as he puts it: 'simultaneously real, like nature, narrated, like discourse and collective, like society' (Latour, 1993: 6).

Contained in this position is a refusal to accept a settled and given distinction between nature and culture (and a recognition that, inter alia, 'the body' and 'childhood' are simultaneously both) and a materialism which, while embracing the importance of representation, classification and symbolic practices, refuses social constructionism's bid to monopolise 'society' as discourse. That sociology sometimes finds it difficult to comprehend the heterogeneous or hybrid character of social life is in part a result of its tendency to delineate the content of social life as that which is not nature. The logic of this position is that the body is difficult to claim as a legitimate topic of social enquiry because if a line were to be drawn between culture and nature there is a strong *prima facie* case for it as part of the latter. Similarly childhood was not much attended to in sociology – although it was appropriated to the degree that socialisation, that is becoming social, was understood precisely as a transition from nature to culture. The concept of socialisation therefore not only tended to place children in a passive relation to culture (a criticism central in the refurbished sociology of childhood and to which I will return) but also rested on a view of children as social only in so far as they gradually ceased being natural.

However, once social life is recognised as heterogeneous, no *a priori* parcelling out of entities (people, bodies, minds, artefacts, animals, plants . . .) into culture or nature is thinkable. Amongst these both the body and childhood become comprehensible as complex phenomena, medleys of culture and nature. My discussion, therefore, has two aspects. The first and more narrow of these focuses on the body and childhood. It takes Turner's (1992) distinction between foundationalist and anti-foundationalist accounts of the body and illustrates it with examples from the literature on childhood. It goes on to discuss Shilling's (1993) notion of the body as biologically and socially 'unfinished', suggesting that this useful formulation, in so far as it recognises children at all, overempha-sises their passivity in social life and underemphasises the specificity of children as social actors. The second aspect broadens the discussion by calling attention to the potential of the sociology of *translation* as an alter-native framework to social constructionism for discussing childhood bodies. This draws into play not only bodies as a constituent of hetero-geneous sociality but also the part played by artefacts, those other materialised hybrids of culture and nature.

Foundationalist and anti-foundationalist accounts of the body

Sociology's turn to the body has proved difficult, plagued by a tendency to fall into either biological or cultural reductionism. In his reviews of the field Turner (1984, 1992) has suggested that contemporary sociological thinking about the body is divided between what he terms 'foundationalist' and 'anti-foundationalist' approaches. These mirror the twin reductionisms mentioned above by making different and contradictory ontological and epistemological assumptions. Whilst Turner argues that both approaches are inadequate in themselves and that some theoretical synthesis or tran-scendence is required, his characterisations make a useful starting point for examining how these different assumptions about the body are present in different analyses of children.

Foundationalists take the view that the body is a real, material entity which is connected with but different from the many different frameworks of meaning in which it is variously represented in human cultures. At its most basic, foundationalists assume that there is something constant (but perhaps changing) which functions independently of the social context within which it is found. The body (and its processes of change) form an entity which is experienced and lived. What is prioritised in this perspective, therefore, is largely phenomenological. The task of sociologists is to document and analyse how the body is experienced and interpreted by different actors in different social and cultural contexts.

Anti-foundationalists, however, are unwilling to make a distinction between the body and its representations. In an extreme form anti-foundationalists might argue in an entirely idealist fashion that there is no material body – only our perceptions, constructions or understandings. Less extreme, but also less consistent, is the view that even if the materiality of the body is conceded we only have access to it through discourse of various kinds. It is these discourses, or ways of representing the body, that structure and shape our experiences of it and the meanings we give to it. In this view, then, the task of social scientists is to analyse these representations and uncover the social processes through which they are made and have their effects.

Childhood bodies

Both foundationalist and anti-foundationalist approaches to the body can be found in the literature on childhood. The work of David Armstrong (1983, 1987) is a prominent example of the latter. In fact Armstrong's interest in the construction of childhood bodies derives from the important role that he argues childhood as a cultural construction has played in the constitution of twentieth-century medicine. Writing from within medical sociology, his purpose is to undermine the idea that human anatomy underlies or is a secure material context for understanding medicine as a social practice. He strongly contests the claim that there is a biology outside of social life to which we might refer when trying to understand the enterprise of biomedicine. Instead the body is seen as a socially constructed knowledge – understood not as a more or less accurate representation of some underlying reality, but as a way of looking and representing which is sustained and is sustaining of social practices: 'What is the nature of the body? . . . The body is what it is perceived to be; it could be otherwise if perception were different' (1987: 66).

The body is a perception, construction, invention, classification or representation that is endlessly perceived anew, reconstructed, reinvented, reclassified and rerepresented. It is from this perspective that Armstrong views the human body and, in particular, the construction of the bodies of children in biomedicine. One of Armstrong's main concerns has been to trace the development of paediatrics as a distinct medical discipline, at first as a speciality concerned with the diseases of children but later in its attempt to claim a concern with the health and development of children as a whole. The emergence of modern biomedicine in the eighteenth century entailed the creation of an anatomy of pathology which could isolate and place disease within specific sites of the body. At this point there was little concern for the age or stage of development of the patient. Although distinctions between adult and childhood versions of a pathological condition gradually came to be made, these classifications did not form the basis of a distinct medical specialism. That development came about in the early twentieth century and was the result, Armstrong argues, of societal changes in the relationships between children and adults.

The establishment of paediatrics at this point turned around a shift from an idea of disease *in* children to the diseases *of* children. As childhood came to be thought of as distinct from adulthood, so medicine came to think of children's disease and children's bodies as different from adult ones. Paediatrics pioneered the panoptical techniques of surveillance and normative regulation through which different versions of the child's body and of children were created: 'Nervous children, delicate children, oversensitive children and unstable children were all essentially inventions of a new way of seeing children' (1983: 15).

Whilst the anti-foundationalist view of children's bodies has a great deal to say about the role of professions such as medicine and their role in the creation of frameworks through which the body is understood, it has little to say about the childhood body as an experienced entity. On the contrary the person with a body in this formulation is construed quite passively, acted upon, regulated, disciplined and determined. This may be thought a problem for any account of the body but it poses a particularly sharp problem in the study of childhood where sociology already has a strong tendency to render children passive. For a countervailing view we have to turn to those who have placed the lived worlds of childhood and the potential of seeing children as social actors more centrally. The foundationalist assumptions of these accounts are often left implicit. In the main these writers are more concerned to enter into the social worlds of children than they are in untangling the theoretical lines of the sociology of the body. Working within a framework which rejects the passive view of children implicit in socialisation theory, and working mostly through intensive ethnographic immersion in the detail of children's lives, they produce what has been called the tribal view of children (James *et al.* 1998). The two examples I discuss below share this approach, although in rather different circumstances. Both show the body as a resource which becomes, as Turner puts it, 'drenched with symbolic significance' for children's relationships with each other and with adults and therefore an important element through which children actively create their identities.

Allison James (1993) deals with the more commonly experienced contexts of children's everyday lives, focusing on how children create and enact categories of significant difference, especially bodily difference at home and in school. She notes that bodily differences (of height, weight etc) have been employed to create 'the child' as an othered category in western cultures. Cultural stereotypes about what constitutes a normally developing body for a child assume, she argues, great importance both for parents and children themselves. Deviations from these normative notions can create intense anxiety. Amongst children themselves, experience of the body, and especially of bodily differences, function as important signifiers for social identity. In her ethnography James noted five aspects of the body that seemed to have particular significance for the children she studied: height, shape, appearance, gender and performance. Each of these acted as a flexible and shifting resource for children's interactions and emergent identities and relationships.

Although cultural stereotypes about each of the five features mentioned by James played a role, children did not simply passively absorb them. Rather, they actively apprehended and used them in, experiencing not only their own body but also its relationship to other bodies and the meanings that were forged from this. One reason for this was that children have to come to terms not only with their own constantly changing bodies and those of their peers, but also with the changing institutional contexts within which meaning is given to these changes. For example, James reports how in the later stages of nursery school, children came to think of themselves as 'big'. Their apprehension of the difference between themselves and children just entering the nursery, together with the significance of the impending transition to primary school signalled this identity. But once they had made the transition and were at the outset of their career in primary school they were catapulted back into being small once again. This relativity produced, therefore, a fluidity about the relationship between size and status that produced what James identifies as a typical 'edginess' among the children about body meanings. The body became a crucial resource for making and breaking identity precisely because it was unstable.

The importance of children's active construction of meanings around the body is also strikingly illustrated by the work of Myra Bluebond-Langner et al. (1991). In her study of a summer camp for North American children with cancer she noted that unconditional acceptance by their peers was one of the most valued aspects of the experience by the children who took part. Whilst hair loss and other effects of therapy were stigmatising in relation to healthy children, those bodily signs were instead taken up as different but shared signs of identity by children in the camp. Like James, this account underlines that children are not simply shaped by ideas about the body but can collectively create their own meanings.

The body unfinished

Both anti-foundationalist and (implicitly) foundationalist accounts of childhood bodies were incorporated into the discussions which gave rise to the renewed sociological interest in childhood which emerged in the 1980s (see, for example, Jenks 1982; James and Prout 1990), but the fundamentally different assumptions on which they were based were not really recognised or resolved. It is noteworthy that a current of uneasiness, not to say evasion, always ran through some social constructionist writings about childhood. Interestingly these often implicit and unresolved reservations were at their most noticeable when it came to childhood bodies. For example, Prout and James (1990) in proposing the study of childhood as social construction acknowledged that the (material) body should be understood as at least a limit or constraint on the possibilities of the social construction of childhood. This posed questions about the extent to which childhood as a discursive construct could be understood independently of childhood as a stage of biological growth and about the weight that should be given to each, but these remained marginal to a discussion which was predominantly concerned to establish childhood as 'social'. As was also the case for studies of the body, social constructionism became something of an orthodoxy in the new sociology of childhood. The reason for its attraction was much the same in both cases: it seemed to provide the most secure defence against attempts to read social relations as epiphenomena of nature. For those intent on seeing either childhood or the body (or both) as part of culture not nature this seemed a congenial position to occupy.

The problem is that, as Turner argues, it is not possible to be simultaneously and consistently foundationalist and anti-foundationalist – because each position is defined in opposition to the other. Turner's suggested way out of this problem is methodological eclecticism: that is to say he suggests accepting the intellectual legitimacy of both approaches, using each as and when it is appropriate and seeing them as in some way different but complementary. Whilst this allows empirical flexibility and diversity of approach, it is not theoretically coherent: different and irreconcilable assumptions are being made about the material character of the body. In taking this point up, Shilling suggests that Turner fails in his ambition to synthesise foundationalist and anti-foundationalist approaches and argues (in effect though not quite in these terms) that this is because his method is additive rather than relational. Turner, he correctly observes, attempts to 'combine foundationalist and anti-foundationalist frameworks without altering any of their basic parameters' (Shilling, 1993: 103). Consequently, he does not examine the relationships between the body in nature and the body in society.

Shilling attempts to synthesise these two approaches and in so doing develops a position that is of great potential for studies of childhood. The

essence of his suggestion is that the human body is socially and biologically unfinished at birth. Over the lifecourse it changes through processes
that are simultaneously biological and social. Drawing on a very wide
range of social theory he suggests two basic elements of a framework.
The first, that the mind-body relationship has to be seen in the wider
context of the culture-nature relationship, is drawn from both anthropological and feminist analyses. Important among the former is the theory
of symbol and metaphor developed by Lakoff and Johnson (1980). They
argue that there is a close, but not one-to-one, relationship between mind
and body as a result of the mind being located in and dependent on bodily
mechanisms for the perception of the natural world. We exist, for example,
in a world where gravity creates phenomena of motion as 'up' or 'down'
and human thought incorporates, draws on and elaborates these phenomena.
Feminist writers have also, though to different degrees, pointed to irreducible biological differences between the sexes which shape experience
differently for men and women. Whilst some feminist analyses tend
towards biological reductionism (often with an inversion of male claims
to superiority), others look to an interaction between biological and social
processes in which natural differences are transformed or distorted into
social ones (Orbach 1988; Chernin 1983). In these accounts the body is
not only shaped by social relations but also enters into their construction
as both a resource and a constraint.

The second, and equally important element of Shilling's approach, is
the suggestion that once we grant the body a biological/physical existence
we can begin to see how it is worked on and by society. Some of this
work occurs through the symbolic and discursive practices highlighted by
social constructionism – the body is represented and classified in various
ways. But there are also social practices which are material ones, for
example diet, exercise and disciplinary regimes, which materially shape
the body. In each case the relationship between the body and society is
reciprocal: society works on the body, just as the body works on society.

In developing this idea of the body as socially and biologically unfinished, Shilling pays little attention to childhood. This is rather surprising
given that childhood suggests itself quite strongly as a stage of the lifecourse in which work on and by the body occurs quite intensively. Children
per se appear in relation to only two substantive topics: Norbert Elias's
account of the 'civilising process', that is, the long-term historical trend
towards individuals practising internalised control and restraint over forms
of behaviour concerned with bodily functions such as eating, copulating
and defecating; and Bourdieu's account of the transmission of class habitus.
But from the point of view of the new social studies of childhood both
Elias and Bourdieu are deficient, or at best ambiguous, in their assumptions
about childhood socialisation. Both treat children as passively and gradually accreting or accumulating embodied dispositions in the transition to

full sociality in adulthood. There is little (or only equivocal) recognition of the possibility that children actively appropriate and transform as well as absorb. Nor is there a sense that childhood and growing up are full of reversals, transformations and inversions rather than being a progression to an ever closer copy of adulthood. In short what is missing is a sense of childhood as a being as a well as a becoming: childhood as staged and children as the active, creative performers described by James and Bluebond-Langner. Once, however, this notion is allowed, it opens up the possibility that childhood itself might be thought of as exhibiting difference at the level of bodily conduct. As Prendergast points out:

> The issue of embodiment as a cultural process surfaces most poignantly at key points in the life cycle: the trajectory of the body is given symbolic and moral value: bodily forms are paradigmatic of social transition . . . Each stage requires that we adjust to and attend to our body, or that of others, in an appropriate and special way . . .
>
> (Prendergast 1992: 1)

We have here the possibility that childhood is created through, even perhaps requires, certain kinds of bodily performance.

This is the direction taken by Toren (1993) and Christensen (1993, 1994). Developing a position broadly similar to Shilling, but owing more to Merleau-Ponty, Toren views children as growing and developing within a historically and socially situated body. Mind she argues, develops in specific social, cultural and historical circumstances that shape it not just as consciousness but also as body, even at the level of the nervous system. Unlike Shilling she stresses the creative activity of children who inhabit a world that stands in paradoxical relationship to the adult one and is not to be taken as an incomplete or faulty version of it. Through its theoretically prepared sensitivity to their position and experience, Christensen's ethnography similarly shows how children might be understanding and expressing bodily experiences in ways quite different from their adult caretakers such as teachers. In her study of Danish primary school children and their actions and relationships during episodes of sickness and minor accidents, she focused on how the children gave help to others. She noticed how teachers and other adults saw children as complaining too much about minor cuts, grazes and bruises acquired during the course of the school day. In response the adults generally tried to teach the children to make less fuss, sometimes by telling them so and sometimes by ignoring their complaints. Observation of the children showed that they frequently drew attention to bodily experiences in very dramatic ways, often with the request from others to 'Look!' For the children, however, this demand was not one for medical attention or first aid or even help – as adults tended to interpret it. Rather, the children were drawing on a wider practice, engaged in during all kinds of games, play and other activities, of asking others to share their experience of the body. In her interactions with the children she, as an adult, came to learn that the culturally appropriate response was not to reprimand the child for over-dramatising, or even give them help, but simply and without fuss to share in the act of looking.

The body translated

Work of this kind, although not formally based upon it, shows how the notion of the body as socially and biologically unfinished might be worked through in relation to children – provided that children's interpretative activity as social beings is also appreciated. Children's bodies then appear in a variety of roles: in the construction of social relations, meanings and experiences between children themselves and with adults; as products of and resources for agency, action and interaction; and as sites for social-isation through embodiment. By emphasising the relationship of the body and society they begin to undermine the notion that it is possible to under-stand social relations as if the body were able to be abstracted from them. In doing this they make an important move towards the hybrid character of social life as it applies to childhood.

Prendergast, in her work on girls' experiences of menarche (1992), also illustrates how the body and society are inextricably woven at a particular moment of the life course. Importantly, however, her study explicitly attends to another source of the hybridity of the social by pointing to the importance of material objects and artefacts in the creation of meaning. Arguing that culturally organised embarrassment, negativity and secrecy (about menstruation) is not only learned attitudinally but is embodied in posture and corporeal demeanour, she shows the way in which shame is transmitted through forms of discourse (for example, teasing and name-calling), social interaction (for example, publicly tipping out the contents of a girls bag to reveal tampons) *and* in the material organisation of school life (for example, inadequate, unhygienic and inaccessible toilets).

Such an insight underlines the necessity of moving beyond the relation-ship between body and society *per se* and locating this as just one instance of the heterogeneity that characterises social life. A highly pertinent example of this approach is found in the work of Bernard Place (1994, 1996). He shows how different approaches to the body might be inte-grated by looking at the processes surrounding the intensive combination of children's bodies with medical technologies. The ethnographic location he chose was the modern hospital, specifically a paediatric intensive care unit. He points out that in this particular location the human body is perfo-rated, cannulated, intubated and catheterised before being connected to sets of technological artefacts which enable detailed examination of the functioning of the heart, kidneys, brain, lungs and other organs. Such artefacts generate sets of symbols (traces, numbers and images) which are manipulated by the doctors and nurses. Changes in these symbols are understood to relate to changes of a similar magnitude occurring within the corporeal body:

> In the process of connection to these artefacts the body is, in the situated vocabulary of the intensive care unit, 'sorted out'. Literally it is 'sorted' (the disordered body is ordered), 'out' (the internal body is externalised). At the same time the boundary of the body is extended and circumscribed by both corporeal (human) and non-corporeal (technological) elements. The body is, in this sense, 'technomorphic', revisable by connection to technological artifacts.
>
> (Place 1994)

In this setting the nurses and doctors, as well as the parents and child patients, are concerned to maintain the integrity of the body. But what is the body in these circumstances? Is it enclosed by the skin or is it bounded by the technologies that treat and monitor it? On the basis of his participant observation Place makes a distinction between what he calls 'child data' (what is happening within the corporeal body) and 'data child' (the visible manifestation of that corporeality through its connection to the surrounding technological artefacts). The coincidence of the two cannot be taken for granted and it is argued that the conditions whereby they are held together is accomplished minute by minute. He argues that the work of the intensive care unit entails maintaining an association between 'child data' and 'data child'.

Place's insights give a fresh perspective on Turner's central divide between foundational and non-foundational views and in it the body and its representations are not mutually exclusive but mutually dependent. The 'child data' and the 'data child' mutually explicate each other so that, at least in this setting, one is unthinkable without the other:

> One does not determine the other, with the necessary implication of prior and post status. They are conjoined, mutually explicating only when juxtaposed. When the two forms do separate, one becomes a set of meaningless symbols, the other a disordered mass of flesh and blood.
>
> (Place 1994)

A concern with this sort of heterogeneity is well developed within one strand of the social study of science and technology (see, for example, Latour and Woolgar 1986: and Latour 1993). Sometimes called the sociology of translation or actor-network theory, this literature is concerned with the materials from which social life is produced and the processes by which these are ordered and patterned. Being substantively interested in science and technology, its object constantly undermines a sharp distinction between culture and nature by focusing on the network of mediations between them. The sociology of translation has much in common with forms of sociology which emphasise the relational, constructed and processual character of social life but is quite distinct in one crucial and radical respect: it rejects the assumption that society is constructed through human action and meaning alone. In this feature it is sharply different from social constructionism. It remains constructivist, but in a radically generalised way; and it restates materialist sociology, but in a way which places the material in relation to the other elements that constitute society. In fact 'society' is seen as produced in and through patterned networks of heterogeneous materials; it is made up through a wide variety of shifting associations (and dissociations) between human *and* non-human entities. Indeed, so ubiquitous are associations between humans and the rest of the material world that all entities are to be seen as hybrids – what Latour (1993) has termed 'quasi-objects' and 'quasi-subjects' – where the boundary between the human and the non-human is shifting, negotiated and empirical.

In this view social life cannot, therefore, be reduced either to the 'purely' human (adult or child) or to the 'purely' animal, vegetable, mineral or abstract. As a general rule (but subject always to detailed empirical examination) we can say that none of these entities alone determines the ordering that results from their combination. Sociological approaches which try to make one kind of entity do all the explanatory work result in some form of reductionism – in the way Turner indicates that foundational and non-foundational approaches to the body have a tendency to do. Like all phenomena, the sociology of translation would see childhoods and bodies as constructed not only from human minds and their interactions, not only from human bodies and their interactions, but also through an unending mutually constituting interaction of a vast array of material and non-material resources.

Analysis focuses on the 'translations' – the network of mediations – between these different entities. It is concerned to trace the processes by which these heterogeneous entities mutually enrol, constitute and order each other, processes which always involve something being retained, something being added and something being taken away. Bodies are included – but alongside aspects of the natural, discursive and material environment, including their orchestration and hybridisation into artefacts of many different types. All of these are to be seen as *a priori* equal (or symmetrical) actants in the creation of society – or more properly 'the networks of the social'. This approach would place childhoods and bodies in relation to not only symbolic but also material culture. What produces them is not simply biological events, not only the phenomenology of bodily experience, and not merely structures of symbolic meaning – although all of these are important – but also the patterns of material organisation and their modes of ordering. Examining childhood bodies in this view becomes a matter of tracing through the means, the varied array of materials and practices (both discursive and non-discursive) involved in their construction and maintenance – and in some circumstances their unravelling and disintegration.

Conclusion

Recent attempts to constitute childhood as a sociological topic emphasised it as a social phenomenon in at least two ways: by pointing to the social construction of childhood as a discursive formation and by ethnographic enquiry into the active and creative capacities of children to shape their collective lives. As with the body, the turn to social constructionism in the sociology of childhood seemed to overturn the assumption that its object of study belongs to the sphere of nature rather than that of culture. However, the attempt to render all things 'social' was problematic in both cases because each needed to work with a more open boundary between concepts of nature and culture.

The literature on childhood bodies produced over the last few years makes sense in terms of the weakening in the body/society and culture/nature divisions theorised by Shilling (1993). In its empirical detail this work has revealed the connection between children as social actors, their creative production of meanings around the body and, emergently, its heterogeneous composition and extended character. Attention to children's bodies and how these act, are experienced and constructed is, then, clearly important to the project of understanding children as social actors. Place's (1994, 1996) account of the intensive care ward, despite the very passive role of children in this particular setting, rests on a theoretical account, the sociology of translation, which is not only able to encompass the corporeal and the representational body but broadens the picture to take in the heterogeneous and hybrid character of all social life. It is a way of looking at children and bodies which might be applied to many other settings – for example, schools, hospitals, households and courts. Its prime demand on the analyst is meticulous empirical enquiry into the network of mediations in which children and their bodies are produced and the varieties of material and symbolic work done in the process. The issue is not whether the body or childhood have both material and representational aspects – for this is a given of heterogeneity. Neither is it contentious to include children as active creators of social life rather than passive products of society – because in the sociology of translation all entities are seen as having this potential. Rather, the stuff of enquiry concerns the extent to which they perform it and the means of its enactment. A programme of research in this mould would, therefore, centre on different claims to 'speak for' the body or children, to translate them and enrol them in collective life. That these themes are already implicit in much of the research discussed in this chapter underlines the potential of the sociology of translation for sharpening and focusing future work in both the sociologies of childhood and the body.

This chapter has not been concerned directly with the sociology of health and illness, although much of the literature discussed above is conventionally placed in this category. Nevertheless, implicit in my argument has been a recognition of the potential value for medical sociology of a theoretical approach which does not counterpose culture and nature. Most obviously health and illness are in large measure empirically concerned with the body, what it does and what is done to it. Medicine involves practices which combine a broad range of entities – indeed activities which do this as intensively are difficult to nominate. Healing is constituted exactly by the mediations between humans, animals, spirits, theories, plants, minerals, beliefs, machines and so on. With more or less resistance these are brought into relationship with each other in the collective orderings we call clinics, treatments, self-help groups, divination ceremonies and the like. In social analysis it is tempting to decide *a priori* that one sort of entity is determinant of such social practices and the sociology of health and illness has certainly known theoretical disputes which turn around the validity or usefulness of the reductionism that results. The debates about social constructionism and medical sociology (Bury 1986, 1997 and Nicolson and McLaughlin 1987) or discussions about the 'medical versus social' model are instances of this. In its insistence on hybridity, the sociology of translation has something to offer here too.

References

Armstrong, D. (1983) *Political Anatomy of the Body: Medical Knowledge in Britain in the Twentieth Century*, Cambridge: Cambridge University Press.

Armstrong, D. (1987) 'Bodies of knowledge: Foucault and the problem of human anatomy', in G. Scambler (ed.) *Sociological Theory and Medical Sociology*, London: Tavistock.

Bluebond-Langner, M., Perkel, D. and Goertzel, T. (1991) 'Paediatric cancer patients' peer relationships: the impact of an oncology camp experience', *Journal of Psychosocial Oncology* 9(2): 67–80.

Bury, M. R. (1986) 'Social constructionism and the development of medical sociology', *Sociology of Health and Illness*, 8(2): 137–69.

—— (1987) 'Social constructionism and medical sociology: a rejoinder to Nicholson and McLaughlin', *Sociology of Health and Illness*, 9(4): 439–41.

Bury, M. (1997) *Health and Illness in a Changing Society*, London: Routledge.

Chernin, K. (1983) *Womansize: the Tyranny of Slenderness*, London: The Women's Press.

Christensen, P. (1993) 'The social construction of help among Danish children: the intentional act and actual content', *Sociology of Health and Illness* 15(4): 488–502.

—— (1994) 'Vulnerable bodies: cultural meanings of child, body and illness', paper given at Children and Families: Research and Policy, 31st International Sociological Association (ISA) Committee on Family Research (CFR) Seminar, London.

James, A. (1993) *Childhood Identities: Self and Social Relationships in the Experience of the Child*, Edinburgh: Edinburgh University Press.

James, A., Jenks, C. and Prout, A. (1998) *Theorizing Childhood*, Oxford: Polity Press.

James, A. and Prout, A. (eds) (1990) *Constructing and Reconstructing Childhood: Contemporary Issues in the Sociological Study of Childhood*, London: Falmer Press.

Jenks, C. (1982) *The Sociology of Childhood: Essential Readings*, London: Batsford.

Lakoff, G. and Johnson, M. (1980) *Metaphors We Live By*, Chicago: University of Chicago Press.

Latour, B. (1993) *We Have Never Been Modern*, Hemel Hempstead: Harvester/ Wheatsheaf.

Latour, B. and Woolgar, S. (1986) *Laboratory Life: the Construction of Scientific Facts*, Princeton, NJ: Princeton University Press.

Nicolson, M. and McLaughlin, C. (1987) 'Social constructionism and medical sociology: a reply to M.R. Bury', *Sociology of Health and Illness* 9(2): 107–26.

Orbach, S. (1988) *Fat is a Feminist Issue*, London: Arrow Books.

Place, B. (1994) 'The constructing of bodies of critically ill children: an ethnography of intensive care', paper to the ESRC Childhood and Society Seminar on Childhood and the Body, Keele University, December. To be published (forthcoming) in Prout, A. (ed.) *Childhood Bodies*, London: Macmillan.

—— (1996) 'Constructing the critically ill body: an investigation into the design and development of a clinical data-logging computer to be used by nurses working on a paediatric intensive care unit', Ph.D. thesis, London: South Bank University.

Prendergast, S. (1992) *'This is the Time to Grow Up': Girls' Experiences of Menstruation in School*, Cambridge: The Health Promotion Trust.

Prout, A. and James, A. (1990) 'A new paradigm for the sociology of childhood? Provenance, problems and prospects', in A. James and A. Prout (eds) *Constructing and Reconstructing Childhood: Contemporary Issues in the Sociological Study of Childhood*, London: Falmer Press.

Qvortrup, J. Bardy, M., Sgritta, G. and Wintersberger, H. (eds) (1994) *Childhood Matters: Social Theory, Practice and Policy*, Aldershot: Avebury.

Shilling, C. (1993) *The Body and Social Theory*, London: Sage.

Toren, C. (1993) 'Making history: the significance of childhood cognition for a comparative anthropology of mind', *Man* 28(3): 1–21.

Turner, B. S. (1984) *The Body and Society: Explorations in Social Theory*, Oxford: Blackwell.

—— (1992) *Regulating Bodies: Essays in Medical Sociology*, London: Routledge.

Chapter 6

Flexible bodies

Science and a new culture of health in the US

Emily Martin

Writing about the development of ideas and practices attached to microbes and the hygiene needed to control them in the nineteenth century, Bruno Latour remarks that he is less interested in the '*application*' of a given power such as hygiene 'on the bodies of the wretched and the poor', than in 'the earlier *composition* of an unpredictable source of power. It is precisely at the time when no one can tell whether he is dealing with a new source of power that the link between science and society is most important. When almost everyone is convinced, then, but only then and afterward, will hygiene be a "power" to discipline and to coerce' (1988: 256). My recent ethnographic fieldwork suggests that we are at precisely such a moment when new sources of power are developing.

In this chapter, I discuss an emerging conception of the body that has the potential to lead to new forms of discipline and coercion. A sign of this emerging conception is that in the US, ordinary people in all walks of life quite commonly see their bodies not as a set of mechanical parts but as complex non-linear systems. This has happened in part by way of an enormous cultural emphasis on the immune system, which has moved to the very centre of the way ordinary people now think of health. Many people are reaching for a way of imaging a fluid, ever-changing body, a body containing turbulence and instability, in constant motion, a body that is the antithesis of a rigid, mechanical set of parts. This new body is also in delicate relationship to its environment, a complex system nested in an infinite series of other complex systems. I will argue below that understanding better the links between medicine, science, health and society may help us avoid one of the bleakest potential consequences of these new models of the ideal body – that, yet again, certain categories of people (women, people of colour) will be found wanting. Certain social groups may be seen as having rigid or unresponsive selves and bodies, which would make them relatively unfit for the kind of society now desired. Another possible consequence no less bleak – is that the old categories of hierarchical discrimination will be reshuffled in fundamental ways. A conception of a new elite may be forged, in which the desirable qualities of flexibility and adaptability to change will be found in certain superior individuals in *any* ethnic, racial, gender, sexual identity or age group in the nation. My research suggests that the 'currency' in which these desirable qualities will be figured is health, especially the health of one's immune system. What may be forged is a conception of 'fitness' in which just as surely as in nineteenth-century social Darwinism (though the terms and mechanisms may differ), some will survive and some will not.

The fieldwork for this project, which mostly took place in Baltimore, MD, involved a variety of activities. Several graduate students and I carried out open-ended interviews on the general topic of health with a significant number of people (about 200) living in diverse kinds of socio-economic settings, who were neither sick (necessarily) nor scientific experts (necessarily). The interviews also served as a sort of probe into the culture, in that the open-ended nature of the conversations allowed issues and ways of thinking we could not anticipate to emerge and be heard. The people we interviewed were not randomly chosen, in the statistical sense. But the range of communities and settings in which we worked insured that they would make up a broad cross-section of the society.

Simultaneous with the interviews, I began participant observation in a research lab in immunology in which I was able to attend classes, lab meetings, journal clubs for the discussion of current articles, lectures, and parties. Later I was taught a technical procedure (the Western Blot) used in the lab, and participated in carrying out part of a series of experiments. I also started to work as a volunteer in one of Baltimore's main AIDS service organisations, HERO (Health Education Resources Organization). As a part of my work at HERO, I was interviewed for and accepted into the 'buddy' training programme, and after a course of instruction, I immediately started work at a residential home for HIV+ people. Over the next three years, I was a primary buddy to three HIV+ individuals, and interacted less intensely with many others. What being a buddy means depends on the circumstances: in my experience it included being a companion, a friend, a nurse, a cook, a chauffeur and an intermediary with doctors. Beginning in the first year of the project, I also joined ACTUP-BALTO, again in the double capacity of anthropologist/volunteer. In addition, several other special realms emerged that we explored through a combination of participation and interviewing: a class of college students who were taking a course in immunology; courses of training for workers and managers in corporations to teach new ways of organising the workforce and new ways of interacting; alternative health clinics and their practitioners. Through activities in all these settings, we sought to put ourselves in places where we would be touched and hopefully pushed along by the same processes affecting other people in the society.

Healthy bodies

In questions of health and illness, life and death, survival and extinction, the immune system has risen to eminence in the US, and perhaps more widely in England and Europe. The immune system is one of 'The great ideas today' in an annual publication of *The Encyclopedia Britannica*, which is meant to supplement and update their more than 50-volume publication, *The Great Books of the Western World*. In 'The great ideas today, 1991' the lead article was entitled, 'The biology of immune responses'. Written by Michael Edidin, a biologist, it is one of only two pieces in the volume that deal with a scientific topic: it sits uneasily among the other articles about modern dance, multiculturalism, music as a liberal art theology, and so on. Edidin begins his article with a powerful image:

> The fortress of [A-kur] Acre rises out of the Mediterranean Sea on the coast of Israel. It is an elaborate and beautiful structure: its great stone seawalls are topped with towers, and its courts connect by arched tunnels. The fortress is a history of the region. Its oldest parts, now half-hidden by sea or earth, were built by the Crusaders, and it was elaborated, extended, and modernized by the Turks. Its structure and complexity remind the immunologist of another great complex that protects against invasion – the complex of organs, cells and molecules that functions as our immune system
>
> (1991: 2)

Apart from the editors of the *Britannica*, no matter how far away from immunology labs and HIV/AIDS contexts my graduate students and I travelled, we found people actively using the immune system to organise their concepts of health and work, and in doing so they were marking a dramatic departure from the taken-for-granted conceptions of health and the body which prevailed only a few decades earlier. This shift is happening for good reason: it dovetails with changes in the kind of person and worker regarded as desirable – indeed, necessary, if one is to survive – in the fiercely competitive and rapidly transforming corporate world of the late twentieth century.[1]

Whether you look in the direction of nutrition, exercise, environmental toxins, stress, cancer or AIDS, these days the health arena is saturated with talk about the immune system. The immune system has begun to function culturally as the key guarantor of health and the key mark of differential survival for the twenty-first century. In our neighbourhood interviews, for example, general discussions of health quickly led people (who were not scientists by profession) to name the immune system as the central player.

[Two men are talking, Bill Walters[2] and Peter Herman] Bill: I don't even think about the heart anymore, I think about the immune system as being the major thing that's keeping the heart going in the first place, and now that I think about it I would have to say yeah the immune system is really ... important ... and the immune system isn't even a vital organ, it's just an act, you know? Peter: It's like a complete network ... if one thing fails, I mean if [Bill:] if something goes wrong, the immune system fixes it. It's like a back up system. It's a perfect balance.

The immune system is the whole body, it's not just the lungs or the abdomen. I mean, if I cut myself, doesn't my immune system start to work right away to prevent infection? So it's in your finger, I mean, it's everywhere. (Steven Baker)

These ways of talking and thinking about the body are significantly different from everyday understandings of the body in the recent past. For example, in 1951, my brother had polio during an epidemic and died at the age of two when I was seven. I can recall vividly my fear of germs in general, the injunctions against being in crowds or swimming pools or having unwashed hands. I recall how I was allowed to see my paralysed brother only from outside, through the closed window of his hospital ward, for fear of his contagion. I recall how my family was quarantined by means of an order from the Department of Public Health for fear of our contagion.

Since those times, something has happened to make public health recommendations for management of the AIDS epidemic today very different. In my recent daily fieldwork as a volunteer in very close proximity to people with advanced cases of AIDS I was taught that HIV's route of transmission, so very different from polio's, makes fear of simple proximity unnecessary. As for all the other 'opportunistic' diseases my companions with HIV/AIDS had – such as tuberculosis, herpes, or toxoplasmosis – I learned I did not have to worry. In my training to be a volunteer, I had often been told that only those with impaired immune systems would be susceptible. The germs themselves posed no threat as long as I took care to maintain the health of my immune system. I began to wonder how this particular taken-for-granted wisdom about the body had been generated, how it was different from the taken-for-granted wisdom of only twenty or thirty years ago, and whether this change might be related to other dramatic contemporary changes in society.

In the 1940s and 1950s, seen through the lens of popular publications, the most important threats to health were considered to lie in the environment just outside the body. Enormous attention was devoted to hygiene, cleaning surfaces in the home, clothing, surfaces of the body and wounds with antiseptics. The most important defence was strictly preventing the entrance of any germs into the interior of the body. This notion was already present in imagery from the early decades of the century. In an illustration of 'The Castle of Health,' *The Primer of Sanitation and Physiology* shows the lines of defence against disease. The two outer defences are: 'keep germs from being spread about' and 'guard the gateways by which they enter the body'. The castle itself represents the body, into which the illustration does not let us see at all, and which is dwarfed by the much larger outer defences (Ritchie 1918: 16).

But in the 1940s and 1950s, the body seems to become even more elaborately defended at its surface. A *Life* article on polio in 1955 shows the body as a seamless whole, besieged on its surface by germs of all sorts, some drilling away with drill bits, and some slain and marked by the victory flags of effective vaccines (Coughlan 1955: 122–3).

Images of the body as a machine abound during this period. A home health book remarked, 'An optimistic view of life . . . acts on the body like oil on the working of machinery . . . it prevents friction' (Peabody and Hunt 1934: 374). Such health manuals often stressed the 'supreme importance' of regular, predictable habits, the good habits of personal hygiene, as well as the good habits learned by cells to produce antibodies (p. 621). Not only health books advocated hygienic habits. Henry Ford, architect of the work process most characteristic of the time, the moving assembly line organised for mass production, sent investigators into workers' homes to scrutinise their private lives. Over 100 investigators visited workers' homes and admonished them to practise thrifty and hygienic habits, as well as to avoid smoking, gambling and drinking. His 'Social Work Department' decided which workers, 'because of unsatisfactory personal habits or home conditions', were not eligible to receive the full five-dollar wage which Ford offered (Gelderman 1981: 56–7).

After the 1940s and 1950s, experts gave greater attention to the defences *within* the body. In books written in the 1960s and 1970s, we begin to find accounts of safeguards within the body, a series of defences within us that are 'arranged in depth like the successive lines of an army entrenched to ward off invaders' (Miller and Goode 1960). In one illustrated book for children, the body is again shown as a castle, complete with a moat, turrets, and armed soldiers to protect it from germs. But the shift from the earlier *Life* illustration is made plain in the cut-away view of what is inside the castle walls. Through the breach in the wall, we can see rank upon rank of soldiers stretching back *inside* the body ready to fight any germs that may enter (Hindley and King 1975: 34–5).

As the interior comes into focus, there is less concern with hygiene and the cleanliness of the outside surfaces of the body. Accordingly, people in our interviews frequently express the notion that the environment surrounding their bodies contains many dangers that could not ever be eliminated. In one interview, Gillian Lewis wiped the top of her soda can before taking a drink. Explaining why she did this, she said:

Oh, because it's dirty, and it's germy. I know even by wiping it, you
noticed I used a wet cloth and then I dried it off? Even by wiping it,
I'm still getting the germs, but at least I don't see that black dirt. I'm
not putting my mouth up to it, but I know that it still gets dirty. I
used to be really neurotic about certain things, like I wouldn't eat, I
was just so, so fussy. If something dropped on the table, I wouldn't
eat it cause it would, you know, probably get germs on it. Now I pick
it up off the floor and eat it. I just know that I'm, you know, ingesting
plenty of germs. I mean when you see the kitchens of some restaurants
and stuff and it just grosses you out. (Gillian Lewis)

It is as if, whatever is out there, and however deadly and dirty it is, the body's
interior lines of defence will be able to handle it. By the time we reach
accounts in contemporary biology, the interior of the body has been enormously elaborated. 'Recognition' of disease-causing microbes is fantasti-
cally honed and refined. The immune system 'tailors' highly specific
responses as needed in almost unimaginably varied ways. Drawing on a
genetically generated and constantly changing arsenal of resources, the body
can hardly rely on mere habit any longer. This body actively relates to the
world, adroitly selects from a cornucopia of continually produced new antibodies that keep the body healthy and flexibly enable it to meet every new
challenge. Possessed of agile responses, and flexible specificity, our adroit,
innovative bodies are poised to anticipate any conceivable challenge.

All these transitions take place within the context of the assumption,
which was gradually more clearly articulated by biologists over the 1960s
and 1970s, that the various parts of the immune response form a single,
interconnected *system*. Today, sometimes immunologists conceptualise this
system as barricaded behind the body's walls, as in Edidin's description
of the fortress of Acre above; and other times immunologists see this
complex system linking the body to its changing external environment.
Some contemporary scientific images provide an arresting contrast to the
1950s body, the interior hidden behind its protective layer of skin. For
example, the 1990s body, as depicted on the cover of *Science*, has no skin
at all on its torso. The protective skin has been stripped away to reveal
gleaming white lymph nodes under the arms and in the groin, key places
where immune system cells are trained and mobilised.

Bodies as complex systems

Not only in immunology and *Science* magazine but also in our interviews
with non-scientists, the body is often conceptualised as a complex system,
dynamically related to its environment. A minister whose parish is in an
inner city neighbourhood has developed a highly articulated way of
explaining the body as a system with vibrancy. In his view, vibrancy

happens when his system works well, and 'moves', when it builds up energy and vigour, but not when it has to expend energy defending its borders, fighting off invaders.

> [What do you mean about vibrancy?]
>   General vitality. You know, I guess good to be alive, I can handle what comes along, I can have enough energy to do what is required of me in this day, and to give what needs to be given, or at least offer it to other people . . . I would rather think about my system, you know, working together for personal strength and vigour, and energy, brightness, that kind of thing. If it is that I have to spend a lot of inner strength fighting things off, that's just like if a group has to spend all of its time dealing with disagreements and dissensions and all like that. It maintains itself, but it tends not to move anywhere. I would rather think of myself as a system that doesn't have to do all that maintenance all the time, but it's a tough environment around here, you know, in terms of bacteria and stuff floating around. And so that has to happen. (Joe Elliott)

Mr Elliott regrets the necessity that his body at times has to defend its borders instead of build its vibrancy. Other people see the enterprise of defending borders as a fruitless one, given that the borders cannot be fixed; they see themselves as persons or bodies in a system with no clear, stable borders within it and no place outside it on which to stand. People frequently make creative use of analogies to recent wars, which have complicated our simple notions of who is friend and who is foe, which is safe territory and which is dangerous. Harry Wilson sees a similarity between the lack of borders in the Vietnam War and the lack of borders in the fight against AIDS:

> See we have to keep in mind – regardless of what you did over there, whether you were a cook, a door gunner, a pilot, a grunt, a radio man, a cook, a typist – you could still get killed any minute, because it was no fun in Vietnam. Like you saw the fronts of World War 1, World War 2, trenches . . . You see all these Vietnam war movies, yeah, there were a small percentage of what they call fire fights, between NVA or Vietcong and Americans, but not like you see on the TV. They boost it up.
>   [There are no borders really?]
>   No borders whatsoever. I was in Saigon many times . . . There was no front, there was no front line. Yeah, my personal opinion, I don't think there's any front line in the war with AIDS. I mean, people say that blacks started it. No, I can't say it's the blacks . . . no, I think it's anywhere – black, yellow, red, green. I don't think there's any particular colour. (Harry Wilson).

Another interviewee produced a drawing of the immune system as a complex system. Vera Michaels objected to the depiction of the immune system on the cover of *Time Magazine* as a boxing match between white blood cells and viruses inside the body. Instead, she said,

> My visualisation would be much more like a piece of almost tides or something . . . the forces, you know, the ebbs and flows.
> [Could you draw anything like that?]
> I could. I don't think anybody would perceive it as a portrayal of the battle within.
> [What is it that ebbs and flows?]
> The two forces, I mean, the forces . . . imbalance and balance.

As she spoke, she drew a picture, labelling it 'the waves' and deftly capturing a sense of a body embedded in a constantly changing environment and unavoidably responding to turbulent motion and change.

A complex systems model of the body carries with it the possibility of catastrophic collapse. Since in complex systems, slight differences in initial conditions can have magnified effects, and since such systems contain randomness and disorder within order, what order there is is local, transient, emergent, like 'a whirlpool appearing in the flow of a river, retaining its shape only for a relatively brief period and only at the expense of incessant metabolism and constant renewal of content' (Bauman 1992: 189).

For many people, at least part of the special horror aroused by the contemplation of AIDS is the horror of system breakdown, which could be seen as the coming of a nightmarish, random disaster, the more horrible because known beforehand to be an ever-present possibility. A young woman explained this in one of our interviews.

> [Can you imagine what it's like to have AIDS?]
> When I do imagine it, it's just one of the most horrifying . . . when I imagine what it's like to have AIDS I imagine dying from within. Just dying from within. All over the body, just dying, every single inch of the body dying from within. Within every finger, within every inch. That's how I look at it, and just shivering up and down.
> [Is that what people have told you that it is like?]
> No. No one's told me what it's like. I mean I've seen, and read a lot, and you see in lots of people, AIDS sufferers on TV and I've known a few, and that's what it looks like, and that's what it made me feel like it would be from inside. All the way into your heart and your mind and everything. (Janey Wilcox)

Causes of this breakdown of the whole body system can come from many places within the larger systems in which we live. The epidemic of immune system dysfunctions, of which AIDS is part (lupus, chronic fatigue syndrome, asthma), is often seen as a result of harmful forces affecting all of our bodies: pesticides in our water and food, background radiation, environmental pollution of all sorts, vaccinations against infectious diseases. As one person put it,

> To me it's all systemic. You can't localize and say this pathology here doesn't affect there. To me it's all one. When you look at what is it that makes the immune system break down, well, there are so many co-factors now, and because we don't want to acknowledge how many co-factors there are, we're always missing the boat. We don't acknowledge the environmental impact. Slowly, we're starting to. We don't acknowledge the background radiation. We don't acknowledge our food supply. We don't acknowledge the breakup of the family. We don't acknowledge the lack of spiritual meaning in people's lives. I mean the bottom line is we don't acknowledge the loss of meaning in people's lives and what that does to the human being. To me the HIV virus is a signature of an already weakened immune system. (Rebecca Patrides)

What are some of the possible or likely consequences of thinking of the body as a complex system? The first consequence might be described as the paradox of feeling responsible for everything and powerless at the same time, a kind of empowered powerlessness. Imagine a person who has learned to feel at least partially responsible for her own health, who feels that personal habits like eating and exercise are things that directly affect her health and are entirely within her control. Now imagine such a person gradually coming to believe that wider and wider circles of her existence – her family relationships, community activities, work situation – are also directly related to personal health. Once the process of linking a complex system to other complex systems begins, there is no reason, logically speaking, to stop. With respect to AIDS, people can simultaneously experience a sense of universal agency (Everything is related to this disease: I will fix everything!) and helplessness (If I can't fix everything, and who could, then I will die from this disease).

Because complex systems can be resilient in the face of change, they are closely associated with the dampening of conflict. Thus another consequence of systems models applied to the body is that conflict can come to seem unthinkable. Like simple systems, complex systems can handle discord (say illness) in one part by making adjustments in another to return to a steady state of harmony (health). The health of the body and the corporate organisation seen as systems seem to require a profound dampening of conflict between husbands and wives, parents and children, management and labour, men and women, whites and minorities.

But the features of a complex system that make it different from a simple system can lead to a different outcome. Because control can suddenly shift from one part of the system to another and because small initial causes can have large effects, health and harmony are by no means guaranteed. Instead, sudden, catastrophic eruption or collapse can, and indeed, eventually *will* occur.

When we see everything made up of systems within systems, humans and human purposes are no longer considered preeminent, as they have typically been seen in western humanistic traditions.

> The systems world may be for humans, *but* it may not be . . . Systems create a certain equivalence between humans and other subsystems of the global system and lead directly to the concept of substitutability among subsystems. There is no priority of human living over any other subsystem within the global system. The subsystem of 'living human beings' is, from a systems perspective, conceptually equivalent to the 'waste management' subsystem, for example.
>
> (Arney 1991: 57–8, emphasis in original)

Immunising (educating and training) the body

The original meaning of the word 'immune' was to be exempt from the requirement of service to the state. It was not until the late nineteenth century that the entity which the 'immune' individual could ward off became not the state, but disease (OED 1989). The two meanings of the word came together when immunisation was developed and brought to us, often without choice, through resources and personnel mobilised by the state and the medical profession. Although people often assume vaccination is beneficial, and indeed the Clinton administration seeks to make vaccination a universal right, not everyone thinks vaccination is a good thing. Vaccination entails the use of state power, within a particular medical view of the body and its immune system.

In immunology, as it is understood in research contexts and as it is presented in popular media, the links among the parts of the immune system are often described as links of communication. In our interviews, people (scientists as well as non-scientists) generally see the immune system as held together by messages communicated among its parts. What determines the efficacy of the communication are such matters as 'recognition' or 'misrecognition,' 'memory' or 'forgetting,' and 'knowledge' or 'ignorance'. Most of the time the immune system 'recognises' or 'identifies' things that are a threat to the body's health and 'knows' what to do in response. Sometimes this is because it 'remembers' the threat from 'seeing' it previously, and having 'learned' about it then.

Since the immune system is perceived as a community of sentient 'beings' who remember and forget, especially in the American context, people readily think of this community on the model of a liberal democracy, in which education plays an important role in allowing its members to achieve their potential. The thymus is often described as the school or college of the immune system, where T cells are educated. Here is how one of my immunology professors described the thymus in a graduate class:

> The thymus doesn't filter anything. It's got a very different function. It's a nursery. It's a T cell nursery. T cells, cells coming from the bone marrow, come into the thymus, settle there, mature, get their antigen receptors, learn who they are, whatever that means. They learn whether they are cytoxin T cell or helper T cell and then another amazing thing happens to the thymus. And these cells that capture antigen receptors that somehow are programmed to react against self protein get eliminated in the thymus – before they leave the thymus they get killed. How that happens we don't know. But about 95 per cent of the cells that enter the thymus never leave. They mature there but they are recognised as a danger to the body and they get killed, right there in the thymus. Only a small percentage of mature cells leave. Another amazing thing about the thymus is that it is very large in the new born and it starts getting smaller at about the teenage years; then in the adult, it is quite small. So the thymus that's sitting above the heart between the lungs is quite large. In contrast, the adult thymus just looks like a twisted rod and it has almost lost its function. All the T cells that have been educated, or while you were a new born or while you were young, are now fed out to lymph nodes and spleen and have already learned who they are and who they are going to react to. So that in the adult thymus there isn't much T cell education going on anymore. T cells can survive outside of the bone marrow. They survive in the lymph node. (Richard Walton)

A harsh school indeed, in which only 5 per cent graduate, and the rest are killed!

Even immune system cells that do not emerge from the thymus are 'educated'. B cells are 'educated' in the bone marrow where they learn enormous specificity (Dwyer 1988: 47). One children's book about the immune system organises its story line around the immature cells in the bone marrow going to school (RubroSchool for the red cells and LeukoSchool for the white cells) until they have learned enough to carry out their functions in the body (Benziger 1989).

Vaccinations play their role in this world as special courses, a designer education for the (usually) young immune system. The vaccine gives the immune system a kind of post-thymus and post-marrow course in recognising a disease organism (smallpox, diphtheria, polio or whatever) In our interviews, some people explain how they understand vaccines as a form of training or education in which the immune system learns:

[OK, go ahead. What's your idea of how a vaccine works?]

I think my most basic idea of how a vaccine works is that you put some dead or severely disabled germs, bad things, bacteria or viruses into your body, that in and of themselves do not pose a threat to disable you. And that your body sends again these little white blood cells to come and check 'em out, and they have some kind of a struggle with them, but they learn, through their struggle, what these bad things are about, so that . . . the next time they chance upon something like this, they're going to have no problem coping with it. (Eliot Green)

[Let's say you have just got a measles vaccination, sort of sketch out the little play. What's going on in your body, imagine what building up resistance looks like, how is your body doing it?]

OK. Back to our little soldiers. The soldiers march around the body trying to keep things cool, you know, and then they like encounter this new species, and it's like, oh shit! We don't know anything about this guy, what are we going to do? Wait, wait, wait, wait, we've got a little bit of an advantage here, you know, *this* is just a small amount of *that*, you know, [there's] a lot of us, and we don't know about them, but you know, maybe we can take them, you know, and let's like send our little spies or whatever and try to figure out what it's all about, what we can do to fight it, and that type of thing. You know, I think that's kind of the way it works. (Charles Kingsley)

Not everyone may desire or even permit the 'education' of their immune systems that vaccinations entail. Sometimes people feel reluctant to accept vaccination, even in the face of government regulations that make it compulsory for school attendance. Sometimes people refuse vaccinations for themselves or their children and take the consequences. It is as if people are saying to the state as purveyor of health education, and of education for the immune system (in the form of a vaccination): thanks anyway, but my immune system and I will learn to adjust to our environment ourselves. As Katherine Johnson put it, 'I will probably never take a flu shot as long as I live. Like what is the point? That's my point, what is the point? Give me the flu to keep me from getting the flu? OK, fine. You know what I mean? So [heavy with sarcasm] – whatever you say'.

In American society, education and training are almost always part of processes of social differentiation (who goes to what schools, for how long, with what result). It was no surprise then to find that education and toning in the body also produced social differentiation. The basic message (which I came upon in many contexts) is: immune systems are not created equal. An acupuncturist told us,

> I tend to believe that, you know, measles, this, that and the other – all these different vaccines, if people don't have a good lifestyle or a living standard, they're very helpful, but aside from that, for most of the middle-class and upper-class people, [they are] total nonsense and they're just asking for much more trouble, you know. They leave the body filled with inactive pathogens to clog it up that are eventually going to change somehow the chemistry. (Barry Folsom)

His point is that the 'well brought up' immune system already knows most of what it needs to know, and even though there are new things coming in all the time, it is a case of overkill to keep bombarding it with unneeded information.

People who decide that they want to avoid the system of 'state education' for their immune systems (vaccines) and develop their own 'private schooling' instead are not so much 'resisting' vaccination as they are developing a positive view of what their health is. This view shares with immunology the basic notion of the body as a training ground for the immune system, but it denies the benefits of crash courses. Such people may have been engaging in a lifetime of preparation, training and nurturing their immune systems through diet, exercise, avoiding stress and other healthy practices. They may quite reasonably believe that they and their immune systems are already able to flexibly change and adapt, rapidly responding as needed to a continuously changing environment. In such a view, a vaccine, bludgeoning the delicate adjustment of the finely tuned immune system with antigen at a time when there is no actual threat, could easily be seen as something undermining health.

Working bodies

In contexts seemingly far removed from neighbourhood discussions about health, similar new conceptions of what kind of person will be able to survive these times are also emerging. Karen-Sue Taussig (one of the graduate students with whom I collaborated in the research) and I learned of a new kind of experiential training method in which workers and management would climb sheer walls and slender tall poles, cross high wires, and jump off cliffs on zip wires. We were invited to attend a day-long experience run by the training company, Vesta (a fictitious name), for the employees of Rockford Company (also a fictitious name), a multi-national corporation in the top 10 of the Fortune 500. Some 22,000 Rockford employees were in the process of going through three days of workshops as well as high and low ropes courses at a rural site on a large bay on the US East Coast. The corporation's human resource director explained to us that this (very costly) investment in the retraining of workers and managers was being undertaken only after severe downsizing during the 1980s.

Protected by sophisticated mountain climbing ropes and harnesses, teams of men and women workers and managers of all ages and physiques (as well as Karen-Sue and I) climbed 40-foot towers and leapt off into space on a zipline, climbed vertical 40-foot high walls and rappelled down again, climbed a 25-foot high telephone pole, which wobbled, stood up on a 12-inch platform at the top, which swivelled, turned around 180 degrees and again leapt off into space. (This last is privately called the 'pamper pole' by the experiential learning staff because people so often defecate in their pants while trying to stand up on it!)

According to the corporation, this was called 'empowered learning'. It is necessary because according to a Rockford Co. brochure, 'We are facing an unprecedented challenge. The world is changing faster than ever before. Our markets are becoming more complex; our products are changing; and we are facing global competition on a scale never before imagined.' The brochure continues, 'Our survival in the 90s depends upon our ability to change our ways of doing things.' Success in the 1990s, 'going over the wall,' will require 'letting go of old patterns and behaviors . . . taking a leap through difficult transitions and working hard at new beginnings'.

The bodily experiences of fear and excitement deliberately aroused on the zipline and the pole are meant to serve as models for what workers will feel in unpredictable work situations. A participant said, 'If we could capture the type of energy we experienced on the tower, at work, there'd be no limit to what we could do.' As a participant in the high ropes course, the experience seemed to me emblematic of a spectacular shift in what it takes to be a successful worker today. Although some of the towers that support the activity were made of huge, solidly constructed frames, some of the apparatus was deliberately left loose and wobbly. Many exercises involved walking across a high wire. Not only did I experience the fear of no visible support at a great height, but on those wobbly poles, wires or platforms, the fear of being unmoored in space was almost intolerable. The exercises combined the vertigo of standing on the edge of a high cliff with the stomach-dropping feeling of the edge of the cliff itself beginning to crumble. I was literally moving from one position of instability to another and experiencing viscerally the need for continuous flexibility.

In this terrified condition, each of us was to jump off into space, only to be caught by our harness (belayed by a co-worker). There we were allowed to hang (very comfortably I can report) for a little while, swinging gently not too far from the ground. The harness completely and securely supported one's whole torso, so that one's reaction was to slump like a baby in a backpack. The experience models physically the nature of the new born workers that corporations desire: individuals – men and women – able to risk the unknown and tolerate fear, willing to explore unknown territories, adrift in space, but simultaneously able to accept their dependence on the help and support of their co-workers.[3] The isomorphism between the bodily experience of this training and the results desired is entirely deliberate. As trainers would often say – we were there to 'experience the metaphor'.

An executive of Rockford Co. was very aware of the change which his employees were being asked to make. Evoking some of the qualities of the passive body and machine-like work organisation familiar from the 1940s and 1950s, he said, 'We made people the way they are! We can't just throw them away like old worn out machinery! . . . We have treated people in the industrial environment as if they had no brain. Now they are becoming whole people, and that is rewarding.' These new 'whole people' are to be active in their willingness to tolerate risk and danger, as well as the insecurity of being literally ungrounded, but passive in their willingness to depend on the work group. Like the shifting poles, platforms, ropes and wires unmoored in space, the nature of the person itself is to shift, and to be able flexibly to tolerate continuing shifts.

When I was participating in these events, I had little idea at first whether they would shed any light at all on other parts of my research concerning the immune system. I had explained my research to the executives and trainers as an ethnographic study of concepts of health and the body in a scientific lab and urban neighbourhoods – without mentioning the immune system specifically. I practically fainted with astonishment when I discovered that trainers elect to use the image of the immune system to convey the kind of flexible, innovative change they desire.

While visiting the headquarters of Vesta in the south west, I was finishing a long interview with Mark Sandler, the head of the company and the person who develops Vesta's training materials. He asked me to tell him more about my research interests. I told him about my research in an immunology lab. He exclaimed, 'That is the very image I use because it works so perfectly to communicate what we want.' What he meant to communicate was the image of a flexible and innovative body poised to respond in a continuously changing environment while constantly communicating with other such bodies.

I later found out that his interest in the immune system was more than pedagogical. The research department of Vesta is carrying out psychoneuroimmunological experiments to determine whether people experiencing fear, such as fear of heights, will actually learn faster. We hear endlessly today that continuous re-education is at a premium for workers, whether through corporate training programmes such as Vesta's or through education of diverse kinds sought and paid for by workers themselves. Any course of training or education that provides speed and efficiency holds appeal, and

Vesta is attempting to harness the complex networks of the mind-brain-immune systems to do this.[4]

The magnitude of the contemporary shift in imagery of the working body we have begun to glimpse in the above descriptions might lead us to suspect it is happening in connection with some major shift in the nature of work or the organisation of the workplace. Certainly, many political economists are trying to describe a major shift in the forces of production that began in the 1970s. This shift, associated with late capitalism, and often termed flexible specialisation, has been called 'the signature of a new economic epoch' (Borgmann 1992: 75).

The 'flexibility' in this new shape of the economy refers both to labour and products: labour markets become more variable over time, as workers move in and out of the workforce more rapidly. The process of labour itself varies too, as workers may take on managerial tasks and managers may spend time on the assembly floor, as dictated by changing production conditions. Products also become more flexible: design processes grow more versatile and technology more able rapidly to adapt to the needs of production. 'Specialisation' refers to the custom marketing of goods produced cheaply in small batches for particular customers ('tailor-made' production) and the consequent end of mass production and standardised products (Smith 1991: 139).

Labourers experience a speed-up in the processes of labour and an intensification in the retraining that is constantly required. New technologies in production reduce turnover time dramatically, entailing similar accelerations in exchange and consumption. Time and space compression occurs, as time horizons of decision-making shrink and instantaneous communications and cheaper transport costs allow decisions to be affected over a global space (Harvey 1989: 147). Space is annihilated through the speed up of time. Multinational capital operates in a globally integrated environment: ideally, capital flows unimpeded across all borders, all points are connected by instantaneous communications and products are made as needed for the momentary and continuously changing market. To emphasise its contrast to the previous era of mass production this era is appropriately called 'post-Fordism.'

The people we met doing fieldwork have become involved in these processes in complex ways, as residents of urban neighbourhoods, scientists in biology labs, and CEOs of major corporations experience the wrenching consequences of the increasing concentration of capital, both nationally and globally, and the decline of former manufacturing systems.

Post-Darwinism

These new depictions of ideal persons/bodies/workers amount to new versions of old hierarchies in which some of us have fit enough immune systems/bodies to survive plagues or downsizing – while some of us are doomed to succumb. One very concrete description of differential survival came to us from a member of an urban community, with high levels of unemployment and poverty. John Marcellino, a community leader, spoke of the community's poor health, bad teeth and general neglect:

> I figure it's one of the ways of distinguishing poor people from the rest of the population is we all got bad teeth (laughs) . . . And so you won't get rid of the drug abuse or the prostitution or the crime or stuff, until the people who live here are no longer here. And that to me is the same as the underclass thing, *disposable* people . . . As soon as they can't figure out a need for us, they'll get rid of us.
> [What's the need for you right now?]
> We still make money for somebody or another. They still need us some, like they needed people to come up out of the South to work in the mills, so they attract them all up. Now there's not as much need for the people to work in the mills, they need some people in the service economy, they try to retrain . . . but if not they're no use, they'll put you in jail . . . they'll choke you off so that you can't make a living doing anything else, so they get rid of you, or you know, hopefully you'll go back to Virginia or somewhere else, right? You know, you'll crawl in a crack or you won't have children or something. (John Marcellino)

Neither the bodies, nor the communities Marcellino is describing, are likely to be able to adapt successfully to serious challenges:

> We think it [AIDS] could kill us. It could just kill a lot of people in our community. That's what I think about . . . I went to the hospital to say you got to do something . . . they said it can be seven years before you know you have HIV, and I thought well Jesus Christ then, we're really in trouble. Cause now, all these people got it, but nobody knows they got it, right? And eventually it's going to be like, you know, all of a sudden it's going to be like, you know, like a butterfly, you know? [it's a] little thing and all of a sudden . . . one day, it's all going to be, you know, all through the community. (John Marcellino)

John Marcellino fears the loss of the life of an entire community, a 'little thing' like a caterpillar that will grow into a big thing like a butterfly, signifying not rebirth but death 'all through the community.'

In a more general sense, the immune system is beginning to function as a measure of health that allows a single standard of comparison among people or among groups of people. In our interviews, there were many instances in which people used the immune system this way. People made comparisons between individuals: 'Some people have stronger immune systems than others, just because of the way they're made up' (Gillian Lewis); you get HIV while another person does not because 'maybe your immune system just isn't as beefed up' (John Parker). And between groups: women don't get AIDS as much as men because they have stronger immune systems (Carol Neilson); people without a good living standard need vaccines, whereas vaccines would only clog up the more refined immune systems of middle class or upper class people (Barry Folsom).

A scale on which people and groups of people can be measured by their immune strength allows some people to feel especially potent. Not a few people we interviewed, especially young male doctors or medical students, expressed a kind of immune-machismo. One medical resident I heard about, dismissing the possibility of contracting HIV infection from blood in the emergency room where he worked, claimed his immune system could 'kick ass'. And in an invidious twist, the local newspaper reported that 'Five Texas girls say they had sex with an HIV-infected male to get into gang'. 'If the test came up negative, then it was like they were brave to have unprotected sex and they were tough enough and their body was tough enough to fight the disease' (*The Sun* 1993).

In addition to this kind of 'given' superiority, people and texts equally often mention the effect of whatever 'training' we give our immune systems: 'like an army which is prepared and waiting but never called into action, an unused immune system may become obsolete, not sufficiently prepared for new types of attack' (Pearsall 1987: 39).

The notion that through practice and training, one could develop an immune system more able to survive is captured by one of our immuno-macho doctors who had his immune system in a training programme:

> Like, for example, eating things that are not particularly well cleaned, or, you know, go on trips and drink water from a river, and, it's sort of, to build up my immune system. Now, I don't know if it has any advantage for me, or, if actually I'm exposing myself to any more danger and, I guess I should think a little bit more about that, but that's sort of my little idiosyncratic attitude about my own immune system. I'm trying to train it, sometimes.
> [To train it?]
> Yeah. (laughs)
> [Do you like to challenge it, or what?]
> Yeah, yeah. (Ken Holden)

The concept of earnable competence, hinging on a core notion of trainability and educability, powerfully reflects the peculiarly American cultural attachment to individual growth and development, as expressed from

Horatio Alger to Bill Clinton. The heights of achievement are open to all who will work hard and apply self-discipline. In an article titled: 'A Brave New Darwinian Workplace,' *Fortune* spells out the following.

- *The problem*: as rigidly hierarchical schemes for organizing work are destroyed, schemes that have limited the ability of 'people, organizations and markets to behave in *natural ways*', the transition will 'be brutal for all concerned, but . . . the workplace will be healthier, saner, more creative, and yet more chaotic – *like nature itself*' (Sherman 1993: 51, emphasis added).
- *The necessary realization*: 'Forget old notions of advancement and loyalty. In a more flexible, more chaotic world of work you're responsible for your career. For the adaptable, it's a good deal' (p. 50).
- *The solution*: 'Specialization is out, a new-style generalism is in. The most employable people will be *flexible folk* who can move easily from one function to another, integrating diverse disciplines and perspectives' (p. 52).

In a sense, 'training' becomes 'natural' here, And like the 'nature' of anything, this different basis for inequality does *not seem arbitrary or artificial to us* but, rather, seems based on good sense, progress, or the fruits of knowledge. To survive, the cherished trait of flexibility must be cultivated in neighbourhoods, hospitals and corporations. Flexibility is an object of desire for nearly everyone's personality, body, and organisation. Flexibility has also become a powerful commodity, something scarce and highly valued, that can be used to discriminate against some people.

In trying to trace the outlines of the selves and bodies populating this scene, the stakes are very large. At issue is what kinds of bodies we imagine will be able to survive the present or next wave of downsizing or onslaught of a microbial epidemic, also: what kind of mechanism we imagine will enable some of us – and not others – to evolve into successful healthy workers, surviving in higher order organisations.

One of the bleakest potential consequences of these new models of the ideal flexible body is that, yet again, certain categories of people (women, people of colour) will be found deficient. Particular social groups may be seen as having rigid or unresponsive selves and bodies, making them relatively unfit for the kind of society we now seem to desire. Another possible consequence – no less bleak – is that the old categories of hierarchical discrimination will be reshuffled in fundamental ways. According to one conception of a new elite, the desirable qualities of flexibility and adaptability may be found in superior individuals of *any* ethnic, racial, gender sexual identity, or age group in the nation. The 'currency' in which these desirable qualities will be figured is health, especially the health of one's immune system. What will be forged is a conception of 'fitness' in which, just as surely as in nineteenth-century social Darwinism (although the terms and mechanisms may differ), some will survive and some will not.

Conclusion

At the beginning of my research, I wondered whether it would be possible to understand how the economic and social formation of late capitalism can influence 'culture,' in particular internal and external forms of the body in health and illness. Certainly others have argued that aspects of late capitalism are responsible for the form taken by such cultural productions as architecture, art, or literature (Jameson 1984; Harvey 1989).[5] At the end of the research, it now seems to me that when it comes to the disciplines of science and medicine, given their cultural preeminence in the US, one could as feasibly argue that the ideal models of being-in-the-world these disciplines generate (i.e. the innovative, agile body) could be acting as templates for ideal forms of conducting business or making products (the innovative, agile firm).[6]

At the beginning of my research I also wondered whether 'scientific' information just travelled out of the lab into the culture and had its effects there, period. As the research went along, I learned how often the effects of scientific information could lack the kind of closure that is often produced inside the lab. Consequently, it seemed possible that there would be many roads by which new cultural constructs of the body and health could return to transform knowledge within the laboratory itself. It is perhaps too much to expect to catch this process 'in the act'; the process is likely to be rather ineffable, made up of implicit understandings that permeate the ideas and practices of scientists in daily life, as in their work.

Despite the difficulty of *proving* the existence of this process, though, there are many suggestive indications that it occurs:

- We have seen the outlines of the emergence of an 'unnerving new view of man's place in the world' (Alpers 1983: 17), taking place in, many arenas involving a variety of forms of systems thinking. Is it unreasonable to think that this new view might have played a part in the shift within science – still underway – to seeing the body as defended by a complex internal *system* in the first place?
- The biologist Mike Edidin chose the image of an ancient fortress, a monumental edifice defended with moats and walls against a hostile enemy, to describe the immune system; Vera Michaels chose the image of 'waves', evoking a turbulent, chaotic, complex phenomenon, in constant change. Edidin's image stresses stable, secure *defence*; Michaels' stresses a complex, turbulent *system*. As models in the science of immunology shift away from the defended castle to the part embedded in a complex whole, this development is influenced by the cultural

environment in which this shift of body image has *already taken place* in many areas outside science and in the private musings of many scientists as well. In this case, immunology is having a path beaten to its door.

- The nearly universal understanding of health in terms of the immune system, a process that is fuelled by the findings of scientific research as translated by the media, surely must influence the thinking of the politicians who approve budgets, the scientists who approve research grant applications, the scientists and editors who select what papers get published, and so on. Finding out more about how the immune system works, or what it influences is understood as a viable and productive activity. Freud used the notion of 'overdetermination' to describe a phenomenon with many causes, none sufficient in itself, but together more than sufficient (Obeyesekere 1990: 56–7). To extend the imagery of roads and paths, we might say that a ten lane super-highway would barely be sufficient to handle the ideas and practices treating the body, self, and world as complex systems, that must be shuttling back and forth between the general culture and scientific research on the immune system.

What is most troubling to me about the new cultural sensibilities I have been describing is the very thoroughness with which (immune) systems thinking has permeated our culture in every direction. Despite all the beguiling attractions of this way of positioning oneself in the world, it also has disturbing implications. There is the propensity to extol harmony within the system and reliance on the group, while paradoxically (and distractingly) allotting individuals a dynamic, ever-changing, flexible role. As we saw earlier, concealing conflict – between those who have different amounts of resources and power, for the sake of the appearance of harmony – usually hurts the disadvantaged. There is a propensity to imagine systems as inexorably evolving wholes, while simultaneously setting up comparisons with other systems that cannot survive. As we saw earlier, this propensity plays its part in an emerging neo-social Darwinism, which again has negative consequences for the disadvantaged.

Perhaps (immune) systems thinking is seductive because it seems to offer an escape from earlier forms of discipline that constrained our bodies and groups in the mass production era. It strictly immobilised the body in rigid postures and limited movements in factories and prisons; detailed rules governed mind and body in schools and the military (Foucault 1979, 1980). Fresh from these experiences, to move gracefully as an agile, dancing, flexible worker/person/body feels like a liberation, even if one is moving across a tightrope. But can we simultaneously realise that the new flexible bodies are also highly constrained? They cannot stop moving, they cannot stabilise or rest, or they will fall off the 'tightrope' of life and die. We need to challenge these implicit constraints, which serve to intensify the contemporary concern about survival of the fittest.

Acknowledgements

This Chapter is adapted from *Flexible Bodies: the Role of Immunity in American Culture from the Age of Polio to the Age of AIDS* (Boston: Beacon Press, 1994). A version of this article was published in *Science as Culture* (1997, vol. 26, part 3, no. 29, pp. 327–62). The research was funded with the generous support of the Spencer Foundation. The graduate students who assisted the research were: Bjorn Cleason, Laury Oakes, Monica Schoch-Spana, Karen-Sue Taussig, Wendy Richardson and Adriane van der Straten.

References

Alpers, S. (1983) *The Art of Describing: Dutch Art in the Seventeenth Century*, Chicago IL: University of Chicago Press.
Arney, William R. (1991) *Experts in the Age of Systems*, Albuquerque, NM: University of New Mexico Press.
Bauman, Z. (1992) *Intimations of Postmodernity*, London: Routledge.
Benziger, J. (1989) *The Corpuscles: Adventures in Innerspace*, Waterville, MN: Corpuscles InterGalactica.
Borgmann, A. (1992) *Crossing the Postmodern Divide*, Chicago, IL: University of Chicago Press.
Coughlan, R. (1955) 'Science moves in on viruses', *Life* 38: 122–36.
Dwyer, J. M. (1988) *The Body at War: the Miracle of the Immune System*, New York: New American Library.
Edidin, M. (1991) 'The biology of immune responses', in *The Great Ideas Today*, Chicago: Encyclopedia Britannica, Inc, 2–59.
Foucault, M. (1979) *Discipline and Punish: the Birth of the Prison*, New York: Vintage Books.
—— (1980) *Power/Knowledge: Selected Interviews and Other Writings 1972–1977*, New York: Pantheon.
Gelderman, C. (1981) *Henry Ford: the Wayward Capitalist*, New York: St Martin's Press.
Harvey, D. (1989) *The Condition of Postmodernity: an Enquiry into the Origins of Social Change*, Oxford: Basil Blackwell.
Hindley, J. and King, C. (1975) *How Your Body Works*, London: Usborne.
Jameson, F. (1984). 'Postmodernism, or the cultural logic of late capitalism', *New Left Review* 146: 52–92.
Miller, B. F., and Goode, R. (1960). *Man and His Body*, New York: Simon and Schuster.
Obeyesekere, G. (1990) *The Work of Culture: Symbolic Transformation in Psychoanalysis and Anthropology*, Chicago, IL: University of Chicago Press.
The Oxford English Dictionary (OED) (1989) 2nd edn, Oxford: Clarendon.

Parker, M., and Slaughter, J. (1990) 'Management-by-stress: the team concept in the US auto industry', *Science as Culture* 8: 27–58.

Peabody, J. E. and Hunt, A. E. (1934) *Biology and Human Welfare*, New York: Macmillan.

Pearsall, P. (1987) *Super Immunity: Master Your Emotions and Improve Your Health*, New York: Fawcett.

Ritchie, J. W. (1918) *The Primer of Sanitation and Physiology*, Yonkers-on-Hudson, NY: World Book Co.

—— (1948) *Biology and Human Affairs*, Yonkers-on-Hudson, NY: World Book Co.

Sherman, S. (1993) 'A brave new Darwinian workplace', *Fortune* 127(2): 50–6.

Smith, C. (1991) 'From 1960s' automation to flexible specialisation: a déjà vu of technological panaceas', in A. Pollert (ed.) *Farewell to Flexibility?*, London: Basil Blackwell, 138–57.

The Sun (1993) Five Texas girls say they had sex with an HIV-infected male to get into gang', April, p. 7.

Chapter 7

'Recombinant' bodies

Narrative, metaphor and the gene

Deborah Lynn Steinberg

> Languages of nature are made and not pre-given.
>
> (Jordanova 1986: 27)

Introduction

In her classic essay, *Illness as Metaphor* (1991), Susan Sontag examined the symbolic economies of disease in order to trace and yet disaggregate the inter-resonances of medical (scientific) discourse and common sense. In the dominant metaphors associated with illness – including for example military, criminological, capitalist and machine metaphors – Sontag intimately mapped what she identified as the conceptual and material preoccupations of modernity. In this context, language, and metaphor specifically, are revealed as mediators of the historically contingent and reciprocal investments between medical scientific discourse and broader cultural processes and meanings. In this reading, illness as metaphor not only articulates the cultural *situatedness* of science and medicine but implicitly posits them as sites of both cultural agency and cultural authorship.

Yet, one of the peculiar contradictions of Sontag's early study, one which Sontag herself later acknowledged, is the contrast posited between metaphoric thinking, as a purely linguistic, extra-scientific and secondary phenomenon, and the scientific standpoint. Language, in this sense, is identified for its capacity to distort the real and subvert scientific inquiry. Indeed, Sontag argues strenuously for the exposure of destructive metaphoric representations of illness as part of a process of conceptual decontamination. This positivistic investment in the (pre)supposedly mimetic and objective qualities of medical scientific standpoint strikes a peculiar note in several respects. For example, while Sontag tracks the political implications of particular kinds of metaphors associated with certain diseases (and disease *per se*), she exonerates medical scientists from complicity in that process. This construction would seem both to reject the ways in which metaphoric thinking demonstrably fuels scientific research (and the scientific imagination) and the ways in which science *resources* the broader cultural take-up of particular disease meanings. Indeed, many of the sources Sontag quotes were authored by medical scientists. In this reading, ironically, metaphor itself becomes metaphor, a pathology against which scientific rationality is posited as antidote.

The positivist and anti-positivist tensions of *Illness as Metaphor* take on a particular poignancy at this contemporary historical moment. On the one hand, three decades on from Sontag's original writing, the notions of science *as* culture, and of the contingent and historically specific relationships between ontology and epistemology, knowledge and power, 'fact' and 'artefact'[1] have complexly reconstituted the epistemic centre of social theory across disciplines. At the same time, resurgent biological explanations of identity, social patterns and social relationships, have harnessed new currency in the iconic configurations of the gene and the neo-positivism of recombinant genetic science. It is this clash of cultures, as it were, which fuels and with which this chapter is, in part, concerned.

Narrative, metaphor and the gene

> Biology is inherently historical, and its form of discourse is inherently narrative. Biology as a way of knowing the world is kin to Romantic literature, with its discourse about organic form and function. Biology is the fiction appropriate to objects called organisms; biology fashions the facts 'discovered' from organic beings. Organisms perform for the biologist, who transforms that performance into a truth attested by disciplined experience; i.e., into a fact, the jointly accomplished deed or feat of the scientist and the organism. Romanticism passes into realism, and realism into naturalism, genius into progress, insight into fact. *Both* the scientist and the organism are actors in a story-telling practice.
>
> (Haraway 1989: 5)

There can be no doubt that the gene, that modern artefact of nearly two centuries of scientific preoccupation with the 'discovery' of life's origins and the 'mechanisms' of its heredity, has become sedimented into the fabric of contemporary popular imagination. We are now well into the third decade of recombinant genetics, heralded by most commentators, as the new biotechnology revolution. The possibilities projected into the manipulation of molecular space are imbricated not only in novel biological and medical practices, but also in a process of grand narrative. The gene has become at once a point of reference and of projective identification, (re)constituted as both a tool and a symbol, *taken* in both literary and literal senses as a rogue and yet domesticated body, a territory, a weapon, a library, a laboratory. The emergence of the gene in and as contemporary commonsense accrues from a complex authorship in which the authoritative accounts of scientific practitioners intersect with older stories. Indeed, emergent discourses of the gene have complexly and contradictorily filtered through the range of representational media (literary, press, televisual and cinematic, professional and lay) and genres (technical, peer review, documentary, sci fi, horror). Similarly, as this chapter will show, gene stories have conscripted and transformed dominant cultural narratives, from origin to adventure stories, dystopian and utopian.

Drawing, then, from a critical engagement with Sontag's original study, this chapter will examine the imagery, metaphors and narratives that have underpinned the emergent cultural primacy of the gene. I do not, in this context, suggest that the narrational dimensions of science are in themselves problematic. Rather, I would argue that what is at issue is a *denial* of science as a site of narrative. What is of critical importance then, are the *particular* narratives embedded in *particular* scientific practices and what they suggest about the power relations accruing to that science. Focusing on a selection of what might be classified as 'high-brow' popular science texts as a case study, I am interested, here, in the representational economies surrounding genes, bodies and embodiment in three respects: the constitution of genes *as* bodies/embodiments, of genetics as a body of knowledge and of geneticists as a body of knowers.

Science, narration and embodiment: a critical standpoint

In reading the metaphors and narratives of genes, this chapter is informed by two particular epistemological trajectories within social theory of science, medicine and the body. First, there has been a veritable explosion of work, recently, on the body and on cultural praxes of embodiment. Such work provides a key theoretical resource for this chapter. As I have noted elsewhere (Steinberg 1996a), the body as *corporealisation* of social and cultural relations has become an increasingly important site of inquiry across a range of (inter)disciplines as well as a field of study in its own right. There has been considerable analytic preoccupation with bodily boundaries – fragile, transgressed, defended, reproduced,[2] with embodied spaces from molecular to cosmic, and with the mapping and remaking of bodily functions and contours. This emergent interest in bodies and embodiment constitutes, in part, an attempt to reconcile materialist and postmodern standpoints within social theory – to re-incorporate bodies in the matrices of imagination, memory and meaning *without* either collapsing or denying the relationship between being and knowing. A central strand of embodiment theory is specifically invested in the analysis of medicine and science as key discourses and disciplinary regimes through which bodies – bodies that matter (Butler 1993) and bodies of knowledge (Foucault 1977) – are constituted.

Second, in taking up the method, but not the positivistic investments of Sontag's original study, this chapter clearly articulates with broader interests in the narrative processes of and within science – and of science itself as a story-telling enterprise. As suggested in Sontag's work, narrative analysis foregrounds discursive processes and power relations of authorship and readership and the textual praxes that constitute the languages, protocols and products of science and medicine. In doing so, the complex embedding of science as product of and as productive of wider social and cultural relations can be intimately mapped. In turn, this growing interest in science as a project of narrative is part of a larger interest in narrative as a cultural process constitutive of competing concepts of kinship (Strathern 1992), of imagined community and nation (Anderson 1982; Yuvall-Davis 1993), of identity (Dawson 1994; Redman 1998) and of the body. As Redman (1998) has argued,

> [N]arrative is a significant mode through which meaning is produced and lived out: in other words . . . narrative is important to the ways in which we understand the world and our place in it. This is a fundamentally anti-positivist view point, and it is therefore unsurprising that much of this work has also stressed the narrative construction of knowledge.
>
> (p. 4)

The association of narrative with science and, more to the point, the investigation of science as a narrative practice, radically reinterprets its epistemic character and radically challenges its status as a privileged (meta)cultural discourse. In such an analysis, moreover, the boundaries of both discipline and genre that are conventionally understood to demarcate expert and popular knowledges are blurred while the profound inequalities that produce their margins and centres can be starkly revealed. Narrative, moreover, as a site of hegemonic struggle, is deeply intertwined with the valedictory dictations of expert tellers and the discursive practices that produce both bodies of knowledge and bodies who know. Thus, a narrative approach to the analysis of medical scientific discourse cannot but reveal its preoccupation with bodies – the very stuff of 'nature', the very bedrock (object and agent) of scientific materialism.

Genes and genre

> [T]hey [scientists] map for us and for themselves the chains of associations that make up their sociologics.
>
> (Latour 1987: 202)

Authoritative accounts of scientific practitioners cannot be easily disentangled from their renderings for popular consumption. Indeed the multiple genres of scientific writing and writing (or other representations) about science seem to merge at various points of nexus. The scientist who writes for peer review may also, for example, write a novel, a newspaper editorial, a film script, a handbook for the lay reader, consumer or patient.[3] As media personalities or speakers on the high-brow lecture circuit, scientists are characteristically produced (and produce themselves) as veritable prophets of modernity: translators and transposers, magicians and democratisers on high who bring science to the people as a downward (and thereby elevating) movement. To draw on the vernacular of the publishing business, the *cross-over* genres of scientific representations, those in which the scientific expert constructs articulations for a lay readership, provide a particularly edifying and rich illustration of the narrative structuring of the scientific imagination. Here even as scientific practice (and practitioners) must necessarily provide the source-point for cultural inscription, wider common senses must also be tapped to provide an intelligible reference point for the bridging (and delineation) of worlds.

The literature I have selected for close study in this chapter belongs to a distinctive strand within popular writing about science. These are typified by their designated readership (highly educated, non-scientific and non-medical but perhaps, otherwise, professional); the credentials of their authors (often well-celebrated scientists); their often glossy and very tasteful production values (with pricing in the upper range, typical of academic books); and their availability in the 'better' bookstores, usually in the 'general science' and 'general medicine' sections (separate, but not far from, the textbooks) and, not infrequently (depending on the celebrity of the author), as special displays at the front of the store. The overwhelming majority of this literature takes a celebratory approach to scientific progress.[4] Here, critique, where it appears, tends to be balanced against projections and estimations of the overwhelming benefits of scientific progress and the virtuosity and ingenuity of science (and scientific medicine). Rationales for new scientific directions are characteristically located in noble goals – the relief of suffering; the quest for knowledge; the forging, in reverential acknowledgement, of the human capacity to grasp and to harness the (recalcitrant/magnificent) forces of nature.

This chapter will focus, then, on three 'serious' genetics advocacy texts, within the wider literature described above, that are characteristic in many respects of the emergent range of progress-orientated texts on this topic. All three of the selected texts make a case for a widening practice of recombinant genetics. All situate their genetics rationales within a broader, albeit many versioned, liberal political framework and tradition. And all cull distinctive cultural narratives, metaphors and common senses that in many respects recall the earliest period of modernist thinking, to articulate utopian visions of the genetics revolution. Stephanie Yanchinski's *Setting Genes to Work* (1985), the earliest text, presents a libertarian, industrial utopia. Capitalist metaphors and narratives dominate the text in an imagined world of perpetual production (of food, chemicals and wealth), a molecular matrix in which discourses of class are both displaced and reinvested in the micro-bodies, the new labouring masses, of the cell. In *Genetics for Beginners* (1993), Steve Jones, with illustrator Borin Van Loon, present what might be termed a liberal imperialist utopia. Here we find a textual and visualised colonial adventure narrative in which the biological landscape is mapped, its resources plundered and the scientist becomes hunter/civiliser of rogue genetic nature(s). Finally, there is *The Lives to Come: the Genetic Revolution and Human Possibilities* (1996), Philip Kitcher's diagnostic utopia in which futures, corporeally mapped, are located in the boundaried, yet metamorphic bodies of the genes. Here is presented the seductive projection of a rational, democratic pharmocracy in which freedom is to be found in the disciplinary regimes of medical diagnosis and rationally planned ('utopian eugenic', in Kitcher's terms) reproductions.

Of monads and machines: Yanchinski's industrial utopia

> **monad:** (n.) the number one; a unit; an ultimate unit of being, material and psychical; spirit; God; a hypothetical primitive living organism or unit of organic life.
>
> (*Chambers English Dictionary* 1990)

In *Volatile Bodies* (1994), Elizabeth Grosz examines Spinoza's concept of the monad as a radical challenge to the disunification of body and agency characteristic of the western Cartesian tradition. In the monad is the ultimate singularity of process, matter and purpose; each attribute or entity only a part, a micocosmic manifestation, of the infinitely possible expressions and overarching unities of nature. Grosz argues that monism thus 'frees the body' from two key aspects of Cartesian thought: its dualism and its 'dominant mechanistic models and metaphors' (p. 11). In Spinoza's conceptualisation of a cell, for example, there is no pre-given structure, animated by an external energy source (as fuel added to a machine), but, rather, its very being-ness *as* a cell is located in a self-generating, continuous metabolic process:

> The forms of determinatedness, temporal and historical continuity, and the relations a thing has with coexisting things provide the entity with its identity. Its unity is not a function of its machine operations as a closed system (i.e. its functional integration) but arises from a sustained sequence of states in a unified plurality.
>
> (pp. 12–13)

Like the atom before it, the commonsense constitution of the gene as an ultimate unit of existence bespeaks a monistic unification of matter and energy, meaning and substance. Yet the molecular manipulations of recombinant genetics would seem to *reinvest* the putative monadic bodies of genes back into the dualistic traditions of modern scientific thought and practice. With recombinant genetics the body of the gene is both conscripted for, and understood to be (re)animated through, the intentionalities of the scientist-engineer and the invented machinery of the recombinant organism. This contradictory fusing of monad and machine is tellingly articulated through the linguistic, organic and industrial metaphors that permeate the dominant literatures, scientific[5] and popular, of contemporary genetics and that are perhaps, most fully realised, in Yanchinski's utopian assessment of recombinant genetics as a new industrial era.

Worker bodies and the industrial metaphor

We are in the middle of another industrial revolution, and most people are only just realizing it. This industrial revolution, called 'biotechnology' depends not on iron and steel but mainly on microbes which scientists are converting into minuscule factories for exotic drugs, industrial chemicals, fuel and even food. The 'bio' in biotechnology refers to bacteria and yeast, mainly, but also to other living cells such as plants, fungi and algae. The 'technology' consists of batteries of gleaming steel vats full of microbes ... [and] hundreds of valves opening and closing to computer-set rhythms, guided by artificial intelligence – all the trappings of our electronics world applied to keeping these microbes producing at top efficiency.

(Yanchinski 1985: 7)

Encapsulated in the notion of 'setting genes to work', the title of Stephanie Yanchinski's appraisal of recombinant genetics, are the key connotations that frame not only her own projected narrative of a new industrial utopia, but also, as we shall see, inform the narrative economies of the later texts by Kitcher and Jones and Van Loon. First is the emphasis on *work*. In this formulation, the significance of genes lies in their perceived productive capacities and, perhaps more to the point, in their projective constitution as *labouring entities*. The notion of 'setting' is also suggestive of the reading that genes do not work *unless* 'set' to. Here the gene is, at least in part, connotatively evoked as idle, undisciplined body, a potential yet resistant energy, animated into its proper (and obligatory) function only by an outside agency (the 'setter'). Such a construction is suggestively reminiscent of Victorian constructions of a recalcitrant working class, defined by the contrast of its muscle but not mind to industry, efficiency and economy. Congruent with industrial logics located in more conventional settings, genes as workers are implicitly constituted as docile[6] and yet resistant, performative objects and objectified subjects in a disciplinary economy that they embody but do not own. Central, then, to Yanchinski's utopian prognostication of mastered microbes in 'gleaming steel' vat-factories are genes as imagined bodies, nostalgically and narratively constituted through a distinctive discourse of class and a decidedly commercial rationality.

The gene as class ideal

So yeasts and bacteria are the new labouring masses toiling to make the wheels of the biotechnology industry run.

(Yanchinski 1985: 20)

Perhaps the most telling linchpin of Yanchinski's industrial narrative is articulated through the distinctive discourse of class characteristic of the metaphors of industrial capitalism. Indeed, the language of class permeates Yanchinski's idealisation of the gene in both its projected commercial and medical applications.[7] Notions of 'toiling labouring masses', 'aristocratic bosses'[8] (p. 20), 'factory foremen' (p. 27)[9] and 'gene machines (p. 49)[10] locate genes as essential(ised) and mechanised components of the transgenic factory.[11] In these projections, class divisions evocative of Marx's dark satanic mill are reconstituted – sanitised and transplanted but still, apparently, intact. The projection of class identities onto the gene has a double movement – naturalising class divisions and yet displacing them onto putatively lesser natures. Implicit in this formulation is a promise of human freedom from class oppression even as such inequalities are recuperated for human investment, conceptual and commercial.

Similarly, the construction of labouring agency is contradictory, both located in the *self-organising* capacities and monadic properties attributed to genes, and yet utilised as functionary cogs in the wheel of a superordinate disciplinary economy. Factory discipline itself is invoked both through the language of intimate precision (to map, cut and paste) attributed to the capabilities of the genetic engineer, and through the idealisation, accruing to such language, of productive efficiency. As Weiss (1987) has noted,[12] a preoccupation with social productivity and rational selection bespeaks a technocratic-managerial logic characteristic of eugenic philosophy. In Yanchinski's utopia, as with the languages of class, the displacement on to genes of the language of selective breeding, also constitutes a recuperation and reinvestment in its historical resonances of productive and reproductive 'fitness', national efficiency and racial hygiene.[13]

To summarise then, the ambivalent construction of a self-governing yet externally governed, self-assembled yet scientifically recombinant, production processes/producer is clearly evocative of industrial logics and

narratives going back to the nineteenth century. Indeed, Yanchinski's idealisation of 'immobilised cell technology' (p. 24)[14] epitomises precisely the
industrial fantasy of continuous production and perpetually renewable (and
essentially expendable) labouring forces.

Dark continents: genetics as colonial conquest

> Heroic narratives have been given a particular inflection in discourses
> of the nation generated since the emergence of the nation-state in
> early-modern Europe.
>
> (Dawson 1994: 1)

Even as Yanchinski's industrial utopia, in its recuperation of the monad
for the machine, focuses on the *gene*, the narrative sweep of Jones and
Van Loon's *Genetics for Beginners* is preoccupied with the genetic *scientist*. Here, as we shall see, the geneticist as heroic (if modest) adventurer
in the uncharted terrains of the molecular world is textually embedded in
a repertoire of eugenic and colonial imagery that is, again, culled from
the Victorian period. Of particular salience in this context are the distinctive motifs – surrounding nation, race and sexuality – which can be traced
through organising narratives of genetic cartography and conquest.

Colonial cartographies: mapping the gene as foreign landscape

> In spite of the new confusion in genetics, it is clear that – just as the
> first explorations of South America – hidden within the genetic map
> there are new and startling facts about genes, about disease and about
> evolution. Now there is a scheme for the great Map of Ourselves –
> a list of the three thousand million letters in the human DNA. It may
> be complete by the year 2000.
>   It will cost a lot: but like many maps will be the first step to
> exploiting the country which it reveals.
>
> (Jones and Van Loon 1993: 112)

The textual investment of genetics in analogies of colonial exploitation is
not incidental to Jones and Van Loon's imagining of the biotechnology
revolution. *Genetics for Beginners* is peppered with images of white colonial hunters, treacherous African and jungle landscapes (see Figure 7.1),
boys-own stories of treasure hunts[15] and Lone Rangers supported by
backwards, but nevertheless complicit, natives. Incorporated in such images
are constructions of both the geneticist and the enterprise of genetics within
the recognisable conventions of the Victorian Quest narrative (see for
example, Showalter 1992 and Dawson 1994), with their themes of dark

Figure 7.1 (Stephen Jones/Borin Van Loon, *Genetics for Beginners*, reproduced courtesy of Icon Books Ltd)

continents to be taken, known and ruled, masculine aspiration and racialised/sexualised imperial fantasy.

The notion of gene-space as a landscape, for example, incorporates Yanchinski's monadic/machine bodies in a subtextual motif of rational domestication. The putative African or jungle genes, for example, are visualised within the conventions of dominant racialised mythologies of the rogue primitive, whose very nativeness seems to demand the cartographic and conquering interventions of white civilisation. The genetic landscape is valued for the dormant, hidden riches of which its native inhabitants are connotatively constituted as both unaware and/or intrinsically incapable of exploiting. The quest for the 'dark continent' is, furthermore, organised around a particular imperial-commercial logic; it is the presumptive institution of western knowhow that locates, cultivates and expropriates the latent economic potential understood to be embedded in the 'alien' landscape.

Civilising missions: metaphoric economies of nation, race and sexuality

If the 'foreign' imaginary discussed above is often coded through controlling myths[16] of colonial Africa and South America, so too is the 'familiar', the imagined genetic coloniser, predominantly visualised through dominant mythologies of white, male (upper class) Britishness. The 'I say, Carruthers' of the generic geneticist of Figure 7.2, for example, melds with the intended humour in another image that re-presents Watson and Crick as Holms and Watson (p. 57). Both representations constitute visual puns grounded in a distinctive version of white British masculinity articulated through its purported 'quaintness', its bumbling (yet incisive) modesty, its idiosyncratic (even ironic) genius and, perhaps most importantly, its taken-for-granted privilege of both entry and ownership.

An investment of genetics in notions of British nation (and white British masculinity) is also suggestively forged through other representative clichés. In their explanations of what genetic scientists regard as 'nonsense DNA' (repeated chains of DNA to which scientists have been unable to attribute an identifiable biological function),[17] Jones and Van Loon take up the Chinese language as a metaphor of generic/genetic incomprehensibility:

> It was as if the owner's manual for an English car was interrupted by sentences in Chinese which had to be nipped out before the instructions could be read properly.

(p. 90)

Englishness thus constitutes not only the presumptive reader and owner of the sought code (and the functional apparatus to which it refers), but the generic properties of functional productivity – Englishness, in other

Figure 7.2 (Stephen Jones/Borin Van Loon, *Genetics for Beginners*, reproduced courtesy of Icon Books Ltd)

words, is deployed here as a metaphor for meaningfulness itself. Chinese, by contrast, is constituted as intrinsically unreadable, as alien interloper, needing to be 'nipped out' for proper order to be restored. A similar Orientalism is also evoked in Jones and Van Loon's representation of boy-preference (constituted as a potential problem accruing from the use of genetic techniques for sex selection) as a function of the putative under-development of Indian culture. Here, the ownership of genetics, is graphically visualised as white, male and Western. India is constituted through the recognisable Orientalist mythology of hyper-patriarchy; its 'extreme' oppression of women iconographic of its 'backwardness'[18] and counterposed to the more enlightened anti-sexism implicitly attributed to British culture (see Figure 7.3).

The racialised imagery of nation that characterises Jones and Van Loon's colonial genetics adventure is clearly mediated through explicitly eugenic textual economies. Figures 7.1 and 7.4, for instance, draw explicitly on what might be described as generic eugenic imagery. There is a double movement here as, for example, Figure 7.1's image of the 'white man

When it comes to women, though, things are different. It is easy to tell the sex of a foetus by looking at its chromosomes. In Britain, parents do not have a strong preference for boys or girls —

To the alarm of geneticists . . .

Figure 7.3 (Stephen Jones/Borin Van Loon, *Genetics for Beginners*, reproduced courtesy of Icon Books Ltd)

Dominant characters seemed simple enough. Soon, characters controlled by recessive genes began to turn up. Only those inheriting two copies of the gene, one from each parent, showed its effects.

Such traits cropped up in families, often skipping generations. This explained an old problem — atavism; the tendency of a child to resemble a remote relative or distant ancestor.

Figure 7.4 (Stephen Jones/Borin Van Loon, *Genetics for Beginners*, reproduced courtesy of Icon Books Ltd)

wrecked on an island inhabited by negroes' is taken up in what might be read as an intended critique of the simplistic wrong-headedness of Victorian eugenics/genetics: '[a] highly favoured white cannot blanch a nation of negroes'. Yet the assumption of heterosexual male access, ('civilised' here as counterposed with 'savage'), characteristic of colonial conquest narratives is reasserted rather than rejected in the white British man's 'humorous' directive 'Ok you chaps let me have the pick of your wives!! I *am* British after all'. Masculinity is the subject, not the object of the joke here. Similarly, what might be described as the classic imagery of constitutional 'degeneracy' evoked in Figure 7.4 is (re)deployed as a light joke, ostensibly now blanched of its historical resonances, on the ways in which mechanisms of inheritance can be recognised in the face of one's offspring. Yet the plundering of racist imagery and language to challenge racism is disingenuous at best. The ironic inflection seemingly intended in the use of this imagery does not work precisely because the images deployed were themselves products of a eugenic colonial enterprise, in which genetics was an organising discourse.[19] However ironic their motivations, Jones and Van Loon's choice to take up of such imagery as a recognisable reference point for the lay-reader bespeaks the continued currency of eugenic/colonial narratives in both popular and scientific common sense. In turn, contemporary genetics is revealed as a hospitable, indeed generative, context for the recuperation of such narratives.

Making the world safe for genetics: Kitcher's diagnostic democracy

> Geneticists warmed easily to their priestly role. The new industrial order had elevated practitioners of the physical sciences to positions of power and public service.
>
> (Kevles 1985: 69)

If Victorian discourses of industrial capitalism and colonial adventure characterise the utopian imaginings of recombinant genetics in the previous texts, their diagnostic implications are elaborately realised in Paul Kitcher's *The Lives to Come*. Here the geneticist as heroic explorer, divining the mysteries of molecular space, also serves a reminiscently 'priestly role' in a narratively projected recuperation of both the physical and social world. In Kitcher's imaginary, genetics is constituted as both a journey, inflected with Biblical import, and a grail of modernist rationality applied both to reproductive practice (what Kitcher terms 'utopian eugenics') and to the forging of a new social order of diagnostic discipline.

Of angels bearing gifts

Another image of a great journey recurs in advertisements for contemporary biomedical research. No less a figure than Walter Gilbert, Nobel Laureate and co-inventor of sequencing technology, has seen genome sequencing not as tedious drudgery, but knightly enterprise. The sequence of the human genome is the 'Grail'.

(Kitcher 1996: 88)

They journey in hope, not knowing for sure that they are playing Christian to the naysayers' Pliable, whether they are Arthurian knights or Don Quixote.

(p. 89)

If there were a sequence-bearing angel, what use could we make of the gift?

(p. 91)

The allegory of the masculine quest, divinely inspired, ennobling and edifying provides the dominant narrative frame for Kitcher's construction of the social importance of both the geneticist and his science. An entire chapter is given over to a sequence of road allegories characterised not only by their quasi-religious overtones but by their investment in a particular version of masculinity: chivalric, exhalted, transcendent and, significantly, seductive. The reader is given, for example, John Bunyan's pilgrim Christian who 'struggles through the mire, goes on to face many other reversals, and ultimately wins his heavenly reward' (p. 21). Christian is the visionary genetic journeyman, his eyes beyond the earthly limitations and 'short term difficulties' of genetic testing, to the 'eventual hope ... to be able to intervene, to treat to cure' (p. 21). As an edifying tale, Christian's journey is taken up as a defensive fable. In his counterpoint to the 'naysayers' Pliable, who loses faith at the first impasse (that genetic testing 'can predict when disease will strike' but is 'helpless to avert or alleviate it'), Christian as 'visionary', embodies the moral high ground (and moral of the story) of genetics' noble purpose, in which the wonder is focused not in the mundaneity of pragmatic outcomes, but in the great journey itself. Similarly, the narratives of knightly quest and angelic prophets bearing gifts, of 'royal roads' (p. 91) and 'maps of destiny' (p. 90) imbue a romanticised metanymic divinity to each localised technical mastery that signposts the molecular path to enlightenment.

The rhetoric of noble purpose – to alleviate suffering – common to all these narratives moreover, implicitly articulates a rescue fantasy that, as Judith Williamson (1997) has suggested, not only 'runs back to medieval chivalry', but in which eroticised projections of 'men doing valiant deeds as a way of courting and 'serving' women' are encoded. As romantic saviour, the persona of the geneticist is not only prefigured male, but is embedded in an intransigently heterosexualised narrative frame. For example, the evocation of the knightly conqueror, indeed even of the romantic outlaw Don Quixote, presents a reminiscent, though perhaps less obviously racialised, heterosexual subtext to the narratives (and penetrative symbolic economies) of colonial conquest taken up by Jones and Van Loon. In this context, genetic science is complexly en-gendered. On the one hand, genetics is graphically masculinised, both as a male preserve and as a journey to a masculinity exalted just short of godhead. At the same time, genetic science is narratively positioned as endangered (by, for example, the 'naysayers' pessimism), an intrinsically feminised construction within the dominant logic of the genre. Indeed, it can be argued that the construction of genetics as 'grail' evokes comparable symbologies of masculine virtue – liberty and justice, for example – that are characteristically embodied female. In turn, the relationship of masculine rescuer to endangered science offers preferred positions of identification in similarly gendered terms. For it is clearly a masculine agency and Eros that is imagined as prime mover of both the science and its narratives: dangerous journeys both, to be braved by brave men. The framing of genetics through romantic fantasies of masculine endeavour clearly link the gendered, heterosexualised imaginaries of Kitcher and Jones and Van Loon. At the same time, there are revealing distinctions to be drawn between narratives of quest and of conquest. If the latter evokes a manful assertion (and man's-own world) of rugged derring-do, the former posits the recuperated conqueror, now protector and humane husband of fragile, but fantastical, futures.

Diagnostic designs

If the romantic quest narrative signals the cosmological import, as it were, of the genetics journey envisaged by Kitcher, more pragmatic imaginings frame the forging of a newly genetified social order. Two themes in particular emerge as significant in this context: the primary location of genetified futures (and rationales) in a medicalised logic and the articulation of its recuperative potentials in a project of 'safe' eugenics. It is in this context that significant distinctions can be drawn between this and the previous two accounts of the genetics revolution. While all three texts, for example, do note problems with genetics (for example accruing to its historical resonances with 'stigmatised' eugenics), Kitcher's concern for the potential for harm emergent in contemporary molecular biology is not a subsidiary focus of the text. Indeed, the alleviation of suffering and the cultivation of an egalitarian society are higher purposes he pointedly invests in the potentials of a genetified future and are themes sustained through (and perhaps behind) the allegorical narratives of noble journeys and protective knights. In addition, although diagnostic implications for the new technologies are taken up by Yanchinski and Jones and Van Loon, this is chiefly as an adjunct to and incorporated within their overarching and respective industrial and conquest logics. By contrast, as has been discussed earlier, while Kitcher's text takes up key metaphoric and narrational economies of the previous texts, it is the diagnostic-medical applications of genetics that are characterised as the dangerous and yet ultimately redeeming centre of the road to molecular enlightenment.

Testing times

> Just after delivery, the nurses took a sample of the baby's blood, and in accordance with the medical standards of 2020, the pediatrician will now give the parents the results of the analysis, the 'genetic report card'. The interview proves more frightening in prospect than in actuality. Although the long columns of statistics are initially baffling, the doctor points out that most of the risks are normal, or below normal, and that the only worrying figures are somewhat elevated probabilities of diabetes and hypertension. She recommends attention to diet from an early age, as well as regular checks of blood sugar levels. Like many others who have experienced the new medicine, the parents are grateful they can take rational steps to promote their child's health.
>
> (Kitcher 1996: 23)

The 'genetics report card' story both leads off and encapsulates Kitcher's utopian imaginings of a world where genetics is the centre-point around which social life is to be rationally re-ordered. As this excerpt suggests, there are a number of key assumptions underpinning the diagnostic logic of a world defined by genetic testing. First, is the unquestioned investment in expertise: genetic science produces accurate facts; doctors explain these facts to patients, who are in turn grateful; and 'rational steps' can then be (and are) taken to accommodate the genetic propensities revealed. Second, is the movement towards universalisation of testing. Indeed, as I discuss further below, Kitcher explores the problematic, but ultimately, in his view, justified projection of genetic screening into widening spheres of social life, from the pre- to post-conceptive, and from the workplace to health and life insurance, to the criminal justice system. In this context, the privileging of medical scientific discourse and agency reaches its apotheosis as genetic diagnostic logics are taken to impel a radical reconstitution of both social order and cultural common sense.

Third, the notion of 'rational steps' is itself invested in the presumption of (expertly read) singularities characteristic of gene discourse more generally. In the scenario outlined above, for example, it is imagined that

UNIVERSITY OF
PAISLEY LIBRARY

a singular 'problematic' predisposition will be the outcome of a battery of genetic testing for which a set of appropriate responses will be clearly available. While Kitcher acknowledges the problem of assuming that all testing will involve 'all of the features that make the perfect test so attractive' (p. 24), his critique never considers either the probability that widening ranges of genetic testing will produce multiple projected propensities, or that the 'rational steps' taken (if indeed there are any at all) for one condition or predisposition may conflict with those to be taken for another. Similarly, while Kitcher notes the problem of 'a world of tests without therapies', his solution is a redoubled investment in genetics: 'the best remedy may be to double our research efforts' (p. 24).

Obscured in Kitcher's idealisation of the possibility that 'we shall be able to test at will – fetuses, couples who plan to marry, people who are sick, and those who show no symptoms' (p. 25) is another story: a dystopia in which 'our' captivation with genetics translates into captivity to a relentless and deeply contradictory disciplinary regime of diagnosis. Read this way, Kitcher's utopia evokes not a rational, healthful and egalitarian society, but an encroaching medicalisation of life (what Illich (1976) termed *diagnostic imperialism*) in which clinical, social and cultural iatrogenic effects (clinical harm, social dependency on experts, and the loss of belief in ones ability to cope with illness or pain) inevitably accrue.

Eugenic recuperations

> Once we have left the garden of genetic innocence, some form of eugenics is inescapable, and our first task must be to discover where among the available options we can find the safest home.
>
> (Kitcher 1996: 204)

> As a theoretical discipline, eugenics responds to our convictions that it is irresponsible not to do what can be done to prevent deep human suffering, yet it must face the challenge of showing that its claims about the values of lives are not the arrogant judgements of an elite group.
>
> (Kitcher 1996: 192)

Kitcher's elaboration of the problems that may accrue to the expansion of genetic testing revolve around its perceived potential to exacerbate existing inequalities – i.e. 'unsafe' eugenics. In this context, he projects a number of dystopian scenarios: from workplace to health and life insurance discrimination: the intensification of class and racialised divisions (which can accrue from diagnostic errors (p. 33) or coercion); a world, as has been mentioned, of tests without therapies and with insufficient demographic and aetiological statistics to make sense of diagnostic data;

and the problematic assumption of utterly rational patients. The answer to these rather overwhelming problems, Kitcher suggests, are to be found in the delicate balancing act of 'utopian eugenics':

> Utopian eugenics would use reliable genetic information in prenatal tests that would be available equally to all citizens. Although there would be widespread public discussion of values and of the social consequences of individual decisions, there would be no societally imposed restrictions on reproductive choices – citizens would be educated but not coerced. Finally, there would be universally shared respect for difference coupled with a public commitment to realizing the potential of all those who are born.
>
> (p. 202)

What is perhaps most striking about 'safe' eugenics is the way in which it is predicated on the, although clearly sincere, nevertheless facile projective assertion of some future equality. We are to assume that genetic screening will not serve only the privileged even as it presages a new class order dividing a small elite of experts from 'grateful' lay-patients. We are to assume that it will not be coercive while at the same time, forced testing in the workplace and in reproductive contexts, according to Kitcher's own assessment, is justified where 'risks' to third parties are involved. We are to assume that 'accurate and adequate information' (about epidemiological probabilities, and the full range of 'environmental factors relevant to the expression of disease') – what Kitcher characterises as 'mountains of statistics' (p. 72) – can simply, albeit with 'considerable ingenuity and immense labour', be provided in order that rational decisions can be made. We are to assume that adequate and independent counselling, 'responsive to the [social and individual] predicaments of all citizens' (p. 86) and fully cognisant of that 'mountain of statistics' can be devised. We are to assume that existing stigmas associated with illness (and social inequality) will be eradicated and that differences constituted through 'genetic disclosures will "spark sympathy" rather than lead to social discrimination' (p. 151). Indeed we are to assume that 'systematic knowledge of the human genome could correct prejudices ... that the catalogue of genetic disabilities is distributed across racial and ethnic groups in roughly equal fashion, engendering the conviction that while there are differences, taken as a whole, all groups are "genetically equal"' (p. 154).

In this context a significant contradiction emerges. On the one hand, a drift to inequality is seen as inherent in genetic screening. At the same time, genetic science is held to herald substantive potentials for democratisation. The extraordinary number of sweeping 'ifs' that must be satisfied in order that genetics does *not* reinforce inequalities, indeed, in order to *make a world safe for genetics* is a testament to the tragic absurdity of such wishful thinking. Kitcher argues that 'without attention to the social surroundings in which molecular medicine is practised [developments in genetic technology] would simply magnify inequalities that are already present, (p. 97). Yet, at the same time, it is in genetics' very propensity to fuel oppressions that Kitcher, rather disturbingly, perceives a bedrock (impetus?) from which such social changes will emerge. Genetics, in this formulation, is both embedded in and yet disagreggated from social relations. Thus we are to understand that while genetic screening will intensify oppressions, it will also transcend them. Perhaps more to the point, the investment of such faith in the utopian fantasy of 2020 seems premised on yet another singularity. This is the notion that a science produced *out* of, and seen as desirable *within*, an unequal social order, would continue to make sense, and for the same reasons, in a profoundly altered social context. Indeed, there seems a further assumption that such a science's acknowledged propensities to do harm would not *undo* a democracy. Kitcher states: '[f]rom the beginning, it will be crucial to prepare the right social settings for the new applications of molecular medicine, (p. 182). Yet as we are well past the beginnings of this project, the good intentions such a claim may reflect, can only be both disquieting and duplicitous.

Conclusion

In its examination of the narrative framing of these selected texts from a wider genre of popular/scientific advocacy of recombinant genetics, this chapter has graphically illustrated the inter-embeddedness of scientific and popular common sense. The issue raised is not, as Sontag's early work suggested, that science is corrupted by metaphor, but rather that the *particular* metaphors invoked *situate* particular scientific perspectives and practices in ways demanding critical evaluation. Perhaps what is most outstanding in the context of this study, is the way in which these narratives reveal the imagined bodies and communities constituted through genetic discourse as both grounded in and contingent upon conditions of social inequality. Common to all of these utopian narratives are investments in elite (classed, gendered and racialised) knowledges and discursive practices that have been historically implicated in both the (re)production and normalisation of social divisions. Indeed, all invest the agency of both social stability and social change in scientific 'readers' and 'writers' – in both the experimental and representational senses of the terms. Similarly, all of these narratives articulate a slight-of-hand through which genetics is on the one hand identified with institutionally oppressive structures (dark satanic mills, colonial invasion, diagnostic imperialism) and yet, on the other, projectively reconstructed as rescuer. The liberal-minded recuperation, for example, of the 'bad' eugenic associations attendant upon recombinant genetics is narratively redeemed through assertive ascriptions of fabulous potentials and noble intent. What is revealed in this context is the extraordinary power of the redemption narrative, whether framed as adventure or romance or pragmatic projection. For it is this narrational frame that makes it possible for the overwhelming dystopian dimensions of the genetics revolution to be acknowledged, embattled and, ultimately, saved.

References

Anderson, Benedict (1982) *Imagined Communities*, London: Verso.

Anthias, Floya and Nira Yuval-Davis (1993) *Racialized Boundaries: Race, Nation, Gender, Colour and Class and the Anti-Racist Struggle*, London: Routledge.

Bordo, Susan (1993) *Unbearable Weight: Feminism, Western Culture and the Body*, Berkeley: University of California Press.

Butler, Judith (1993) *Bodies that Matter: on the Discursive Limits of Sex*, New York: Routledge.

Chambers English Dictionary (1990) Edinburgh: Chambers.

Collins, Patricia Hill (1990) *Black Feminist Thought: Knowledge, Consciousness, and the Politics of Empowerment*, Boston, MA: Unwin Hyman.

Crichton, Michael (1991) *Jurassic Park*, London: Random House.

—— (1995) *The Lost World*, London: Random House.

Dawson, Graham (1994) *Soldier Heroes: British Adventure, Empire and the Imagining of Masculinities*, London: Routledge.

Elkington, John (1985) *The Poisoned Womb: Human Reproduction in a Polluted World*, Harmondsworth: Penguin.

Foucault, Michel (1977) *Discipline and Punish: the Birth of the Prison*, London: Allen Lane.

Garrett, Laurie (1994) *The Coming Plague: Newly Emerging Diseases in a World out of Balance*, New York: Penguin.

Gilman, Sander (1991) *The Jew's Body*, New York: Routledge.

Grosz, Elisabeth (1994) *Volatile Bodies: towards a Corporeal Feminism*, Bloomington, IL: Indiana University Press.

Haraway, Donna (1989) *Primate Visions: Gender, Race and Nature in the World of Modern Science*, London: Verso.

Illich, Ivan (1976) *Limits to Medicine. Medical Nemesis: the Expropriation of Health*, Harmondsworth: Penguin.

Jones, Steve and Borin Van Loon (1993) *Genetics for Beginners*, Cambridge: Icon Books.

Jordanova, Ludmilla (1986) *Languages of Nature: Critical Essays on Science and Literature*, London: Free Association Press.

Kevles, Daniel J. (1985) *In the Name of Eugenics: Genetics and the Uses of Human Heredity*, Harmondsworth: Penguin.

Kitcher, Philip (1996) *The Lives to Come: the Genetic Revolution and Human Possibilities*, London: Penguin.

Latour, Bruno (1987) *Science in Action*, Cambridge, MA: Harvard University Press.

Martin, Emily (1994) *Flexible Bodies: Tracking Immunity in American Culture from the Days of Polio to the Age of AIDS*, Boston: Beacon Press.

Piller, Charles and Keith R. Yamamoto (1988) *Gene Wars: Military Control over the New Genetic Technologies*, New York: Beech Tree Books, William Morrow.

Redman, Peter (1998) 'Narrative and the production of subjectivity' (draft chapter of) *Boys in Love: Narrative, Genre and the Production of Heterosexual Masculinities*, unpublished Ph.D. thesis, School of English, University of Birmingham, England.

Showalter, Elaine (1992) *Sexual Anarchy: Gender and Culture at the Fin de Siècle*, London: Virago.

Sontag, Susan (1991) *Illness as Metaphor/AIDS and its Metaphors*, London: Penguin.

Steinberg, Deborah Lynn (1996a) 'Cultural regimes of the body: introduction', in D. L. Steinberg (guest editor) 'Cultural regimes of the body' (special issue) *Women: a Cultural Review* 7(3): 225–8.

—— (1996b) 'Languages of risk: genetic encryptions of the female body', in D. L. Steinberg (guest editor) 'Cultural regimes of the body' (special issue) *Women: a Cultural Review* 7(3): 259–70.

—— (1997) *Bodies in Glass: Genetics, Eugenics, Embryo Ethics*, Manchester: Manchester University Press.

—— (1997) 'Genetics of criminal and anti-social behaviour' (book review), *Sociology* 31(1): 187–9.

Steinberg, Deborah Lynn, Debbie Epstein and Richard Johnson (eds) (1997) *Border Patrols: Policing the Boundaries of Heterosexuality*, London: Cassell.

Strathern, Marilyn (1992) *Reproducing the Future: Anthropology, Kinship and the New Reproductive Technologies*, Manchester: Manchester University Press.

Strobel, Margaret (1991) *European Women and the Second British Empire*, Bloomington, IN: Indiana University Press.

Waldby, Catherine (1996) *AIDS and the Body Politic: Biomedicine and Sexual Difference*, London: Routledge.

Weiss, Sheila Faith (1987) *Race Hygiene and National Efficiency: The Eugenics of William Schallmayer*, Berkeley: University of California Press.

Williamson, Judith (1997) 'Saving grace', *The Guardian* (Weekend Magazine), 30 August, p. 6.

Yanchinski, Stephanie (1985) *Setting Genes to Work: The Industrial Era of Biotechnology*, Harmondsworth; Penguin.

Chapter 8

The politics of 'disabled' bodies

Gareth Williams and Helen Busby

Introduction

The language of disability has changed in recent years. The de-regulation of the health and welfare services in capitalist societies, the development of social movements of disabled people, the continuing challenges to medical dominance within and outside the health care system, and the influence of post-structuralism and postmodernism have led to a situation in which many different ways of writing about disability have emerged, each with its own lexicon. Any discussion of the politics of disability and disabled bodies carries the possibility of transgression and controversy. There is no neutral language and analysis of language itself is central to any discussion of how we approach 'disability' (Zola 1993). Impairment and disability; illness and handicap; suffering and oppression; victim and survivor: the only uncontested terms are those which have been erased from the vocabulary; and even they are likely to be excavated by the archaeology of disability studies.

In this chapter we examine the different ways in which medical sociology and 'disability studies' or 'disability theory' have approached an analysis of disability. Disabled people and others who were formerly objects of study and research by medical practitioners, social scientists and other 'experts', are now involved not only in challenging policy and practice, but also in defining what disability is and how it should be conceptualised and researched (Barnes and Mercer 1997). Sociology – so often self-consciously the discipline of the underdog – has itself become the target of a sharp critique from 'disability theorists' and disabled people working within the disability movement (Barton 1996; Barnes and Mercer 1996, 1997).[1]

Although an emphasis on the powerful role of society in the 'oppression' of disabled people is important, it is not possible, we suggest, to encompass all experiences of chronic illness and impairment within a social model that sometimes seems to deny the relevance to disability of bodily damage and decay. Culture and experience remain central to understanding illness and disability (Shakespeare 1997), and disability theorists cannot altogether pretend that the body has nothing to do with disability. We consider whether new ways of thinking within sociology and cultural studies can help the body find its way back into the picture. Taking the work of Irving Zola as a point of reference, we suggest that a more plural-istic politics of disability, including impaired bodies and oppressive societies, provides the basis for more creative developments in sociolog-ical analysis of chronic illness and disability. However, writing on the one hundred and fiftieth anniversary of the publication of *The Communist Manifesto*, we also argue that it is important to recognise the ineluctable power of global economic forces in shaping people's experiences of disability.

We begin by looking briefly at the way in which disability is conven-tionally understood within medicine. Medicine is important in under-standing the politics of disability because it is a hegemonic source of knowledge and set of practices which exerts direct control over many aspects of people's lives and, perhaps more importantly, influences the way in which we define the boundaries between normality and abnormality. Moreover, although people are more sceptical of doctors as they are of other socially sanctioned experts than they were in the past (Gabe *et al.* 1994), there is still a relatively high degree of trust in their motives, their competencies and the legitimacy of their claims to expertise.

The medical model

The medical model which informs traditional approaches to disability takes the biological reality of impairment as its fundamental starting point. This biological reality is taken to be the foundation of all forms of illness and impairment, whether 'mental' or 'physical'. Although ill health may arise from sources outside, it is the body within which illness is situated. In relation to the rehabilitation of disabled people, the focus of the analysis and the intervention is on the functional limitations which an individual 'has', the effect of these on activities of daily living, and attempts '. . . to find ways of preventing, curing, or (failing these) caring for disabled people' (Marks 1997: 86).

Although rehabilitation practitioners may make reference to the way in which disability affects the 'whole person' or 'all aspects of an individual's life', the nature of this wider context is rarely built systematically into analysis or recommendations for intervention (Gloag 1985; College Committee on Disability 1986). From the early 1970s onwards, those professionally engaged in rehabilitation recognised the need to move away from the highly reductive conceptions of functional limitations focusing on deficits in limbs and organs which had traditionally characterised phys-ical medicine and physical therapy. This newly discovered holism was enshrined in official reports, with the promulgation of broader definitions of rehabilitation as the restoration of patients to their fullest physical, mental and social capability (Mair 1972; Tunbridge 1972).

Increasingly, broader definitions of health status in patients with chronic illness and disability were used for two main reasons (Williams 1987). First, to assess needs for treatment, therapy, services, or benefits; and, second, to provide a baseline from which to perform more realistic evaluations of change in the health and functional status of patients, both informally and as part of research and evaluation. The focus of these evaluations was still very much on the individual, but with a recognition that it was the person who could or could not perform certain kinds of activities rather than the organ, the limb, or the body conceived abstractly as a bundle of capacities and incapacities. The idea of individual deficit continued to have a profound influence on policies, notwithstanding the influence of some other models of disability and associated reforms.

New types of descriptor (developed by sociologists, amongst others) consisted of assessments of performances in daily living stressing those activities which are purportedly carried out habitually and universally (Williams 1987); and this measurement of a range of daily activities extended the conventional clinical measures of 'functional capacity'. However, the fact that they are deemed to be universal rather than context-bound implies that they can be used across multiple settings without any substantial reconsideration of their validity, and without consideration being given to the meaning of the items for the person with the impairment. The Barthel Index, for example, asks only whether a person can walk 50 yards on level ground regardless of whether he or she wants to, needs to, or has anywhere to walk to (Granger et al. 1979).

In line with the positivistic underpinnings of medical science the emphasis of traditional assessments is on some universal definition and measure that can be applied by appropriately qualified people without reference to the disabled person's own perspective, the roles they occupy, the relationships in which they are embedded, their circumstances and milieux, or the wider political context of barriers, attitudes and power.

However broad their frames of reference, measures of health, disability, well-being and quality of life continue to be driven by classical positivist concerns with universality and generalisability. In other words, such assessments provide a picture of 'activities of daily living' devoid of a phenomenological grasp of the individual's own experience, on the one hand and any political analysis of the structures and contexts within which the activity takes place on the other.

In the period immediately after the Second World War health and social welfare for disabled people were characterised by a mixture of formal, institutional neglect and charitable, humanitarian concerns for those who had been maimed in war (Bury 1996). In this context, assessments of function were orientated towards simple arithmetic calculations regarding the effect of damage and deficit in particular limbs. However, medical sociologists became increasingly disillusioned with the positivist assumptions of rehabilitation research, and were concerned to develop specifically sociological ways of thinking about disability and chronic illness. In particular, sociologists began to emphasise the social context of disability, and the meaning of the experience of living with impairments and disabilities (Blaxter 1976; Strauss and Glaser 1975). In the next section, we explore the direction of this critique.

Chronic illness and disability: sociological perspectives

In contrast to class, gender and race, disability has been conspicuous largely by its absence from mainstream sociology (Barton 1996). Within the sociology of health and illness, however, there have been numerous examinations of the experience and social basis of chronic illness and disability. The attempt to understand the meaning of experience by looking at it in its context lies at the heart of work in the sociology of chronic illness and disability (Bury 1991).

The focus on chronic illness and the experience of disability associated with it can be seen as an attempt to move away from the rehabilitation models which were rather static, reductionist, and focused on the mechanics of functional limitations and activity restriction. While the experience of 'adaptation' to a limb amputation or some other trauma-induced impairment clearly has its own dynamics, influenced by personal, situational and treatment factors, chronic illness contributed new dimensions of variation, unpredictability and uncertainty (Bury 1982; Strauss and Glaser 1975).

Sociologists of health and illness have engaged in a wide range of studies of chronic illness and disability. These have been marked by an interest in listening to the point of view of the individual with illness or disability, and using methods that allow this to be done. The outcome is studies which claim in some sense to have explored 'meaning', either by charting the *consequences* of illness, or by examining the *significance* of illness in the wider context of culture and society (Bury 1991).

Some have used these points of view largely as a source of empirical data to comment on problems defined to some extent by the sociologists (Blaxter 1976; Locker 1983; Anderson and Bury 1988). The emphasis is on using what people say to provide better understanding of topics or issues: employment, sexuality, environmental barriers and so forth. Other work using the same kind of data is more methodological or epistemological in its orientation. Rather than looking at what people say, it looks at the way in which they say it, or how their understanding of their illness or disability is constructed. The emphasis in this kind of work is to explore the nature of the lay knowledge people with chronic illness or disability develop, and what they use it for (Williams 1984). A third variation on this theme is work which uses the accounts of lay people ontologically, to explore the way in which illness is a condition of having a story to tell. Such work attempts to grasp the depth of the meanings of illness and disability as they affect the foundations of a person's being-in-the-world, as a sort of existential sociology (Frank 1995).

These three versions of sociological work are, of course, not mutually exclusive, and the hallmark of each is a focus on the symbolic and material interaction between the individual and society or the social 'environment' and the interpretive processes whereby individuals construct meaning from their experiences. The environment is that which *emerges* in the meaning-giving processes of interaction between the individual, their milieux, and the wider society. Disability, (or 'handicap') in the World Health Organization's (1980) sense, is the product of complex processes of interaction between an individual with an impairment and the discriminating, disadvantaging and stigmatising society. It is neither inside the individual nor 'outside' the individual and 'inside' society:

> The extent to which functional limitations and activity restrictions constitute a problem, or are otherwise handicapping, is not only variable historically and culturally but is also somewhat dependent upon more immediate contexts; their meaning is not the same across different social and environmental settings.
>
> (Locker 1983: 5)

The argument put forward by Locker, and other sociologists developing work on chronic illness and disability in the 1970s and 1980s, was that the development of 'disability' or 'handicap' is not a simple linear process of cause and effect. Disability is caused neither by the external environment, nor any 'facts' of biological trauma or deterioration. It is a relational phenomenon that emerges out of the interaction between a person with impairments and an 'environment' which includes everything from low income and inaccessible transport to a pitying glance from a passing stranger. This kind of analysis is primarily concerned, in Bury's (1991) terms, with the meaning of chronic illness in terms of its consequences – but without implying that the consequences follow in a straightforward way from the illness. It is about the empirical consequences which emerge from the person's relationship with their everyday world when chronic illness develops.

Recent sociological studies of illness have attempted to probe more deeply into the existential interstices between self and world and make their analytical focus the epistemological qualities of the knowledge lay people produced about illness, or the ontological conditions of the stories

they tell. Many of these analyses are either interpretations by sociologists
and anthropologists of people's narratives (Williams 1984; Kleinman 1988;
Hyden 1997), or 'socio-biographies' (Zola 1982; Murphy 1987), 'pathogra-
phies' (Hawkins 1993) or 'autopathographies' (Couser 1997). While much
of this work retains an interest in the interaction between an individual
and other people or society more generally, it often leads away from the
empirical features of the impaired individual's interaction with the material
world into the individual's 'self' and 'body'.

There has been some attempt within the sociology of health and illness
to incorporate a more satisfactory theorisation of the 'physicality of the
body' through making the relationship between body, identity and social
experience more explicit (Zola 1991; Kelly and Field 1996; Watson *et al.*
1996; Seymour 1998). But these developments within the sociology of
health and illness have been to some extent limited by sociology's desire
to distance itself from the corporeal basis of the body as part of its resistance to biomedicine (Williams, S. 1996).

The danger that lies in wait for social scientists who go in search of
the holy grail of embodiment in health and illness is that a view is lost
of the structures which shape the experience. History and even biography
are dissolved into a quasi-religious or spiritual quest for the truth which
illness is supposed to reveal. So profound is the truth of illness that even
the person experiencing the illness is merely a vehicle for allowing the
body to speak of its suffering. This is the body incarnate:

> The body is not mute, but it is inarticulate; it does not use speech yet
> begets it. The speech that the body begets includes illness stories; the
> problem of hearing these stories is to hear the body speaking in them.
> (Frank 1995: 27)

These analyses certainly provide rich languages for exploring questions
of ultimate concern, but they also reduce the individual to a speaking
body, and limit the social reality of illness and disability to a personal
quest for meaning and truth. While the testimonies contained within auto-
biographical accounts can themselves be regarded as political, many of
them become so absorbed in the minutiae of experiences on the edge that
the politics and history of illness and disability are marginalised and the
realities of health and social care are forgotten.

To say that work of this sort neglects power and structure is mistaken,
however, because it allows for the development of an understanding of
the experience of power and structure. Taking the distinction employed
above between three forms of sociological analysis of the experience of
disability, the empirical version is political in the sense that it allows for
a better understanding of the problems and obstacles people face in their
dealings with the outside world. The methodological or epistemological

version is political in the sense that it privileges lay knowledge, and points to its equal worth and equal weight as a way of understanding and challenging the explanation for experiences provided by the medical model and other normative models. The ontological version is political in the sense that it is rooted in people's embodied experiences in the world, their sense of pain and loss described in their own terms, bearing witness to oppression in accounts which 'connect' with the experiences of others in similar situations, and seeks to 'recover' the body from the dominance of biomedicine (Couser 1997).

Nonetheless, although politics is immanent in these accounts it remains implicit: stories of self and body standing as testimony to the objectifying, reifying, commodifying forces of science and capitalism. It is an ethical or a religious politics, a politics of redemption which resists alienation but leaves the structures of hegemony intact, and does not in itself form a political programme or strategy for change. In focusing on telling it like it is for individuals, such accounts – however contextualised and politicised – do not directly take on the structures of power and knowledge which the medical model of disability represents. These stories provide solidarity of meaning but do not in themselves lead to solidarity in action.

The politics of disability and disability theory

With the alienating power of the medical model, and the focus on 'experience' of much phenomenological sociology, it is perhaps not surprising that those who regard disability studies as a political as much as an intellectual project (Davis 1997), should want to distance themselves from sociological or any other 'scientific' contributions to the study of chronic illness and disability. As Davis has argued:

> People with disabilities have been isolated, incarcerated, observed, written about, operated on, instructed, implanted, regulated, treated, institutionalized, and controlled to a degree probably unequal to that experienced by any other minority group.
>
> (Davis 1997: 1)

For many disability theorists in Britain and elsewhere the cause of disability is neither the illness, nor the individual in a state of tragic adaptive 'failure', but the oppressive society in which disabled people live. If disability is seen as a personal tragedy, disabled people are treated as individual victims of unfortunate circumstances. If disability is defined as a form of social oppression, disabled people can be seen collectively as the victims of an uncaring, discriminatory society, whose most effective remedy for their conditions is protest and resistance. This fundamental position is that which has underpinned most of the writing by disability theorists in Britain.

> Dependency is created amongst disabled people, not because of the effects of functional limitations on their capacities for self-care, but because their lives are shaped by a variety of economic, political and social forces which produce it.
>
> (Oliver 1990: 94)

The problem to be overcome is not anything within the individual's body, mind or soul. There is no personal road to redemption and salvation. The problems are unequivocally located in the structures, attitudes and beliefs which exist in a society run by able-bodied people. However, in this case, the relationship between the individual and society is much more clearly stated: disability and dependency are caused by society, and 'hostile environments and disabling barriers – institutional discrimination' – are seen as the 'primary cause of the problem' (Barnes 1992: 20). Proponents of this 'social model' of disability argue that disability is caused by society, and if you change society you can eliminate disability.

The causal relation is reversed and, as a consequence, the traditional models and practices of those engaged in rehabilitation come to be seen as part of the problem. If the dominant ideology of the medical model informing rehabilitation defines the focus as what has happened to an individual and what can be done 'for the patient', attention is distracted from the primary structural causes; and the medical profession and those working along side them become key figures in the perpetuation of oppression. For example, the World Health Organization's (1980) classification that was developed to clarify the terms used to describe disablement through the differentiation of 'impairment', 'disability' and 'handicap', and to enhance understanding of the needs arising out of the interaction between chronic illness or impairment and the wider environment (Bury 1996), is seen as an extension of the medical model focused on individuals (Oliver 1990; Marks 1997). Sociological analysis of what disability is like, from the point of view of someone with an impairment or disability – the phenomenological or interactionist exploration of the construction of reality – becomes another ideological justification for the oppression of disabled people.

In recent years the original formulation of what has come to be known in Britain as 'the social model' (UPIAS 1976; Finkelstein 1980; Oliver 1983) has been developed and elaborated through seminars and workshops, books, and journals like *Disability and Society* (Oliver 1990; Barnes and Mercer 1996; Barton 1996; Barton and Oliver 1997) and increasingly through lively and combative debate on the internet (disability-research @mailbase.ac.uk). These publications show increasing internal differentiation in discussions about the social model (Swain *et al.* 1993; Barnes and Mercer 1997; Barton 1996). Through various media many different voices, definitions of disability, and subjects for research and strategic development can be found amongst people who have come to disability theory at different times and from a variety of places. While there is common agreement on the need for resistance to 'disability oppression', criticism of the biomedical model and rejection of the primacy of impairment in thinking about disability, Marxism, feminism and post-structuralism provide variations on the theme.

Although the principles of the 'social model' have been used to inform the work of transnational organisations such as Disabled People's International, there is still a rather parochial quality to it. Those whose perspectives have been forged within an American civil rights context (Charlton 1998), have a different way of thinking about the relationships between impaired bodies and disabling societies from those developed in the British context, and recent feminist developments of the social model point to the patriarchy embedded in its original assumptions (Morris 1991). In addition there are those who feel that the materialist analysis of the original model is over-simplistic, and are now drawing on a wider range of philosophical and other sources in cultural studies in order to elaborate new versions of the origin and nature of oppression for disabled people (Shakespeare 1996a, 1996b, 1997).

Although its base rests on resistance to the medical model, and the giving of epistemological and political primacy to society over the body, there is a growing recognition that a strict social model excludes 'personal tragedy' and discussion of 'impairment' to a point where bodies and identities – the experience of being ill and disabled in society – are discounted as subjects for discussion. It is the development of thinking at the interfaces of body, identity and society – situated knowledge – that provide for the kind of exploration of the divide between sociologists and disability theorists that are needed to move this subject forward (Crow 1996; Peters 1996; Shakespeare 1996a, 1996b).

Situated knowledge

Sociological perspectives on disability have been criticised by disability theorists on a number of different (and sometimes seemingly contradictory) grounds: for not paying attention to disability, for enhancing rather than rejecting the medical model, and for becoming obsessed with the details of illnesses and impairments. All these concerns contain some truth: disability has not excited the same interest in mainstream sociology as class, gender, or race. Early work on disability by social scientists was undertaken in collaboration with rehabilitation specialists and epidemiologists which took the reality of individual impairments as its starting point (Bury 1996). And some of the more phenomenologically orientated work on chronic illness has attempted to reach the deepest interiors of people's subjective experiences to a point where the connection between those experiences and the outside world is not easy to see. But these criticisms contain a truth that depends to a large extent on the setting up and knocking down of straw men and women.

Mainstream sociology may have neglected disability, but the large and growing constituency of the sociology of health and illness has not (even if the conceptualisation of its interest has not been to everyone's taste). Social scientists' early work on the conceptualisation and measurement of need amongst disabled people was to some extent individualistic, medically orientated and 'paternalistic', but much of this work was important politically in drawing attention to large numbers of people whose needs were not being met by the health service or the welfare state more generally. Moreover, the work of sociologists like Blaxter (1976) in the UK and Strauss and Glaser (1975) in the USA, did start an important process of using lay people's own accounts of life with symptoms and difficulties with professionals. This work was used as the basis for developing an understanding of chronic illness and disability and making recommendations for how doctors, health services and society should be educated, organised or constituted differently. While such studies may be criticised from the viewpoint of the social model for having looked at social aspects by starting with the individual (Oliver 1996), this is only to say that if you allow individuals with chronic illness or disability to speak, they will start with themselves, autobiographically, and the virtue of this kind of work is that it allows that to be possible.

Increasingly, knowledge and frameworks developed by sociologists are interrogated, interpreted and made use of by groups who were formerly its objects. More recent critiques of sociology by disability theorists, point to the assumptions which have framed much of the research agenda, with the methods which are used producing answers which reinforce predominant models of disability (Barnes and Mercer 1997).

Taking as his example some of the questions used in the OPCS survey to ascertain 'levels' of disability, Oliver (1990) suggests how questions which ask about an individual's 'difficulty in holding, gripping or turning things' could be reframed as a questions about defects in the design of everyday equipment which limit a person's activities; or how a question about an individual's 'scar or blemish' could be reframed to ask about difficulties caused by other peoples' reactions to any such blemish.

While the extent to which these questions offer any practical alternative to current survey items is debatable (Bury 1996), and is being tested empirically (Zarb 1997), they do turn the world upside down in a manner which requires us to question our framing of the relationship between individual experiences and social circumstances. Oliver's satire also raises questions about the relationship between lay and professional expertise within the processes whereby knowledge about 'disability' is produced. However, we need to be sensitive to the way in which methods and research questions are embedded in the political economy and culture of a certain time and place, whether postwar collectivism, 1970s corporatism, or Thatcherite monetarism, while also being the product of decisions by particular politicians, civil servants and researchers, to ask questions in one way rather than another (Abberley 1996a).

The critique of the dominant methods used in the social sciences for understanding disability goes beyond a replacement of one set of survey questions by another. It seeks to contextualise the concept of disability within '. . . knowledge which arises from the position of the oppressed and seeks to understand that oppression. Such sociology requires an intimate involvement with the real historical movement of disabled people if it is to be of use' (Abberley 1996b: 77). However, to imply that the position of disabled people is uniquely oppressive replaces one kind of exclusivity with another, and defines disabled people as an undifferentiated class in itself, without the differences of body and identity which clearly have cultural significance for disabled and able-bodied people alike (Hughes and Paterson 1997).

Recent post-structuralist, neo-Foucauldian analysis attempts to bring the body back in by conceptualising it as the object of knowledge and the target of power. In Hughes and Paterson's terms: 'Post-structuralism can be useful in theorising impairment outwith a medical frame of reference' (1997: 333). Proponents of a social model who ignore impairment because of its clinical connotations miss the opportunity to develop a social model that applies to a wider range of disabling experiences and can inform a more inclusive disability politics. If the embodied person were conceptualised as the site of oppression, impairment could be brought back into the analysis without compromising the social model. Such developments would mean that some of the current difficulties involved in including people with learning disabilities, mental health problems, and other less visible forms of impairment into the disability movement might be reduced, allowing an understanding of politics that is as much about aesthetics as economics (Hughes and Paterson 1997). It would also allow for 'the near universality of disability' and the diverse 'chorus of voices' which disability represents to be part of the movement in the manner championed by Zola (1989, 1994).

However, there are other ways of situating knowledge and praxis in relation to disability which cut across this post-structuralist conceptualisation. For example, it has recently been argued that a more productive way to think of the oppression of disabled people is within a materialist conception of history which places disability in a broader context:

> Political economy is crucial in constructing a theory of disability oppression because poverty and powerlessness are cornerstones of the dependency people with disabilities experience.
>
> (Charlton 1998: 23)

Charlton goes on to argue that we need to see the oppression experienced by disabled people as a worldwide reality – 80 per cent of the world's 500 million disabled people live in 'developing countries'. This oppression, Charlton argues, results from structures of domination and subordination and ideologies of superiority and inferiority. The oppression of disabled people – defined as exploitation, marginalisation and powerlessness – cannot be understood within a post-structuralist framework. While there are cross-cutting identities and relationships of disability, gender, race, age, and class, these cannot be understood in a non-structural way. As Charlton puts it:

> Foucault's paradigm, which situates the body as the only verifiable 'truth' or site of oppression, contradicts the political thrust of the disability rights movement, which posits that disability is an oppressed social condition ... The oppression of individual disabled bodies is not the basis for the oppression of people with disabilities, it is the oppression of people collectively that is the basis for the oppression of their bodies.
>
> (Charlton 1998: 57)

Towards an understanding of living in bodies in places

Placing too great an emphasis on the politics of exclusion obscures the real effects of different impairments and the complex, 'negotiated' aspects of everyday life, and creates a spurious impression of homogeneity. Crow has written about the discounting of the experience of impairment resulting from 'keeping our experiences of impairment private, and failing to incorporate them into our public analysis' (Crow 1996: 66). Others have emphasised the need to explore the nature and status of impairments, without being restricted by seeing them as either purely biological, or simply social (Kelly and Field 1996; Williams, S. 1996).

Closure of debate about the body has been characteristic of the disability movement, and perhaps for good reasons. As Benoist and Cathebras (1993) point out, closure of 'the body' is characteristic of most systems of thinking underpinning utopian projects and visions. Pinder's (1995) work about how fixed definitions of disability may have obscured the experiences of some disabled people at work draws attention to some of the consequences of excluding the dimension of lived experience. Pinder argues that many fall into 'no-man's land' between definitions of able/disabled, and that these have done some disservice to the task of promoting the interests of disabled/differently abled people at work. Similarly, Zola has argued that the exclusivist leaning of some of the writing about disability has led to the marginalisation of the growing numbers of older people whose bodies will slowly, but surely, let them down (Zola 1991).

Increasingly post-structuralist, postmodernist and feminist analyses have argued that all-encompassing theories of disability and oppression can never account for the diversity of lived experiences (Hughes and Paterson 1997; Crow 1996). As Radley (1995: 19) argues, being disabled involves distinctive bodily experiences, but such experiences cannot be seen as unique inasmuch as they 'symbolize and are symptomatic of social contradictions and struggles sited on the body'. Peters (1996) draws on the postmodern perspective for the development of what she calls a critical pedagogy which involves working towards an understanding of the world and one's relation to the world with disabled people and others. In Peters' interpretation of postmodernity one implication is that different, insider voices can be articulated and heard and can challenge those of the academy (in this case professional sociologists). For her, as for other feminists, making private experience speak to public policies is a radical act.

Within sociology the work of Irving Zola, a sociologist and disability activist, represents an important attempt to link the material, social and cultural dimensions of disability (Williams, G. 1996). During the early 1980s, Zola recognised that while his politics had to be unwavering in the articulation of demands for independence and an end to discrimination, there was more to a sociological analysis of disabled people's oppression than an empirical identification of environmental barriers conjoined with a conspiracy theory regarding the interests of professionals engaged in rehabilitation. In line with many other activists in both Britain and the USA, Zola recognised the undermining power of the dominant ideology of disability which regarded 'it' – that is the thing from which the individual 'suffers' – as a personal tragedy.

Zola resisted the temptation to sociological solipsism, and recognised the implications of ageing societies peppered with chronic illnesses for the development of the disability movement (Zola 1991), pointing out that the processes of ageing were something that linked the interests of 'the able-bodied' to those of 'the disabled'. However imperative it may be politically to define people with disabilities as a minority group, it is a curious minority which will include us all if not today, then tomorrow, or the day after, and that:

> only when we acknowledge the near universality of disability and that all its dimensions (including the biomedical) are part of the social process by which the meanings of disability are negotiated, will it be possible fully to appreciate how general public policy can affect this issue.
>
> (Zola 1989: 420)

In place of the reification of the 'medical model' on the one hand and the 'social model' on the other, we find in Zola a willingness to examine disability from many points of view, and a desire to understand the contribution the different voices have to make to our discussions about disability. Zola's work was a bold attempt to hold firm to the politics of disability while remaining free to explore its darker phenomenological waters. He wanted to place at the forefront of any discussion of disability the bleak realities of economic deprivation, disenfranchisement, and marginalisation, while insisting on the continuing need to find a place for research in clinical rehabilitation and an interpretive phenomenology of the personal worlds of people with disability and chronic illness. Within this context the ontological reality of the impaired body is central to the development of any social theory of disability.

In conclusion, we suggest that while the attempt to bring the body back into the sociology of disability can overemphasise the self-authorship of possibilities, thinking about the lived body forces a recognition of the constraints as well as the possibilities of interpretation. As the philosopher Martha Nussbaum argues: 'We all live our lives in bodies of a certain sort, whose possibilities and vulnerabilities do not as such belong to one human society rather than another' (Nussbaum 1995: 76).

Any theory, whether expounded by sociologists or by disability theorists and activists, which overdetermines social control risks paralysing the possibilities for change. Within sociology, the turn towards 'the body' can be seen as representing a longing for community, for connection, and for meaningful participation (Kirkmayer 1992) – a turn away from some of the more sterile territories of critical theory. But if theory is not to incapacitate meaningful politics altogether (Hallsworth 1996), then it must use the insight of lived experience as grit for its development, and closure of the subject of the body is no longer possible. The dangers of incapacitating meaningful politics are recognised by Charlton when he argues that it is important to work for unity in the theory and practice of disability politics while recognising individual difference and self-identity:

> [The] postmodern or poststructuralist position revels in diversity . . . When universality is abandoned, when difference becomes everything at the expense of collectivity, only the lonely, isolated individual remains.
>
> (1998: 157–8)

Post-structuralist theorising about the body will not reproduce the methodological and political individualism of the medical model unless it remains connected to the material basis of embodiment. We hope we have indicated how work in both sociology and disability studies attempts in different ways to retain that connection.

References

Abberley, P. (1996a) 'Disabled by numbers', in R. Levitas and W. Guy (eds) *Interpreting Official Statistics*, London: Routledge, 166–84.

—— (1996b) 'Work, utopia and impairment', in L. Barton (ed.) *Disability and Society: Emerging Issues and Insights*, Harlow: Longman, 61–82.

Anderson, R. and Bury, M. (1988) *Living with Chronic Illness: the Experience of Patients and their Families*, London: Unwin Hyman.

Barnes, C. (1992) 'Institutional discrimination against disabled people and the campaign for anti-discrimination legislation', *Critical Social Policy* 34: 20.

Barnes, C. and Mercer, G. (eds) (1996) *Exploring the Divide: Illness and Disability*, Leeds: The Disability Press.

—— (eds) (1997) *Doing Disability Research*, Leeds: The Disability Press.

Barton, L. (ed.) (1996) *Disability and Society: Emerging Issues and Insights*, Harlow: Longman.

Barton, L. and Oliver, M. (eds) (1997) *Disability Studies: Past, Present, and Future*, Leeds: The Disability Press.

Benoist, J. and Cathebras, P. (1993) 'The body: from one immateriality to another', *Social Science and Medicine* 36(7): 857–65.

Blaxter, M. (1976) *The Meaning of Disability*, London: Heinemann.

Bury, M. (1982) 'Chronic illness as biographical disruption', *Sociology of Health and Illness* 4: 167–82.

—— (1991) 'The sociology of chronic illness: a review of research and prospects', *Sociology of Health and Illness* 13: 451–68.

—— (1996) 'Defining and researching disability: challenges and responses', in C. Barnes and G. Mercer (eds) *Exploring the Divide: Illness and Disability*, Leeds: The Disability Press.

Charlton, J. (1998) *Nothing About Us Without Us: Disability, Oppression, and Empowerment*, London: University of California Press.

College Committee on Disability (1986) 'Physical disability in 1986 and beyond: a report of the Royal College of Physicians', *Journal of the Royal College of Physicians* 20: 160–94.

Couser, G. T. (1997) *Recovering Bodies: Illness, Disability and Life Writing*, London: The University of Wisconsin Press.

Crow, L. (1996) 'Including all of our lives: renewing the social model of disability', in C. Barnes and G. Mercer (eds) *Exploring the Divide: Illness and Disability*, Leeds: The Disability Press, 55–73.

Davis, L. (ed.) (1997) *The Disability Studies Reader*, London: Routledge.

Finkelstein, V. (1980) *Attitudes and Disabled People*, New York: World Rehabilitation Fund.

Frank, A. (1991) *At the Will of the Body: Reflections on Illness*, Boston: Houghton Mifflin.

—— (1995) *The Wounded Storyteller: Body, Illness and Ethics*, London: The University of Chicago Press.

Gabe, J., Kelleher, D. and Williams, G. (eds) (1994) *Challenging Medicine*, London: Routledge.

Gloag, D. (1985) 'Severe disability: tasks of rehabilitation', *British Medical Journal* 290: 301–3.

Granger C. V., Albrecht G. L. and Hamilton B. B (1979) 'Outcome of comprehensive medical rehabilitation: measurement by PULSES profile and the Barthel Index', *Archives of Physical Medicine and Rehabilitation* 60: 145–54.

Hallsworth, S. (1996) 'Confronting control: finding a space for resistance in theory', *Aldgate Papers in Social and Cultural Theory*, no. 1, 1996–7, Department of Sociology and Applied Social Studies, London Guildhall University.

Hawkins, A. H. (1993) *Reconstructing Illness: Studies in Pathography*, West Lafayette, IN: Purdue University Press.

Hughes, B. and Paterson, K. (1997) 'The social model of disability and the disappearing body: towards a sociology of impairment', *Disability and Society* 12: 325–40.

Hyden, L.-C. (1997) 'Illness and narrative', *Sociology of Health and Illness* 19: 48–69.

Kelly, D. and Field, D. (1996) 'Medical sociology, chronic illness and the body', *Sociology of Health and Illness* 18: 241–57.

Kirkmayer, J. (1992) 'The body's insistence on meaning: metaphor as presentation and representation in illness experience', *Medical Anthropology Quarterly* 6(5): 323–46.

Kleinman, A. (1988) *The Illness Narratives: Suffering, Healing and the Human Condition*, New York: Basic Books.

Locker, D. (1983) *Disability and Disadvantage: the Consequences of Chronic Illness*, London: Tavistock.

Mair, A. (1972) *Medical Rehabilitation: the Pattern for the Future.* Report on the subcommittee of the standing medical advisory committee, Scottish Health Services Council on Rehabilitation, Edinburgh: HMSO.

Marks, D. (1997) 'Models of disability', *Disability and Rehabilitation* 19: 85–91.

Morris, J. (1991) *Pride Against Prejudice*, London: Women's Press.

Murphy, R. (1987) *The Body Silent*, New York: Henry Bolt.

Nussbaum, M. C. (1995) 'Human capabilities, female human beings', in M. C. Nussbaum and J. Glover (eds) *Women, Culture and Development: a Study of Human Capabilities*, Oxford: Clarendon, 61–104.

Oliver, M. (1983) *Social Work with Disabled People*, London: Macmillan.

—— (1990) *The Politics of Disablement*, Basingstoke: Macmillan and St Martin's Press.

—— (1996) 'A sociology of disability or a disablist sociology?', in L. Barton (ed.) *Disability and Society: Emerging Issues and Insights*, London: Longman.

Peters, S. (1996) 'The politics of disability identity', in L. Barton (ed.) *Disability and Society: Emerging Issues and Insights*, London: Longman, 215–34.

Pinder, R. (1995) 'Bringing back the body without the blame? The experience of ill and disabled people at work', *Sociology of Health and Illness* 17(5): 605–31.

Radley, A. (1995) 'The elusory body and social constructionist theory', *Body and Society* 1: 3–23.

Riddell, S. (1996) 'Theorising special educational needs in a changing political climate', in L. Barton (ed.) *Disability and Society: Emerging Issues and Insights*, Harlow: Longman.

Seymour, W. (1998) *Remaking the Body: Rehabilitation and Change*, London: Routledge.

Shakespeare, T. (1996a) 'Disability, identity, difference', in C. Barnes and G. Mercer (eds) *Exploring the Divide: Illness and Disability*, Leeds: The Disability Press.

—— (1996b) 'Power and prejudice: issues of gender, sexuality and disability', in L. Barton (ed.) *Disability and Society: Emerging Issues and Insights*, Harlow: Longman.

—— (1997) 'Cultural representation of disabled people: dustbins for disavowal?', in L. Barton and M. Oliver (eds) *Disability Studies: Past, Present, and Future*, Leeds: The Disability Press.

Strauss, A. and Glaser, B. (1975) *Chronic illness and the Quality of Life*, 2nd edn, 1984, St Louis: Mosby.

Swain, J., Finkelstein, V., French, S. and Oliver, M. (1993) *Disabling Barriers: Enabling Environments*, London: Sage (in association with the Open University).

Tunbridge, R. (1972) *Rehabilitation* (Report of a subcommittee of the standing medical advisory committee), Department of Health and Social Security, London: HMSO.

UPIAS (Union for the Physically Impaired Against Segregation) (1976) *Fundamental Principles of Disability*, London: UPIAS.

Watson, J., Cunningham-Burley, S. Watson, N. and Milburn, K. (1996) 'Lay theorizing about "the body" and implications for health promotion', *Health Education Research* 11: 161–72.

Williams, G. H. (1984) 'The genesis of chronic illness: narrative reconstruction', *Sociology of Health and Illness* 6: 175–200.

—— (1987) 'Disablement and the social context of daily activity', *International Disability Studies* 9: 97–102.

—— (1996) 'Irving Kenneth Zola (1935–1994): an appreciation', *Sociology of Health and Illness* 18: 107–25.

Williams, S. J. (1996) 'The vicissitudes of embodiment across the chronic illness trajectory', *Body and Society* 2: 23–47.

World Health Organization (1980) *International Classification of Impairments, Disabilities and Handicaps*, Geneva: WHO.

Zarb, G. (1997) 'Researching disabling barriers', in C. Barnes and G. Mercer (eds) *Doing Disability Research*, Leeds: The Disability Press.

Zola, I. K. (1982) *Missing Pieces: a Chronicle of Living with a Disability*, Philadelphia: Temple University Press.

—— (1988) 'Whose voice is this anyway? A commentary on recent collections about the experience of disability', *Medical Humanities Review* 2: 6–15.

—— (1989) 'Towards the necessary universalizing of disability policy', *The Milbank Memorial Fund Quarterly* 67(Supplement 2): 401–28.

—— (1991) 'Bringing our bodies and ourselves back in: reflections on past, present and future of "medical sociology"', *Journal of Health and Social Behaviour* 32: 1–16.

—— (1993) 'Self, identity and the naming question: reflections on the language of disability', *Social Science and Medicine* 36: 167–73.

—— (1994) 'Towards inclusion: the role of people with disabilities in policy and research in the United States: a historical and political analysis', in M. H. Rioux and M. Bach (eds) *Disability is Not Measles: New Research Paradigms in Disability*, Ontario, Canada: Roeher Institute.

Chapter 9

Reflections on the 'mortal' body in late modernity

Lindsay Prior

> Everywhere journeying, inexperienced and without issue,
> [man] comes to nothingness.
> Through no flight can he resist
> the one assault of death,
> even if he has succeeded in cleverly evading
> painful sickness.
>
> Sophocles, *Antigone*, lines 359–65

In 1798 Thomas Robert Malthus anonymously published his first *Essay on the Principles of Population*. His insistence on anonymity is characteristically pre-modern, but the contents and claims of the *Essay* itself are distinctively modern – not least because they reflect a focus on objects of study that dominated social scientific discourse from the beginning of the nineteenth century until well into the twentieth century. The objects of study to which I refer are properly called 'collectives', and the particular collective in which Malthus invested intellectual curiosity was, of course, a population.

A population, suggested Malthus, has only two parameters worthy of serious and long-term consideration: the birth rate and the death rate. If the birth rate remains unchecked then the 'laws of nature' will ensure that the death rate increases so as to calibrate the size of a population to the means of available subsistence. Empirically this calibration might occur through the appearance of famines, pestilence or war. However, the mode of transmission is irrelevant for it is ultimately death which will bring a population back to its natural level. For death invariably and inevitably imposes itself as a limit on the expansion of human designs. In the face of death, therefore, we must chose the path of moral restraint or the control of life (births) as the route to moderating human numbers.

Both the focus on the collective and the appeal to natural laws was characteristic of the nascent science of population that nineteenth-century political economists sought to develop. Such a 'demography', (the word appears in the English language only in 1880), necessarily embraced a study of mortality, and that study revolved primarily around the analysis of *rates* of death. The concept of a rate as applied to social events was, of course, a distinctive nineteenth century invention and one that was very successfully extended to the study of marriage patterns, patterns of birth, crime and suicide as well as endless other phenomena. Naturally, in the realm of the socially determined rate, questions surrounding the personal meaning of death (and other social events) were irrelevant. For the death of an individual, though disruptive of intimate social relations, had no implications for the continuity of populations. That is perhaps why Durkheim, at the end of Malthus's century, was to focus on collectives (in every sense of that word) in his study of suicide, and deliberately attempt to evade all considerations relating to the fates of mere individuals. Indeed, for both Durkheim (1952) and Malthus (1970), as for almost every other nineteenth century social scientist, individuals were merely the atoms that constituted the properties of the collective. Puzzles relating to the personal meaning of death or suicide or whatever were, therefore, superfluous to social scientific discourse. For, ultimately, the meaning of death lay in a realm that was extraneous to temporal existence. Indeed, such meaning could be revealed only by an omniscient God. And this was precisely the position adopted by Parson Malthus in the final chapter to his first *Essay*.

This is not the occasion for dwelling on that long and relentless process of secularisation that has characterised the history of the modern world – a process that has recently been called into question by some. (See, for example, Mellor and Shilling (1997: 188) who refer to a process of 'resacrilisation' in the modern world). We need merely note that it is only during the mid-twentieth century that questions relating to a personal and this-worldly meaning of death (as distinct from a religious and other-worldly meaning) are picked up within the human sciences. It is only then that a sociology of death and dying, as distinct from a social scientific study of mortality patterns, becomes feasible. In this respect, the elevation of death to a central position in life is, perhaps, underlined most forcibly in the philosophy of Martin Heidegger. And it is an emphasis that is given further consideration in the writings of those who sought to extend and mimic Heidegger's ontological theses – and particularly his claim that death forms the 'limit beyond all limits' that defines being in the world. In fact this reference to death as limit, together with the lines of Sophocles' *Antigone* that opened this section, are taken directly from Heidegger's *Introduction to Metaphysics* (1959: 158 and 147). I have cited them precisely because they form the origin for all subsequent claims to the effect that human identity is structured only in the face of death. (See, for example, Bataille 1957: 13; Foucault 1972: 26; Deleuze 1983: 174–5; Derrida 1994: xviii.)

Yet, in so far as death may be considered a limit – a 'black border', as Foucault would have it – it is a limit only for persons. So, whilst death marks out a point of personal disjuncture and a point of disruption of personal relations (as Bataille (1986) was so keen to note), the death of an individual is entirely irrelevant to the trajectory of a population. And it is, in many ways, this tension between personal disjuncture and collective continuity that has underpinned the social scientific study of death in the twentieth century. Indeed, it is a tension that has given rise to and carried along two entirely different frames of understanding for dealing with human finitude. The first of these frames has circulated around technical (mainly statistical) assessments of mortality in its collective sense, whilst the second has expressed humanistic and hermeneutic endeavour to comprehend the meaning of death for self and others.

Sociology/social science, of course, not only reflects on the world but is reflective of the social order in which it is embedded. To that extent one can detect in the modern sociological preoccupation with the meaning of death the presence of a much wider and more general twentieth-century concern. It is a concern to discover a new legitimisation for death. For whilst Parson Malthus may have been able to rest content with a meaning of death buried deep in divine purpose, the same cannot be said for our contemporaries. Indeed, those who have followed in the wake of Gorer (1965) and Ariès (1983), for example, have argued that modernity has deprived death of collective significance and thrust the burden of dealing with human transience on to the privatised individual. In consequence the isolated individual is forced to legitimise death in terms of a personal quest for self-identity. Modern individuals are thereby left exposed and unprotected in the face of death. There is, in other words, no longer a collective canopy (sacred or otherwise) under which individuals can shade themselves from the oblivion of extinction.

I will return to these gloomy pronouncements later. For now, we need simply note that a sociology of death and dying arose in a culture concerned to search for a personal meaning to the end of life – a culture troubled with notions of self-identity and directed towards the discovery or fulfilment of self in this world. Only in such a context – where individuals come to consider death as an end; a culture characterised by what Kierkegaard (1989) called 'the sickness unto death' – could a science of death and dying emerge from a science of human mortality.

In the subsequent sections of this chapter I intend to explore the opposition between the collective and the personal in a number of ways. Initially, I shall examine the opposition in relation to narratives of death. As I shall indicate, official narratives of death are almost invariably couched in materialist (biological or pathological) terms. And one significant consequence of the adoption of a materialist discourse of death – as interpreted at a personal level – has been a proclivity to view human transience as, at the very least, controllable, and possibly avoidable. Added to this distinctly twentieth-century vision of death as subjugated to human will and purpose, there has been a parallel tendency to demote death from a certainty into a risk. Such a demotion has had consequences for the manner in which self and being are understood in the late modern world. Among these one is forced to include the singular desire to centre all sources of health, illness, death, disease and personal misfortune on the isolated and sovereign individual. In addition, of course, one needs to recognise the late modern tendency to demand personal authority over the very manner, timing and process of dying. This last characteristic has been referred to by Walter (1994) in terms of the 'revival' of death. A revival, he states, '[that] takes individualism to its logical conclusion and asserts the authority of the individual not only over religion but also over medicine; only individuals can determine how they want to die and grieve' (1994: 185). Finally, of course, we will be drawn to note that the tension between the individual and collective further extends itself into the very nature and structure of immortality. For the sovereign individual of modern society seeks not only to control death but further seeks (in modest ways) to move beyond the limits of which I spoke earlier, and to insert themselves into a future that will never be experienced. In its most popular and banal form such appropriation is achieved by little more than the adoption of personal and individual strategies of remembrance. In more elaborate forms it involves the manufacture of celebrity as a lasting monument to 'self'.

Death, disease and the body in the modern world

> The dead aren't dead until the living have recorded their deaths in narratives. Death is a matter of archives.
>
> (Lyotard 1989: 126)

Case 1463:
Cause of Death:

> I   (a) Bronchopneumonia
>   (b) Secondary deposits in brain
>   (c) Primary carcinoma of prostate
> II Chronic Obstructive Airways Disease

This transcript of a medical certificate of cause of death locates the causes of death very plainly in human anatomy. It points towards both a set of disease entities and anatomical sites affected by those entities. As such, it alludes to the presence of infectious agents such as the pneumococcus, and the co-existence of malign processes associated with cancers. These agents and processes are argued to have been variously distributed in the bronchial tract and the brain and the prostate gland. The implication to be drawn is that the physiology of this particular human body became overwhelmed by the identified agents and processes, and consequently the person died. In that sense the death of this individual man has been bolted very firmly on to his anatomical frame.

The sequence as written may be said to provide a narrative of death. It is, for example, a narrative that allocates explicit causes to the death and which links such causes into a time flow of primary (Ic,b,a) and secondary (II) causes. In some part it is a narrative that guarantees the 'naturalness' of death in the sense that it points to the fact that this man died of disease processes alone – and not as the result of human inter-vention. We may further note that the certificate on which this sequence was written provided an imprimatur of death. That is to say, the certificate underpinned and ensured the legality of the death and enabled the bereaved to tie up the loose ends of the person's earthly existence. Naturally, side by side with this official narrative, there will have existed other, personal, narratives that attempted in various guises to provide an explanation as to why this person died now rather than later, died of this disease rather than another, and why death should occur in the world at all. Unlike the materialist narrative, however, such parallel accounts are unlikely to be recorded in any considerable numbers. Moreover, we can rest assured that it is only the materialist account that will be lodged in the official archives of the dead, for it is only the materialist account that is given credence in the modern world.

This particular death also forms a part of a larger, collective and much wider narrative. It is a narrative that will be written up in the books of official Mortality Statistics. Such books will contain summary tables and charts and accounts of patterns and trends of mortality. Table 9.1, for example, which is taken from an official publication (OPCS 1994), provides a near facsimile of the kind of representation that routinely appears in such narrative accounts. Indeed, in so far as we will ever find a trace of our selected death, it is likely that it will be found buried in a collective narrative of this kind.

Now, Table 9.1 is clearly constructed as a mosaic of personal narra-tives – of which the sequence that opened this sub-section represents but one small 'tile'. Moreover, whilst the personal narrative is written in terms of individual diseases and personal names, the collective narrative will be so composed as to reflect a picture framed in terms of gender and social class, town and country, age and marital status. In brief, a distinctively social, as compared to a personal picture.

Table 9.1, of course, provides, at one and the same time, a source of data (on mortality patterns in Wales, 1992), a nosology of disease and an image of what does and what does not cause human beings to die. Clearly, the nosology contained herein takes as its starting point the human frame

Table 9.1 Deaths by gender in each nosological category, Wales, 1992 (%)

Nosological category		Males	Females
I	Infectious and parasitic diseases	0.6	0.5
II	Neoplasms	28.2	24.2
III	Endocrine, nutritional and metabolic diseases and immunity disorders	1.7	2.0
IV	Diseases of the blood and blood forming organs	0.4	0.5
V	Mental disorders	1.4	2.8
VI	Diseases of the nervous system and sense organs	1.8	2.3
VII	Diseases of the circulatory system	46.1	47.7
VIII	Diseases of the respiratory system	10.5	10.4
IX	Diseases of the digestive system	2.7	3.4
X	Diseases of the genito-urinary system	0.8	1.1
XI	Complications of pregnancy childbirth, and puerperium		0.0
XII	Diseases of the skin and subcutaneous system	0.1	0.2
XIII	Diseases of the musculo-skeletal system	0.3	1.0
XIV	Congenital anomalies	0.3	0.3
XV	Certain conditions originating in the perinatal period	0.0	0.0
XVI	Signs, symptoms and ill-defined conditions	0.4	0.9
XVII	Injury and poisoning	4.2	2.2
All deaths all causes (total):		16,383	17,424

Source. Derived from: *Mortality Statistics (Area)*, London: OPCS, 1994.

and builds on it an anatomical geography of disease. Of the seventeen great orders contained in the nosology, ten are clearly related to anatomical seat. Diseases of the genitourinary system sit next to diseases of the digestive system; diseases of the circulatory system next to diseases of the nervous system and so on. Furthermore, many of the sub-divisions in the nosology (such as those for neoplasms) depend on even finer anatomical distinctions – here the kidney, there the anus, yet again the stomach, lungs, uterus, bladder and pancreas. The causes of death therefore are not only discovered in human anatomy, but are further classified according to anatomical parts. The human body in this sense serves both as a site for discovery and as a frame for classification. Death is written on the body. Indeed, representations of death such as are given in Table 9.2, can more properly be said to be written on the gendered body. Thus, whilst looking at Table 9.2., one may be usefully reminded of Foucault's claim that, if for us '[T]he human body defines, by natural right, the space of origin and of distribution of disease. . . . this order of the solid, visible body is only one way – in all likelihood neither the first, nor the most fundamental – in which one spatializes disease. There have been, and will be, other distributions of illness' (1973: 3).

Table 9.2 Causes of death, sub-divisions of Chapter II (neoplasm), Wales, 1992

II ICD number[b]	Neoplasms Anatomical site	SMR[a]	
		Females	Males
140–9	Lip, oral cavity and pharynx	87	132
150–9	Digestive organs and peritoneum	106	109
150	Oesophagus	113	111
151	Stomach	114	119
153	Colon	102	105
154	Rectum, rectosigmoid junction and anus	101	112
157	Pancreas	100	98
161	Larynx	140	123
162	Trachea, bronchus and lung	98	97
174	Female breast	100	
179–89	Genitourinary organs	100	100
180	Cervix uteri	99	
179, 182	Uterus, other and unspecified	99	
183	Ovary	100	
185	Prostate		100
188	Bladder	100	101
189	Kidney	99	100
200–8	Lymphatic and haemotopoietic tissue	99	99
204–8	Leukaemia	98	97
205	Myeloid leukaemia	98	98
210–39	Benign, in situ and unspecified	100	99

Source: *Mortality Statistics (Area)*, Series DH5, Number 19, London: OPCS, 1994.
Notes: [a] A brief explanation of how Standardised Mortality Ratios (SMRs) might be calculated is
        provided in Charlton and Murphy (1997: Ch. 1).
        [b] International Classification of Diseases, Injuries and Causes of Death (ICD). 10th revi-
        sion. World Health Organization.

Naturally, and as with all narratives, there are rules for composition that
need to be followed in the construction of such a table. The rules are
routinely contained within the official nosologies and nomenclatures of
the type furnished by the World Health Organization (WHO 1992). I have
discussed the nature and application of such rules elsewhere (Prior 1989),
and demonstrated how changes in the rules alter the structure and content
of any given narrative product. Thus, for example, between 1984 and 1993
the number of deaths attributed to pneumonia and especially bronchopneumonia in the UK, declined because of changes in the automatic coding
rules. The latter required that specific pathological conditions listed in Part
2 of the death certificate take precedence over conditions such as bronchopneumonia that might be entered into Part 1 of the certificate. This was
recommended on the grounds that bronchopneumonia is only the final
stage in a sequence of illness and not, therefore, a primary cause. (The
certificate that opens this section partly illustrates the point in question).

Some of these implications are discussed more fully in Charlton and Murphy (Vol. 1, 1997). I leave these issues to one side, however, because I merely wish to emphasise here how the international nosologies and nomenclatures of disease offer the means of manufacturing a simulacrum of mortality patterns rather than a reflection of such patterns. That is to say, I wish to emphasise how tables of the kind presented herein are not mirror images of the way the world actually is, but representations of that world according to a set of narrative rules. In particular, they are representations that reduce death to nothing more than a series of anatomical and physiological processes (mostly of a pathological nature). And it is, above all, in this reduction of death to its pathological essentials that we locate what Bauman (1992) has referred to as the modernist deconstruction of mortality.

By using such a phrase Bauman intends to draw our attention to the fact that in the modern world, the explanation of death (one of the great imponderables of life) in terms of a set of distinct and limited number of disease forms, helps to generate the illusion that death can somehow be controlled. In other words, since death is caused by disease and since, in theory, all diseases are conquerable through human praxis, then death itself is conquerable. For example, many of the WHO nosologies to which I have previously alluded list some 999.999 forms of disease, injury and causes of death – each one of which is *in theory* curable, or surmountable. (The reader may be delighted to hear that 'old age' is not included among the 999 causes). It is but a small step to then conclude that 'in theory', death itself can be cured. That once we have fathomed out the causes of cancers and pneumonia and wasting diseases we will have overcome death itself. Thus, as Bauman (1992: 137) states, 'From the existential and *unavoidable* predicament of humanity, mortality [has] been deconstructed into diverse events of private death, each with its own *avoidable* cause' (emphasis in original).

Nowhere is this line of reasoning more forcefully expressed than in certain forms of late twentieth-century public health discourse. Indeed, these are commonly characterised by two major themes. First, that ill health and its ultimate consequences (early death) are avoidable. Second, that the key to good health lies within the grasp of the actions of individuals. So death and misfortune can be avoided if people behave properly – eat the right things, exercise, stop smoking and so on. This is undoubtedly the message contained in the British government's document *Health of the Nation* (Dept of Health 1991). Death, it seems, stalks only those who are careless of their personal health. This, despite the fact that the mortality rates of those who are careless of their health and those who are fastidious remains stubbornly similar (viz. 100 per cent). It is, perhaps, a frame of mind epitomised by the use among epidemiologists of the phrase 'avoidable death' – you too can avoid death if you behave yourself.

Such a denial of death (Ariès 1983) is expressed in contemporary culture in various ways. Indeed, the numerous strategies used by contemporary societies to deny and hide death have been referred to by Giddens (1991) and, subsequently others such as Mellor and Shilling (1993), as a form of the sequestration of death. Where, in the words of Giddens (1991: 156), 'The term "sequestration of experience" refers to connected processes of concealment which set apart the routines of ordinary life from the following phenomena: madness, criminality; sickness and death; sexuality and nature.' One consequence of such a sequestration process is that, at the end of the twentieth century, individuals confront death in a segregated and privatised world. The basis of such segregation is in all likelihood, as Elias (1985) has argued, the great improvement in life expectancy that has characterised the short history of the industrial world. An improvement that in a British context, has been particularly well documented by Charlton and Murphy (Vol. 1, 1997). As a result, death has been effectively confined to old age. In turn, it has been further confined to the nursing home, the hospital, and the hospice. Indeed this latter institution – specialised and dedicated to the dying – undoubtedly gives expression to one of the most characteristic themes of modern culture: the desire to exert control over each and every experience in the world – including death itself.

In the hospice the struggle to come to terms with death will of course be executed in a framework that seeks to answer the conundrum of what death means for 'me' rather than for us. And, in increasing numbers, the meaning of death for both the dying and the bereaved will no longer be mediated through a priesthood but through a bereavement counsellor (professional or otherwise). The grand Judeo-Christian narrative of a collective fate and a collective resurrection, is thereby replaced by a quest for personal immortality and personal meaning negotiated by a secular agent (see, for example, Seale 1995).

The denial of death thesis has, of course, many persuasive features. Thus, in the modern western world the dead and dying are routinely and ordinarily set apart from the living. They are sequestered into 'chapels of rest', and hidden behind cemetery walls. And the ritual surrounding death and disposal is routinely pared down, privatised and restricted to the attentions of a limited 'family circle'. (In this respect it is of interest that even in one of the most public of all funerals – that of Diana, Princess of Wales – the moments of disposal were restricted to a very private domain). In like manner, the dying are sequestered and processed through specialised institutional settings – such as hospitals and hospices. Yet, for all that, it seems more plausible to suggest that the denial of death occurs most forcefully at the level of individual consciousness than collective procedure. People rarely talk about their own deaths because death does indeed mark the limit of personal experience, but that does not necessarily imply that talk about death is limited or suppressed. Indeed, and as I have already demonstrated, there is a public narrative structure in which death is freely and easily discussed. It is, however, a narrative structure that draws on a vocabulary of medicine and science, of mortality statistics and actuarial assessments concerning life chances. Above all, it is a discourse that centres on the collective causes of death, rather than the personal meaning of death. It is not, therefore, a narrative structure that sits easily with the demands of a late modern culture that remains obsessed with issues of lifestyle rather than life chances, and of personal fate rather than collective destiny.

In the modern world, then, we come to know death through the body, and we come to understand and confront all forms of illness through the human frame. All of our perceptions about illness, disease, and death are filtered through what Merleau-Ponty (1962) referred to as our 'corporeality'. It is not perhaps surprising therefore that we appropriate our knowledge of death in terms of an anatomical framework. Indeed, as I have already shown, death is written on the body. Yet, as sociologists, we are also aware that the categorisation of body parts is in itself an essentially social affair. That there is a sense in which our comprehension of anatomy and physiology is constantly mediated through aspects of (collective) social structure and social relations (see, for example, Hertz 1960; Mauss 1979). In the words of Nietzsche (1973: 31), 'Our body is only a social structure'. Nevertheless, in late twentieth-century culture, it is the individual and personal that has come to dominate our relationship to death. Issues concerning the collective meaning of death together with the meaning of death for the collective have been shunted into the sidelines. Elevated above all else is the consideration of death for 'me'. And that shift from the collective to the personal is one that is evidenced in both social life at large and sociology in particular.

The certainty of mortality is transformed into a personal risk

During the twentieth century death has become a 'risk' rather than a certainty. Naturally, and as J. M. Keynes supposedly observed, in the long run we are all dead, yet none of us can predict the exact date or time or place of death. It is in the context of the latter kinds of uncertainty that we can legitimately consider our chances of dying. For risks are calculable, and the promise of modernity is that all events – no matter how remote they may seem – can be calculated with precision.

Over a century ago, Karl Pearson (1897) published an essay on death. It was an essay in which he invoked the medieval metaphor of the dance of death in an attempt to explain the vagaries of human mortality. The dance of death as depicted on the walls of Europe's medieval monasteries and churches, and in the manuscripts of Europe's libraries, had of course represented death as a random and capricious creature that could strike anyone, anywhere, at any time with equal possibility. In homage to such a vision Pearson, too, personified death. On this occasion as a marksman firing at people crossing a bridge. Yet, in Pearson's world it proved not only possible to calculate (with considerable accuracy) the hit rate of the marksman, but to assess (within precise limits) the marksman's margin of error. In other words, Pearson was arguing that for any given human group, we could calculate more or less exactly how many would die and survive on different sections of the bridge. Pearson, of course, used the bridge as a metaphor for the lifespan itself, and it is also clear that it was the rate of mortality that truly interested Pearson, rather than the fates of individuals. By implication, his focus was on a property of populations rather than of persons. Indeed, by adopting such a focus, Pearson also alluded to another important feature of nineteenth century mathematical thinking, namely the idea of probability.

During recent years, various historians of mathematics and statistics (such as Hacking 1990; Hald 1990; Daston 1988; and Crombie 1994) have argued about the existence of what they call the revolution in probability theory. The arguments relate to the appearance – from the 1660s onward – of a new concept of chance. In terms of the latter, chance was conceived as something calculable and determinate rather than as something shrouded in fate and mystery. Consequently it was argued that chance belonged to the realm of things which could be examined and discussed in a scientific manner. It was a revolution of world view that was to affect all aspects of human inquiry. Above all, during the nineteenth century the new concept of chance was to find itself linked to life and death in a new object. That object was the life table. Both the history of the life table and its individual elements deserve more detailed attention than we can offer here. Its history is to be partly located in the history of mathematics to which I have just referred, and partly in the empirical concerns of demographers and epidemiologists such as Graunt (1620–1674), Halley (1656–1742), and Farr (1807–1883). Most important of all, the life table served to underline a vision of death as an orderly, regular and predictable event. In fact, it seems safe to say that from the point at which the first life table was published, death was divested of its capricious nature. The irregular and random dance of death could be no more.

William Farr's English Life Table 'Number 1', was published in the *Fifth Annual Report of the Registrar General in England*, 1843. Life Table Number 1, was by no means the first life table, but it was the first to incorporate the concept of a death rate, and also the first to apply mathematical concepts of probability to patterns of death in an entire nation (as opposed to a town or city). Apart from the use of simple ratios – such as the number of deaths per 1,000 living – Farr's genius lay in the application of the principles of Newtonian calculus to matters of human existence. This later served to provide an image of a human lifespan in terms of smooth and gentle geometric curves so that life and death no longer appeared as a reckless gamble with fate. Indeed, one might say that with the life table we witness a significant shift in cultural constructions of risk. So much so that, in the words of Daston (1987), with the new picture of human mortality, risk became 'domesticated'. Domesticated in the sense that it was this mathematical vision of order and stability that facilitated the growth and adoption of family centred systems of life assurance and pension provision. Indeed, following Giddens (1991: 146–8), we can claim that it is the life table that enables us to place lifespan, rather than the lifecycle as the focal point of our everyday projects. That is to say, the existence of a predictable future has enabled us to replace a concern with the collective destiny of generations with an interest in a limited, bounded and personal expectation of life years.

The life table, then, is one of the most significant representations of life and death that our own culture has produced. It not only expresses a modernist vision of life as a rationally calculable object, but also provides a set of background expectancies of normal, natural lifespans. It forms an essential part of that mesh within which death is explained. Those who report on and who analyse death – especially in the medico-legal community – are dependent on it for their everyday judgements of what is and what is not a normal, natural death. Individuals, of course, pick up the associated calculations in the context of personal expectation rather than in the context of population projections. And in the culture of control that modernity has engendered, individuals believe that they can expand or contract their personal quota of temporal days by personal action – and especially action on the body. In fact, it is this potential for calculability that enables us to draw the future into the present – to 'colonize the future' (Giddens, 1991: 111) – and thereby execute plans for future action in ongoing projects.

Life planning and lifestyle choices can only be made in the stable framework of life table assessments. In late modern society such planning, however, also occurs in the context of a reflexive individualism (Giddens 1991). In that sense, the well/spring of human longevity is commonly regarded as being located within the isolated individual, and especially in the amounts of physical and genetic capital that an individual can muster for life's long journey. Such physical and genetic capital, as with all forms of capital, is further seen as requiring a systematic form of investment and re-investment.

Investment and reinvestment in the body can follow many paths. Exercise, cosmetics, dietary regimes and lifestyle are all called upon to play their part. Featherstone (1982) has argued that such routes are commonly followed in the pursuit of a particular bodily ideal. That ideal is one that exudes and exemplifies a sense of health, fitness and youth. It is also an ideal that retains the highest form of 'exchange-value' in consumer culture. Be that as it may, it is perhaps more important to note that in late modern society, the state itself entices us to focus on the body as the source of health and longevity. Thus, whether it be the US government's *Healthy People* (1979) or the UK government's *Health of the Nation* (Department of Health 1991), or any similar publication, the message is the same: we can improve our health status by adapting and changing our personal behaviour. In particular, we can make ourselves healthy by embracing particular forms of dietary and nutritional regimes; by controlling intakes of tobacco and alcohol, fatty foods and dietary fibre. For our life, our health and our time of death lies in our very own hands. In that sense we strive to put back the moment of death by adopting a series of what Bauman (1992) has called 'survival strategies'.

In short, then, the personal body is regarded as a temple of health, to which the social body is merely a backdrop, adjunct or irrelevance. Health is thereby viewed as a personal and not a social matter. In this framework the fate of the collective supposedly impinges little or not at all on the fate of the individual. The personal is everything – even to the extent that we can distinguish between the deserving and undeserving ill on the grounds of whether or not they are cigarette smokers, people who drink alcohol beyond the recommended limits, practise safe sex and so on. It is an understanding of health and illness that ignores the effects of the collective. Yet, as Wilkinson (1996) has recently demonstrated, the structure of the collective has a very real and decisive impact on the destiny of individuals.

The cult of reflexive individualism is especially apparent in discussions concerning genetics where the role of collectives *vis à vis* those of individuals are daily confused and conflated. Consequently, genetic material, as with health in general, comes to be understood as a form of bodily capital that is passed on from person to person, or from individual to individual within the same family. Indeed, in matters of genetics, materials that belong to a population are readily and commonly 'privatised' and regarded as a matter of personal inheritance. (Attempts by pharmaceutical companies to patent body products, and segments of genetic sequences are simply starker, and more legalistic forms of this privatisation process.)

Yet genetic materials (and the associated 'risk' that might be associated with such materials) must also be considered as a property of populations as well as of singular individuals. Indeed it was this insight which enabled the English geneticist G. H. Hardy and (independently) the German mathematician-geneticist, Weinberg, to propose, during the first half of this century, the use of simple probability models in population genetics. For example, according to the Hardy–Weinberg law of genetic equilibrium, in any large population where discrete generations reproduce by random mating, the distribution of a gene with two alleles can be modelled by the function $(p + q)^2$. That is to say, the distribution of the genetic combinations AA, Aa, and aa would be evident in the following proportions: p^2, $2pq$, q^2.

It is a truly magnificent proposition and not least because it highlights the poverty of thought which was and is associated with those who advocate a focus on the individual as a source of genetic 'risk'. Indeed, it was results of this kind which enabled Penrose finally to understand why haemophiliacs are always with us and why those with 'amentia' (later called mental handicap), are present in all populations despite the fact that such individuals rarely reproduce in any numbers. To follow their insight simply assume that a recessive and 'damaging' allele has a low probability (say 0.01), and carry out the calculations. The results will tell you that the unwanted condition will be evident in only 0.0001 (1 in 10,000) of the population. The recessive allele, however, will be carried by 0.0198 (roughly 2 in every 100) of the population (that is the Aa's). In other words, the risk belongs to all and not simply to the singular and isolated individual.

Unfortunately, in the late modern world, the ways in which genetic risks are identified, framed, packaged and translated for public consumption frequently serve so as to block out the problems relating to collectivities and to highlight merely the particular, the singular and the personal. Indeed, one might reasonably argue that the ways in which genetic risks are understood and perceived in everyday late twentieth century life have relatively little to do with genetics or bio-chemistry *per se*. For the processes of identification and translation are ultimately social, cultural and political ones. In that respect, public discourse about genetic risks merely echoes the public understanding of health, illness, disease and death in general. Genetic material is appropriated as personal capital – carried in and transmitted through individual bodies. The concept of genetics as a science of populations, and the concept of a gene as a property of collectives are thereby anathema to political, social and even scientific discourse as they are constituted in the late modern world.

Conclusion

One of the grandest contributions that social scientists ever made to nineteenth century scientific developments hinged on the way in which they advertised the collective as the key to understanding social processes. Indeed, it was their concern with collective properties and, in particular, the manner in which they 'kept track of death' (Daston 1988: 126) that provided the impetus for the development of the modern mathematical theory of probability. More importantly, from our point of view, it was a tracking process that emphasised the need for the systematic study of mortality processes; a study that was executed, for the most part, under the canopy of demography.

It was, of course, the concerns of the demographers that gave rise to the technologies through which we came to know death in the modern world. That is to say, it was the demographers who insisted on the necessity for a recording and classifying process that has enabled us to talk about rates of death, chances of death and causes of death. And for a large part of the twentieth century the vocabulary of rate, cause and chance seemed to provide a perfectly adequate framework for the expression of what we now refer to as the sociology of death and dying. Indeed, it is only during the second half of the century that sociology has turned away from a focus on cause and rate (understood in terms of the activities of populations), and towards a concern with the meaning of death (understood in terms of personalised and individualised fate). In this latter framework, of course, sociology has also adopted very different styles of study and analysis – mostly forsaking the tools of the mathematical demographer and embracing the tools of the ethnographer in their place.

This switch of focus away from the study of populations and towards the study of individuals has been paralleled in every other field of sociology, and one might even argue that it merely reflects trends and movements that have occurred in the world of everyday social interaction at large. This is presumably why Bauman (1992) is able to observe that a concern with the study of life chances has been replaced with a focus on lifestyles, and why Giddens (1991) argues that an interest in personal lifespan has come to override a concern with (generational) lifecycles.

These forces that channel our attention from life chances to lifestyle, and from lifecycle to lifespan are, perhaps, expressed most forcefully in our attitudes towards the personal body as the font of health and longevity. And, as I have pointed out above, such attitudes are nowhere better exemplified than in contemporary lay and expert discussions concerning the role of genetic factors in health and mortality. For, in the modern genetics clinic, it is assessments of risks to health in terms of singular and individual bodies that structures everyday discourse, whilst assessments of population genetics are held in abeyance. Risks to health and well-being, including the risk of death, are thereby personalised and individualised in such a manner that the analysis and significance of the collective is abandoned.

In the last act of Ibsen's *The Doll's House*, Nora asserts that, 'I want to be me.' In retrospect, we can clearly regard it as the cry of the twentieth century. I want to be me, and I want it now.

> 'Now' is the site of happiness – its only site. Life duration is split into a succession of such 'nows', none less significant than any other, each equally deserving to be lived to the full, enjoyed to the full,

squeezed to the full of all its pleasure giving juices. One may say that inequality of life chances, no more attacked point-blank, no more challenged directly, seeks its compensation in the new spirit of egalitarianism of life moments.

(Bauman 1992: 193)

References

Ariès, P. (1983) *The Hour of Our Death*, trans. H. Weaver, Harmondsworth: Penguin.

Bataille, G. (1957) *La Litterature et Le mal*, Paris: Gallimard.

—— (1986) *Erotism, Death and Sensuality*, trans. M. Dalwood, San Francisco: City Lights.

Bauman, Z. (1992) *Mortality and Immortality and Other Life Strategies*, Cambridge: Polity Press.

Charlton, J. and Murphy, M. (eds) (1997) *The Health of Adult Britain 1841–1994*, 2 vols, London: ONS.

Crombie, A. C. 1994. *Styles of Scientific Thinking in the European Tradition*, Vol. 2, London: Duckworth.

Daston, L. J. (1987) 'The domestication of risk: mathematical probability and insurance 1650–1830', in L. Krüger, L. J. Daston, and M. Heidelberger (eds) *The Probabilistic Revolution*, Vol. 1, *Ideas in History*, London: MIT Press, 241–60.

—— (1988) *Classical Probability in the Enlightenment*, Princeton, NJ: Princeton University Press.

Deleuze, G. (1983) *Nietzsche and Philosophy*, trans. H. Tomlinson, London: Athlone Press.

Department of Health (1991) *The Health of the Nation. A Consultative Document for Health in England*, London: HMSO.

Derrida, J. (1994) *Specters of Marx*, trans. P. Kamuf, London: Routledge.

Durkheim, E. (1952) *Suicide: a Study in Sociology*, trans. J.A. Spaulding and G. Simpson, London: Routledge and Kegan Paul.

Elias, N. (1985) *The Loneliness of the Dying*, trans. E. Jephcott, Oxford: Blackwell.

Featherstone, M. (1982) 'The body in consumer culture', *Theory, Culture and Society* 1(1): 18–33.

Foucault, M. (1972) *Histoire de la folie à l'Âge Classique*, Paris: Gallimard.

—— (1973) *The Birth of the Clinic*, trans. A. M. Sheridan, London: Tavistock.

Giddens, A. (1991) *Modernity and Self-Identity: Self and Society in the Late Modern Age*, Stanford, CA: Stanford University Press.

Gorer, G. (1965) *Death, Grief and Mourning in Contemporary Britain*, London: Cresset Press.

Hacking, I. (1990) *The Taming of Chance*, Cambridge: Cambridge University Press.

Hald, A. (1990) *A History of Probability and Statistics and their Applications before 1750*, New York: John Wiley.

Heidegger, M. (1959) *An Introduction to Metaphysics*, trans. R. Manheim, New Haven: Yale University Press.

Hertz, R. (1960) *Death and the Right Hand: a Contribution to the Study of the Collective Representations of Death*, trans. R. and C. Needham, London: Cohen and West.

Kierkegaard, S. (1989) *The Sickness Unto Death*, trans. A. Harvey, Harmondsworth: Penguin.

Lyotard, J.-F. (1989) *The Lyotard Reader*, ed. A. Benjamin, Oxford: Blackwell.

Malthus, T. R. (1970) *An Essay on the Principle of Population and a Summary View of the Principle of Population*, Harmondsworth: Penguin.

Mauss, M. (1979) *Sociology and Psychology: Essays*, trans. B. Brewster, London: Routledge and Kegan Paul.

——— (1997) *Re-forming the Body: Religion, Community and Modernity*, London: Sage.

Mellor, P. A. and Shilling, C. (1993) 'Modernity, self-identity and the sequestration of death', *Sociology* 27(3): 411–31.

Merleau-Ponty, M. (1962) *Phenomenology of Perception*, trans. C. Smith, London: Routledge.

Nietzsche, F. (1973) *Beyond Good and Evil*, trans. R. J. Hollingdale, Harmondsworth: Penguin.

OPCS (1994) *Mortality Statistics*, (Area), Series DH5, no. 19, London: HMSO.

Pearson, K. (1897) *The Chances of Death and Other Studies in Evolution*, Vol. 1, London: Edward Arnold.

Prior, L. (1989) *The Social Organization of Death. Medical Discourse and Social Practices in Belfast*, Basingstoke: Macmillan.

Seale, C. (1995) 'Heroic death', *Sociology* 4(29): 597–613.

US Department of Health, Education and Welfare (1979) *Healthy People: the Surgeon General's Report on Health Promotion and Disease Prevention*, Washington DC: US Government Printing Office.

Walter, T. (1994) *The Revival of Death*, London: Routledge.

Wilkinson, R. G. (1996) *Unhealthy Societies: The Afflictions of Inequality*, London: Routledge.

World Health Organization (WHO) (1992) *International Statistical Classification of Diseases and Related Health Problems*, 3 vols, 10th edn, Geneva: WHO.

Part III

Risk and consumption

Chapter 10

Food, risk and subjectivity

Deborah Lupton

Introduction

In recent times, sociocultural theorists have turned their attention to examining the role played by concepts of 'risk' in contemporary western societies. It has been argued that discourses on risk have become pervasive, and are now widely used to explain deviations from the norm, misfortune and frightening events. Unlike in previous times, when misfortunes were often attributed to something out of individuals' control, such as the gods or fate, the concept of risk in late modernity assumes that 'something can be done' to prevent misfortune. Risk, therefore, is associated with notions of choice, responsibility and blame. It has become a means by which institutions and authorities, as well as individuals, are held accountable and encouraged to regulate themselves.

This chapter takes up some aspects of these theoretical perspectives in relation to the risks associated with food consumption as they are represented, perceived, negotiated and experienced. People in modern western societies demonstrate an obsession with the content and quantity of foodstuffs and the relationship between health states and the consumption of food. Hardly a day goes by without a report in the news media either on the linking of a food substance with illness or disease, or a claim that a foodstuff serves to protect against ill health. The linking of health states with food consumption is constantly made in such forums as commercial advertising for foodstuffs and health promotional media campaigns. As a consequence, food has become profoundly medicalised in its association with health, illness and disease.

At a more symbolic level of meaning, the risks associated with food consumption involve challenges to our sense of self, including our maintenance of self-autonomy and self-control and our membership of social groups. Because eating is an act that involves the incorporation of a substance that begins as 'other' into the 'self', it is fraught with risk. Anything we may seek to take into our mouths, chew and swallow, implicitly poses a threat, and requires careful evaluation before we allow it into our bodies. What might be termed 'social' risks are also fundamental to notions of the body and the self in relation to food. These risks are associated with understandings about how people should conduct themselves when eating and the shape and size of bodies in terms of attractiveness and issues of self-control.

In discussing these dimensions and meanings of risk and food consumption, a number of major theoretical perspectives are examined in this chapter. These include the 'risk society' approach put forward by sociologists such as Ulrich Beck and Anthony Giddens, the 'cultural' approach, which draws principally upon the work of the anthropologist Mary Douglas and the 'civility' perspective based on the writings of the sociologist Norbert Elias. The perspectives offered by these theorists and those who have taken up and elaborated upon their work provide important insights into how individuals and social groups come to define 'risk' in relation to foodstuffs and eating practices and how they deal with, or manage, such risk as part of everyday life. They discuss the issues at various conceptual levels, ranging from a focus on the social structural, political and institutional aspects to the more symbolic and cultural dimensions of risk.

An important premise underpinning the theories covered in this chapter is that risk is a socio-cultural construction rather than an objective 'fact' that can be identified via scientific procedures. The primary interest for socio-cultural perspectives is in exploring the ways in which certain phenomena are singled out and described as 'risks', and the implications that this process of selection has for how we conceptualise and experience our bodies, our selves and others. This approach to risk departs in significant and important ways from the individualised and asocial method that tends to dominate in policy, psychological and public health accounts of lay responses to risk. In the latter literature, risk assessment is viewed as an individual's response to objective health threats, and those who refuse to respond to expert communications on risk are routinely positioned as 'ignorant', 'apathetic' or lacking 'self-efficacy' (Lupton 1995). Aspects of social and cultural context and of symbolic meaning are rarely incorporated into these models of risk.

Food and health risks in the 'risk society'

Sociologists who have adopted the 'risk society' approach generally tend to focus on issues of the political and economic organisation of late modern societies and the implications for individuals' conduct of everyday life and relationships with others. In his well-known book *Risk Society* (1992), Ulrich Beck described the constant state of concern, anxiety and even dread people in western countries feel in relation to such environmental threats to human health as air and water pollution, ionising radiation and food contamination. Beck argues that people living in western societies have moved towards a greater awareness of threats and hazards (now commonly called 'risks') and that therefore they should be described as inhabiting a 'risk society' rather than an 'industrial society'. The major difference he perceives between the two types of society is that in 'risk society', unlike 'industrial society', the drawbacks and ill-effects of modernisation are continually confronted and challenged.

Anthony Giddens (1990, 1994) has also written at length on the uncertainty with which individuals approach life in contemporary western societies. Like Beck, Giddens sees this uncertainty as springing from the realisation that the claims of modernity for human progress have been shown to be not quite as utopian as once was thought. Giddens argues that the greater knowledge which is an outcome of modernity has led in turn to greater uncertainty and many people's subsequent search for alternative expertise and knowledge claims. While awareness of threats and hazards may always have been part of life, the difference in late modernity is that many of them are seen to arise from (rather than being assuaged by) the very growth in human knowledge.

Both Beck and Giddens agree that those aspects and incidents of late modern life that are identified as 'risks' are closely linked to accountability and responsibility. The prevalence of discourses on risk is a central feature of a society which has come to reflect upon itself, to critique itself. Judgements on risk represent implicit moral judgements (albeit masked in the discourse of objective, quantitative 'facts'), on the ways in which human societies have developed. Beck and Giddens also see risk as a major theme through which the body and the self are monitored, both by the self and by others. They argue that concepts of risk and how best to manage it is a central part of subjectivity, for it is often in response to risk that we seek to act in certain ways, whether it is in relation to human relationships, sexuality, commodity consumption, employment and financial issues, emotional states or physical health.

In relation to food consumption, in risk society what may previously have been seen to be the advantages of industrialisation are overweighed by the hazards and threats that are viewed to be an outcome of producing and processing food on a massive scale. From this perspective, risks related to food are associated with contemporary anxieties about the side-effects of industrialisation, including such phenomena as the pollution and environmental degradation caused by factory-farming, the use of hormones, pesticides and fertilisers and genetic manipulation in food production and the industrial processing of food. Foodstuffs are viewed as increasingly being taken from their ideal 'natural' state and rendered dangerous through human intervention. Contemporary processed food products are portrayed as hazardous to health in their lack of fibre and vitamins, their high fat, sugar and salt levels and their added components of chemicals. The food industry is represented as blindly seeking profits to the detriment of the quality of food they produce, the welfare of the animals they farm and the environment in general, while the government is viewed as pandering to agribusiness, lacking the conviction to introduce strict regulations ensuring the safety and health value of food products (see, for example, critiques by Jenkins (1991) and Singer (1992)).

One example of current concerns about the side-effects of industrialisation in food production is the high level of attention paid in public forums to the invisible dangers in familiar foods over the past decade. The publicity given to 'mad cow disease' (bovine spongiform encephalopathy [BSE]) by the news media is a particularly vivid instance of the intensity of concern and anxiety that appear to surround 'risky' foods. The presence of BSE in British cattle first became identified in 1986, and the news media in Britain have periodically devoted their attention to it since 1990 (Miller and Reilly 1995; Newsinger 1997). A spate of intense media coverage occurred in early 1996, following the release of a British government report which discussed a possible link between BSE and cases of the degenerative brain disorder Creutzfeld Jakob Disease in a number of British people who had consumed beef products. In response to the publicity, and despite government assurances that the public was not endangered by eating beef, levels of beef consumption in Britain fell dramatically in the weeks following the media reports and British beef was banned from sale in world markets (Marris and Langford 1996: 39; Newsinger 1997: 245).

Much of the publicity over this particular BSE outbreak revolved around what was seen as a 'natural' outcome of 'unnatural' practices: that is, feeding cattle with the ground remains of other mammals (sheep contaminated with the infective agent believed to cause BSE). As one English columnist put it, 'A horrified public now realises that cows have been fed on sheep, other cows and chicken dung. And one step along the chain we have been feeding it to our children' (quoted in the *Australian*, 27 March 1996). Another newsworthy feature of the outbreak was the controversy concerning the British government's apparent attempts to ignore the problem and avoid introducing regulations to prevent against the spread of BSE. It was not only the idea that thousands of Britons and others who had consumed British meat or meat products may be harbouring a potentially fatal brain disease that constituted the 'risk' of BSE, but also the economic losses the British beef and dairy industries faced and the related threat of job losses.

As the media coverage of BSE demonstrates, industry and government may often be singled out as being responsible for creating the threats that render foods hazardous to consumers. This dimension of risk sees risks as being external threats, posed by others to oneself. Risks, however, are not always located externally. Risk discourse also positions dangers to health as the personal responsibility of members of the public to control.

This is particularly the case in medical and public health discourses, in which individuals are constantly exhorted to seek out information on the health risks associated with food and to conform to diets that avoid these risks (Lupton 1993, 1996: Chapter 3). Indeed, there is generally far more emphasis placed on individual behaviour change in response to food risks than on changing the food production system or encouraging political activism to address the hazards associated with food.

While risks may be debated at the level of expertise and public account-ability, therefore, they are dealt with by most individuals at the level of the local, the private and the everyday. This is clearly so in the case of health risks associated with foodstuffs, for people most often respond to anxieties about food by making changes to their personal consumption and preparation of food. Recent studies involving interviews with people about their diet have found that food is closely associated with health states. A survey of 420 adults in Leicestershire found that well over half (64 per cent) of the respondents reported having made dietary changes due to their increased awareness of the relationship between diet and health (Goode *et al.* 1996). Like the young Canadian girls in Chapman and Maclean's (1993) research, the Welsh women in Murcott's (1993) study and the Australian men and women interviewed by Santich (1994) and Lupton (1996), the Leicestershire sample evinced awareness of health messages about the need to avoid dietary fat and sweet foods, and to eat more fruit and vegetables.

Despite the emphasis in risk society on expert knowledges in identi-fying risks and providing solutions for their management, disputes and uncertainties among experts are also common (Giddens 1990). This uncer-tainty is often conveyed to the public via the mass media. The news media, for example, frequently report controversies such as debates among experts over whether controlling one's diet for cholesterol helps to prevent heart disease (Lupton and Chapman 1995). With this awareness of uncertainty in the ranks of experts, it is difficult for members of the lay public to know which advice to 'believe in'. Lay people often express distrust of the pronouncements of 'experts' in relation to health risks associated with food. They say that they prefer trusted and known lay sources, such as family members and friends, to inform their judgement of risk rather than scientists or government officials, who they see as having vested interests in communicating certain knowledges about risk (Marris and Langford 1996). In the Leicestershire study conducted by Goode *et al.* (1996), 84 per cent of the respondents agreed that 'I find there are a lot of conflicting messages around concerning a healthy diet.' As this suggests, the rela-tionship lay people have with expert knowledges in the context of risk is complex and ambivalent.

While foodstuffs may not be directly referred to as 'risky' or 'safe' by lay informants, they frequently use synonyms that convey similar meanings.

Certain foods are routinely singled out as being 'good' or 'bad'. Santich (1994) concluded from her interviews with lay people that 'good' foods included those foods that were seen as trusted, homemade, pure, natural and expensive as well as healthy. 'Bad' foods, in contrast, were those that were distrusted, bought from takeaway outlets, contaminated, manufactured and unhealthy. Other binary oppositions appear in cultural concepts of 'good' and 'bad' foods, such as whole/refined, wholesome/junk, organic/chemical, traditional/modern, rural/urban, folk/technological and small/mass (Hamilton *et al.*, 1995). Although expert knowledge may be used as part of the development of these distinctions, people also often draw upon their lived experience and their own perception of the world. People refer to the need to 'trust their own bodies' in dealing with conflicting expert advice (Sellerberg 1991; Murcott 1993; Lupton and Chapman 1995; Good *et al.* 1996).

Drawing distinctions between 'good' and 'bad' food is part of lay people's construction of conceptual 'strategies of confidence' (Sellerberg 1991: 196), which serve to develop and maintain boundaries around what foodstuffs are trusted. Once a food is established as 'trusted', then it may be eaten with confidence, and all other substances are positioned as outside these boundaries. These distinctions serve to provide some certainty and degree of predictability in a context in which the health risks of foods are constantly broadcast and debated.

Breaching boundaries: food, risk and cultural transgression

The primary focus of Beck's and Giddens's writings on 'risk society' is on the 'rational' strategies that people adopt when conceptualising and dealing with risk. They have much less to say about the ways in which risk discourse tends to operate at a more latent, extra-rational level of meaning. It is here that cultural theorists, drawing particularly on the work of Mary Douglas, have some important insights to offer.

As noted above, binary oppositions tend to be used in lay people's accounts of the risks associated with food. However, the construction of trust around foodstuffs and the positioning of certain substances as 'outside' the boundaries of acceptable foods go beyond judgements about health risks. At a more latent level of meaning, 'bad' or 'risky' foods are not only those that are perceived to be 'unhealthy' or 'unnatural', but are also those foods that challenge our sense of self-autonomy and self-identity.

Cultural theorists have dealt with issues around the notion of conceptual body boundaries and the ingestion of food. From this approach, food is viewed as a potentially risky substance because it constantly breaches the body boundaries, moving from 'outside' to 'inside', from that which is 'alien' or 'other' to that which is 'self'. Douglas's book *Purity and*

Danger, first published in 1966, has become a classic reference in relation to defining the symbolic nature of boundaries across cultures. For Douglas, the human body stands as a metaphor for human societies: 'The body is a model which can stand for any bounded system. Its boundaries can represent any boundaries which are threatened or precarious' (Douglas 1966/1980: 115). Just as we regulate what goes 'in' and 'out' of our own bodies, so too do human societies and groups seek to position themselves as bounded, needing closely to monitor and regulate which people and objects travel 'in' and 'out'. In *Purity and Danger*, Douglas explores the taboos and rules around what is considered 'food' and 'non-food' in different social groups in relation to this symbolic conceptualisation of the importance of boundaries. As she notes, central to these definitions is the binary opposition between 'purity' and 'contamination' or between 'clean' and 'dirty'. Douglas argues that these oppositions are socially constructed, and therefore differ between societies and historical periods.

'Contamination' occurs when boundaries are transgressed; when a substance that is understood to be properly 'outside' the body goes inside, for example, or if a substance is consumed, taken inside the body, and then comes outside. This point is underlined if we think about the cultural meanings associated with vomit. Vomit is semi-digested food that once 'inside' the body, comes 'outside'. This movement from 'inside' to 'outside' challenges our sense of what is culturally appropriate to be considered a foodstuff. Once food is placed into the mouth, we consider it highly inappropriate to remove it. Once it has been chewed, it becomes disgusting, and once it has been swallowed, it loses the status of food, and becomes a bodily substance. Vomit, therefore, in cultural terms is considered an extremely impure substance. While it retains the organic composition and nutritional value of the food that was originally swallowed, it is unthinkable that it should be considered as a foodstuff. The status of vomit as a 'risky' substance lies in the notion that any contact with it will contaminate us.

At the heart of the disgust and fear we have concerning such substances is their liminal or 'in-between' nature, which makes them difficult to properly categorise. In terms of their organic composition, liminal substances that arouse our disgust are not necessarily poisonous or contaminated. They will not kill us if we eat them (although they might make us feel queasy). Their danger lies in their cultural status as contaminating and unclean and the threat they pose to our sense of bodily or self integrity. Julia Kristeva (1982) refers to such liminal substances as 'abject', that which is neither 'self' nor 'other', neither 'inside' nor 'outside'. As she notes, the negative emotions aroused by the abject go way beyond concerns about health: 'It is thus not lack of cleanliness or health that causes abjection but what disturbs identity, system, order. What does not respect borders, positions, rules. The in-between, the ambiguous, the composite'

(1982: 4). What seems uncategorisable, in some way, is greeted with fear and loathing, because it appears to be less controllable, challenging the apparent order of things. Kristeva describes the emotional and bodily responses that the abject incurs as a means of 'protection': loathing, spasms, vomiting, repugnance, retching. Sticky, slimy and viscous foods, because they blur the distinction between 'wet' and 'dry' and seem difficult to contain, are a particular source of anxiety, disgust and fear in their liminality (Lupton 1996: 114–16).

The anthropologist Claude Fischler has extended Douglas's perspectives on contamination and bodily boundaries to explore what he calls the 'omnivore's paradox', or the need for humans to include diversity in their diets but simultaneously to be conservative in their eating habits: 'The omnivore's paradox lives in the tension, the oscillation between the two poles of neophobia (prudence, fear of the unknown, resistance to change) and neophilia (the tendency to explore, the need for change, novelty, variety)' (Fischler 1988: 278). Underlying the anxiety behind this tension is the notion that the act of incorporation, or the passing of a foodstuff between the 'inside' of our bodies and the 'outside' of the external world is 'both banal and fraught with potentially irreversible consequences' (Fischler 1988: 279). When we take in a substance, it becomes part of us. This is the case both at the individual and at the social level, because acts of food consumption serve to define and reinforce collective identity: 'Thus, not only does the eater incorporate the properties of food, but, symmetrically, it can be said that the absorption of a food incorporates the eater into a culinary system and therefore into the group which practises it' (Fischler 1988: 280–1).

Fischler contends that the increasing gap between the production and consumption of food in industrialised societies has meant that consumers are less able to be certain about the nature of the food they buy. He relates this uncertainty to the intensification of anxiety about the content of food, noting that 'if one does not know what one is eating, one is liable to lose the awareness of certainty of what one is oneself' (1988: 290). A particular risk of incorporation is in eating something which is too close to the human, such as pet animals, or which pose a threat, such as wild animals. Both kinds of animals confuse the distinction between 'eater' and 'food', and therefore arouse revulsion (Falk 1994: 76–7). An example of this source of revulsion was demonstrated in an article published in a Sydney newspaper addressing the issue of the controversies and anxieties aroused by genetic manipulation of foodstuffs. One specific problem, asserted the author, was that a type of pig has been produced using some modified human DNA. If consumers knew this, he argued, they would find this disgusting, as it would be close to cannibalism: 'tell someone the pork they just ate contained a bit of human genetic material and most likely you will see one shocked consumer' (Gilchrist 1996).

It is not just the health and immediate physical well-being of the eater which are risked when a foodstuff is consumed, therefore, but also her or his cultural, social and self identity. If an individual cannot find a cultural place for a substance as an edible food, then, regardless of its nutritional value, it is simply not acceptable as a food and cannot be incorporated into the self because it is viewed as dangerous, and therefore takes on the status of 'risky'.

The risks of the 'uncivilised' body

I have emphasised in the above section the challenges to concepts of identity raised by the incorporation of substances into the body. A related perspective on the link between food and risk presents the view that changing ideas about the body, manners and social status have contributed to the ways in which we currently conceptualise food and eating practices. These risks include the potential to appear 'uncontrolled' in one's eating habits or to lack the appropriate refinement in one's tastes or manners. It has also become a 'social' risk to appear to allow one's appetite to overcome one's ability for self-control. Here again, the symbolic basis of anxiety is the threat of disorder, the loss of control over our bodies and the negative cultural meanings associated with this, rather than more manifest concerns about the threat of illness or disease. Nonetheless, these issues of bodily control and deportment have relevance for health, because they impose norms about desirable body shape and size which influence dietary practices.

One of the dominant writers here is the historical sociologist Norbert Elias (1978), who wrote detailed accounts of how the notions of 'civility' and 'manners' developed in Europe in the Renaissance. While Elias may not have overtly referred to 'risk', his writings have relevance for a discussion of concepts of risk in relation to food. This is because of the implicit social risks involved with appearing to lack self-control that are associated with the meanings of the 'civilised' body. Elias contends that the 'civilised' person, as the notion developed in European societies in the sixteenth century, began to be viewed as an individual who could set himself or herself apart as an autonomous, contained entity and who could exert a high degree of control over such bodily functions as eating, drinking and excretion. This concept of the body/self differs dramatically from the medieval or 'uncivilised' body/self. The 'civilised' body is much more 'closed in' than the medieval body, its boundaries more tightly regulated in the effort to maintain an individualised subjectivity. As Shilling notes:

> The civilized body can be contrasted with the 'uncivilized' body of early medieval times which was only weakly demarcated from its social and natural environment. The uncivilized body was constrained

by few behavioural norms, gave immediate physical expression to
emotions, and sought to satisfy bodily desires without restraint or
regard for the welfare of others.

(1993: 151)

Notions of embarrassment and shame, linked to perceptions of social
conventions and how others might judge oneself, according to Elias, were
central to the regulation of behaviour; one behaved in certain ways so as
to avoid shame or embarrassment. Mennell (1985, 1991) has taken up
Elias' ideas to explore changes in conventions around diet and cuisine in
Britain and France from medieval times. Mennell argues that what he
describes as a 'civilizing of appetite' began to emerge in the eighteenth
century in those countries. Among those classes who had access to plentiful foodstuffs it was considered more refined to restrain one's food intake,
avoiding the public displays of gluttony that were common in previous
centuries. Matters of health were not so much the concern as were matters
of social decorum, of delicacy and manners. Simultaneously, obesity
became a less desirable mode of bodily presentation, again not principally
because of health concerns but because it was associated with gluttony,
excess and lack of self-control and refinement.

Using this notion of the importance of 'civilised' behaviour to modern
concepts of embodiment and self-hood, it may be seen that one integral
dimension of the risky nature of food and eating is the threat of social
opprobrium, of shame and embarrassment incurred through engaging in
inappropriate eating practices or table manners. Styles of eating, including
food preferences, preparation and presentation, as well as table manners,
are commonly associated with social class distinctions. 'Good taste' in
food preferences and manners denotes social superiority (Bourdieu 1984).
Being seen to eat the 'wrong' kinds of foods, displaying little knowledge
of how to behave in expensive restaurants, are all potent sources of shame
and embarrassment, and therefore potential social 'risks'.

So too, the link between eating practices and the size of the body
produces certain 'risks' related to self-presentation and others' judgement
of oneself. Because tight control over body size is understood to be both
a mark of a 'civilised' person and a route to physical attractiveness,
apparent loss of control over eating, leading to overweight or obesity, is
viewed as a material embodiment of one's laziness and inability to control
one's desires. The sight of an obese body, or the thought of oneself as
obese, may provoke the emotions of disgust, revulsion and fear (Bordo
1993; Heywood 1996). Such a body is conceptualised as chaotic, disorderly and unruly, a direct antithesis of the notion of the self-contained
and highly disciplined body that is the ideal in western societies. It is
therefore a highly socially stigmatised body, a type of body that we seek
strenuously to avoid. Leslie Heywood (1996) has referred to this approach

to the body as the 'anorexic aesthetic'. This aesthetic privileges reason over emotion, mind over body, and because the feminine is associated with emotion and the body, the masculine over the feminine. Heywood argues that the currency of the anorexic aesthetic in contemporary western societies underlies why 'a ripple of fat tissue over the ribs or the protrusion of a stomach is the source of anxiety, self-loathing, unreasonable fear' (1996: xii).

The cultural meanings underpinning these notions of the body/self have a long history in western societies. Historical accounts of people who deprived themselves of food for religious reasons suggest that hunger was understood as a contaminating force, pushing base bodily desire ahead of spiritual concerns. To be able to overcome the desire for food was regarded by religious fasters as evidence that one had become more pure, less flesh and more soul, and thus closer to God (Bynum 1987). To consume food, to take it into the body, was thus conceptualised as giving into fleshly desires and contaminating the purity of reason. These meanings around food have also been identified in the accounts of modern-day people who engage in self-starvation (now generally diagnosed as having anorexia nervosa). Food, for such people, is viewed as contaminating, impure, a source of pollution and defilement because it underline the base desires and material needs of the body (Bordo 1993).

Evidence from interview studies, however, would suggest that these meanings are also prevalent (if at a somewhat lower level of intensity) among those people who do not suffer from anorexia nervosa or bulimia (see, for example, Charles and Kerr 1988, McKie et al. 1993; Chapman and Maclean 1993; Lupton 1996). Most women and many men, such studies suggest, constantly struggle with their desire to eat foods they find pleasurable and their desire to control their urges and avoid overweight, to adhere to the 'anorexic aesthetic'. They may describe feelings of self-disgust and guilt if they think they have over-eaten or have consumed 'junk' foods. It would appear that many people in western societies find it difficult to consume foods, particularly those that are categorised as 'bad' because they are fatty, sugary or salty, without worrying about how they might affect either their health or their physical attractiveness, or both. The ingestion of animal fat has come to be viewed with particular anxiety, not only because it has constantly been publicised in medical and public health discourses as clogging the arteries and contributing to heart disease, but also because it is seen to cause the ugly, uncontrolled obese body (Lupton 1996: 138).

There is, therefore, a close interrelationship between notions of diet, health, body size and physical attractiveness – what I have referred to elsewhere as the 'food/health/beauty' triplex (Lupton 1996: 137). Because of the increasing focus placed on individuals' responsibility for their own health states (discussed above), both good health and slimness are viewed as accomplishments of self-discipline, the outcome of a well-regulated lifestyle. People who are overweight or obese by contemporary standards of physical attractiveness are often described as 'unhealthy', while a 'healthy' body size is that which is slim (but not excessively slim, as this would imply that the person is suffering from malnutrition, has a terminal illness such as cancer or HIV/AIDS, or is suffering from anorexia nervosa). This linking can often be seen in advertisements for food products that claim to be 'light' in fat, in which the food is represented as assisting the consumer to lose weight in the interests of both good health and good looks.

We can see in contemporary times, thus, the intertwinings of the notions of restrained eating as part of the presentation of oneself as civilised, displaying proper decorum and moderation in appetite, and notions of the health effects of diet that became important following the emergence of nutritional science: 'Just as the attainment and preservation of good health is perceived as a moral accomplishment, the achievement of a slim body represents the privileged values of self-control and self-denial' (Lupton 1996: 137). In these discourses, the 'risks' associated with food consumption are not simply health-related, but are associated with the loss of rationality and self-control, the privileging of the body over the mind, and the associated self-hate and anxiety that eating and appetite bring with them.

Conclusion

All three major theoretical perspectives discussed in this chapter throw light upon various aspects of the association between the sociocultural meanings around food consumption and risk. While they address the topic from differing positions and interests, and at varying levels of conceptual depth, these perspectives are insightful in underlining that notions of risk are integral to notions of the body, self-hood and social relations. The 'risk society' thesis draws attention to the macro-level and political aspects of risk discourse, locating the major cause of the current intensification of anxiety about the health risks of food within broader concerns about the negative outcomes of modernisation and industrialisation. Concern about risk, from this perspective, is a rational response to individuals' perceptions of the uncertainties and growing hazards of life in late modernity. The 'cultural' approach directs attention at the more latent meanings underpinning anxieties around food. Exponents of this perspective highlight the symbolic role that food plays in passing across cultural boundaries, and the risks that are integral to this act of incorporation of 'other' into 'self'. From the 'civility' perspective, the consumption of food is surrounded with the 'social' risks of incurring embarrassment, shame or humiliation through inappropriate eating practices or in demonstrating to oneself and others one's lack of self-control.

These perspectives move towards a more complex understanding of social and individual responses to the threats and dangers that are identified in relation to food consumption than is generally presented in research addressing food habits and preferences. Perhaps most importantly, they emphasise that simply devoting attention to people's overt concerns about the health implications of various foodstuffs is only scratching the surface of the sociocultural meanings and implications of food and risk. The perspectives discussed here underline that the risks associated with eating may be understood as far more than the biological effects of poisonous, indigestible or carcinogenic substances that may be contained in foodstuffs. Indeed, as discussed above, foods may be conceptualised as 'risky' by some individuals or social groups even when there is no apparent biological link to ill health or disease. Their danger is founded far more on social norms and cultural conventions associated with the need for individuals to maintain some sense of certainty and order, preserve self-integrity, present themselves as 'civilised' and defend their bodily and symbolic boundaries against transgression.

References

Beck, U. (1992) *Risk Society: Towards a New Modernity*, London: Sage.

Bordo, S. (1993) *Unbearable Weight: Feminism, Western Culture, and the Body*, Berkeley, CA: University of California Press.

Bourdieu, P. (1984) *Distinction: a Social Critique of the Judgement of Taste*, London: Routledge and Kegan Paul.

Bynum, C. (1987) *Holy Feast and Holy Fast: the Religious Significance of Food to Medieval Women*, Berkeley, CA: University of California Press.

Chapman, G. and Maclean, H. (1993) '"Junk food" and "healthy food": meanings of food in adolescent women's culture', *Journal of Nutrition Education* 25: 108–13.

Charles, N. and Kerr, M. (1988) *Women, Food and Families*, Manchester: Manchester University Press.

Douglas, M. (1966/1980) *Purity and Danger: an Analysis of Concepts of Pollution and Taboo*, London: Routledge and Kegan Paul.

Elias, N. (1978) *The History of Manners: the Civilizing Process*, Volume 1, Oxford: Blackwell.

Falk, P. (1994) *The Consuming Body*, London: Sage.

Fischler, C. (1988) 'Food, self and identity', *Social Science Information* 27(2): 275–92.

Giddens, A. (1990) *The Consequences of Modernity*, Cambridge: Polity Press.

—— (1994) 'Living in a post-traditional society', in U. Beck, A. Giddens and S. Lash (eds) *Reflexive Modernization: Politics, Tradition and Aesthetics in the Modern Social Order*, Cambridge: Polity Press, 56–109.

Gilchrist, G. (1996) 'Future food: is it so hard to swallow?', *Sydney Morning Herald*, 27 March.

Goode, J., Beardsworth, A., Keil, T., Sherratt, E. and Haslam, C. (1996) 'Changing the nation's diet: a study of responses to current nutritional messages', *Health Education Journal* 55: 285–99.

Hamilton, M., Waddington, P., Gregory, S. and Walker, A. (1995) 'Eat, drink and be saved: the spiritual significance of alternative diets', *Social Compass* 42(4): 497–511.

Heywood, L. (1996) *Dedication to Hunger: the Anorexic Aesthetic in Modern Cultures*, Berkeley, CA: University of California Press.

Jenkins, R. (1991) *Food for Wealth or Health?: Towards Equality in Health*, London: Socialist Health Association.

Kristeva, J. (1982) *Powers of Horror: an Essay on Abjection*, New York: Columbia University Press.

Lupton, D. (1993) 'Risk as moral danger: the social and political functions of risk discourse in public health', *International Journal of Health Services*, 23(3): 425–35.

—— (1995) *The Imperative of Health: Public Health and the Regulated Body*, London: Sage.

—— (1996) *Food, the Body and the Self*, London: Sage.

Lupton, D. and Chapman, S. (1995) '"A healthy lifestyle might be the death of you": discourses on diet, cholesterol control and heart disease in the press and among the lay public', *Sociology of Health and Illness* 17(4): 477–94.

McKie, L., Wood, R. and Gregory, S. (1993) 'Women defining health: food, diet and body image', *Health Education Research: Theory and Practice* 8(1): 35–41.

Marris, C. and Langford, I. (1996) 'No cause for alarm', *New Scientist*, 28 September: 36–9.

Mennell, S. (1985) *All Manners of Food: Eating and Taste in England and France from the Middle Ages to the Present*, Oxford: Basil Blackwell.

—— (1991) 'On the civilizing of appetite', in M. Featherstone, M. Hepworth and B. Turner (eds) *The Body: Social Process and Cultural Theory*, London: Sage, 126–56.

Miller, D. and Reilly, J. (1995) 'Making an issue of food safety: the media, pressure groups, and the public sphere', in D. Maura and J. Sobal (eds) *Food, Eating and Nutrition as Social Problems: Constructivist Perspectives*, New York: Aldine de Gruyter, 305–36.

Murcott, A. (1993) 'Talking of good food: an empirical study of women's conceptualizations', *Food and Foodways* 5(3): 305–18.

Newsinger, J. (1997) 'The roast beef of old England', *International Journal of Health Services* 27(2): 243–6.

Santich, B. (1994) 'Good for you: beliefs about food and their relation to eating habits', *Australian Journal of Nutrition and Dietetics* 51(2): 68–73.

Sellerberg, A.-M. (1991) 'In food we trust? Vitally necessary confidence: and unfamiliar ways of attaining it', in E. Furst, R. Prattala, M. Ekstrom, L. Holm and U. Kjaernes (eds) *Palatable Worlds: Sociocultural Food Studies*, Oslo: Solum, 193–201.

Shilling, C. (1993) *The Body and Social Theory*, London: Sage.

Singer, P. (1992) 'Becoming a vegetarian', in D. Curtin and L. Heldke (eds) *Cooking, Eating, Thinking: Transformative Philosophies of Food*, Bloomington, IN: Indiana University Press, 172–93.

Chapter 11

The ritual of health promotion

Robert Crawford

> We look to medicine to provide us with key symbols for constructing a framework of meaning – a mythology of our state of being.
>
> (Comaroff 1982: 55)

Since the mid-1970s, there has been a turn towards health in the United States and in other western cultures. The pursuit of health has become an important activity, especially for the American middle class. Millions of people have become concerned about their health and have changed their behaviour in order to protect or improve it. Millions more continue to act as always or with minor changes but now with an awareness that such behaviour puts them 'at risk'. In either case, health has become an important topic in everyday conversation, reflecting an extraordinary expansion of medical, political, and educative discourses about health hazards and ways to protect individuals and populations against them. There are several kinds of health discourse. My topic is health promotion, by which I mean the set of discourses and practices concerned with individual behaviours, attitudes, dispositions or lifestyle choices said to affect health. Protecting and improving individual health appear to be prototypical acts of practical reason and personal responsibility – a matter of common sense. The appearance is based on the assumption that, given accurate medical information about hazards to health and naturally desiring to live a long life free from debilitating disease, the rational person will act to avoid unnecessary dangers and adopt healthy behaviours. Yet, there is a parallel appearance. No matter how much or how little is undertaken in the name of health, we all know that the attempt falls short. Health promotion is an imperfect practice, an experience of conflicting urges and varied outcomes. Few of us live consistently healthy lifestyles and those who approach that ideal seem to be engaged in an unhealthy obsession. In short, we are both ambivalent and inconsistent in following the rules of health. As an interviewee told me in the early 1980s, 'there are other things, you know'. It is this entire set of signifying practices – characteristic of our present age – that begs interpretation.

In this chapter, I will consider health promotion as ritual. The ritual is performed in various settings – medical encounters, at work, through the media, advertisements, and, crucially, in everyday conversations among friends, family, and colleagues. I am not suggesting that health promotion is in any sense a formal ritual, only that it shares certain properties with ritual and that the exploration of such similarities opens a window on the symbolic practices undertaken in its name. David Armstrong (1993), for example, has recently taken up an aspect of ritual made popular by anthropologist Mary Douglas (1966, 1982). 'Pollution rituals', including ritual prescriptions and proscriptions that appear to be about hygiene, Douglas asserts, are concerned with 'matter out of place', mixing what should be kept separate, dangerous transgressions of a culture's symbolic order, its most sacred categories. Dangers are ritually featured in order to reassert and reaffirm the proper order of things and thereby control imagined threats to that order. Armstrong constructs a Foucauldian account of 'contemporary hygiene rituals' by focusing on public health discourse. In the twentieth century, Armstrong argues, public health has continually widened the 'unruly regions' of danger, the conditions of life said to adversely affect health. For Armstrong, the expansive identification of danger in the name of health is an opportunity to extend regions of rule. The creation of a 'reflexive subject', conscious of her own health and willing to undertake rational self-surveillance and self-reform is an essential part of a ritual act that serves a disciplinary social order – that is, an order in which new forms of power-knowledge move, more or less continuously, towards incorporating more of life within nets of surveillance and control.

Douglas's notion of 'matter out of place' will be my point of departure as well. However, unlike Armstrong's Foucauldian logic of a continuous 'deployment' of the 'technologies' of power via the ritual identification of 'unruly regions', my approach to ritual emphasises symbolic practices that give expression to – and provide a repertoire for managing – problems which are at once institutional and individual. Structured in domination, rituals work to imprint and legitimate prevailing arrangements, roles, and agendas; they are a means for extending power through incorporating individuals within institutional projects. However, as stylised evocations of experience, rituals also rehearse and provide repertoires for making sense of widely shared conflicts or dilemmas. Rituals are employed as a means for situating individual experience in relation to the experience of others. They provide moral commentary on the conditions and possibilities for a 'good life' and equip people with practical rules (models of and models for) living. Thus, rituals not only extend or revitalise system 'imperatives'; they are also practices the outcomes or significance of which are ambiguous.

Health promotion, including the conflicted and inconsistent adoption or rejection of medical prescriptions and proscriptions, can be understood as a ritual which attends to 'matter out of place': a *contradiction in structure*

– at once material and symbolic – which is the source of a *conflict in experience* for contemporary Americans. Advanced capitalist societies are beset by a contradiction between production and consumption, which in its cultural form defines the parameters for crucial conflicts of individual behaviour, morality and identity (Bell 1976). Health promotion is meaningfully situated on an 'axis of continuity' (Bordo 1993: 142) with the cultural contradictions of capitalism – an axis in that those contradictions and their experiential conflicts 'meet and converge' in health promotion and continuity because the two domains of experience have 'family resemblances and connections'.[1] I am proposing that the collectively fashioned, mutually recognised, and endlessly rehearsed predicaments of attempting to improve health in a world of apparently unhealthy enticements provide a template of meaning for our larger predicament. Injunctions to promote health, ambivalence about the effort, inconsistency in adopting health promoting practices, and moralised talk about matters of health are the ingredients of a highly stylised endeavour to make sense of and come to terms with experiences residing at the centre of contemporary American life. My argument is that the 'ritual' of health promotion can be understood as a pedagogy for living with, managing and commenting upon conflicts intensely felt in a historical period when the relations between their underlying antithetical terms are being reordered. In taking up and dramatising concerns that evoke the unresolvable disorder at the heart of capitalist culture, the discursive field of health promotion furnishes 'key symbols for constructing a framework of meaning – a mythology of our state of being' (Comaroff 1982: 55).

Modern capitalism requires both workers and consumers and therefore two fundamentally different behavioural patterns, two opposing personality structures, indeed, two ethics. What is beneficial to the managers of production – an ethic, personality and behavioural patterns compatible with disciplined work – is ruinous to the managers of consumption. Behaviours and motivations that are optimal for continuous consumption – loosening the restraints of utility, rationality, and self-denial; activating tastes for pleasure, variety, convenience – impede the workplace goals of efficiency, applied effort, compliance, motivated initiative and perseverance. The mandates of production acquire their psychocultural power through a secularised work ethic – an ideal of self-realisation through applied effort, delayed gratification, self-control, self-discipline, and will power. Individuals as workers are expected to control their urges in the name of job performance, productivity and efficiency, expectations that are reinforced by the labour market, the distribution of material and status rewards and the satisfactions of career. For the professional middle class, disciplinary virtues are linked to autonomy and self-direction at work, to the ideals of professionalism and the legitimation of class privilege (Rodgers 1974; Ehrenreich 1989). In the United States, 'middle-class' identity requires that one embrace and conspicuously display the values associated with 'personal responsibility', 'self-determination', and applied effort. Throughout the twentieth century, however, the ethic of work has been joined by an ethic of consumption which, although framed as a complement to work, has also functioned as its symbolic adversary. The ethic of consumption offers an ideal of self-fulfilment through the satisfaction of desires and substitutes an emotional logic of pleasure and individual expression for a practical logic of utility, necessity and achievement. Consumer capitalism relies on a change in cultural psychology – from a modal personality premised on the virtues of denial, delayed gratification, and sobriety to a personality disposed towards fun, immediate gratification, and a propensity to exceed limits (Marchand 1985). Ideals of the 'good life' tied to the American Dream of abundance and the belief in its progressive realisation have steadily displaced or, at the very least, have come to compete with definitions of well-being rooted in work and restrained respectability. These ideals also provide the marks of 'distinction' tied to class identity.

In various forms, the interplay of control and release is certainly characteristic of experience in every culture.[2] In advanced capitalist societies, however, their continuous co-presence is a system requirement. Influenced by sub-cultural values, family history, work experience, class, age and other circumstances, individuals variably internalise each mandate, making them more or less their own. They attempt to fulfil aspirations and demands associated with each. But simultaneous and contradictory internalisations make such efforts problematic. Opposing personality constellations or dispositions and the moralised investments of identity that go with them cannot be neatly segmented by temporal divisions, such as on-the-job and off or week and week-end. Individuals must manage the undertow of each opposing mandate, each a part of the self – the tensions of denial and pleasure; self-control and letting oneself go, fulfilment through work or the fulfilments offered by the purveyors of commodified enjoyments. The social ideals of complimentarity and balance are elusive, subject to tensions and ambivalences which in the context of contemporary experiences of work and consumption are continually aggravated by disappointments, resentments and anxieties related to each sphere.

Moreover, the values, hopes, and desires – indeed, the identities – associated with each side of the contradiction have become the location of a highly politicised struggle as the terms of work and consumption are reordered in the present era. The dramatic reversal in the long wave of postwar expansion, beginning in the United States in the mid-1970s, inaugurated a disciplining of labour (speed up, wage containment, cuts in benefits and social programmes, a marked increase in technological replacement of workers, out-sourcing and 'downsizing') affecting virtually every economic sector and all but the highest levels of employment. The disciplinary mandate has necessarily been internalised as workers scramble for credentials and marketable skills in an effort to find positions safe from the proletarianising tide. In the absence of collective resistance, most individuals have no other choice. Individual strategies for maintaining position appear to be the only hope for meaningful work and for the promise of fulfilment through consumption. Seeking to maintain previous or expected levels of consumption, more Americans are working over-time, taking more than one job and putting more family members in the workforce. Leisure and vacation time have been curtailed (Schor 1992). Declining or stagnating real wages along with increasing job insecurity and forced part-time work have also dictated a disciplining of consumption. The ability to purchase high-cost consumer items, especially a home, has significantly declined, disproportionately affecting the 'baby-boomer' generation. The freeze in wages has been accompanied by steep increases in the costs not only of homes, but also education, automobiles, and medical care (Newman 1993; *The New York Times* 1996).

American workers-consumers must attempt to integrate and balance the opposing behavioural mandates and their internalised ideals; that is, manage the ambivalences, resentments and anxieties they generate. The effort is not new. In the 1950s and 1960s, for example, an expanding economy and advertising industry prompted and scripted desire – an appetite for goods, services, entertainment and leisure among an expanding middle class. Abundance, however, was accompanied by ambivalence: anxieties about 'excess' or becoming too 'soft', on the one hand, resent-ments about 'ascetic' or 'repressive' restraints on behaviour, on the other (Ehrenreich 1989). Likewise, the shift towards more disciplined work and consumption beginning in the mid-1970s fostered a renewed work ethic and a revaluing of discipline and denial in many spheres of American life – a 'new temperance', as sociologist David Wagner (1997) calls it, but not without resentment and anxiety about restraints on the good life as it had come to be lived and desired. For those who have come to expect but are unable to sustain or achieve a given level of consumption or main-tain it only by an expansion of working time, the injunction that a new global economy requires 'realistic' belt-tightening is, at best, partially inter-nalised. The competition to get or keep relatively well-paid and prestigious jobs fuels a psychology of disciplinary retooling, but also resentment, as the effort consumes time, energy and resources, and as the pay-offs for such efforts recede or become more uncertain. Anxiety about job security and income has become more common (Newman 1993). For those who, in Barbara Ehrenreich's (1989) apt phrase, live in 'fear of falling', the imposed constraints are a source of distress. In the midst of a radical restructuring of class relations, the 'cultural contradictions of capitalism' are lived through a prism of heightened tensions and anger.

The contradiction must be managed at the top as well. The same corpo-rate managers who implement the logic of globalisation, seizing the histor-ical moment to restructure the workplace, discipline workers, and reform the polity, must also respond to the new economic realities in the market-place. Advertising, for example, both picks up on the new disciplinary mood, providing images of 'fitness' for a more competitive labour market, and plays off the contradiction, offering commodified releases from the 'stresses' of work and pleasurable compensations for the 'deprivations' of sustained effort. The logic of desire is strengthened by its denial and the managers of consumption, who understand the psychology of the contradiction perfectly well, amplify the tension. As both capital and capitalist state advance the 'common sense' of disciplinary economic restructuring, they must also find ways to sustain consumer confidence and spending.

My argument is that health promotion is a professionally mediated, popular ritual that provides a deeply resonant and believable framework for making sense of and morally managing 'matter out of place'– the contradictory and internalised mandates of work and consumption as these are being reworked in the present era. Metaphorically homologous with the conflict-generating logic of economic restructuring, health promotion can be understood as a ritualised displacement of the middle class's anxious ambivalence about discipline and pleasure onto the medicalised body and the language of somatic well-being. My use of the concept of displacement does not entail the psychoanalytic implication of substitution. Tensions associated with work and consumption are widely apprehended in their own terms (Newman 1993; *The New York Times* 1996). Likewise, health consciousness and health promoting practices reflect diverse concerns and personal goals that are largely explainable by a practical account of the vast increase in communication about health hazards and the dissemination of medical information about how to protect against them. Displacement occurs by way of symbolic articulation and the psycho-cultural capacity for experiencing one thing in terms of another and for one thing to be an expression of another. Health experience and economic experience, I am suggesting, form a metaphorical homology – a parallel set of symbolic oppositions with similar moral and ideological connotations along with homologies of experiential tensions, ambivalence and conflicts. I do not want to overstate the homologies; there are certainly disjunctions as well as resemblances, refractions as well as reflections. Nonetheless, continuities of meaning provide for experiential coherence in ways that are often unconscious. The world of symbols, and therefore practice, is a world in which boundaries are honoured in the breach. Displacement, in this sense, works both ways. If economically structured experience and its symbolic frames inform or model somatic well-being and its symbolic frames, the transference is also reversed. Indeed, it is this circularity or symbolic reverberation that accounts for the cogency of ritual form. Rituals – formal or informal – impart deeper meaning to experience by acting out in one symbolically charged domain the experience of another. Ritual practices are effective, among other reasons, because

they condense and express experience, because they resonate. In identi-
fying and solving problems of health, in expressing commitment,
frustration and ambivalence about the project of health promotion, and in
moralising every step and misstep, middle-class Americans are employing
a highly stylised blend of discursive practices that address matters far
beyond the domain of health.

Certain characteristics of 'health' augment its ritual significance. Health
is a 'key word' in modern cultures, a metaphor rich in its power to signify
a range of meanings and values close to the centre of the symbolic order.
In mobilising anxieties and energies that speak to life and death, social
action in the name of health validates individual worth and autonomy
along with the institutions and forms of knowledge that are employed to
protect and improve the body's health. In our largely secular culture, health
has become a key marker of identity and well-being – a code for signifying persons, qualities, moral capacities and situations. Health reveals the
truth of a body that 'cannot lie' and continues to provide one of modernity's most effective 'natural alibis' for masking the politically protected
privileges of class, race and gender. In the body's health, we search for
and find confirmation of a life well lived or lived poorly, a nature within
that discloses through signs and symptoms individual biographies and
social trajectories. Health points to the order of things and to their disorder,
to transgressive 'dirt' and to purifying acts of restitution.

Pleasure or denial: the ritualisation of ambivalence

> To those of you who may think I always eat right and take the best
> possible care of my body, I say, not so. I am not a fanatic who lives
> by a string of 'thou shalt nots'. And so I must say mea culpa for any
> number of bodily sins to which I am about to confess in the hope
> that they will make you feel more relaxed about your own. After all,
> perfection is stressful, and stress is to be avoided, isn't it? So relax,
> and let's not worry so much about the little transgressions. ... I
> decided my only salvation was to incorporate 'sins' into my normal
> eating plan.
>
> (Jane Brody, *New York Times*'
> Personal Health columnist, 1996: B7)

> In a culture where rationality and self-control are supremely valued,
> a person who affirms that he cannot control himself loses face and is
> ridiculed. However, a person who intends to exert control, but cannot
> despite his best 'will power', is admired and excused for his failing.
> One is only condemned if one does not try.
>
> (Stein 1985: 210)

Jane Brody's 'confession' and Howard Stein's comment about alcohol exemplify a ritual that takes place in a space *between* the symbolic polarities it evokes, for it is there – in the unresolved and necessarily unresolvable space of contradiction – that the structured disorder of contemporary social life resides. Because health promotion is in part an expression of that disorder, not an autonomous subsystem of 'health beliefs', the solutions to problems of health offered by the pole of control or the pole of pleasurable fulfilment and release are elusive. Contemporary social life cannot provide viable solutions for the experiential tensions it creates.

The social impasse becomes a site for imagined solutions or for rehearsing the difficulty or impossibility of achieving them – ambivalent valuations of persons and behaviours in relation to each of the offending polarities, stories and dramatisations, often humorous, of personal binds, accounts of successes and failures in managing daily struggles. The ritual of health promotion is thus a collective act speaking to a collective experience. It sets out the symbolic-practical polarities of conflict, provides guideposts for making sense of their entanglement, improvises rules for practical action, including transgressions, and supplies scripts for moralising various outcomes.

The tidal turn towards discipline, as I argued in 1984, supplied a key motivation for the embrace of a self-practice in which self-control could find everyday expression. Accelerating dramatically in the mid-1970s, health promotion became a middle-class preoccupation which both reflected and reinforced mandates for a more disciplined self. Working on oneself in the name of health replicated the need to recreate oneself in conformity with the rapidly changing requirements for successful social functioning. The 'symbolic capital' necessary for middle-class identity could be demonstrated through efforts aimed at somatic self-improvement. The work ethic found a metaphorical expression in the work of making the body healthy. On the one hand, then, what I am calling the ritual of health promotion assembles and conspicuously displays a set of disciplinary values, practices and individual characteristics professionally encouraged and popularly understood as necessary in order to achieve health – practices that are homologous with structurally generated mandates for discipline and control. Health as a goal, as a state to be achieved, requires a sustained mobilisation of effort. Time must be reallocated, information obtained, practices undertaken. High risk activities must be discontinued or contained. These virtues are situated in relation to what often appears as a negative pole – 'bodily sins', traits that are generally believed to undermine the goal of health.

Yet, the rehearsal and attempted management of structurally generated ambivalences are as much the subject of ritual action as the evocation of preferred 'solutions'. Or, as suggested by Stein, preferred solutions cannot be achieved without incorporating contrary, *positively* valorised or otherwise compelling dispositions that are held to be 'solutions' as well. Health promotion as ritual assimilates and valorises meanings that, on the surface, appear to be negated. The 'positive' virtues of health promotion are revealed as relative rather than essential values. It is not only that 'other things', other notions of well-being, compete with the disciplinary goals of health promotion; not only that the effort falls short for lack of sufficient resolve. Competing definitions of well-being are also refigured as means to health or as simply healthy in themselves – though in complex relation to their somatic effects. The meaning of health and the means to health become integral to ritual performance – the nodes of a moralising discourse in which virtue and vice are engaged in epic struggle. But it is a contest in which juxtaposition, reversals, and masks (virtue appearing as vice and vice as virtue) can change the expected inflections of meaning. Ritual performance, therefore, employs plural and 'flexible' (Martin 1994) meanings of health, multiple conceptions of the causal pathways of disease, and the 'immunological' or other resources that are believed to enhance resistance to disease. The still mysterious but imaginatively rich relations of mind and body are incorporated into a script which, in endlessly playing out the moral tensions between denial and pleasure, must remain improvisational. Both denial and pleasure, the achievements of work and pleasurable fulfilments are essential to the perceived well-being of contemporary Americans. The dual conditions of a 'healthy economy' are replicated in two expressions of 'healthy' disposition. Like the ambivalence generated by opposing economic mandates, middle-class Americans *want both* the 'health' promised by a medicalised regime of self-control and the 'health' of pleasurable escapes from the 'stress' of renunciations.[3]

The drama enacted, however, is not simply the struggle between a medicalised morality of health-promoting habits and competing definitions and epidemiologies of health. The ritual also provides for the containment of health promotion, a repertoire for restricting its imperial or 'healthist' reach. Along with the moralisation of health-promoting choices there appears a heightened moralisation of medically proscribed pleasures. In this aspect of the ritual, health promotion is equated with Puritan denial and violation of health injunctions with the freedom to pursue the good life. Health-endangering enjoyments are experienced and promoted as 'deserved': 'Life is short. Eat what you want' (sign at a roadside diner). In this dimension, the ritual features a contest between a virtuous 'should' and a 'compensatory' or 'rightfully' earned want – one that is also prescriptive – between a self capable of self-denial and a self that should not and ultimately will not be denied.

The entanglement of psychic and symbolic oppositions is taken up by Richard Klein in his provocative reflection on cigarette smoking and the health campaign against it (Klein 1993). Klein explores how the struggle against 'temptations' provokes a reversal of the religiously connoted sign, transforming somatic sins into pleasures of transgression. Both smoking and the resolve to quit smoking activate different parts of the self. One part is invested in the resolution to control the unhealthy habit; the other is derived from the self who is free to choose in the present, to escape any decision made in the past. Unlike yesterday's resolve to act for health, the smoker must confront his temptation in the present:

> For his resolution to help him, [he] would have to re-create in the present all those feelings of anxiety about his health, relive the unhappiness occasioned by social disapproval that he felt yesterday . . . The smoker had believed that [the resolution] would prevent him from smoking in the future, but standing now before the temptation to smoke he realizes that he is as naked and alone as he was before, with no barriers between him and the cigarette, which he can smoke if he wants to. And he does.
>
> (1993: 94)

Klein's theme here is that interdiction incites transgression; the freedom to choose, an expression of self, will be exercised in opposition to social constraint and its internalised voice. Two parts of the self, each representing and expressing a socially valued definition, are locked in struggle. Klein believes the individual can escape this psychocultural ambivalence only by embracing that which is condemned, thereby neutralising the attractive charge of negation and eventually enabling a rational choice for health.

Ritual efficacy relies on repetition as well as the capacity to condense and re-present the engagement of oppositional poles of meaning. In the ritual of health promotion, time is circular; action continually moves from one charged pole to the other. Emotions and self concepts are incited in service of each phase of the ritual – the resolution and its subversion, the freedom to consume what is pleasurable and freely chosen self-denial. The pleasure of violating the interdiction is countered by the pleasure of resolving to abstain and the repeated demonstration of will power. Acting in conformity with the expectations of medicine, friends and family, the health conscious person 'feels good', but, in turn, is excited by transgressing the interdiction – an action that also enjoys the company, understanding, and approval of others. Conversely, each side of the ritual – the denial and the desire to escape the denial – also arouses feelings of 'anguish'. Denial in our consumer culture cannot be extracted from a sense of deprivation and yet the freedom to indulge activates, in the very moment of pleasure, consciousness of the interdiction and the consequences of its violation. Risk-taking is, thus, the mirror of health promotion – doubly charged – an effervescence of pleasure-pain – in short, ritualised ambivalence. Howard Stein argues that something similar is at work with alcohol:

> Behind the proscription lies the prescription; beneath the admonition against the behavior lies the tacit injunction to go ahead and engage in the behavior. The plea for inhibition or restraint vies with the command to indulge. Taboo contends with the wish to which the repetition of the taboo draws attention . . . That which is forbidden is most attractive.
>
> (Stein 1985: 207)

Transgression is linked with command. The 'autonomous' individual *may* disobey the injunction not to drink; the scripted occupant of a role *must* disobey. The 'sovereign' subject is capable of renouncing alcohol; the socialised subject is required to seek restitution. In a culture that is fundamentally ambivalent about alcohol – one of this culture's chief means for 'relinquishing control' and 'exceeding limits' (Stein 1985: 207–8) – interdiction kindles desire while indulgence strengthens taboo. They are part of a single system – one, I am arguing, that is structurally sustained by the contradictory mandates of contemporary capitalism. The assertion of control 'can be seen not only as the opposite of loss of control but as a *stage* in its loss' (Stein 1985: 211). Control is the necessary condition for the loss of control, its *legitimation*, just as the loss of control sets in motion required restitutions.

As health-conscious participants endlessly re-enact their conflicts of 'compliance' and 'resistance', 'restitution' and 'revolt', in relation to the mandates for discipline and denial, they create themselves as kinds of persons that are recognised and valued and that provide a position from which they can act and speak with social authority. First, participants assert their individual autonomy in the freedom to choose one's pleasures and an equal assertion of freedom to deny pleasure and command one's own destiny in the name of health. The two freedoms are constituent of modern selfhood. Second, however, individuals are not free to do as they please: each choice is infused with moral significance; one must exercise freedom 'responsibly'. Identities are formed and re-formed, valued and re-valued, in relation to shifting requirements and expectations. Moral (and physical, psychological, spiritual) jeopardy is represented, on one side, as 'a failure of will' (Sedgwick 1992). Instances of loss of control raise a moral question and are carefully evaluated by self and others. These are often nuanced accounts of personal histories and social contexts. 'Failure of will' also calls up its nemesis – an overly controlled self who cannot enjoy life and who *pathologically* pursues the cultural ideal. Loss of control in this frame takes on different moral connotations. The self that must be distanced from conventional images of 'dependency', 'addiction', or 'female voraciousness' (Bordo 1993) is countered by a self that must be distanced from the extremity of renunciation or the dangers of obsession (Backett 1992). Addiction is stigmatised as the disease of loss of control but it is also normalised by application to a broad range of behaviours and by playful self-ascription. 'I'm addicted to . . .' has become a statement about desire, an assertion/confession of the desiring self. People with 'no addictions' are thought to be 'addicted to perfection'. Anorexia and obesity point to the perils of each pole and bulimia to their dangerous oscillation but in more moderate forms they become expressions of healthy dispositions or cycles of 'loosening-' and 'tightening-up'. In these ways, moral dangers are domesticated and the *order* of 'healthy balance' repeatedly asserted.

Thus, the condition of autonomy and freedom in health is a continuous moral management of the 'inner' tendencies towards the 'extremity' represented by each opposing pole of identity. In proclaiming and *occasionally* following the rules of health, we recreate ourselves in the heroic mode of overcoming our inner weaknesses. As cultural historian Phillip Rieff (1966: 72) might say, we are involved in a kind of 'commitment therapy', a 'mystical' union with the 'saving agency' of discipline and control and 'the community that stands behind it'. Stein (1985) refers to 'ritual desecration' (of alcoholism and the alcoholic) and 'restitution'. But at the same time, is there not also a ritual desecration of the health or fitness 'fanatic'? Amendatory binges? Deserved rewards for strenuous efforts undertaken? Restitution for loss of pleasure? We also embrace, I am suggesting, a therapeutics of compensation (Marchand 1985), letting go, putting aside 'unhealthy' interdictions and discontents as we 'learn' how to enjoy life in the moment. And in professing the health of pleasure, we thereby also assert an identity that has become essential to our socially recognised and supported freedom to pursue the good life.

Health consciousness and action, I am proposing, is a site for reflexive commentary, providing an opportunity – in the company of others – for commenting and acting upon diverse and opposing definitions of well-being. Drawing on widely shared notions and flexible repertoires, the ritual of health promotion provides a map for evaluating self and others. In managing health risks, ritual participants are managing the meanings and emotions aroused by symbolically charged – because structurally pivotal – domains of experience. The ritual attends to matter out of place. The 'unruly region' requiring ritual management is not simply the disorderly 'pollution' of health-denying pleasure. Rather, the focus of attention is the unresolvable instability of the conflict between denial and pleasure, the tensed vacillation of identity. Neither side of the conflict can be embraced without raising the intimation of psychic costs and moral danger. The embrace of one value without the 'balance' of the other endangers the conflicting imperatives of behaviour and identity generated by the contemporary social and economic order. The 'reflexive subject' of health promotion is an individual who must be willing to undertake self-reform but at the same time rationally manage the experiential conflicts produced by that reform (Martin 1994). The 'imperative of health' is in maintaining the healthy 'centre' – even, or especially, as the imposed and internalised mandates for control move the normative centre towards one pole of the ambivalence. In that movement, there must be a cultivation of 'exceptions', limited by time, scope, or magnitude, but affirmed or 'forgiven' as necessary (that is, 'healthy') correctives to excessive virtue. These remissions become the essential ingredients of 'stress management'. The psychic costs and resentments about controls and renunciations are addressed through their repeated and supported violation.

Thus, the contradictory terms of the social and cultural order are precariously sustained even as they are reordered towards the pole of control. The healthy self is likely to become more disciplined while continuing to assert her freedom to consume, relax, and have fun. Anxiety and resentment are momentarily managed both by the assertion of control *and* by the continued 'resistance' to health norms in the name of pleasure. The antinomies of capitalist culture are bridged in a ritual which, though momentarily subordinating the enjoyment of one to the virtue of the other, infuse both – in a putative relation of 'balance' – with the sign of health. Never mind that the bridge is precarious to stand on; that is our abiding predicament.

Conclusion

What are the ideological implications of the ritual of health promotion? Performed in the space between the crucial metaphors it mobilises, the ritual provides a model of and model for our contemporary ambivalence. It is a way for an experiential conflict emblematic of the sociocultural order and its present reordering to be re-presented and individually managed – not resolved but managed. In the name of health, dominant institutions extend surveillance and enforce compliance for a variety of disciplinary agendas. Individuals, also in the name of health, voluntarily comply by adopting a more disciplinary approach to daily life. On the other hand, health promotion situates compliance in relation to what is universally acknowledged to be inevitable – and, more to the point, desirable, socially supported, and structurally mandated – non-compliance. Thus, it is also a ritual about a self that *must* seek its own fulfilment. The reformation of self towards control inevitably incites its opposite and, further, could not be achieved without the continued expression and legitimation of a self that can no longer live in denial. Likewise, the continuing and necessary formation of a self compatible with consumption necessarily incites its opposite and also could not be secured without its disciplinary containment. Participation in a ritual that emphasises control and allows for its conspicuous display legitimises the promise, underneath a necessity, that one can have it both ways. As long as individuals comply with disciplinary norms, that is, as long as they make a good enough effort, the pursuit of pleasures and giving into indulgences take on the connotation of an earned reward; having conspicuously asserted the intention, the health-conscious individual is 'admired and excused for his failing' (Stein 1985: 210). Thus, ritual repetition sustains the prevailing categories by naturalising their social logic in the domain of somatic insecurity and medicalised well-being.

Yet, the symbolic reformation of contradictory system imperatives cannot possibly go smoothly. Unresolvable within the structured culture of contemporary capitalism, anxiety, ambivalence and resentment will remain unresolved in the ritualised expression of the contradiction. 'Balance' is ephemeral and unstable in a society that mandates both modal personalities and yet demands their radical reordering. 'Proper order' – the learned capacity to straddle happily and healthfully both mandates, to manage ambivalence, to reside in the healthy centre, or in Emily Martin's (1994) words, to achieve an adaptive 'flexibility' – will not likely be achieved. Matter will remain out of place. The chaotic nature of contemporary social life will continually provoke new ritual formulations, including creative inflections of meaning, for addressing the experiential consequences and, perhaps, on occasion, for identifying and redressing their structural sources.

Deborah Lupton (1995: 131–57), who also considers the problem of ambivalence to disciplinary mandates of health promotion, frames her discussion by the concept of resistance. I do not deny her point. Modern individuals, suspicious of authority in general, do not take kindly to moral regimes that appear to be externally imposed, even those camouflaged by biomedical naturalism. Moreover, ambivalence towards medical authority is not only a matter of scepticism towards expertise or hostility towards governmental and corporate intrusions into 'private matters'; there is also resentment about the 'bad news' of medical knowledge. Many people adopt a 'too much to worry about' or even an 'I'd rather not know' response; and most only selectively follow medical advice (Crawford 1984; Backett 1992). The continuous stream of new findings about risks poses a challenge to life as presently lived. The message that there is hell to pay for a consumer lifestyle is not welcomed. Moreover, medical 'bad news' is consumed on top of what may be experienced as a litany of such messages about the good life – limits to growth, environmental damage, declining work ethic, declining standards, breakdown of traditional values. I imagine that, for many, the mandates for health promotion sound too much like the disciplinary mandates of a downsizing economy, a perception that would partially explain the more extensive resistance to those mandates among working-class people subjected to external disciplines and controls. Further, even though support for government action to reduce exposure to environmental or occupational hazards and concerns about lifestyle and health frequently reinforce each other, there are certainly people for whom resentment towards corporations or government and/or a sense of pervasive and unavoidable threat are sufficient grounds for rejecting disciplinary lifestyle changes (Douglas and Wildavsky 1982).

I am arguing, however, that health promotion, viewed from the perspective of ritual, incorporates from the beginning ambivalences about medical prescriptions and proscriptions and the cultural metaphors employed through its discourse. Rather than the 'non-discursive or unconscious' sources of 'resistance' emphasised by Lupton, I am suggesting (without dismissing those sources) that both conformity with and resistance to health promotion mandates are essential to the ritual performance. What may appear to be resistance and feel like resistance may emerge from the dialectic of a social contradiction of which health discourse is an expression. Health promotion cannot be adequately conceived, as the Foucauldians would have it, as only a 'deployment' of disciplinary 'technologies' against which 'resistances' spring up. In the play of compliance and resistance, the conflicting subjectivities (identities, perceptions, practices, dispositions) required by the existing social order and its present reordering are recruited and recreated as healthy virtues, unhealthy extremities or, in the hopeful imagery of balance, a healthy achievement. Resistance may also be structured in domination.

Where does power reside in such a conception? What becomes of agency? Is there a capacity to act in ways that are not simply reflective of discursive 'regimes'? I am not suggesting that individuals are determined – mere objects of the disciplining and pleasuring mandates of contemporary capitalism or fully scripted actors in a ritual performance 'directed' to achieve political effects. In the assertion of our freedom, we sometimes 'deservedly', sometimes defiantly or with the delight of disobedience, and sometimes with anguish, violate the injunctions of our 'doctors'. Occasionally, or in partial and subtle ways, the effect may be emancipatory. I am arguing, however, that these mandates are internalised and perpetuated as ethics and that they become 'moral sources of the self' (Taylor, 1989). The struggle for alternative perceptions and meanings in the life-worlds of individuals – and there are many[4] – must contend with the meaningful cognitions that are structured by prevailing economic, political, and cultural discourses. The ideological significance, let alone motivations, of symbolic practices are notoriously enigmatic. Signs are fluid and reversible and rituals can be put to transformative ends. Yet, surely, in consuming so much of our conscious attention and effort for the attainment of well-being, in moralising its uneven achievements among individuals and social groups – that is, in providing a natural alibi (the sanction of health or illness) for problems and resentments that are social and cultural – the ritual of health promotion provides symbolic substance to mandates that are designed to achieve the well-being of capital. Brokered by expert authority and yet 'chosen' by individuals, the ritual becomes a lifelong project, gaining power in repetition. If alternative, more emancipatory (healthful?) conceptions of self-control and discipline, release and pleasure are to emerge and find in culture sustainable support, including the achievement of a 'healthy' combination of their various possibilities, the 'surplus repression' and the 'repressive desublimation' of contemporary capitalism will require more direct interrogation (Marcuse 1955). Middle-class Americans are preoccupied instead with an individualised and medicalised somatic practice, when as Lewis Thomas put it, 'just outside, the whole of society is coming undone' (Thomas 1979: 46).

Acknowledgements

Thanks to Bill Arney, Sam Parker, Ike Balbus, and the editors for their helpful comments.

References

Armstrong, D. (1993) 'Public health spaces and the fabrication of identity', *Sociology* 27(3): 393–410.

Backett, K. (1992) 'Taboos and excesses: lay health moralities in middle class families', *Sociology of Health and Illness* 14: 255–74.

Bell, D. (1976) *The Cultural Contradictions of Capitalism*, New York: Basic Books.

Bordo, S. (1993) *Unbearable Weight: Feminism, Western Culture, and the Body*, Berkeley, CA: University of California.

Brody, J. (1996) *New York Times*, 31 July.

Bury, M. (1994) 'Health promotion and lay epidemiology: a sociological view', *Health Care Analysis* 2: 23–30.

Comaroff, J. (1982) 'Medicine: symbol and ideology', in P. Wright and A. Treacher (eds) *The Problem of Medical Knowledge*, Edinburgh: Edinburgh University Press.

Crawford, R. (1984) 'A cultural account of health: control, release and the social body', in J. McKinlay (ed.) *Issues in the Political Economy of Health Care*, New York: Tavistock.

Davison, C., Davey Smith, G. and Frankel, S. (1991) 'Lay epidemiology and the prevention paradox', *Sociology of Health and Illness* 13: 1–19.

Davison, C., Frankel, S. and Davey Smith, G. (1992) 'The limits of lifestyle: reassessing "fatalism" in the popular culture of illness prevention', *Social Science and Medicine* 34: 675–85.

Douglas, M. (1966) *Purity and Danger*, London: Routledge.

—— (1982) *Natural Symbols*, New York: Pantheon.

Douglas, M. and Wildavsky, A. (1982) *Risk and Culture*, Berkeley, CA: University of California.

Ehrenreich, B. (1989) *Fear of Falling*, New York: Pantheon.

Klein, R. (1993) *Cigarettes are Sublime*, London: Duke University Press.

Lupton, D. (1995) *The Imperative of Health: Public Health and the Regulated Body*, London: Sage Publications.

Marchand, R. (1985) *Advertising the American Dream*, Berkeley, CA: University of California.

Marcuse, H. (1955) *Eros and Civilization*, Boston: Beacon Press.

Martin, E. (1994) *Flexible Bodies*, Boston: Beacon Press.

Newman, K. (1993) *Declining Fortunes: the Withering of the American Dream*, New York: Basic Books.

The New York Times (1996) *The Downsizing of America*, New York: Times Books.

Rieff, P. (1966) *The Triumph of the Therapeutic*, New York: Harper and Row.

Rodgers, D. (1974) *The Work Ethic in Industrial America: 1850–1920*, Chicago: University of Chicago.

Schor, J. (1992) *The Overworked American: the Unexpected Decline of Leisure*, New York: Basic Books.

Sedgwick, E. K. (1992) 'Epidemics of the will', in J. Crary and S. Kwinter (eds) *Incorporations*, New York: Urzone.

Stein, H. (1985) 'Alcoholism as metaphor in American culture' *Ethos* 13(3): 195–235.

Taylor, C. (1989) *Sources of the Self*, Cambridge: Harvard University Press.

Thomas, L. (1979) *The Medusa and the Snail*, New York: Bantam.

Wagner, D. (1997) *The New Temperance*, Boulder, CO: Westview Press.

Chapter 12

Drugs and risk

Developing a sociology of HIV risk behaviour

Graham Hart and Simon Carter

Introduction

The postwar period has seen a change in the focus of socio-cultural theory from identity formation being defined by relation to processes of production (e.g. job, profession or class) to a situation where the processes of consumption are often considered to be of more importance (Featherstone 1991; Bauman 1992). Consumption, as used here, is not simply concerned with the purchase of material commodities but refers also to broader 'lifestyle' choices and practices including ideas, beliefs, attitudes and desires relating to obtaining and making use of symbolic goods. In other words the social meanings which become attached to commodities are seen as important in shaping individuals' identities. It has been argued that an understanding of these developments in socio-cultural theory is of importance for two reasons: first, the design and delivery of interventions to modify peoples' risk behaviours (such as health promotion) will be more adequate if such strategies connect with the meanings shaping peoples social identities and lifestyle choices (Lupton 1994); and, second, there are well established associations between many forms of individual consumption and health risks (for instance smoking and drinking).

This chapter is concerned to describe the relationship between drug consumption, a specific life-threatening disease associated with the injection of illicit drugs (HIV/AIDS) and how we might understand better and therefore intervene to modify the social context and social relations of drug consumption to reduce its attendant health risks. We do this by undertaking analysis at three levels of society: the macro-social, meso-social and micro-social. The chapter begins with a brief overview of this approach, continues with an example of how a recent drug scare raises a range of issues that are important for our understanding of drug consumption, and then provides a social analysis of drug culture at these three levels of society. Such an approach offers an understanding of risk practices that can help with the development and evaluation of preventative programmes designed to attenuate the negative social and health effects of this form of illicit consumption.

Current paradigms of non-medical drug consumption

The importance, to socio-cultural theory, of the emerging analytical focus on consumption remains to be seen and is still the subject of debate (Edgell *et al.* 1996). However there is one particular class of consumption which has a very long association, at least at the level of the popular representation, with identity formation – namely recreational drug use. The 'junkie', 'dope fiend', 'speed freak' or 'alcoholic' are all recognisable categories of identity which are based on the person's perceived consumption of particular substances. Moreover, such constructions of identity are seen as totally saturating all aspects of a person's personality (and this is reflected in popular sayings such as 'never trust a junkie' or 'once an alcoholic, always an alcoholic'). Such categorisations implicitly define an individual's personality as an empty vessel to be filled by the features, demands and attributes of their drug of choice and any risk choices they may make will follow a pharmacokinetic rather than any social or cultural logic.

While such views of non-medical drug consumers still enjoy a widespread currency (Stepney 1996) there is also a relatively long history of social research into drug consumption, and its related risks, which reveals a more complex picture. For example, Howard Becker's now classic study of marijuana consumers in the 1950s uncovered an intricate culture of users with their own associated rituals and shared symbolic meanings. Someone becomes a marijuana user by transforming a set of 'vague impulses and desires' into a pleasurable activity and this is a socially *learned* process (Becker 1963). A similar situation exists for all drugs (legal or not) consumed for recreational purposes. Such consumption exists in a cultural context in which social meanings, rituals and rules have to be learned and negotiated. Some of the rituals and rules around drug use enjoy a formal legal sanction but many more are the result of locally negotiated cultural meanings. Any understanding of the risk behaviours connected with drug consumption has to take account of this cultural background if it is to help reduce the potential harm that can follow drug use.

One way to approach a sociological examination of drug consumption and risk is to carry out an analysis at three levels of society: the macro- or supra-structural level, the mid- or meso-structural level and finally the micro-social level. Previously used primarily to understand sexual risk behaviour and HIV infection (Hart and Flowers 1996) this approach can also contribute to our understanding of the relationship between drug use and risk. We could illustrate this by considering the case of alcohol consumption. At the macro level most cultures seek to modify risk behaviour by strictly regulating alcohol consumption using formal laws. These may specify places where alcoholic beverages can be used and purchased or activities that are prohibited after ingesting alcohol (such as driving). In addition the macro level of analysis would take account of economic factors such as the way the industry promotes products or how different socio-economic groups consume different types and amounts of alcohol. At the meso level it would be important to look at institutional controls – such as how different organisations police the formal laws or how professional bodies deliver health messages or services. At the micro level we would need to consider how group use of alcohol is a feature of many human interactions and how these are regulated by local social rituals and rules.

Alcohol, in many countries, is legally sanctioned; however, consumption of state authorised drugs is not the only source of health problems and risk. On a global basis one form of predominantly illicit consumption has had dire health consequences, primarily because of its role in the transmission of HIV and other infections, and this is the use of opiate and stimulant drugs. Such drugs are not necessarily of themselves a risk factor for HIV infection. Some researchers have found an association between drug use and unprotected sexual intercourse, and suggest that one of the effects of such use is disinhibition in relation to sex (Klee 1990). However, this has not been demonstrated to be a causal link; people who are exposed to multiple risks, or engage in a constellation of risk behaviours, may do so because behaviours happen to coincide in particular cultural contexts, and so drug use alone may not 'cause' unprotected sex. For instance, in an analysis of the putative disinhibitory role of alcohol in gay men's sexual behaviour, no relationship between alcohol use and unsafe sex could be demonstrated (Weatherburn *et al.* 1993). It may simply be that the venues where alcohol is consumed are also the places where people looking for sexual contact are likely to meet.

However, where there does exist a clear causal relationship is in the route of drug administration and HIV infection. The shared use of injection equipment or drug paraphernalia by an HIV positive person with other people can result in micro-injections of serum infected with live virus. Not only is this a significant route of HIV infection in its own right but, as many drug users are also sexually active, this can be an important path by which HIV infection can be passed to non-drug users. There is then a direct link between particular forms of drug consumption and infection with a life threatening pathogen. When other types of consumption are linked, often through less durable scientific evidence, to the spread of dangerous pathogens it is not unusual to see declines in consumption and action to limit harm. The spread of HIV by drug consumption appears more complex than this: intravenous consumption of drugs continues and even limited measures to reduce the harm associated with HIV spread can arouse controversy. So what is special about drug consumption that makes risk reduction problematic? The key questions in relation to drug consumption and risk of HIV infection, therefore, relate to cultures of drug use and the availability of sterile injecting equipment.

Yet despite being well into the second decade of AIDS, the under-standing of risk in relation to drug use and HIV infection is still dominated by two other paradigms. These are epidemiological and social psycho-logical. Epidemiology was the first biomedical science to recognise the syndrome of diseases constituting AIDS, and it soon became apparent that these were secondary to a primary infection with an unidentified pathogen, now known as HIV infection. With the identification of HIV antibodies and the availability from 1985 of the HIV antibody test, the sophistica-tion and clarity of epidemiological studies was such that infection could be demonstrated to be present in populations of intravenous drug users around the world. This epidemiological information proved invaluable to prevention programmes, in that absence of infection or low prevalence could be shown to be extremely short-lived if the behaviours associated with transmission – unprotected sexual intercourse, sharing of used needles and syringes – were in place.

In terms of social psychology, models of health behaviour were already in the process of development when HIV infection was recognised to be the cause of AIDS. That the primary transmission modes of the virus depend upon human behaviours and interactions means that risk of expo-sure to HIV can be understood in terms of human agency and action, and therefore amenable to analysis using a social psychological paradigm. Thus, the central tenet of individual decision-making (premised upon human volition and the ability to determine personal risk exposure) led to the wide scale employment of theories like the Health Belief Model (Rosenstock 1974) or the Theory of Reasoned Action (Fishbein and Ajzen 1975) in attempting to understand HIV-risk related behaviours. Yet, the psycho-social factors which structure these models have been shown to have, at best, limited predictive validity (Flowers *et al.* 1997) and, at worst, rely on naïve models of human identity and action (Carter 1997a).

Both epidemiological and social psychological perspectives have informed HIV prevention, and drugs-related harm minimisation pro-grammes throughout the world. Although directed at individuals, and aiming to change individual behaviour, these approaches are not entirely asocial. The demographic data collected by epidemiological studies, and recognition of the role of peers in influencing choices in social psycho-logical models, demonstrate that the distribution of HIV and AIDS is both socially patterned and subject to local and immediate social context. Yet, despite these elements of the social at the heart of HIV transmission, there has been concern expressed regarding the focus of these theories on the individual and his/her health 'choices', and the paucity of systematic inves-tigations of the social determinants of risk exposure (Bloor 1995; Hart and Boulton 1995; Parker 1994; Rhodes 1995).

The advent of the HIV epidemic is one reason why there has been an increased interest in risk and risk behaviours within the sociology of health and illness. Much of this interest has sought to understand HIV exposure from a sociological perspective. The remainder of this chapter describes sociological perspectives that have been used to understand the risks associated with the consumption of intravenous drug use and HIV infection, and determines the extent to which there exists a sufficiently cohesive body of literature to inform future research on, and prevention programmes for, drug-related behaviours associated with HIV.

Understanding drug use: the example of Ecstasy

Recent years have seen substantial media interest in the drug Ecstasy (MDMA), or more particularly its life-threatening potential. The unfortunate parents of young people who have died after taking Ecstasy are presented to the nation to plead with those who use, or may be tempted to use, this drug not to do so. By way of contrast there are those who compare the number of deaths from Ecstasy with the morbidity and mortality associated with legal drug use (cigarettes, and alcohol), both of which, it is claimed, take many more lives than Ecstasy. The problem with this kind of 'debate' and many other discussions associated with illicit drug use is the absence of a clear set of understandings and agreements regarding the parameters of discussion. For example, post mortems of young people who have reportedly died of the complications of Ecstasy use have found evidence of multiple drug combinations, rather than 'pure' MDMA. It is unknown how many, if any, deaths have been caused by reactions to pharmaceutically supplied MDMA. Similarly, it is unknown what, even in fairly pure form, are the health consequences of short and long term use of Ecstasy. This renders comparisons with alcohol-related morbidity and mortality difficult, if not impossible.

A number of sociological points can be made about Ecstasy which also apply to other aspects of illicit drug use. The first is that there are clearly *cultures* of drug use, with the use of substances being patterned by class, ethnicity, and social context. Ecstasy is a 'dance' drug, consumed by young men and women, and experienced with other young people in a shared culture also involving the consumption of music, dress, commercial clubs and other recreational drugs. The next is that drug use generates multiple *impacts*, notably in relation to health and health care systems, the social circumstances of those who use or are indirectly affected by drug use, and the publicity given to the negative aspects of use, such as those associated with crime, through the media and in political discussion. Finally, there are competing *explanations* or accounts of the causes and consequences of drug use, which include the pharmacokinetics of drug effects, the psychology of addiction or dependency, and the sociology and demography of use. The latter emphasise the highly patterned and discrete nature of drug usage. Indeed recent studies suggest the use of 'dance' drugs among particular groups of young people is both widespread and becoming normalised – to the extent that there is a considerable overlap between the legal and illegal economies of consumption (Measham *et al.* 1994; Parker and Measham 1994).

Employing Ecstasy as an example of illicit drug use allows us to see the shared attributes of any discussion of a range of drugs. However, as a relatively 'new' drug, at least in its current appeal, little is known of its health sequelae, except that public 'expert' disagreements about the safety of the drug are a frequent feature of media reports. The same cannot be said for heroin use, the effects of which have been well described since opiates were used both socially and for medical purposes in the last century (Berridge and Edwards 1987). It is the injection of heroin or indeed any drug for non-medical purposes that has recently been of interest, particularly in the use of equipment shared with one or more partners. This includes damage to veins as a result of repeated use, and the transmission of specific blood-borne pathogens, including the life-threatening diseases of Hepatitis B and HIV. We will now go on to consider in more detail the consumption of illicit drugs by injection. Later sections will consider the meso and microanalysis of risk and drug consumption; however, we will begin with a consideration of macro-social analyses of drug cultures.

Macro-social analyses

The analysis of risk, at the macro-social level, has been influenced by Ulrich Beck's *Risk Society* (1992). To determine whether this is useful for an understanding of risk and drug consumption we need to explore briefly Beck's writings on risk. According to Beck, society is in a period of transition not towards postmodernity but to a second modernity in which the logic of industrial production and distribution (i.e. wealth) is becoming increasingly tied to the logic of 'the social production of risk'. In the first modernity, concerns focused on the distribution of wealth, but as material inadequacy is reduced we move to a more complex modernity, or 'risk society', where consideration has to be given to the distribution of risks – a move from class position to risk position, from underproduction of goods to overproduction of harm. These are qualitatively different conditions. In the former, one is dealing with desirable items in scarcity but conversely, in the latter, one has an undesirable abundance. The traditional inequalities of strata and class in the West are broken up by a 'boomerang effect' in which 'sooner or later the risks also catch up with those who produce or profit from them' (Beck 1992: 37). Ultimately, this boomerang effect generates a 'dynamics that destroys boundaries' (Beck 1992: 47) because risks such as radioactivity or pesticides have no respect for class position or national boundaries in this new modernity.

Within this 'new society' a person's risk cognition is strongly mediated by the consumption of expert knowledge which is both external to the individual and socially disputable. The externalisation of risk knowledge, into the hands of risk experts, is a social process thwarted by public disputes and disagreements between the experts and the public and between the experts themselves. This leads to a situation in which the very divide between expert and non-expert becomes turbid and amorphous. This results in what Beck characterises as a learning process in which victims no longer believe risks to be acts of fate. Instead, these people become 'small, private alternative experts in the risks of modernisation'(Beck 1989: 61).

An example of this could be the situation described by Patton (1990) concerning the strategies adopted by people living with AIDS. Arguably, in the greater part of this century people suffering from illness were largely silenced by the knowledge formations which establish an unbreachable boundary around scientific medical wisdom. However the advent of the AIDS epidemic has led activists themselves, at least within the United States, to gain considerable medical proficiency. The circulation of newsletters and self-help books provides information about clinical trials, including criteria of inclusion and exclusion, to those people living with AIDS. In addition, the 'underground' consumption of experimental therapeutic drugs has become established in some communities. As Patton says 'it is the medical knowledge of the person living with HIV/AIDS ... which has become today's ticket to experimental treatments' (Patton 1990: 52). A similar argument is put forward by Anthony Giddens (1991) when he writes of the reflexivity of modernity. Within the late modern period there is a 're-appropriation' of expert knowledge by individuals who have undergone a process of 're-skilling' and 'empowerment'. Giddens (1991: 141) illustrates this by citing the medical example of a patient suffering from back pain who can choose between the consumption of a range of traditional and alternative therapies.

The problem with these accounts is that the process (of reflexive modernisation) that they describe may only be found in limited cultural contexts. Specific and discrete risks may become politicised by certain social actors – but how far this is applicable to understandings of either HIV risk in general or intravenous drug use in particular must be seriously questioned. Some sufferers of back pain, or some groups of people infected with HIV, may have the cultural and economic capital to use reflexively and re-appropriate expert knowledge but, as we will show, for the majority of intravenous drug users, and people with HIV infection, the scope for therapeutic 'choice', 'empowerment' or 'reflexivity' is severely limited.

To use Beck's words, there may be many new types of risk which display a 'boomerang' effect that 'destroys boundaries'; however, HIV risk is not one of them. Worldwide, HIV is found in groups that have been marginalised either culturally or economically and often both. At the macro-social level of the political economy of HIV we find that globally AIDS is a disease of both relative and absolute poverty (Altman 1995). There are more cases *per capita* in the world's poorest economies than in the richest; within both developed and developing countries the majority of people with HIV and AIDS are the poorest members of those societies (Mann *et al.* 1992). In the USA and the countries of Western Europe, drug dependency is primarily a problem of lower socio-economic groups, and injecting drug users and their heterosexual partners now constitute the majority of people with HIV infection. In developing countries HIV is associated with poverty in both urban and rural communities and is both a heterosexual and parenterally transmitted disease. Its spread is associated with war, famine, societal breakdown, debt-crises, political change (Low *et al.* 1993) and the more mundane cross-border movements of peoples in search of greater economic security.

It is clear, therefore, from a passing acquaintance with the demography that HIV/AIDS, as with so many life-threatening infectious diseases, is patterned by economic and social inequality. What in western cultures are considered to be the most individual and private of domains – sexuality and drug consumption – are in fact subject to social and economic forces beyond the immediate control of individuals, local communities and, often, nation states. Gillies *et al.* (1996) clearly illustrate that, in many developing countries, industrialisation has led to shifts in systems of labour, caused migration (rural to urban) and homelessness. This, in turn, has led to social upheaval which impacts upon the breakdown of social mores regarding sexual behaviour and drug use, thereby facilitating the transmission of HIV.

In terms of the *cultures* of injecting drug use, certain shared features are apparent, even on a global scale. Despite media interest in the heroin use of the rich and famous, it is mostly in poor communities throughout the world that heroin is both smoked and injected. This includes users in the housing schemes of Glasgow, the streets of New York and in the northern hill tribes of Thailand (Des Jarlais *et al.* 1993). Poverty and deprivation provide the ideal conditions for a drug that generates feelings of warmth and contentment and, prior to dependence, even euphoria. In the developed world heroin use is associated with inner cities, high unemployment and extremely poor housing (Parker *et al.* 1988). In those developing countries where it is prevalent, notably in South East Asia, whilst drug use is a feature of city life, it is just as likely to be seen in rural areas, particularly those in which people are engaged in subsistence farming.

There are, however, no inherent qualities of cultures at risk of heroin epidemics. An often unconsidered feature are the global factors affecting the consumption and availability of drugs. Heroin use spread rapidly in

British inner city areas in the late 1970s and early 1980s because of the availability of cheap, plentiful and good quality heroin. Availability is clearly an issue in other parts of the world. The epidemic of cocaine and crack-cocaine use in the United States is intimately related to its proximity to and political and economic links with South American countries such as Colombia. The location of Thailand's northern hills tribes in one corner of South East Asia's golden triangle of heroin production is evidently a factor in the high local prevalence of use. Indeed, we know from the molecular epidemiology of HIV infection that in Thailand there are two quite distinct variations of the virus, associated with quite different sources of primary infection. Thus, HIV sub-type E is to be found in the country's commercial sex workers (reflecting Thailand's historical position as a western sex tourist destination) whilst sub-type B of the virus is more prevalent in Thai drug users (suggesting that this infection is associated with other geographical and biological routes of transmission) (Quinn 1996).

The global economies of heroin supply and consumption also have consequences for risk practices. In most western countries heroin, on the street, is an extremely valuable commodity, costing between 4 to 20 times more than gold (Grund 1993). But as a commodity it does not follow the classical laws of consumption in economics – demand for heroin is relatively inelastic and rises in price do not translate into falls in demand in a linear way. Rather, changes in availability and price lead to changes in risks practices. Earlier it was suggested that there was an increase in heroin use in UK cities because it was available cheaply, and the quality was good. Although initially heroin was smoked, any decrease in availability and the consequent increase in price, is often associated with more 'economic' usage of the drug, notably by injecting (Parker *et al.* 1988). On the other hand, in a western country such as the Netherlands, intravenous drug use is relatively rare with less than 25 per cent heroin users injecting. This could be explained by the stability of the Dutch illegal drug market with high levels of supply and moderate prices (Grund 1993).

Thus, at the macro-social level, the global problem of HIV infection and drug consumption is associated with economic relations between nations, inequalities and social conditions in particular countries, and factors such as production, export and availability at the local level. What can be done to attenuate the health effects of these larger social and economic processes?

Meso-social considerations

The meso-social level of social structure is the organisational level. This can be formal organisations, such as organised religion (churches), industries (individual businesses), education (schools, colleges) and health care (clinics, hospitals). The meso-social can also refer to social organisation, such as socio-political groupings (e.g. the *junkiebonden* of Amsterdam, who argued for increased availability of injecting equipment to prevent Hepatitis B). How does the meso-social, whether formal or social organisational, affect risk? The examples given above of the way in which the macro-social context can impact upon risk – through inter- and intranational economic forces, and the availability of drugs – are represented at the meso-social level through organisational constraints and opportunities. For drug users, this means organisational responses to the harm consequent upon drug use, notably through treatment, prevention and harm-minimisation programmes.

An example of the latter is the organised provision of needle and syringe exchange. For instance, in Edinburgh the shared use of injecting equipment in city housing schemes was followed by epidemics of Hepatitis B and HIV (Robertson *et al.* 1985). It was this that first alerted General Practitioners and Public Health doctors to the widespread consumption of drugs by injection. The change from smoking to injecting of heroin and other drugs, and the viral epidemics associated with this, demonstrated that if there was a dearth of injecting equipment there would also be shared use of whatever equipment was available (Hart 1989). Initially the sharing of injecting equipment was thought to be a strong feature of sub-cultures of heroin users, the act of sharing injecting equipment was a mark of shared community (Des Jarlais *et al.* 1986). Whilst this may have applied on New York's lower east side, it was not however, a universal feature. For example, in the housing schemes of Edinburgh (Hart 1989) and in parts of South East Asia (Robert Power, personal communication), injectors would go to the houses or known locations of drug dealers and use the equipment made available to them, not necessarily considering that this might have been used only minutes earlier by another injector. Thus, 'sharing' does not require the direct presence of another person for equipment to be 'passed on to' or be 'borrowed by' a drug user.

It soon became clear that if clean needles and syringes could be provided to drug users, through needle-exchange schemes, they would attend these projects in large numbers and, over time, report reduced incidence of needle-sharing (Donoghoe *et al.* 1989; Hart *et al.* 1989). This is not to deny that sharing of equipment has cultural elements. McKeganey and Barnard (1992) found, for example, that the sharing of injecting equipment in a deprived Glasgow housing scheme was less connected to a sub-culture of drug use, and far more to a wider working-class ethic of sharing in communities where individuals had few personal resources. However, with the setting up of needle exchange in this culture, the need to do this has been dramatically reduced (Bloor *et al.* 1994).

Indeed, it is at the meso-social, the organisational level, that there is the greatest optimism, and increasing evidence, that risks connected with drug consumption can be modified through social interventions. As well as making organisational provisions for the supply of sterile injecting equipment for drug consumers, much can also be done at the meso-social level with regard to police policy towards drug consumption. At the macro level heroin and other opiate consumption and trafficking is a criminal offence in many, if not most, countries worldwide. In some (e.g. Philippines, Jamaica, Malaysia, and Singapore) this extends to making drug trafficking a crime punishable by death (Manderson 1994). However at the meso-level there is considerable police discretion about how criminal law is applied. Studies in Connecticut and Baltimore have demonstrated a reduction in both the sharing of injecting equipment and needle stick injuries to police officers after possession of drug paraphernalia was no longer treated as a criminal offence (Groseclose *et al.* 1995; Latkin *et al.* 1995). In Rotterdam police policy extends to tolerating the consumption and sale of heroin and cocaine at known premises as long as certain conditions are met (e.g. no sale of stolen goods, no large quantities of drugs and no nuisance for surrounding residents). The strategy is based on the Dutch drug policy of formally classifying heroin use as illegal but in practice seeking to contain and manage drug problems rather than eradicating them (Engelsman 1991). It has been argued that normalisation policies, such as these, allow drug consumers to reflect social responsibility and so reduce a number of interrelated physical, economic and social risks (Grund 1993).

There are by now many examples of how meso-social interventions can achieve an overall reduction of the risks of drug consumption. One can, for example, learn a great deal in relation to the prevention of HIV/AIDS in injecting drug users by looking at, *inter alia*, Des Jarlais and colleagues' work on 'prevented epidemics' (1993), Bloor *et al.*'s work on Glasgow's low and stable prevalence (1994) or Gray (1995) on Thailand's reduced incidence. These authors demonstrate that a particular approach or combination of approaches – including the provision of needle exchange – have resulted in low or stable prevalence of HIV in regions or cities that, in other circumstances and because of local conditions (including levels of risk behaviour), should have been candidates for exponential HIV incidence.

Micro-social accounts

Earlier it was suggested that there are any number of 'explanations' or accounts of the causes and consequences of drug use. British empirical sociology has a respectable history of describing and seeking to account for different phases of the postwar heroin epidemic (Stimson and Oppenheimer 1982; Parker *et al.* 1988). A socio-historical perspective has been taken (Berridge and Edwards 1987), and the development of social policy in this field has also been described (Berridge 1990). The greatest number of recent accounts, however, have been at the micro-social level, with the social context and social relations of drug use forming the focus of investigation.

Robert Power (1989) has focused on the social context of drug use, and particularly on the immediate and local factors that affect drug using behaviour. For example, he refers to the 'pragmatism' attached to the change from smoking to injecting heroin in the context of dependency and the need to maintain a drug habit, the socialisation of young people into drug use which differs according to local culture, and the situational and circumstantial constraints which impact upon the means of drug administration, particularly the sharing of equipment. Thus, in prison the health proscription on sharing injecting equipment is overridden by the craving for a drug effect in a situation where needles and syringes are scarce.

Other anthropological research into the sharing of injecting equipment shows that even when clean syringes and needles are available there are still significant risks for spreading the HIV virus. This is because most drugs used for recreational injecting are purchased in powder form and so need skilled preparation through several distinct stages to produce an injectable solution – the drug is measured out, heated to dissolve in acidified water, filtered into a syringe and then injected. Sharing equipment at many of these stages can potentially lead to the spread of infection. In addition, a convenient and accurate way in which to divide drugs between users is to do so when they are in aqueous solution by either 'frontloading' or 'backloading' syringes. In either case the needle of one syringe is used to fill the barrel of another and so this can be an alternative route of viral infection. This may be a particularly important route of transmission as drugs are often cheaper to consume if bought in greater quantities. While large scale collective purchasing may be rare, there is good evidence to suppose that many users share drugs with specific others in this way (e.g. sexual partners, family, those who live in the same premises and friend or 'mate' dyads). In such contexts drug consumers, who have clean or personalised equipment, may be unaware of the additional risks of sharing (Grund 1993).

Tim Rhodes (1995) has also focused on the social meanings of drug use, and the process by which the medically accepted risks of drug use are subsumed or accepted alongside other risks. Drug users interviewed in London perceived there to be a hierarchy of 'risk priorities', many but not all of which were health related. Thus, whilst HIV infection is a primary public health concern in relation to illicit drug use, for users themselves other issues are of greater and more immediate priority. There is the routine and daily risk of over-dose, given fluctuations in the quality and amount of drug available. This increases the proximity of mortality, with one user pointing out that 'death is . . . a normal thing . . . an everyday thing. If you take heroin you can be dead at any moment and it's not very frightening – you live with that' (Rhodes 1995: 134). A number of other dangers and uncertainties in the lives of drug users can at any time eclipse worries about HIV infection. For instance, the possibility of being duped into buying poor quality heroin; long term dependency; and getting money to buy drugs – all these are risks that need to be prioritised alongside the risk of HIV infection.

At the micro-social level, changes in social norms through diffusion of safer sex and safer injecting messages have the potential to make a major impact on risk exposure. Bloor (1995), for example, has employed the phenomenology of Alfred Schutz to understand how norms of safer sex are translated into changed behaviours, notably through an understanding of 'systems of relevance' and 'recipes for action'. In doing so, he draws a crucial distinction between decision-making that is monothetic (a single flash) and that which is polythetic (step wise). Monothetic thinking can be thought of as habit or routine, requiring little attention and, as Rhodes suggests (1995: 129), 'is often a product of socialised habituation rather than calculation'. Much needle sharing in the 1980s was reportedly habitual and unconsidered, and reflected simply the way in which a drug user had first learned how to inject drugs (as the first injection is rarely considered to the point of buying injecting equipment prior to the event, and use of another's injecting equipment is common). Polythetic decision-making is much more akin to the social psychological paradigm of cognitive processes or steps, though calculated decisions are made according to the immediate situation. An example of this would be needle sharing with a sexual partner. Many drug users in the 1980s continued to share with their partners long after they had stopped sharing with friends and acquaintances because they were having unprotected sex with them. In making this polythetic decision they could maintain that, as they were at risk through engaging in unprotected sex, further risk was unlikely consequent on sharing with a partner. In addition, positive benefits (of togetherness and intimacy) also informed the decision to continue to share injecting equipment. Both the kind of decision-making which occurs (monothetic or polythetic) and the response that is elicited (the recipes for action) are highly subject to normative influence.

Davison *et al.* (1992), although writing about risk for coronary heart disease, have noted how people react to risk in terms of its perceived proximity, and their own power to modify the situation to avoid risk. Their concept of 'risk landscapes' exemplifies this notion of proximity, with some risks close by and others far away on the horizon. Much micro-sociological research is concerned to determine the topography of risk landscapes. Thus interventions such as needle and syringe exchange seek to modify perceptions of the proximity of harm and encourage a sense that it is possible to respond constructively to risk by changing behaviour if this is endorsed by respected others. This model has been used with injecting drug users with regard to the cleaning of injecting equipment, and not sharing used needles and syringes, and has also been found to result in behaviour change (Rietmeijer *et al.* 1996). In Schutzean terms, these aim to change decision-making in the first instance from monothetic to polythetic, and introduce new recipes for action. The final intention is to render habitual the act of not sharing needles and syringes.

From the micro to the macro: pleasure, risk and health

Finally at the micro level of analysis it is possible to start making connections back to the macro or supra structural level. Although lip service is paid to the notion of positive health status, and the need to avoid a pathologising bio-medical perspective, much writing on 'health' is in fact concerned only with disease. This chapter is no exception, given its explicit focus on HIV/AIDS. This paradigm is one that dominates public discussions of health issues – newspaper articles, parliamentary debates and health care professionals are understandably exercised more by disease than the factors that contribute to positive health. By tacit implication, health within this paradigm becomes little more than a 'lack' – the absence of disease or potential disease (risk). Such a model of health must be seen as overly restrictive and negative given the many different ways in which cultures and groups define 'good' health. Yet, by implication, health as lack of disease is at least evident in public discussions, given its frequent appearance in various media, public and political pronouncements.

The same cannot be said of a discourse of pleasure in relation to drug use and sexual behaviour. Pleasure as a concept or experience is entirely absent from public discussion of health and risks. Yet people take illicit drugs, in the first instance at least, because it is a pleasurable experience and, as with sex, is sought after and paid for because of positively enjoyable sensations (Eisler 1995). Thus the search for gratification through these particular forms of consumption should be seen as integral to their occurrence, and should inform our understanding of the context and sites in which these activities take place. It is in consideration of the processes of consumption that we can understand the nexus of pleasure, risk and health.

It has been pointed out that health has increasingly become a 'central plank of contemporary consumer culture' in a way that would not have been recognisable even as recently as the 1960's (Burrows *et al.* 1995). That health today touches on such a wide range of consumption means that its definition is far more open to wider debate than before. Two possible frames of reference are suggested: the global and the local. The global refers to risk reducing health consumption which offers long term or distant benefits and seeks to maintain the absence of undesirable qualities. This could include activities such as dietary choice, exercise, and prophylactic behaviour. On the other hand, the local refers to health consumption which gives an immediate, and often physical sense, of well-being or pleasure. Much health consumption involves elements from both frames of reference – someone may exercise or do sport both for the perceived long term benefits of body maintenance and for the immediate physical sensations that are produced. However, other types of consumption, such as cosmetic surgery (Balsamo 1993) or sun tanning (Carter 1997b), are undertaken for the local and immediate sensation of health they foster.

The pleasures of drug consumption also exists in this local and immediate category of sensation and pleasure. On the other hand, many of the health dangers connected with drug taking exist in a global frame of reference. The fact that health discourses on drug consumption exist almost solely in a global frame of reference can only impede public discussion of local pleasures and the risks that follow from them. If the pleasures associated with artificially altered states of consciousness are socially learned then public debate could be one path to a more informed understanding of the relation between global risk and local pleasure. The absence of a discourse of pleasure from public discussions of drug use and commercial sex work should not render it invisible in every account of their relationship with HIV infection.

Conclusion

Risk analysis is constantly subject to revision and, no matter how much information is available, there can be no final certainty in making decisions about the chance of harm occurring (Adams 1995) and, as we have seen, this is particularly true of behaviours associated with consumption. Yet some of the social psychological models used to understand drug use and sexual behaviour treat the individual as if such certainty was achievable – social subjects are treated as if they move in a context-free landscape engaging only in volitional dealings with other similar human beings. The utility of such an approach will however always remain questionable when the constraints of many people's everyday lives are addressed and, as we have seen, such constraints affect people's consumption and the risks associated with them. For example, situational constraints structure the micro-level of the social relations of drug users; at the meso-level, opportunities to use clean needles and syringes depend upon the policies of organisations such as prisons, the police or health authorities; and at the macro level international economics and national policing dictate the availability of illicit drugs for any individual.

What this chapter has attempted to demonstrate is the existence of an alternative to unduly individualised understandings of risk exposure, and that sociologically-based models of human behaviour can be used to inform interventions that reduce the level of risk taking in populations affected by HIV/AIDS. There now exists a body of descriptive work which can be used to understand the macro-, meso- and micro-social contexts of risk behaviour and consumption, and a series of practical interventions which have been demonstrated to be effective in modifying the environment in which risk exposure occurs.

The emphasis here has been upon factors other than the constituents of personal psychological make-up that are important in our understanding of drug use and HIV infection. It is perhaps understandable that research on HIV risk is individually oriented because the concept 'risk' has become so directly concerned with actual or potential harm associated with an individual's behaviour. Even within epidemiology, however, and its biomedical focus (on the individual body), it is understood that harm does not necessarily occur as a consequence of individual human action, because environmental factors so often determine 'risk exposure'. Sociologists, unconstrained by an exclusively individual focus – indeed, spurred on by disciplinary imperatives to seek explanations beyond the level of the psyche, self or will – have both the obligation and opportunity to explore the social dimensions of human relations and action, with the study of drug use and sexuality offering many possibilities for the disclosure of the social dynamics of intimate and personal interactions. By understanding that drug use is an example of social action and interaction it becomes possible to determine the nature of any risk, associated with consumption, in terms of primarily social relations. Risk can be considered as situated *between* people, rather than as residing within their individual cognition. It is the expressed aim of a sociological perspective to recognise that it is the links shared by and connecting social actors, and the context in which action occurs, that are significant. The broader social structure should be the starting point rather than an after-thought for those who wish to study the social dynamics of risk.

References

Adams, J. (1995) *Risk*, London: UCL Press.

Altman, D. (1995) 'Communities, governments and AIDS: making partnerships work', in P. Aggleton, P. Davies, and G. Hart (eds) *AIDS: Safety, Sexuality and Risk*, London: Taylor & Francis.

Balsamo, A. (1993) 'On the cutting edge: cosmetic surgery and the technological production of the gendered body', *Camera Obscura* 28: 207–39.

Bauman, Z. (1992) *Intimations of Postmodernity*, London and New York: Routledge.

Beck, U. (1989). 'On the way to the industrial risk-society? Outline of an argument', *Thesis Eleven* 23: 86–103.

—— (1992) *Risk Society: Towards a New Modernity*, London: Sage.

Becker, H. (1963) *Outsiders: Studies in the Sociology of Deviance*, New York: Macmillan.

Berridge, V. (1990) *Drug Research and Policy in Britain*, Aldershot: Avebury.

Berridge, V. and Edwards, G. (1987) *Opium and the People*, London: Yale.

Bloor, M. (1995) *The Sociology of HIV Transmission*, London: Sage.

Bloor, M., Frischer, M., Taylor, A., Covell, R., Goldberg, D., Green, S., McKeganey, N. and Platt, S. (1994) 'Tideline and turn: possible reasons for the continuing low HIV prevalence among Glasgow's injecting drug users', *Sociological Review* 42: 738–57.

Burrows, R., Nettleton, S. and Burrows, R. (1995). 'Sociology and health promotion: health, risk and consumption under late modernism', in R. Bunton, S. Nettleton and R. Burrows (eds) *The Sociology of Health Promotion: Critical Analyses of Consumption, Lifestyle and Risk*, London: Routledge.

Carter, S. (1997a) 'Reducing AIDS risk: a case of mistaken identity?', *Science as Culture* 6(2): 220–45.

Carter, S. (1997b) 'Who wants to be "peelie wally"? Glaswegian tourists' attitudes to sun tans and sun exposure', in S. Clift (ed.) *Tourism and Health: Risks, Responses and Research*, London: Pinter.

Davison, C., Frankel, S. and Davey Smith, G.(1992) 'To hell with tomorrow: coronary heart disease risk and the ethnography of fatalism', in S. Scott, G. Williams, S. Platt and H. Thomas (eds) *Private Risks and Public Dangers*, Aldershot: Avebury.

Des Jarlais, D., Friedman, S. R. and Strug, D. (1986) 'AIDS and needle-sharing within the IV-drug use subculture', in D. A. Feldman and T. M. Johnson (eds) *The Social Dimensions of AIDS*, New York: Praeger.

Des Jarlais, D., Goldberg, D., Tunving, K., Wodak, A., Hagan, H. and Friedman, S. R. (1993) 'Characteristics of prevented HIV epidemics', Ninth International Conference on AIDS/IV STD World Congress, Berlin, June (abstract WS-C15–6).

Donoghoe, M. C., Stimson, G. V., Dolan, K. and Alldritt, L. (1989) 'Changes in HIV risk behaviour in clients of syringe-exchange schemes in England and Scotland', *AIDS* 3: 267–72.

Edgell, S., Hetherington, K. and Warde, A. (eds) (1996). *Consumption Matters*, Oxford: Blackwell.

Eisler, R. (1995) *Sacred Pleasure: Sex, Myth, and the Politics of the Body*, New York: Harper Collins.

Engelsman, E. (1991) 'Drug misuse and the Dutch: a matter of social wellbeing and not primarily a problem for the police and the courts', *British Medical Journal* 302: 484–5.

Featherstone, M. (1991). 'The body in consumer culture', in M. Featherstone, M. Hepworth and B. Turner (eds) *The Body: Social Process and Cultural Theory*, London: Sage.

Fishbein, M. and Ajzen, I. (1975) *Belief, Attitude, Intent and Behaviour: an Introduction to Theory and Research*, Reading, MA: Addison-Wesley.

Flowers, P., Sheeran, P., Beail, N., and Smith, J. A. (1997) 'The role of psycho-social factors in HIV risk reduction among gay and bisexual men: a quantitative review', *Psychology and Health* 12: 197–230.

Giddens, A. (1991). *Modernity and Self-Identity: Self and Society in the Late Modern Age*, Cambridge: Polity Press.

Gillies, P., Tolley, K. and Wolstenholme, J. (1996) 'Is AIDS a disease of poverty?', *AIDS Care* 8: 351–63.

Gray, J. (1995) 'Operating needle exchange programmes in the hills of Thailand', *AIDS Care* 7: 498–9.

Groseclose, S. L., Weinstein, S., Jones, T. S., Valleroy, L. A., Sehrs, L. G. and Kassler, W. J. (1995) 'Impact of increased legal access to needles and syringes on practices of injecting-drug users and police officers – Connecticut, 1992–1993', *Journal of Aquired Immune Deficiency Syndromes and Human Retrovirology* 10(1): 82–9.

Grund, J. (1993) *Drug Use as a Social Ritual: Functionality, Symbolism and Determinants of Self-Regulation*, Rotterdam: Instituut voor Verslavingsonderzoek.

Hart, G. (1989) 'HIV and the injecting drug user', in P. Aggleton, G. Hart and P. Davies (eds) *AIDS: Social Representations, Social Practices*, London: Falmer Press.

Hart, G. J., Carvell, A. L. M., Woodward, N., Johnson, A. M., Williams, P. and Parry, J. V. (1989) 'Evaluation of needle-exchange in central London: behaviour change and anti-HIV status over 1 year', *AIDS* 3: 261–5.

Hart, G. and Boulton, M. (1995) 'Sexual behaviour in gay men: towards a sociology of risk', in P. Aggleton, P. Davies and G. Hart (eds) *AIDS: Safety, Sexuality and Risk*, London: Taylor & Francis.

Hart, G. and Flowers, P. (1996) 'Recent developments in the sociology of HIV risk behaviour', *Risk, Decision and Policy* 1: 153–65.

Klee, H. (1990) 'Some observations on the sexual behaviour of injecting drug users: implications for the spread of HIV infection', in P. Aggleton, P. Davies and G. Hart (eds) *AIDS: Individual, Cultural and Policy Dimensions*, London: Falmer Press

Latkin, C. A., Mandell, W., Vlahov, D., Knowlton, A. R., Oziemkowska, M. and Celentano, D. D. (1995) 'Self-reported reasons for needle sharing and not carrying bleach among injection-drug users in Baltimore, Maryland.' *Journal of Drug Issues* 25(4): 865–70.

Low, N., Egger, M., Gorter, A., Sandiford, P., Gonzalez, A., Pauw, J., Ferrie, J. and Davey Smith, G. (1993) 'AIDS in Nicaragua: epidemiological, political and sociocultural perspectives', *International Journal of Public Health Services* 23: 685–702.

Lupton, D. (1994) 'Consumerism, commodity culture and health promotion', *Health Promotion International* 9(2): 111–18.

Manderson, D. (1994) 'An archaeology of drug laws', *International Journal of Drug Policy* 5(4): 1–8.

Mann, M., Tarantola, D. J. M. and Netter, T. W. (1992) *AIDS in the World*, Cambridge, MA: Harvard University Press.

McKeganey, N. and Barnard, M. (1992) *AIDS, Drugs and Sexual Risk*, Buckingham: Open University Press.

Measham, F., Newcombe, R. and Parker, H. (1994) 'The normalisation of recreational drug-use amongst young people in north-west England', *British Journal of Sociology* 45(2): 287–312.

Parker, H., Bakx, K. and Newcombe, R. (1988) *Living with Heroin*, Milton Keynes: Open University.

Parker, H. and F. Measham (1994) 'Pick 'n' mix – changing patterns of illicit drug-use amongst 1990's adolescents', *Drugs Education, Prevention and Policy* 1(1): 5–13.

Parker, R. (1994) 'Sexual cultures, HIV transmission, and AIDS prevention', *AIDS* 8: S309–S314.

Patton, C. (1990) *Inventing AIDS*, New York: Routledge.

Power, R. (1989) 'Methods of drug use: injecting and sharing', in P. Aggleton, G. Hart and P. Davies (eds) *AIDS: Social Representations, Social Practices*, London: Falmer Press.

Quinn, T. C. (1996) 'Global burden of the HIV pandemic', *Lancet* 348: 99–106.

Rhodes, T. (1995) 'Theorising and researching "risk": notes on the social relations of risk in heroin users' lifestyles', in P. Aggleton, P. Davies and G. Hart (eds) *AIDS: Safety, Sexuality and Risk*, Taylor & Francis: London.

Rietmeijer, C. A., Kane, M. S., Simons, P. Z., Corby, N. H., Wolitski, R. J., Higgins, D. L., Judson, F. N. and Cohn, D. L. (1996) 'Increasing the use of bleach and condoms among injecting drug users in Denver: outcomes of a targeted community-level HIV prevention program', *AIDS* 10: 291–8.

Robertson, R., Bucknall, A. B. V., Welsby, W. J. *et al.* (1985) 'Epidemic of AIDS-related virus (HTLV-III/LAV) infection among intravenous drug abusers', *Lancet* 2: 449–50.

Rosenstock, I. (1974) 'Historic origins of the health belief model', *Health Education Monographs* 2: 328–35.

Stepney, R. (1996). 'The concept of addiction – its use and abuse in the media and science', *Human Psychopharmacology and Experiment* 11(S1): S15–S20.

Stimson, G. V. and Oppenheimer, E. (1982) *Heroin Addiction: Treatment and Control in Britain*, London: Tavistock.

Weatherburn, P., Davies, P. M., Hickson, F. C. I., Hunt, A. J, Coxon, A. P. M. and McManus, T. J. (1993) 'No connection between alcohol use and unsafe sex among gay and bisexual men, *AIDS* 7: 115–9.

Chapter 13

Health care and consumption

Jonathan Gabe and Michael Calnan

Introduction

A striking feature of recent times has been the growth in popularity of the term 'consumer'. Whereas before people were cinema goers, football spectators, shoppers or television viewers they are now all described as consumers (Keat *et al.* 1994), acquiring and/or using goods and services for their own benefit.

Initially applied to purchasers of private sector goods and services the term has, since the 1980s, also been employed to describe users of public sector services such as the British National Health Service (NHS) (Seale 1993). It has had particular appeal for Conservative governments which, faced with underlying weaknesses in the British economy in the context of both global recession and capital restructuring (Clarke 1996), have sought to reduce or at least keep in check public expenditure on health care by shifting some of the responsibility for health onto individual citizens.

Such a policy is in line with New Right thinking which has identified a 'dependency culture' encouraged by the Welfare State as a major problem, and sees greater emphasis on self-reliance and individual choice exercised through the marketplace as a way of tackling this problem. Consumerism is not, however, restricted to the New Right. It also resonates with New Left thinking which has been critical of paternalistic welfare agencies and has advocated reforms which draw on voluntary and cooperative forms of mutual aid (Flynn 1992).

Faced with the growing emphasis on consumerism in policy circles and in popular discourse sociologists (and other social scientists) have perhaps rather belatedly been giving increased attention to the concept (Gabriel and Lang 1995; Warde 1996). This has resulted in the realisation that a rather 'loose consumerist perspective' has been employed 'to frame the discussion' (Campbell 1995: 101), that production and consumption are not necessarily exclusive categories (p. 101) and that the mode of provision of a good or service can influence access to it, the manner of its delivery and the way in which it is experienced (Warde 1990, 1992). With these concerns in mind an attempt has been made to establish a theoretical framework for understanding consumption and it is to this that we now turn.

Warde's model of production/consumption cycles

Warde (1990, 1992) is one of the few people to attempt to provide an ideal-type model which links production and consumption and aims to throw light on the impact of the mode of provision for a good or service. According to him the way that goods and services are produced can affect, although not in a simple 'determinist way' (Edgell and Hetherington 1996), the experience of consumption. Four modes of provision are identified – market, state, household and communal – and these are said to have potential consequences for social relations governing access, the manner of delivery and the experience of consumption (see Table 13.1).

Applying this model to health care we can see that the NHS, as established under the 1946 NHS Act, was organised by the state as a producer of health care with access being provided as a right. The need for care was determined by doctors and delivered by them and other health care professionals, with users of the service being treated as clients and as citizens (Taylor-Gooby 1993). Since the late 1940s the NHS has markedly changed, especially following the 1990 NHS and Community Care Act which established an internal market for health care and an enhanced role for both consumers and the private sector (see below). One of the issues to be addressed in this chapter is therefore whether this distinction between state and market provision can be sustained in the 1990s. Has the 'state' version of provision ceased to exist and if so what should the new hybrid be called? Second, if the mode of provision has changed, what have been the consequences for the users of health care and for citizenship rights? Have users been empowered or have social divisions been increased?[1]

These questions will be addressed by considering three changes in the structure of NHS provision introduced by Conservative governments during the 1980s and 1990s, namely: (1) the implementation of the internal market;

Table 13.1 Warde's model of production/consumption cycles

Mode of provision	Access/social relations	Manner of delivery	Experience of consumption
Market	Price/exchange	Managerial	Customer/consumer
State	Need/right	Professional	Citizen/client
Household	Family/obligation	Family	Self/family/kin
Communal	Network/reciprocity	Volunteer	Friend/neighbour/acquaintance

Source: Expanded and amended version of Warde (1992) reproduced in Edgell and Hetherington (1996).

(2) the introduction of new managerialism; and (3) and the development of welfare pluralism.

In answering these questions we shall be able to test Warde's model and comment on its heuristic value when applied to health care provision. More generally we also hope to demonstrate that the sociology of consumption has much to offer medical sociologists with an interest in health care organisation.

The internal market

The idea of a market for health care was first spelt out in the 1989 White Paper, *Working for Patients* and subsequently enacted in the 1990 NHS and Community Care Act. Premised on the assumption that competition enhances efficiency, the White Paper divided the NHS into purchasers and providers of health care, while reaffirming the principle of providing health care free at the point of use. The purchasing and providing functions of health authorities (HAs) were separated, with district HAs now expected to seek out the lowest cost providers while providers competed with each other to offer the services sought by purchasers at the cheapest price. To make the market work, supply side providers such as large hospitals and community units were given the opportunity to become self governing trusts with the promise of increased financial freedom and greater autonomy. On the demand side, general practitioners were permitted to become fundholders, able to place contracts for non-emergency care for their patients.

One of the justifications for the development of the market for health care was that it would shift the culture of the NHS from one determined by the preferences and decisions of professionals to one shaped by the views and wishes of its users (Hunter 1994). To what extent has this turned out to be the case?

GP fundholders were of course purchasing services on their patients' behalf. Thus they were acting as proxy or surrogate consumers, with individual patients having no purchasing rights of their own (Paton 1992; Clarke and Newman 1997). It was assumed that these fundholders had the incentive to fulfil this role effectively as otherwise their patients would simply have switched to a competing practice (Klein 1995). However, commentators have questioned patients' motivation to shop around (Leavey *et al.* 1989; Shackley and Ryan 1994). Many people's contact with their GP is minimal and spasmodic, perhaps seeking an appointment once a year for a minor complaint or a prescription, so it may seem a waste of time to think of alternatives. If an urgent condition does arise then it would preclude the possibility of shopping around. For those with chronic conditions, a relationship of interpersonal trust and confidence may have been built up during the course of an illness (Mechanic 1996) which provides a powerful incentive to stay put. Given that patients lack the necessary inclination to shop around in the medical marketplace and often do not have a great choice of alternative GPs with which to register, it is therefore not surprising that there is little evidence that this aspect of the reforms markedly increased consumer choice (Klein 1995).

As proxy consumers, however, there is some evidence that fundholding GPs have acted in their patients' best interest. For example, it seems that they achieved shorter waiting times, quicker test results and a more responsive service (Glennerster *et al.* 1992). In part this may have been due to the extra funds provided by the Conservative government to fundholders, but it was also a consequence of the advantageous contracts that fundholders managed to sign with trusts eager for business. At the same time the achievement of shorter waiting times for fundholding patients may well have been achieved at the expense of non-fundholders' patients, with the former being given accelerated admissions which were not available to the patients of other purchasers (Francome and Marks 1996). Thus a two-tier GP service seems to have developed, with fundholding patients, usually living in suburban middle-class areas reaping the benefits at other patients' expense (Gabe 1997).

Moreover, for those patients who remained with non-fundholding GPs the 1990 reforms may have had the perverse effect of actually restricting choice. These patients' GPs were no longer free to refer their patients to a consultant of their choice but instead had to refer them to providers with whom the district had a contract.

However, this situation is likely to change in the light of the current Labour government's decision, announced in the 1997 White Paper *The New NHS*, to abolish the distinction between fundholding and non-fundholding GPs and replace them with primary care commissioning groups, consisting of local networks of GPs and community nurses. This system, while maintaining the role of GPs as proxy consumers, may help address the concerns about equity noted above (Annandale 1998).

Turning to the supply side, the creation of hospital and community NHS trusts have had some benefits for users of the service. For instance, the number of patients waiting over a year for hospital treatment has been reduced, although those waiting under a year – the largest category on the waiting list – have increased in number, as have the total number waiting (Baggott 1994).

At the same time, these possible gains must be set against certain potential disadvantages for users. In particular there is a danger that trusts will respond to purchasing power at the expense of social need. Given the requirement to generate income, trusts may concentrate on more profitable areas of work to the detriment of others, and in the process discriminate against certain categories of patients (Ranade 1994). Patients may also be disadvantaged if local specialist services are cut back because a trust has lost a contract with a DHA, or a primary care commissioning group which has now replaced HAs' purchasing role to a large extent, in favour of one located some distance away. In such circumstances two of the core principles on which the NHS was founded, namely equity of access for all and comprehensiveness would appear to be threatened.

Furthermore, the introduction of an internal market with winners and losers means that some trusts run the risk of not having sufficient contracts to remain financially viable. A few have already closed and others have run short of money, being forced to cut back on treatment for non-urgent conditions and temporarily closing wards (Mohan 1995). Again, this threatens the NHS's commitment to provide comprehensive health care for all wherever they live, thereby fostering inequalities between consumers and closing or running down assets in which, as citizens, they had a vested interest (Gabriel and Lang 1995).

Overall, the internal market under the Conservatives would seem to have produced a decentralised and fragmented system with numerous buyers and sellers, in place of a centrally planned, uniform, top down approach. However, it must be emphasised that the NHS system was never 'uniform' due to covert rationing decisions by GPs and clinicians and geographical variations in services (e.g. teaching hospitals). This has had some benefits for individual consumers but these have been offset by a series of problems stemming from a system which has put efficiency before equity and, in the process, accelerated the dilution of citizenship. The new reforms of the Labour administration will remove some of the worst excesses but do not involve the dissolution of the internal market, just its regulation. In such circumstances citizenship rights are unlikely to be fully restored.

The new managerialism

The application of consumerist principles to the NHS was given a major impetus with the Conservative government's decision to implement the recommendations of the *Griffiths Report* of 1983. This report advocated altering the organisational culture of the NHS by appointing general managers at each level of the service who would give pride of place to the preferences of patients', or as they were re-named 'consumers', when making health care decisions. Griffiths argued that managers should try to establish how well the service for which they were responsible was being delivered by employing a range of research techniques and other methods to find out their customers' needs and their views about service standards and its quality. They were to act on this information by amending policy and monitoring subsequent performance against it. Thereafter this management-led consumerist approach was promoted vigorously, with Directors of Quality Assurance appointed by Health Authorities to establish users' views and staff sent on customer relations courses and encouraged to follow newly established 'mission statements' outlining their organisations' common goals. While these activities may have legitimated managers' claims to knowledge about their customers and what they wanted (Clarke and Newman 1997), the kind of information collected seems to have been of limited benefit to patients, as the focus appears to have been on their views of hotel aspects of care (e.g. cleanliness and food) rather than their assessment of clinical effectiveness (Seale 1993).

Service standards have also been enshrined in the *Patient's Charter* (Dept of Health 1991), one of a number planned by the Conservatives to transform the management of public services. The Patient's Charter was designed to make the health service more responsive to individual consumers and raise quality overall at nil cost (Taylor 1992) by setting rights and service standards which consumers could expect. These standards were to provide the basis for targets against which the performance of managers could be measured. Three new rights were established. These were the right to: detailed information about local health services, including quality standards and waiting lists; guaranteed admission to hospital within two years of being put on the waiting list; and having any complaint about the service fully investigated and promptly dealt with. As these rights were not legally binding, doubts were subsequently expressed about whether they would be realised in practice (Gabe 1997), especially as there were no specific mechanisms set up to implement them, apart from an attempt to simplify the complaints system.

What benefits has the Patient's Charter had for users of the NHS? Survey evidence suggests that the impact of the Charter has been mixed. For example, Bruster *et al.* (1994), in their national study of patient views about hospital care, have shown that Patient's Charter rights are not being met in areas such as being given access to health records; choosing whether they wished to take part in student training; and being guaranteed admission within two years of being placed on a waiting list. Also, it has been suggested that the limit on waiting list times may be focusing on the less important aspect of waiting. Cartwright and Windsor (1992) have reported that patients are more dissatisfied with the delay between referral by the general practitioners and being seen at an outpatient department and less by the decision to put them on a waiting list.

Survey evidence suggests that, apart from a short period after the NHS reforms were introduced, dissatisfaction with the overall running of the NHS has risen dramatically (18 per cent in 1991/2 to 29 per cent in 1996/7), with the highest levels of dissatisfaction being observed in London (Mulligan and Judge 1997). While dissatisfaction with general practice has constantly remained low (10–15 per cent) there has been a marked increase in dissatisfaction with general dental care. The reasons for this appear to lie with the increasing privatisation of dentistry and the barriers of access to and cost of dental care. For example, evidence from a recent study (Dickinson *et al.* 1999) of the public's views and experiences of general dental care showed that current dissatisfaction is rooted in perceived barriers to accessibility created by an apparent lack of availability of NHS dentists and the concern about the cost of care (nearly two-fifths of those surveyed believed that the expense generally restricted how often they visited the dentist). In addition, three-fifths of those who reported a complaint about the dental service were concerned about lack of access to general dental care.

At the same time, the number of people complaining has increased since these reforms were put in place, as have the number of medical negligence claims. For example complaints to the General Medical Council rose by almost 50 per cent between 1991 and 1994 (Agnew and Lyall 1997), while spending on awards for clinical negligence rose from an estimated £60 million in 1990/1 to £155 million in 1994/5 (Annandale 1998). This suggests either that the quality of care has not improved or that individuals are responding to the rhetoric of consumerism and increasingly holding health care providers to account (Wilder 1997). Or, more prosaically, it may be that it is now simply easier for patients to complain with the changes in the complaints procedures. The last possibility is perhaps the least likely because the failure to resource these changes adequately has arguably restricted the benefits to patients (Wratten 1996). However, the impact of the 'new' managerialism may have led to the increase in the official recording of and responding to complaints.

Nor are things likely to change significantly under Labour. The new government, despite committing itself to dismantling the Patient's Charter while in opposition, now seems prepared to retain it, while adding certain clinical outcome measures based on mortality rates (Crinson 1998). A new Patient's Charter is to be published, although it appears that this is likely simply to dress up the old charter with a slightly different set of standards rather than replace it with a strong commitment to patients' rights and access to health care according to need.

While the Patient's Charter may have increased individual users' right to information, it is premised on the dubious assumption that making such information available to the public will of itself change the practice of clinicians and managers. Such an approach can be criticised as 'consumer essentialism' (Crinson 1998), in that it ignores the vested interests which different health care occupations have in the maintenance of the status quo.

According to Crinson, seeing the Patient's Charter merely as a way of empowering patients through the provision of information misses the point that a primary aim of the Charter was to create a management tool for indirectly re-imposing central government control over the performance of trusts, albeit in the name of the consumer. In reality it therefore gave more power to managers than it did to patients (Crinson 1998).

Moreover, the planned introduction of crude measures of clinical performance (such as deaths in hospital) may have the unintended effect of
creating a climate of fear, defensiveness and mistrust between hospitals
and the public, as happened in the US following the publication of league
tables in the late 1980s.

It is thus unlikely to bring about significant improvements in the quality
of care which might be achieved if the service was made directly accountable to users through community participation in decision-making, in line
with local health needs. But this would involve a different view of the
citizen as a member of a community with rights and duties balanced by
mutuality and control (Walsh 1994; Gabriel and Lang 1995).

Arguably this community participation has been more to the fore with
other policy initiatives to enhance consumer choice, such as *Local Voices*
(NHSME 1992). Building on the requirements of the 1990 NHS and
Community Care Act, this advisory document encouraged Health Authority
managers to listen to the views of local people, including community
groups, about their priorities for health care before making rationing decisions (Allsop 1995). A number of methods for ascertaining local views
were suggested such as the use of focus groups drawn from the local
population, surveys, opinion polls and health forums. These would enable
managers to obtain advice from local people who would then act as 'champions of the people'. Thus users' views were to be mediated and interpreted
by management, limiting their power to influence rationing decisions
directly (Clarke and Newman 1997).

The *Local Voices* document was just a prelude to a series of political
exhortations that continued well into the 1990s. For example, the
Conservative administration's planning document for the whole NHS for
1996/7 continued the theme of local people as 'health advisers' by encouraging health authorities and their managers to place an emphasis upon
'giving greater voice and influence to users of NHS services and their
position in their own care'. The new Labour government likewise
committed itself to involving local people but seems to have taken a more
collectivist position in that they have given a much greater role to
Community Health Councils (CHCs). These bodies are now to be turned
into 'local health advocates' with a membership that will reflect the interests of the community (Hunter and Harrison 1997). Their role will be to
scrutinise the strategies of health authorities to 'ensure that processes are
in place to enable patient's views to be heard' (Labour Party 1996: 294).
This shift in approach, from local 'advice' to direct involvement by CHCs
representing local people in the determination of health service priorities,
would seem to increase 'the voice and influence' or 'views' of health
service users and their carers and constitutes a policy environment which
may have important policy implications. For the first time with regard to
health care local populations are being invited to contemplate and influence

the burden of responsibility between the state, market and the 'private sphere' of self-reliance, community, family and household support.

But what have been the effects of recent efforts by purchasing authorities to consult local people? The evidence available to assess the impact of these consultations is presently limited and it is difficult to know whether they are genuine attempts to take on board the views of local people or token strategies reflecting managerial manipulation.

A study (Milewa *et al.* 1998) examining the scope and nature of the initiatives being adopted by health authorities during the Major Conservative administration to take greater account of local people's views in the purchasing of health care, showed that users may play an important role in decision-making about qualitative aspects of the delivery of health services, such as hotel accommodation, and also about issues such as the re-siting of geriatric wards. However, simply asking the public to comment on a complete set of commissioning intentions was often seen as unrealistic. Managers suggested that valuable and 'usable' local input arose from ongoing informal and formal dialogue with interested parties through the development of local contacts and networks.

In terms of local advice, however, two general observations arose from the investigation. First, managerial attitudes seemed to exert considerable influence over the demarcation of and response to 'local issues'. This resulted in inevitable geographical variability in efforts made to address and respond to local public views and preferences with regard to purchasing.

Second, local public preferences were weighed against a number of other influences before health care was purchased. These included the geographical limits to the purchase of services and the need to maintain or develop relationships with local health care providers. Thus the development of participatory mechanisms will not in themselves necessarily increase the influence of the local population over decisions with regard to the purchase of health services. However, the apparently limited impact of participatory mechanisms cannot necessarily be cast as a continued marginalisation of user views. A process of professionalisation and the growth of active or 'representative' management may in part be off setting the so called 'democratic deficit' (Milewa *et al.* 1999).

It is clear that despite central government exhortation to consult, the institutional boundaries within which health authorities operate effectively exclude the possibility of such change occurring. Health authorities remain formally accountable upwards to the Secretary of State, not downwards to the public.

Thus public participation carries with it certain in-built difficulties. It may be appropriate where there is a genuine interest in becoming involved in the service in question (e.g. mental health services) but not otherwise. People may be committed to the NHS but are not generally interested in becoming involved in its management (Milewa *et al.* 1998; Pickard *et al.* 1995).

This has implications for primary care groups which are expected to involve users and the public in decision-making. It suggests that mechanisms to facilitate user involvement to date have been primarily a technology of legitimation (Mort and Harrison 1998), enabling the state to justify its policy on health care provision. However, one might question why the idea of public and user involvement has been deployed rather than some other means of legitimation such as medical expertise. According to Mort and Harrison (1998), one explanation may be that the previous government was no longer able to pretend that the state could meet all demand and used explicit rationing and prioritisation, informed by consultations with the public, as a means of legitimising constraints on health care provision. Hence, the public's views were presented as significant in rationing and prioritisation debates while giving the impression that the public still owned the NHS by casting it in the role of stakeholder. However, some doubts have been expressed (Doyal 1998), in the interests of equity, about whether the public should be the final arbiter of decisions about rationing health care.

How far, then, has the introduction of new managerialism in the National Health Service affected the process of consumption of health care? The evidence suggests that despite the rhetoric there has been little change in the position of the user or the public. There may have been an increase in information available about certain aspects of health care delivery, particularly about accessibility, but there has been little change in the status or power of the individual user or citizens as a whole (Clarke and Newman 1997). While the health service agenda may now be influenced more by managerialist than professional interests, this has not affected users at least in terms of their influence on the purchase and provision of health services. The lack of impact of the introduction of managerialism and market principles might indicate that these organisational changes have been marginal and insignificant for patient empowerment. Alternatively, it might reflect the unique position of the user in the health care market whose dependency is accepted and is inevitable given the uncertainty involved with illness and the information gap between professional and user. Thus, informed choice is never a real option because of the special characteristics of health care which distinguish it from other consumption goods (Calnan *et al.* 1998).

Promoting welfare pluralism

Another reform with major implications for users of the NHS has been the attempt during the 1980s and 1990s by Conservative administrations to shift the balance between public and private funding profoundly in the direction of greater private sector involvement (Davies 1987; Harrison *et al.* 1990). Of course acknowledging the fact that the NHS was a mix of public and private funding, planning and provision before these reforms were implemented has implications for Warde's model which distinguishes state from market provision. In reality, as we have just noted, the British health service has always been pluralist – a mix of public/state provision and private/market provision. What changed as result of the reforms we are about to discuss was the balance of the mix.

In order to illustrate the shift in the public/private mix and the consequences for consumers we shall concentrate on two particular developments: (1) the promotion of the private acute sector, and (2) collaboration between the NHS and the private health care sector.

The promotion of the private sector

One strategy employed by the Conservatives while in power to shift the balance between the public and private sector was to encourage the growth of private medicine. For instance they relaxed controls on private hospital development by requiring private developers only to seek authorisation for larger hospitals (100 or more beds outside London – 120 in the capital), and they even waived this requirement in the 1990 NHS and Community Care Act. Similarly, they limited local authorities' powers to object to developments, making profitability the main criterion instead of local health care needs (Gabe 1997).

They also revised NHS consultants' contracts so that they had more scope to undertake private practice, and they encouraged a growth in private health insurance by making it more attractive. The latter was achieved by making premiums paid by employers on behalf of their employees, and low paid workers with individual subscription plans, tax deductible (Calnan *et al.* 1993). In 1990 tax relief on private health insurance was provided for those over 60. This may have helped to increase the level of private health cover from 5 per cent of the British population in 1979 to around 13 per cent in 1994 (Mohan 1995), although the current evidence suggests that the boom in private health insurance subscriptions experienced in the 1980s has now levelled off.

These changes created a climate favouring private hospital development and provided opportunities which were fully exploited by the private sector. Between 1979 and 1989 the number of private hospitals increased by 30 per cent and the number of private beds by 58 per cent (Calnan *et al.* 1993). Many of these hospitals were located in the prosperous south east of England, compounding existing geographical inequalities in the distribution of resources.

From the point of view of the New Right, with its emphasis on individuals exercising choice through the market, the expansion of the private sector increased opportunities for consumers to shop around for the health care which best met their needs. In reality such an option has mainly been the preserve of the well off and better educated, suggesting that choice and equity are inversely related.

Evidence from a study of private health insurance in the south east of England also suggests that the use of private health insurance increases 'consumer choice' only slightly (Calnan *et al.* 1993). Those who had experienced private health care in this study stressed the quality of the facilities and the individualised nature of care and timing of visit, but there was little evidence of shopping around between the private and public sectors. Also, subscribers had limited knowledge of the costs of treatment and felt they lacked the competence to evaluate the skills of different consultants in order to make an informed choice. Rather than shopping around for the best deal, they depended on their NHS GP to decide whether they should go privately and, if so, which consultant they should see. Thus, the notion of consumer sovereignty, in this context, was problematic and individuals did not feel more empowered (Calnan *et al.* 1993). Instead they used their NHS GP as a proxy consumer, in the same way as those who did not have the option of 'going private'.

Private health insurance, on this evidence, does not confer on the individual greater choice and autonomy in decision-making about private health care. However, did the study show any evidence of the consumption of private health insurance being associated with new social divisions which are independent of or related to social class, and was consumption associated with a particular political ideology? Further, was the cultural significance attached to private health insurance similar to other consumption goods? On the first question, there was little support for the proposition that private health insurance highlights social divisions independent of class. While there was some evidence of support for the neo-liberal strand of New Right ideology (personal control, self-reliance and individual responsibility) this was not confined to subscribers of private health insurance. Moreover, even those who subscribed to private health insurance held the NHS in high regard and expressed a strong attachment in principle to the egalitarian values underpinning it. Also, while subscribers did attach social significance to private health insurance, these values were related to class, income and occupation. This suggests that the consumption of private health care is a symbol of socio-economic position rather than a substitute for it. It is thus best seen as dependent on class rather than cutting across it.

Additional evidence from a study of doctor–patient relations in the private sector suggests that private patients tend to have relationships which contain elements of what the authors call 'mutuality' and 'consumerism' rather than the paternalism generally found in the NHS (Wiles and Higgins 1996). However, they argue that moving the relationship further in the direction of a consumerist approach is constrained because of the 'knowledge gap' between doctor and patient and the dependency of the patient on doctors for treatment and care.

Collaboration between the NHS and the private sector

Shifting the balance between the public and private sector was also enhanced by reforms which encouraged greater collaboration between the two sectors. Again, did this enhance the quality of care and increase choice for patients, and was this at the expense of their rights as citizens?

An early attempt was the requirement that NHS District Health Authorities introduce competitive tendering for domestic, catering and laundry services in 1983. The intention was to challenge the monopoly of the in-house providers of services in the expectation that costs would be reduced and greater 'value for money' would be achieved. This contracting out was given a new lease of life by the internal market and has been extended to clinical and clinical support services (e.g. pathology and pharmacy services) (Ruane 1997). In practice the financial benefits have been relatively modest, at least initially, and whatever savings have been achieved seem to have been at the expense of quality of service (Gabe 1997).

A second form of collaboration has involved the NHS contracting out patient care to the private sector. Such co-operative arrangements were first allowed on a voluntary basis in 1981, partly as a way of dealing with capacity constraints in the NHS (Rayner 1987). Subsequently, Health Authorities were directed by the Conservatives to use private hospitals as a way of reducing NHS waiting lists for non-urgent cases and those waiting more than one year. The creation of an internal market, allowing GP fundholders, DHAs and now primary care commissioning groups to buy services from the private sector as well as public providers, has enhanced the prospects of the independent sector treating NHS short stay patients. To date, however, most of this work has come from DHAs.

A third form of collaboration involves the use of private finance instead of public borrowing to undertake capital projects for the NHS. The Private Finance Initiative (PFI), as it is called, was introduced by the Conservatives in 1992 and, after a slow start, provided a major source of finance in the last years of that government and has continued under Labour. Under the initiative, new hospitals, new technologies and equipment are all designed and paid for by the private sector and leased back to the NHS for a specific period (Annandale 1998). Some projects are also to be privately or jointly maintained by the private sector, thereby giving this sector much greater involvement in the day-to-day running of the NHS (Ruane 1997). Such arrangements are to be agreed to only if it can be demonstrated that they increase value for money and transfer risk to the private sector. While this may help governments keep down the cost of the NHS to the public purse it arguably has the effect of transforming the NHS into a private service by stealth (Hunter 1995).

Of course, from the patient's viewpoint, the PFI has the advantage of providing the level of resourcing that should help the NHS maintain a high standard of care. However, in so far as it involves the privatising of a national asset, this initiative could be said to be dismantling their owner-ship rights as citizens over such an asset.

In sum, the attempt to shift the balance between public and private funding in the direction of the private sector has had mixed consequences for users of health care. While the growth of private health insurance has increased the choice of the better off to a limited extent, there is little evidence that it has encouraged shopping around, nor has it created social divisions independent of social class. At the same time the encourage-ment of greater collaboration between the public and private sectors has increased resources for individual NHS patients at the expense of patients' rights as citizens.

Conclusion

In this chapter we have explored the relevance of arguments from the soci-ology of consumption for health care, within the context of the changing structure of health care provision in Britain during the 1980s and 1990s. Three changes to the NHS have been considered: namely, the implementa-tion of the internal market, the introduction of new managerialism and the development of welfare pluralism, and their consequence for users of the service have been considered.

On the basis of this analysis we are now in a position to answer the questions posed in our introduction. First, is the state mode of provision, identified by Warde applicable to the NHS? As we noted in our discus-sion of welfare pluralism, the fact that the NHS has involved a mix of public and private funding, planning and provision from the outset suggests that Warde's model never adequately portrayed the complex nature of the production and consumption of health care in the NHS. It was however more accurate to characterise the NHS as an example of state provision before the recent reforms than subsequently. Since the 1980s the nature of the mix between public and private has changed significantly with the balance swinging strongly towards the private sector. In such circum-stances it would be far more accurate to suggest that the British NHS reflects a new mode of provision – that of the marketised state – and that this set of arrangements has had an effect on the social relations of health care, the manner of its delivery and the experience of consumption.

In the new NHS access is still based on need rather than price but the right to equitable provision has been challenged by the development of a two-tier system of general practice (although this inequity might be reduced with primary care commissioning groups) and the possibility that socially stigmatised groups' health care needs may no longer be met as a result of rationing implemented in the name of local consumer preferences. Moreover, given the growing geographical disparities in provision resulting from the internal market, the choice of doctor or hospital available to people is dependent on where they live (Walsh 1994).

The manner of delivery has also changed with state professionals having to defend themselves against the growing power of health service managers, as predicted with a move towards a market for health care. However, the growth of new managerialism has not greatly empowered the users of the health service as these managers still have the final say, along with doctors, in any rationing decisions that are taken. Nor has the power of doctors been totally eclipsed as Warde's model would suggest, not least because patients lack the information to be able to judge the clinical skills of doctors and hence still defer to their expertise (even if they are more prepared to complain if things go wrong). Moreover, given the way in which the internal market works, patients continue to rely on GPs to act as proxy consumers and organise health care on their behalf.

In addition, despite the shift in mode of provision, there has not been a radical change in the experience of consumption. Admittedly, developments such as the Patient's Charter have presented users of health care as individual consumers rather than as citizens with a collective voice (Taylor 1992; Barnes 1997), but in practice such users have not found themselves more empowered. While there has been an increase in information about certain aspects of health care such as access, there still remains a considerable asymmetry between patients and providers (Shackley and Ryan 1994). Moreover, neither private nor NHS health care users seem keen to shop around for care and, faced with the uncertainty of illness, continue to prefer doctors to take responsibility for health care decisions. Thus, as far as users of the health service are concerned, informed choice does not appear to be a real option. According to Barnes and Walker (1998) empowerment would involve power sharing between professionals and users and would lead to the user ideally being involved in the development, management and operation of services as well as in the assessment of need. These authors argue that the 'supermarket' consumerist model and the marketisation of the public sector is an insufficient basis on which to empower service users because they are not involved in decision-making. Users are particularly vulnerable in the private sector because they do not have the protection of legal rights which can guarantee service users a 'voice'.

In the light of these comments we can also address the second question of the nature of the impact of the changes in the mode of provision on citizenship rights and social divisions. Developments such as the growth of private medicine, the contracting out of services and the Private Finance

Initiative, have all challenged the collectivism on which the NHS was founded and with it citizens' rights to ownership of a national asset. Moreover, social rights to equity and justice and the obligations these create have been undermined to an extent by the changes to the structure of provision. As Ruane (1997: 70) argues, the fragmentation of the health service may well be undermining the 'lateral solidarities' between service users and workers, 'breaking down the sense of communality and collectivity which surrounded the NHS and out of which it was born'.

At the same time social divisions have certainly not been reduced by the changes in health service provision and, if anything, have worsened as a result of them. Under the fundholding system access to primary and secondary care appeared to be more restricted for non-fundholding patients, the majority of whom were working class, while the better off have benefited from the growth in private health insurance and health care during the 1980s. As we noted earlier, consumption of private health care is a symbol of socio-economic position rather than a substitute for it. It is thus best seen as dependent on class and certainly does not reflect new social divisions independent of class as some have argued (Saunders 1989).

It is also worth noting, however, that being a subscriber to private health insurance does not result in ideological opposition to the NHS. On the contrary, those who have such insurance generally seem to hold the NHS in high regard and use it when possible. It would thus appear that changing the mode of provision does not, in some deterministic way, necessarily result in a particular attitude towards and experience of consumption. However, it must be remembered that private health insurance in the UK only applies to a relatively small minority of the population: it covers mainly acute care and seldom chronic illnesses, childbirth or major surgery, and those subscribers can still rely on the NHS when needed. Hence, the UK may not be the best example to evaluate whether a change in mode of provision shapes experience of consumption.

Finally, what of the wider cultural changes in people's views of medicine and their consumption of it that Warde's model seems to neglect? It has been suggested that lay views of modern medicine in the current period are far more critical and dynamic and that the notions of blanket professional dominance and the 'fabrication' of docile bodies are now of limited explanatory power (Williams and Calnan 1996). In late modernity doubt is said to be a defining feature of critical reasoning, with trust in experts no longer being taken for granted but needing to be won. However, this argument, has been shown to be of limited value in the 'unique' context of medicine and the doctor-patient relationship. For example, Lupton (1997: 379) shows in her empirical research on lay perceptions of medicine that lay people, even when they have adopted 'consumerist' orientations in some contexts, in others are willing to 'invest their trust and faith in a particular doctor, should that doctor earn this trust'. For, Lupton this suggests the need to acknowledge the importance of affective aspects of illness particularly in the context of doctor–patient encounters. Dependency, as Wiles and Higgins (1996) have shown in the context of 'private' medicine is, it appears, a fundamental character of the doctor–patient encounter regardless of the mode of provision.

References

Agnew, T. and Lyall, J. (1997) 'Doctors who don't deliver', *Health Service Journal* 17 April: 24–6.

Allsop, J. (1995) *Health Policy and the NHS, Towards 2000*, Harlow: Longman.

Annandale, A. (1998) *The Sociology of Health and Medicine*, Cambridge: Polity Press.

Baggott, R. (1994) *Health and Health Care in Britain*, London: Macmillan.

Barnes, M. (1997) *Care, Communities and Citizens*, London: Longman.

Barnes, M. and Walker, A. (1998) 'Consumerism versus empowerment: a principled approach to the involvement of older service users', *Policy and Politics* 24(4): 375–95.

Bruster, S., Jarman, B., Bosanquet, N., Weston, D., Erens, R. and Delbanco, T. L. (1994) 'National survey of hospital patients', *British Medical Journal* 309: 1,542–9.

Calnan, M., Cant, S., and Gabe, J. (1993) *Going Private, Why People Pay for their Health Care*, Buckingham: Open University Press.

Calnan, M., Halik, J. and Sabbat, J. (1998) 'Citizen participation and patient choice in health reform', in R. Saltman *et al.* (eds) *Critical Challenges for Health Care Reform in Europe*, Milton Keynes: Open University Press.

Campbell, C. (1995) 'The sociology of consumption', in D. Miller (ed.) *Acknowledging Consumption: A Review of New Studies*, London: Routledge.

Cartwright, A. and Windsor J. (1992) *Outpatients and Their Doctors*, London: HMSO.

Clarke, J. (1996) 'Public nightmares and communitarian dreams: the crisis of the social in social welfare', in S. Edgell, K. Hetherington and A. Warde (eds) *Consumption Matters: the Production and Experience of Consumption*, Oxford: Blackwell Publishers/*The Sociological Review*.

Clarke, J. and Newman, J. (1997) *The Managerial State*, London: Sage.

Crinson, I. (1998) 'Putting patients first: the continuity of the consumerist discourse in health policy, from the radical right to New Labour', *Critical Social Policy* 18(2): 227–39.

Davies, C. (1987) 'Things to come: the NHS in the next decade', *Sociology of Health and Illness* 9: 302–17.

Department of Health (1991) *The Patient's Charter*, London: HMSO.

Dickinson, M., Calnan, M. and Manley, G. (1999) 'Private or NHS General Dental Service care in the United Kingdom? A study of public perceptions and experiences', *Journal of Public Health Medicine* 16.

Doyal, L. (1998) 'Public participation and the moral quality of health care rationing', *Quality in the Health Care* 7: 98–102.

Edgell, S. and Hetherington, K. (1996) 'Introduction: consumption matters', in S. Edgell, K. Hetherington and A. Warde (eds) *Consumption Matters: The*

Production and Experience of Consumption, Oxford: Blackwell Publishers/*The Sociological Review.*

Flynn, R. (1992) 'Managed markets: consumers and producers in the National Health Service', in R. Burrows and C. Marsh (eds), *Consumption and Class: Divisions and Change,* Basingstoke: Macmillan.

Francome, C. and Marks, D. (1996) *Improving the Health of the Nation,* London: Middlesex University Press.

Gabe, J. (1997) 'Continuity and change in the British National Health Service', in P. Conrad (ed.) *The Sociology of Health and Illness: Critical Perspectives,* New York: St Martin's Press.

Gabriel, Y. and Lang, T. (1995) *The Unmanageable Consumer: Contemporary Consumption and its Fragmentation,* London: Sage.

Glennerster, H., Matsaganis, M. and Owens, P. (1992) *A Foothold in Fundraising,* London: King's Fund Institute.

Griffiths, R. (1983) *NHS Management Inquiry,* Report, London: DHSS.

Harrison, S., Hunter, D. and Pollitt, C. (1990) *The Dynamics of British Health Policy,* London: Unwin Hyman.

Hunter, D. (1994) 'From tribalism to corporatism: the challenge to medical dominance', in J. Gabe, D. Kelleher and G. Williams (eds) *Challenging Medicine,* London: Routledge.

—— (1995) 'Making a virtue out of chaos', *Health Service Journal* 23 March: 23.

Hunter D. J. and Harrison, S. (1997). 'Democracy, accountability and consumerism', in S. Iliffe and J. Munro (eds) *Healthy Choices: Future Options for the NHS,* London: Lawrence and Wishart.

Keat, R., Whiteley, N. and Abercrombie (1994) 'Introduction', in R. Keat, N. Whiteley and N. Abercrombie (eds) *The Authority of the Consumer,* London: Routledge.

Klein, R. (1995) *The Politics of the NHS,* 3rd edn, London: Longman.

Labour Party (1996) 'Renewing the National Health Service: Labour's agenda for a healthier Britain', *International Journal of Health Services* 26(2): 269–308.

Leavey, R., Wilkin, D. and Metcalfe, D. H. H. (1989) 'Consumerism and general practice', *British Medical Journal* 298: 737–9.

Lupton, D. (1997) 'Consumerism, reflexivity and the medical encounter', *Social Science and Medicine* 45(3): 373–81.

Mechanic, D. (1996) 'Changing medical organisation and the erosion of trust', *The Milbank Quarterly* 74(2): 171–89.

Milewa, T., Valentine, J. and Calnan, M. (1998) 'Managerialism and active citizenship in Britain's reformed health service: power and community in an era of decentralisation', *Social Science and Medicine* 47: 507–18.

—— (1999) 'Community participation and citizenship in British health care planning: narratives of power and involvement in the changing welfare state', *Sociology of Health and Illness,* 21(4): 445–65.

Mohan, J. (1995) *A National Health Service? The Restructuring of Health Care in Britain since 1979,* Basingstoke: Macmillan.

Mort, M. and Harrison, S. (1998) 'Which champions, which people? Public and user involvement in health care as a technology of legitimations', *Social Policy and Administration* 32(1): 66–70.

Mulligan, J. A. and Judge, K. (1997) *Public Opinion and the NHS in Health Care UK 1996/7*, Kings Fund: London.

National Health Service Management Executive (1992) *Local Voices: the Views of Local People in Commissioning for Health*, London: NHS Management Executive.

Paton, C. (1992) *Competition and Planning in the NHS: The Dangers of Unplanned Markets*, London: Chapman and Hall.

Pickard, S., Williams, G. and Flynn, R. (1995) 'Local voices in the internal market: the case of community health services', *Social Policy and Administration* 29: 135–49.

Ranade, W. (1994) *A Future for the NHS?*, Harlow: Longman.

Rayner, G. (1987) 'Lessons from America? Commercialization and growth of private medicine in Britain', *International Journal of Health Services* 17: 197–216.

Ruane, S. (1997) 'Public–private boundaries and the transformation of the NHS', *Critical Social Policy* 17: 53–78.

Saunders, P. (1989) 'Beyond housing classes: the sociological significance of private property rights in means of consumption', in L. McDowell, P. Sarre and C. Hamnett (eds) *Divided Nation: Social and Cultural Change in Britain*, London: Open University Press.

Seale, C. (1993) 'The consumer voice', in B. Davey and J. Popay (eds) *Dilemmas in Health Care*, Buckingham: Open University Press.

Shackely, P. and Ryan, M. (1994) 'What is the role of the consumer in health care?' *Journal of Social Policy* 23: 517–41.

Taylor, D. (1992) 'A big idea for the nineties? The rise of the citizens' charters', *Critical Social Policy* 33: 87–94.

Taylor-Gooby, P. (1993) 'Citizenship, dependency and the welfare mix: problems of inclusion and exclusion', *International Journal of Health Services* 23(3): 455–74.

Walsh, K. (1994) 'Citizens, charters and contracts', in R. Keat, N. Whiteley and N Abercrombie (eds) *The Authority of the Consumer*, London: Routledge.

Warde, A. (1990) 'Introduction to the sociology of consumption', *Sociology* 24(1): 1–4.

—— (1992) 'Notes on the relationship between production and consumption', in R. Burrows and C. Marsh (eds) *Consumption and Class: Divisions and Change*, Basingstoke: Macmillan.

—— (1996) 'Afterword: the future of the sociology of consumption', in S. Edgell, K. Hetherington and Alan Warde (eds) *Consumption Matters: The Production and Experience of Consumption*, Oxford: Blackwell Publishers/*The Sociological Review*.

Wilder, G. (1997) 'Pay-back time', *Health Service Journal* 20 March: 28–31.

Wiles, R. and Higgins, J. (1996) 'Doctor–patient relationships in the private sector: patients perspectives', *Sociology of Health and Illness* 18(5): 341–51.

Williams, S. and Calnan, M. (1996) 'The limits of "medicalization?": modern medicine and the lay populace in "late" modernity', *Social Science and Medicine* 42: 1,609–20.

Wratten, L. (1996) 'When things go wrong', *Health Matters* 25: 10–11.

Part IV

Emotions

Chapter 14

Emotions, psychiatry and social order

A Habermasian approach

Nick Crossley

The focus of this chapter is the growth, during the postwar period, of an 'emotion industry', consisting of pharmaceutical companies, psychiatric and GP services, psychotherapy and counselling, psychological services and the sales boom in psychological self-help manuals. Aspects of this industry have been analysed elswhere, either in terms of its medical (Rose *et al.* 1984) or psychological and psychotherapeutic components (Rose 1985, 1989; Giddens 1991, 1992; Craib 1994; Pilgrim 1997). The broader picture of the industry as a whole has not been considered, however, and it is one of my chief aims to correct this. Moreover, I aim to broaden and deepen the picture by considering the situation of the emotion industry within the complex relations which hold between emotion, psychiatry and the social order.

Theoretically my argument draws upon Habermas (1987, 1991) and upon my own previous attempts to introduce a more corporeal and affective dimension into his otherwise predominantly cognitive approach (Crossley 1996, 1997, 1998). The strength of the Habermasian approach is that it allows us to consider the emotion–psychiatry–order nexus from both a systems and a lifeworld perspective; that is, to consider it in terms of the socially and normatively integrated sphere of communicative action, and in terms of economic and political systems. Habermas's approach is unique in affording the opportunity for considered reflection at both of these levels. All other major perspectives tend to approach psychiatry from either one or the other; the ethnomethodologists (e.g. Coulter 1973, 1975, 1979; Pollner 1975) and interactionists (e.g. Goffman 1961, 1971; Scheff 1984), for example, examine the lifeworld dimension, focusing upon the process and consequences of insanity ascription at the level of intersubjective human praxes, whilst the Marxists (e.g. Scull 1984, 1993) and Foucauldians (Foucault 1965; Castel 1988; Rose 1985, 1989) adopt a more systemic focus, examining the 'unintended' contribution of psy-services to the securing of social order and the process of governance, as well, in the case of the Marxists, as their relation to economic and political systems. Furthermore, the Habermasian approach allows us to put the technical control of emotion, promised by the emotion industry, into a critical perspective, by contrasting it with an alternative: *the rational regulation of emotion in the lifeworld*. Much of my argument in the chapter rests upon the notion of 'rational emotion' and the 'rational regulation of emotion'. I therefore begin with a detailed account of what I mean by these terms.

Reason and emotion

Emotion and reason are, as Williams and Bendelow (1998) critically note, often portrayed as mutually exclusive opposites. This portrayal is problematic for a number of reasons. First, it fails to consider that emotions may not be the sort of things that one can step out of and thus that the calculating attitude of seriousness associated with reason may itself be regarded as an emotional attitude. When we oppose reason to emotion, I contend, we rely upon one very specific use of the term 'emotion', a use which designates excessive or inappropriate emotional states. To this there corresponds a notion of being 'unemotional', which is applied in instances where an individual might be expected to display a sense of heightened emotion but doesn't. There is also a sense, however, in which we must always adopt an emotional attitude towards the world, whether that be an attitude of gravity, elation or whatever. Everyday discourse clearly admits the claim of 'feeling' calm, for example, and even 'feeling rational'. Second, the juxtaposition of reason and emotion rests upon mind/body dualism; reason being assigned to the mind, emotion to the body. This basis is problematic because it crumbles if we take contemporary challenges to dualism seriously (Merleau-Ponty 1962; Crossley 1994, 1995). If mind and body are not separate Cartesian 'substances', then our basis for seeing reason and emotion as belonging to different realms collapses also. Third, the juxtaposition of reason and emotion assumes a very narrow, instrumental view of reason. If reason is simply a matter of linking means to ends then many of the wide range of human emotional responses to situations may indeed be deemed irrational because they are often not good means of resolving problem situations. Crying at funerals would be irrational, for example, because it does not bring the deceased back to life. If we adopt a broader and wider definition of rationality, such as Habermas's (1987, 1991) 'communicative rationality', however, then this mutual exclusion and opposition are by no means as evident and it becomes possible to think of emotions as having the potential to be either rational or irrational. Furthermore, there are good reasons, additional to the purposes of this paper, for us to broaden our conception of reason. The attempt to narrow 'reason' down to an instrumental core has the disadvantage of departing significantly from our common uses of the terms 'reason' and 'rational', which is problematic as common usage is the only meaningful benchmark we have for making sense of a concept (Wittgenstein 1953). Moreover, many central aspects of social life are irrational by this view definition (Habermas 1991; Hindess 1988; White 1988). It is this third point that I wish to expand upon in this chapter.

Rational emotion

As a first step it should be noted that we routinely judge emotions in terms of their reasonableness in everyday life. It seems *reasonable* to us, for example, that an individual would be upset if they hear of the death of a loved one. In such cases we are inclined to say that they *have good reasons* to feel as they do. Conversely, it is not so reasonable if they become very upset after a minor mishap and we might judge this *irrational* because they 'blew up *for no reason*'. Reason, in this context, is clearly linked to mutual, intersubjective understanding and contextual appropriateness. An emotional response strikes us as reasonable insofar as it seems to have been occasioned by circumstances and insofar as we can understand it as the sort of reaction that we or anybody else might have had to such circumstances.

Another integral element of this notion of reasonable emotion is that we are often inclined to try to argue individuals out of seemingly unreasonable emotions. We may suggest to them that they are mistaken, that they have *no reason* to feel as they do, and we might be successful in changing their response by these means. Conversely, they might inform us of circumstances that we are unaware of, persuading us that their response is rational. Either way emotion is rooted, as a rationally accountable phenomenon, within the communicative praxes which are constitutive of the lifeworld.

In saying this I do not mean to deny the embodiment of emotion. Emotional responses clearly are embodied. It is significant, however, that they enter into the communicative praxes of the lifeworld in a way which distinguishes them from certain other embodied phenomena (see also Crossley 1998). One would not ordinarily expect to talk an individual out of a toothache, for example, as one might their anger. At most one expects to be able to take a person's mind off their toothache through talk but with emotion one genuinely expects to be able to 'talk them around'. Likewise, although one might feel justified in criticising an individual for their emotional attitude, one would not ordinarily expect the same with respect to pain. One might be tempted to suggest that a person is overreacting to pain but such criticism is directed at the emotional response to the pain and not to the pain itself. It is for this reason, because emotions fall on this side of the line of bodily phenomena, that I suggest they be deemed rational. Moreover, I would further suggest, on the same grounds, that emotions belong to the subject side of our embodiment, to the body-subject (Merleau-Ponty 1962; Crossley 1994, 1995) rather than the mechanistic body-object; that is, they belong to 'the body' considered as a purposive being, oriented to intersubjectively constituted systems of meaning. With this said we can explore the rationality of emotion in a little more depth.

Emotion and the three validity claims

Habermas (1991) outlines three types of 'validity claims' which, he argues, can be raised, differentiated and contested in rational discourse and which, as such, define it. Rational discourses raise, in either tacit or explicit forms, *truth claims* about the world, *sincerity claims* in respect of the speaker and *normative claims* about both the social world and the rights of the speaker *qua* speaker. It is my contention, and central to my claim that emotions can be reasonable, that emotional conduct is potentially open to argumentation on exactly these terms. As responses occasioned by specific situations, for example, emotions raise claims about those situations. Worry, for example, raises the claim that the individual has something to be worried about. Likewise, the sincerity of another's emotional conduct can always be called into question and argued over. Finally, emotions raise normative claims. One 'ought' to have certain emotions in certain circumstances, for example, such as sadness at a time of loss, and if one doesn't then one may be subject to moral criticism. Furthermore, having certain feelings about a person, such as love, typically involves assumption of specific obligations towards them which, in many cases, may themselves be fulfilled through the expression of particular emotions. As with the previous two claims, there will always be room for argument in such cases. Individuals who do not show the feelings they ought might be asked why they don't and if they don't think that they should, but they may respond with convincing arguments regarding the moral justification for their feeling and acting as they do.

Not every expression of emotion will necessarily raise each of these three claims and it is certainly true that, in many cases, the type of debate I have outlined will not take place. It is sufficient for my argument, however, that they can and do take place in some form, some of the time. This illustrates that emotions are bound up with the rational communicative exchanges that are largely constitutive of the lifeworld. Communicative rationality is central to the process of social integration according to Habermas. Social integration is achieved through intersubjective relations of mutual understanding and negotiation, which facilitate co-ordination and co-operation, and through the common recognition of certain core norms which can be appealed to in everyday interaction. It rests upon the process whereby situations are made *rationally accountable* to their participants by way of communication. As such it relies strongly upon both the mundane reasoning skills of participants and upon the possibility that ordinary events in the social world can be accounted for and *argued over*. Having established the communicatively rational nature of emotion, therefore, we have also indicated the manner in which it is bound into the process of social integration. As a rational, accountable phenomenon it is regulated by recourse to practical reason and discourse.

Irrational emotion, social order and psychiatry

None of what I have said implies that emotions don't get out of hand and cause disruption in the lifeworld. To define emotion as rational in the sense that I have, however, is to suggest that it is something which is understandable and to an extent therefore manageable for social agents. When emotions pose a threat agents are able to engage in the types of debates I have mentioned, contesting the claims to validity which are tacitly raised and thereby attempting to restore order. As with cognitive processes, however, emotions can transcend the boundaries of communicative rationality to a socially intolerable extent. Like hallucinatory perceptions or delusional beliefs, they can prove resistant to the efforts of lifeworld members to understand and reason with those who express and experience them. Extreme feelings of depression or elation, lasting over an extended period time, which bear no obvious relation to occasioning circumstances and cannot be accounted for by the person experiencing them, provide one example of this, as do instances of what psychiatrists refer to as 'inappropriate affect'; that is, emotional responses which do not 'fit' with their circumstances, such as laughing at a sad event or becoming upset at happy circumstances.

Given what I have said about the importance of communicative reasoning for social integration, it should be evident that these irrational emotions can pose a threat to social order (see Goffman 1971, for an illustration). For present purposes it will suffice to make three brief points about this threat and its significance. First, the individual who is affected in this way doesn't behave as they ought to behave if social order is to be secured. They cease to be a co-ordinated part of interaction sequences and become something of a loose cannon. This creates a basic disturbance in the process of social integration and, consequently, in the social order. Moreover, given what I have said about the moral claims that emotional behaviour raises, there is a potential for moral injury which stems from this. This is made worse by the second factor, which is that the usual mechanisms for righting wrongs in the social world don't work in these cases. Indeed, this is precisely what separates these cases from 'ordinary emotional deviance'; the deviant can't be talked back into line and can't be made accountable and understandable in the usual ways. The implication of this, and this is my third point, is that it can generate great anxiety for all those involved, as Goffman (1971) shows and, indeed, as was discovered in the planned breaches of convention organised by Garfinkel (1967) and his students. Anxiety is a common experience when the rules of normal inter-action and the intersubjective understanding they facilitate break down.

It is at this point, where the threat to social integration is great, that psy-chiatry usually steps in. Psychiatry is precisely concerned with irrational emotions, emotions which defy ordinary attempts to understand or regulate them. And, at least in its biomedical form, it short-circuits the search for reason and understanding by offering explanations of emotional conduct at the level of the third-person processes of the brain and nervous system: e.g. neurotransmitter activity. Within this technical, instrumentally rational dis-course, emotion is stripped of its claim to reasonableness or meaning and reduced to a cause within the body, where the latter is understood as a phys-ical system. A gestalt shift is effected in which the reasonable, meaningful and purposive aura of the body-subject is eclipsed by the complex causal relations and mechanisms which comprise the body-object. The body no longer secretes meanings, it manifests symptoms which point to underlying mechanical faults. This shift in discourse and perception can be helpful for the relatives of individuals 'explained' in these ways, as indeed for the indi-viduals themselves. For as long as the 'sick' individual is perceived within the frame of communicative rationality their behaviour has the potential to create the anxiety and moral injury discussed above, but when the gestalt shifts and they are objectified this potential is removed. Their behaviour no longer causes moral injury because it is no longer attributed to a moral agent. And it no longer causes (as much) confusion and anxiety because the requirement to understand and judge it against the standards of commu-nicative reason is removed. It is clear to see in this case how psychiatric diagnosis conforms to Parsons's (1951) claim that the sick role removes blame from the individual and it is equally clear to see why this may be a pressing matter in relation to so-called 'mental illness', where conduct is capable of generating a great deal of moral injury.

It is important to add here that the psychotherapies work in a similar way. They too are technologies of emotion which short-circuit the process of com-municative reasoning, as I have defined it. This is perhaps evident with respect to behaviourist techniques, like 'flooding' or 'systematic desensiti-sation', which closely conform to a positivistic scientific model, but it applies equally to other therapies (for psychoanalysis see Kendall and Crossley 1996). All suspend the process of open communicative exchange, restructuring the dialogical process and suspending the assumptions of normal interaction, in accordance with the rules and roles appropriate to their technique. Moreover, models are employed which allow the therapist to reframe the utterances of the client in such a way that it is amenable to diag-nosis and intervention; utterances become signs or symptoms of the work-ings of a psychological system. As with drugs this has a demoralising effect;

behaviours which might otherwise be deemed immoral are reframed as indicators of psychological problems which require cure rather than reprimand.

This process of technologising is where the efficacy of both psychotherapy and psycho-pharmacology is said to lie and, as I have already noted, it is a process which enables diffusion of at least some of the difficulties which emotional problems can generate within the process of social integration. This is also where the potential danger of psychiatry lies, however, both for the individual defined in this way and for society more generally. The danger for the individual is that their conduct ceases to be understood as that of a reasonable and responsible moral agent. This may be attractive to such individuals if it allows them to avoid culpability for their actions but it is nevertheless a form of dehumanisation and disempowerment which some individuals seek to avoid. On the side of society the danger is that areas of conduct are torn loose from the fabric of the lifeworld and deemed 'off-limits' to ordinary methods of understanding, judging and managing them, and to the norms and values which underpin such methods. The lifeworld and its members are effectively disempowered in this respect, as a limit is set to the range of behaviours which are accountable to and controllable by them, making them dependent upon experts and specialised forms of technical intervention. A new form of non-accountable power is constituted. Moreover, this involves a substitution of technical for moral solutions and thus constitutes a demoralisation of the lifeworld. The range of behaviours expected to be morally accountable is subject to a limiting factor.

I describe these tendencies as 'dangers' rather than 'problems' since there is no problem if the line between rational and irrational emotion is 'correctly' drawn within psychiatric practice. Insofar as this is the case technical interventions may be justified because they would only be applied to those individuals whose emotions defy communicative understanding and reason. There is a danger, however, *because there can be no hard and fast criteria for differentiating the rational and the irrational*. Although it is easy to think of paradigm cases at each extreme, the judgement of reason necessarily occurs in an intersubjective situation and rests upon the mutual understanding that is built between interlocutors (Habermas 1991), relying, as all such situations do, upon culturally specific and often ambiguous assumptions, 'et cetera clauses' (Garfinkel 1967) and forms of taken for granted knowledge (Coulter 1973; Ingleby 1981). Moreover, there is at least cause for concern, given the historical evidence which suggests both a shrinkage in the range of emotions deemed reasonable and acceptable in society (Elias 1994; Newton 1998), and an increasing reliance upon technical forms of intervention into emotional life.

In relation to this latter trend we can point to the growth of a massive 'emotion industry', consisting of pharmaceutical companies, public sector psychiatric and GP services, psychotherapy and counselling, psychological services, as well as the sales boom in psychological self-help manuals. In terms of the private sector, this industry can be traced back to the private madhouses and fashionable 'nerve doctors' of the eighteenth century (Porter 1987), with public sector involvement developing in the following century, in the form of the asylum system (Scull 1993). These developments, with the exception of the nerve doctors and the related growth of 'office psychiatry', both of which were relatively small scale before the 1950's, functioned primarily by way of exclusion and, in theory at least, were focused only upon the extreme edge of emotional and psychological disturbance: 'lunacy'. In the period since the 1950's, however, the focus of psy-services has moved out into the community and has widened the scope of its interventions considerably, incorporating what have become known as neurotic problems (Busfield 1986), as well as more general psychological and emotional problems and issues associated with the twists and turns of the lifecycle (Rose 1985, 1989).

The development of new psychoactive drugs is an important part of this. During the mid-1960s there was a sharp rise in the number of individuals, particularly women, being prescribed tranquillisers such as Valium for emotional problems (Gabe and Williams 1986). More recently it is Prozac, 'the wonder drug', which has served this market, and widened it to include more men and children (Rose *et al.* 1984). Furthermore, since the 1970s a number of drugs, most notably Ritalin, have been developed to address 'problems' of hyperactivity or 'attention deficit disorder' in infants, children and young people, and are now used quite widely, particularly in the USA (Armstrong 1993).

In addition to drugs, however, there has been a massive expansion in psychotherapy, counselling and a variety of self-help books and audio-cassettes which claim either to resolve emotional problems or to maximise aspects of an individual's emotional potential (Rose 1989; Giddens 1991, 1992; Craib 1994; Pilgrim 1997). In contrast to the drugs, these emotional technologies are not monopolised or regulated by the medical profession, who in many cases remain suspicious of them, and have tended, therefore, to proliferate within the private sector. Increasingly, however, the sectors, approaches and technologies have merged. As the NHS has been marketised, GPs in particular have elected to buy in counselling and psychotherapeutic services. The trend looks set to consolidate and continue, moreover, as various forms of emotional 'injury' are increasingly being recognised within the courts and compensation and insurance claims are starting to bite. Where employers were once expected to protect only their employees' physical health, there is now an increased expectation that they are responsible also for some aspects of emotional health, a factor which generates great potential for commercial development.

It is not immediately obvious how we should interpret this trend. It is arguably worrying whichever way one looks at it, unless it simply represents an increased recognition of previously undetected problems – which seems unlikely given the unrelenting longevity of the trend. But what should we be worried about? Should we be worried because society is causing an increase in emotional problems or because professionals are pathologising and monopolising an increasing range of emotional vicissitudes? Is irrational and pathological emotion on the increase, in real terms, or are professionals shifting the boundaries of the rational and the irrational and, in the process, undermining the capacity of lifeworld members to deal with emotions? In what remains of this chapter, drawing on further aspects of Habermas's theory, I suggest that there is reason to believe that both may be true and, indeed, that each are twin aspects of the same process. As a necessary first step, however, we must briefly outline the central tenets of Habermas's social theory in more detail.

System and lifeworld

The aspect of Habermas's theory that we have engaged with hitherto is his analysis of the rationalised lifeworld; that is, the aspect of the social world which is integrated and reproduced through communicative action and the mutual orientations it involves. The term 'rationalised' is used by Habermas to indicate the extent to which areas of social life have been secularised and opened up to linguistic contestation in terms of the three aforementioned validity claims. Many areas of our lives, which were once governed by indisputable religious prescriptions are now open to debate and demands for accountability, he argues, and are thus subject to rational regulation. This generates great potential, he continues. Rationalisation affords us the possibility of greater control over our lives and also accountability, democracy and justice. This potential has been obscured, however, by the unilateral way in which rationalisation has progressed and the side-effects which this has created: specifically 'colonisation of the lifeworld' and 'cultural impoverishment'.

To understand 'colonisation of the lifeworld' we must first understand the distinction between lifeworld and system. Habermas draws this distinction at a number of levels. First, he argues that our understanding of 'social integration' must be complemented with a notion of 'system integration'. The former was discussed above. It involves rational communicative negotiation and, as such, is *coextensive with the lifeworld*. The latter, by contrast, refers to the harmonisation of the unintended consequences of action that is achieved by way of 'emergent' social mechanisms which operate 'behind the back' of the actor. The economy is a key example of this: it co-ordinates the distribution of goods in society without requiring that any of the agents involved in it (i.e. the entire population) understands how this is done or orients to it *qua* co-ordinating mechanism. As Adam Smith (1950) famously suggested, economic agents act selfishly, without due consideration for the consequences of their action, but the consequences of their action are nevertheless co-ordinated by way of the 'invisible hand' of the market. *Such system integration mechanisms are an integral element of Habermas's understanding of systems.* Moreover, he gives the name 'strategic action' to the type of action orientation noted by Smith, and he contrasts it with both 'communicative action' and 'labour'. Strategic and communicative action both entail human interaction. They differ in the respect that the former is oriented to success and operates with a purposive, means-end type of rationality, whilst the latter is oriented to mutual understanding and operates with a communicatively rational form of interaction. Communicative actions, Habermas argues, typically involve the securing of consent between actors in order to be effective. Strategic action, by contrast, depends upon forms of power or manipulation for its efficacy. What differentiates strategic action from labour is that the latter involves interaction with the physical world. Like strategic action it is oriented to success but to achieve this it must manipulate physical forces rather than social conventions.

The second level at which Habermas draws his distinction concerns the symbolic and material reproduction of society. The symbolic reproduction of society, which involves the reproduction of personalities, culture and the normative order, necessarily relies upon communicative action. The processes of socialisation, cultural transmission and normative regeneration can only be achieved by way of actions which are oriented towards mutual understanding. In this sense symbolic reproduction belongs very much to the lifeworld, since *the lifeworld consists precisely in those symbolic elements and the communicative actions which reproduce them.* Material reproduction, however, which involves the provision and distribution of the means of physical survival for a society, requires labour, which transforms the physical world in accordance with instrumentally rational plans. Moreover, in large-scale societies it relies upon mechanisms of system integration and upon strategically rational interactions. Thus *there is a close affinity between material reproduction and the system level* in Habermas's theory.

The third level at which Habermas draws his distinction is historical. In traditional societies, he argues, the processes of symbolic and material reproduction were closely interwoven. Economic exchanges, for example, were regulated according to religious lore. One aspect of the process of societal modernisation and rationalisation, however, has been an 'uncoupling' of certain parts of the process of material reproduction from the communicatively negotiated order of the lifeworld, by way of the emergence of reified and objectified action contexts, such as the 'marketplace', which accommodate strategic action. Economic actors, for example, are not bound by traditional value systems, nor must they strive to achieve communicatively rational consensus with their interactants. Money talks in the economic system and everything has a price. Moreover, although the law sets boundaries for economic action, the only moral expectation for actors is that they stay within these bounds: whatever is not prohibited is allowed. Integral to this is the emergence of what Habermas calls 'delinguistified' media of exchange, such as money, which generate, by way of the pricing mechanism, a reification of exchange processes, and which facilitate the emergence of 'system integration' mechanisms like the market. Money, as a standardised indicator of exchange value, allows for the co-ordination of the vast number of (economic) transactions that occur within any society at any time, in a way that does not depend upon a communicatively achieved co-ordination plan.

These media, their related action contexts and the mechanisms of system integration they effect form the basis of Habermasian 'systems' and he suggests that two such systems have emerged in the process of modernisation and rationalisation, along with two delinguistified mediums of exchange (money and power) and four system-roles. The first system is the economy. In this system individuals sell their labour power in return for a wage, which they then use to purchase the goods that they need or to pursue more money through investment etc. The relations involved here are strategic and do not depend, as such, upon communicative action. The consumer, for example, does not consult the shopkeeper with respect to the goods that they buy, nor do they seek their consent or understanding. They orient to the shopkeeper either as another individual or as an incumbent of a social role but they nevertheless buy what they want, where they want, from whom they want, when they want. And they reserve the non-negotiable right to do so. The second system identified by Habermas is the modern administrative-political system. In this system individuals pay taxes in return for services (e.g. welfare services) provided by the state, and they both bestow power upon the state, through their authorisation and legitimation of its rule, and are subject to and benefit from its power in the form of the political decisions that it effectively imposes upon them.

The colonisation of the lifeworld and cultural impoverishment

This 'uncoupling' of system mechanisms from the lifeworld is, to some extent, both necessary and desirable for Habermas. It provides a relatively effective way of co-ordinating material reproduction. There are instabilities in the system, however, which have led to pathological consequences. These instabilities stem, in the first instance, from economic crisis tendencies and the potential for class conflict these generate, but in contemporary societies, where systems of economic management and welfare provision have emerged, they have shifted to the political level. A situation has been created in which workers endure the problems they experience in the labour market because and to the extent that they are placated by the welfare goods provided for them by the state. In combination with continuing economic demands, however, this generates a colonisation of the lifeworld by economic and political relations. If the economy is to survive, the argument runs, then it needs to expand existing markets and develop new ones, with the consequence that an increasing number of regions of the lifeworld are subject to commodification, including many which are central for social integration and symbolic reproduction. Likewise in relation to the political-administrative system: the dynamics of 'legitimation politics', which require the state to take on ever more roles if it is to pacify citizens, coupled with the requirement for social control, have led to an increasing expansion of the administrative machine into the lifeworld. In relation to ever more areas of their lives, individuals find themselves as either *clients* or *consumers*.

This is coupled with a process of 'cultural impoverishment'. What Habermas means by this is that a wide range of areas of life have, by virtue of a process of increasing cultural differentiation and specialisation, become the preserve of various forms of 'expert', whose knowledge is, by definition, esoteric and is often closely guarded and protected. This has the consequence of deskilling individuals in relation to a wide range of spheres of action and of fragmenting their sense of the world. They are unable to form a coherent worldview as the complexity of the social world and the specialisation of discourses it entails defies synthesis.

These processes of colonisation and impoverishment have pathological consequences for Habermas. At one level this entails a 'demoralisation' of society. Like Weber (1978), he recognises the incapacity of strategically rational action systems to generate valid normative frameworks and he thus perceives their increased predominance as a loss to the moral core of society (which is otherwise constituted by the aforementioned normative structure of the lifeworld). In addition, however, he identifies directly psychopathological consequences (see also Sloan 1996). This idea is not very well developed in his work. It is clear that what he intends has some relation to Weber's (1978) notion of the 'loss of freedom' and 'loss of meaning' created by societal rationalisation, and to both Durkheim's (1952) understanding of anomie and the Marxist notion of alienation (Marx 1977), but how this works in practice is not spelled out. What Habermas seems to mean, however, can be postulated in terms of a number of plausible hypotheses. First, he is suggesting that the 'strategic relations' required by the roles of client and consumer do not engender the types of relationship and interaction required for the stabilisation of personalities and are corrosive of lifeworld traditions which, in the past, have given individuals a sense of purpose, meaning and direction in life. When all is reduced to the cash nexus, formal contract or to self-interested political exchange, the basis from which a meaningful life can be constructed is considerably diminished. Second, Habermas holds some version of the thesis that the 'client' role engenders an unhealthy dependence upon the part of those who adopt it and that welfare, therefore, can have a detrimental effect upon autonomy. Third, there is a sense in which, for Habermas, cultural impoverishment undermines an individual's capacity to construct a coherent narrative about their self and world. They are alienated from the types of knowledge that they need to construct a satisfying and legitimate story about their self or indeed to experience that sense of autonomy which is central to well-being.

The emotion industry

From this position it is possible to offer, albeit tentatively, a two-pronged approach to the question of the growth of the emotion industry, focusing both upon supply and demand. From the demand side, Habermas identifies certain (psycho)pathological consequences with the colonisation of the lifeworld and cultural impoverishment, and the growth of the 'emotion industry' can be seen as a response to the need that this creates. Social changes are making people unhappy and entrepreneurs within psychology and psycho-pharmacology are responding to this. Supply follows demand. From this point of view the expansion of the emotion industry does not indicate that our criteria for judging emotions rational or otherwise have changed. It suggests that people are more distressed than they used to be. The growth of the emotion industry is a systemic solution to a systemically induced problem (psychopathology). This conclusion is interesting from Habermas's point of view, but also challenging, since it suggests that the system is more durable than he suggests and is, in fact, able to compensate for the damage it does to the process of social integration by providing psycho-technological alternatives.

Habermas might also want to put forward a supply-led explanation, however, not least because many sectors of the emotion industry do not strictly offer 'cures' for 'problems'(Rose 1989). The rise of the industry is easily mapped on to the twin track dynamic of economic and administrative expansion that he identifies, whilst the specialisation of 'psy' knowledge conforms to the process of 'cultural impoverishment'. The expansion of psychiatric services during the postwar period is clearly linked to the incorporation of welfare provision into the remit of the state (Busfield 1986), for example, whilst there is an evident financial logic to both recent psycho-pharmacological 'advances', such as the invention of Ritalin and Prozac (Rose et al. 1984), and the expansion of psychotherapy, counselling and self-help books (Craib 1994). Whatever the motives of the people who write such books or become psychotherapists, their opportunity to do so must be explained in terms of the emergence of a new 'psycho-sector' within the service economy. Likewise with the pharmaceutical companies; as Abraham (1995) (albeit with somewhat different intent), has shown, the economically competitive environment within which these companies work generates a considerable pressure for the expansion and domination of markets. Pharmaceutical companies have a vested interest in the extension of the remit of psychiatric intervention and constitute a powerful force for bringing this about.

Furthermore, it is not only the postwar trends that can be interpreted in this way. Roy Porter (1987), for example, explains both the rise of the private madhouses, in the eighteenth century, and the emergence of 'nerve doctors' in terms of 'service sector' expansion and increased affluence amongst the bourgeoisie:

> In the 'birth of the consumer society', one growing item of consumption was the services of madhouses, not because affluence drove people crazy, but because its commercial ethos made trading in insanity feasible.
>
> (Porter 1987: 165)

Similarly, it is evident from the work of Scull (1984, 1993), Busfield (1986) and Goodwin (1993, 1997), that the development of public sector psychiatric services has been strongly affected by the dynamics of the political-administrative system and its attempt to secure stability within the context of the capitalist economy. The location of the nineteenth-century public asylums within the poor law (Busfield 1986; Scull 1993), illustrates this clearly for the early history of psychiatry, whilst Goodwin's (1993) focus on the economic and legitimation demands which had to be balanced in and by the process of decarceration provides a more contemporary illustration.

Another interesting dimension to the longer term historical perspective, moreover, is that the emergence of public sector psychiatry appears to have been quite closely linked to a threat to system (rather than social) integration. Scull (1993), for example, pointing to the integral link of the asylum with the poor law, has suggested that asylums emerged in response to the need to discipline the workforce and distinguish the deserving and undeserving poor; that is, he suggests that the mad had to be sequestered because they were unable to assume the newly emerging (systemic) role of industrial labourer. Furthermore, from another perspective, Castel (1988) has argued that the emergence of the asylum system in France was very closely linked to the emergence of the new political system, following the 1789 revolution. Again the case he makes is that 'lunatics' were unable to assume the (systemic) role expected of them in this new order. In both cases 'lunatics' were an obstacle to the smooth running of the newly emerging mechanisms of system integration.

This is where the danger that I discussed earlier could become reality. Pressure to expand markets, secure legitimacy or eradicate 'system problems' may lead to an extension of psy-services into areas where there is no demand for them but where such demand can be created, at the cost of undermining the potential for managing emotion within the lifeworld and a consequent diminution of the boundaries of reasonable emotion. As Craib (1994) notes, for example, the sales tactics of many of the new forms of psychotherapy actively encourage individuals to be less tolerant of the range of emotions they might experience and encourages them to believe that they could and should always feel good, a right which psychotherapy purports to guarantee for them. History is again illustrative here. Porter (1987), for example, has suggested that the demand for private madhouses was largely a consequence of supply-side machinations:

> When Ticehurst was founded, custom was initially a mere trickle, indicating that demand had to be 'created' or at least nursed, rather than being a damned-up lake seeking outlet. Nevertheless, once a 'supply' was created, demand soon rose to capacity.
>
> (Porter 1987: 165)

Likewise Scull (1993) notes the considerable growth in the proportion of the population officially deemed insane, following the development of the public asylum system. He attributes this trend to both doctors, who were willing to expand the boundaries of 'caseness' when they had the beds available, and the community, whose tolerance of unusual behaviour decreased as a consequence of the availability of asylum places. In both cases we can see how psychiatric technologies displace lifeworld skills and competencies, shifting the boundaries of tolerance and changing, or rather diminishing, the definition of what is reasonable. Seeing a counsellor or taking a pill begin to move their way up the list of possible responses that individuals have for the emotionally difficult situations they face and the definition of emotional difficulty is widened. Or to put it another way, sorting emotional problems in communicatively rational ways becomes as unattractive as getting off the sofa to change TV channels is in the remote control era. This is problematic, to reiterate, because it generates a relation of dependence and power between ordinary lifeworld members and the new experts, undermining the (communicatively rational) way of living and dealing with emotions that members themselves can control.

The Habermasian argument I am developing here bears some similarity to that of Rose (1989), who suggests that the modern preoccupation with emotion and the 'inner world' is a consequence of the proliferation of discourses and technologies which constitute an individuals' relation to their self in precisely these ways. It adds to this account in a number of respects, however. First, it allows us to identify the growth of the emotion industry with a shift from communicatively achieved regulation within the lifeworld (social integration) towards politically and economically driven regulation by expert powers (system integration), with the above mentioned consequences that this entails. In doing this, moreover, it raises the possibility that something valuable is being lost by this process, and thus generates at least some potential for critique. Second, Habermas allows us to identify the dynamics which fuel this shift; that is, the dynamics of economic and administrative expansion. Rose says very little about the reason for the expansion of psy-industries, focusing rather upon its effects. Third, where Rose concentrates mainly upon the psychotherapeutic and psychological wings of the emotion industry, the Habermasian position incorporates the medical and pharmacological wings too, suggesting that the growth of both relates to the same dynamic process (colonisation of the lifeworld). Finally, by identifying the possibility of both supply and demand side factors (in the growth of the emotion industry), the Habermasian position allows us to consider the rather peculiar possibility that the growth of the emotion industry may be part of exactly the same social process that generates the problems it claims to alleviate: that is, the growth of the emotion industry is a response to the psychological problems generated by the colonisation of the lifeworld and cultural impoverishment but is at the same time part of that colonisation and impoverishment. Furthermore, as such, it allows us to hypothesise that the industry creates exactly the same sorts of problems that it claims to resolve. The most obvious of these, for which there is some evidence, is dependency. Psychotherapy, for example, has been shown, in some cases, to generate dependency, whilst the danger of addiction and dependency is ever present in relation to psychiatric drugs. In addition to dependency, however, it is clear that the new technologies of emotion may fall well short of providing the types of interaction required for individuals to sustain meaningful narratives about self and world; relationships within psychotherapy, for example, are generally very strictly 'contracted', i.e. reduced to the cash nexus, with many of the territories of 'normal' lifeworld relations being out of bounds. Furthermore, the authoritative nature of therapeutic discourse may, in itself, undermine the capacity of the consumer or client to construct their own narrative of self and world. These ideas need to be tested empirically before we can accept them but they are, nevertheless, interesting hypotheses generated by the Habermasian programme.

Conclusion: the colonisation of emotional life

The final stages of my argument, in this chapter, have brought me to the familiar claim that emotional life is increasingly 'colonised' by various forms of expert knowledge and intervention. The specifically Habermasian perspective that I have developed has done more than offer a new gloss upon a now quite worn observation, however. It has allowed us to link this process into the logic of advanced capitalism and the conflict, therein, between two distinct principles of societal organisation: social integration and system integration. The colonisation that I have discussed involves an erosion of the mechanisms for socially integrating emotion, through the advance of system mechanisms and imperatives. Integral to this, moreover, the Habermasian approach has allowed us to consider that emotions are not just technical objects of intervention, that they have a rational character too, but that the colonisation of emotional life increasingly eclipses this rational dimension in the name of technical intervention. Our 'inner nature' is ever more subject to a process of instrumentally rational domination, at the cost of a loss to its communicatively rational accountability. The costs of this, at the social level, are a loss of autonomy at the level of everyday life: the capacity for regulation of emotion within the lifeworld is being lost to the system. Furthermore, this involves a demoralisation of the lifeworld, as emotion passes from the normatively regulated sphere of the lifeworld into the rather more anomic and instrumentally rational functioning of the system. In outlining this case I hope that I have both alerted the reader to certain of the dangers of advanced capitalist societies and, at the same time, illustrated the value of the Habermasian perspective for the sociology of psychiatry and mental health.

References

Abraham, J. (1995) *Science, Politics and the Pharmaceutical Industry*, London: UCL.

Adorno, T. and Horkheimer, M. (1979) *The Dialectic of Enlightenment*, London: Verso.

Armstrong, L. (1993) *And They Call It Help*, New York: Addison Wesley.

Bendelow, G. and Williams, S. (eds) (1998) *Emotions in Social Life: Critical Themes and Contemporary Issues*, London: Routledge.

Busfield, J. (1986) *Managing Madness: Changing Ideas and Practice*, London: Hutchinson.

Castel, R. (1988) *The Regulation of Madness*, Cambridge: Polity Press.

Coulter, J. (1973) *Approaches to Insanity*, London: Martin Robertson.

—— (1975) 'Perceptual accounts and interpretative asymmetries', *Sociology* 9: 885–96.

—— (1979) *The Social Construction of Mind*, London: Macmillan.

Craib, I. (1994) *The Importance of Disappointment*, London: Routledge.

Crossley, N. (1994) *The Politics of Subjectivity: between Foucault and Merleau-Ponty*, Aldershot: Avebury.

—— (1995) 'Merleau-Ponty: the elusive body and carnal sociology', *Body and Society* 1(1): 43–63.

—— (1996) *Intersubjectivity: the Fabric of Social Becoming*, London: Sage.

—— (1997) 'Corporeality and communicative action: embodying the renewal of critical theory', *Body and Society* 3(1), 17–47.

—— (1998) 'Emotion and communicative action: Habermas, linguistic philosophy and existentialism', in G. Bendelow and S. Williams *Emotions in Social Life*, London: Routledge, 16–38.

Durkheim, E. (1952) *Suicide: A Study in Sociology*, London: Routledge and Kegan Paul.

Elias, N. (1994) *The Civilising Process*, Oxford: Blackwell.

Foucault, M. (1965) *Madness and Civilisation*, London: Tavistock.

Gabe, J. and Williams, P. (eds) (1986) *Tranquillisers: Social, Psychological and Clinical Perspectives*, London: Tavistock.

Garfinkel, H. (1967) *Studies in Ethnomethodology*, Cambridge: Polity Press.

Giddens, A. (1991) *Modernity and Self-Identity: Self and Society in the Late Modern Age*, Cambridge: Polity Press.

—— (1992) *The Transformation of Intimacy: Sexuality, Love and Eroticism in Modern Societies*, Cambridge: Polity Press.

Goffman, E. (1961) *Asylums*, Harmondsworth: Penguin.

—— (1971) 'The insanity of place', in his *Relations in Public: Microstudies of the Public Order*, Harmondsworth: Penguin, 389–450.

Goodwin, S. (1993) *Community Care and the Future of Mental Health Provision*, Aldershot: Avebury.

—— (1997) *Comparative Mental Health Policy: from Institutional to Community Care*, London: Sage.

Habermas, J. (1987) *The Theory of Communicative Action*, Vol. 2, *The Critique of Functionalist Reason*, Cambridge: Polity Press.

—— (1988) *Legitimation Crisis*, Cambridge, Polity Press.

—— (1991) *The Theory of Communicative Action*, Vol. 1, *Reason and the Rationalisation of Society*, Cambridge: Polity Press.

—— (1992) *Moral Consciousness and Communicative Action*, Cambridge: Polity Press.

Hindess, B. (1988) *Choice, Rationality and Social Theory*, London: Unwin Hyman.

Ingleby, D. (1981) 'Understanding mental illness', in his *Critical Psychiatry: the Politics of Mental Health*, Harmondsworth: Penguin, 23–71.

Kendall, T. and Crossley, N. (1996) 'Governing love: on the tactical control of counter-transference in the psychoanalytic community', *Economy and Society* 25(2): 178–94.

Marx, K. (1977) 'Economic and philosophical manuscripts', in *Selected Writings* ed. D. McLellan, Oxford: Oxford University Press.

Mead, G. H. (1967) *Mind, Self and Society*, Chicago: Chicago University Press.

Merleau-Ponty, M. (1962) *The Phenomenology of Perception*, London: Routledge.

Newton, T. (1998) 'The socio-genesis of emotion: a historical sociology', in Bendelow, G. and Williams, S., *Emotions in Social Life*, London: Routledge, 60–82.

Parsons, T. (1951) *The Social System*, New York: Free Press.

Pilgrim, D. (1997) *Psychotherapy and Society*, London: Sage.

Pollner, M. (1975) 'The Very Coinage of Your Brain', *Philosophy of the Social Sciences* 5: 411–30.

Porter, R. (1987) *Mind Forg'd Manacles*, Harmondsworth: Penguin.

Rose, N. (1985) *The Psychological Complex*, London: Routledge and Kegan Paul.

—— (1989) *Governing the Soul: the Shaping of the Private Self*, London: Routledge.

Rose, S., Lewontin, R. and Kamin, L. (1984) *Not in Our Genes: Biology, Ideology and Human Nature*, Harmondsworth: Penguin.

Scheff, T. (1984) *Being Mentally Ill*, New York: Aldine.

Scull, A. (1984) *Decarceration*, Cambridge: Polity Press.

—— (1993) *The Most Solitary of Afflictions*, New Haven, CT: Yale University Press.

Sloan, T. (1996) *Damaged Life*, London: Routledge.

Smith, A. (1950) *The Wealth of Nations*, London: Methuen.

Weber, M. (1978) *Economy and Society*, 2 vols, Berkeley: University of California Press.

White, S. (1988) *The Recent Work of Jürgen Habermas*, Cambridge: Cambridge University Press.

Williams, S. and Bendelow, G. (1998) 'Introduction', in G. Bendelow and S. Williams *Emotions in Social Life*, London: Routledge.

Wittgenstein, L. (1953) *Philosophical Investigation*, Oxford: Blackwell.

Chapter 15

Emotions, social structure and health

Re-thinking the class inequalities debate

Simon J. Williams

Introduction

Two decades have passed since the Black Report (DHSS 1980) first revealed the gap in health as well as wealth, from birth to old age, which divides the rich from the poor. Whilst research continues to extend, refine and develop its four-fold explanatory frame of reference on class inequalities – from the critical reassessment of artefact (Bloor *et al.* 1987) and health-selection explanations (West 1991; Blane *et al.* 1993), to the 'biological programming' of social disadvantage *in utero* (Barker 1991), and the importance of longitudinal research across the lifecourse (Wadsworth 1991, 1997; see also Blaxter in this volume) – researchers and policy-makers alike must now confront a central paradox; namely, that once a certain level of material wealth has been reached, and the 'epidemiological transition' completed, other more diffuse and intangible factors come into play as the main determinants of socially patterned disease and illness in advanced western societies. Central to these developments, has been a growing interest in the so-called 'psychosocial pathways' to disease, including the impact of relative versus absolute deprivation and the corrosive effects of an increasingly 'individualised' society (i.e. an 'unravelling' of the social fabric, and a dissolution of communal bonds which bind members of society together) (Wilkinson 1996).

Talk of psychosocial factors and subjective process of meaning construction place emotions centre-stage, linking as they do the private realm of personal feeling to broader public issues of social structure. Yet like the body to which they are so closely tied, emotions have remained, until quite recently, a neglected sociological topic in general, and an under-researched and theorised aspect of the inequalities debate in particular. Emotions lie at the juncture of a number of traditional divisions and debates, opening up alternative ways of being and knowing which promise to free us from former rigid, binarised modes of western thought and practice. The choice here should not be framed in either/or terms. Rather, emotions are in fact central to the rational pursuit of (scientific) knowledge.

Seen in this light, the irrational passion for dispassionate rationality is itself, like all ideologies, unreasonable. The central issue is, therefore, how to re-incorporate emotions and to re-embody the research agendas of those working both inside and outside the academy.

It is this challenge and opportunity which forms the starting point of the present chapter[1]. Having briefly outlined the contours and contemporary debates in the sociology of emotions, including the biology/society question, I then proceed to illustrate the relevance of this newly emerging field of sociological inquiry in relation to the aetiology and psychosocial patterning of disease in contemporary western society. Not only, as I shall argue, does attention to the importance of emotions in social life shed important new light on these health-related issues, it also, as suggested above, enables us to transcend formerly rigid dualities through a unified conception of the 'mindful', emotionally 'expressive' body as an ongoing structure of lived experience and the existential basis of culture and self, structure and agency. It is to these 'neglected emotions' that I now turn as a backdrop to the discussion which follows.

The sociology of emotions

As suggested above, emotions lie at the juncture of a number of classical and contemporary debates in sociology including the micro–macro divide, postivism versus anti–positivism, quantitative versus qualititative, prediction versus description, managing versus accounting for emotions, and biosocial versus social constructionist perspectives (Kemper 1990). Central questions here include the following: Can emotions be isolated, defined, observed and understood as universal 'things' in themselves or as 'social constructs'? Can we delineate a distinct, autonomous realm of 'measureable' emotions, or are they instead culturally specific products of particular contexts, beliefs and value-systems (McCarthy 1989)? How, precisely, given their complexity, are we to relate micro-interactional processes of emotion management to broader macro-structural issues of power and status, conflict and control?

Broadly speaking, approaches to emotions can be conceptualised on a continuum ranging from the 'organismic'[2] at one end to the 'social constructionist' at the other, with 'interactionist' approaches, as the term implies, somewhere in between. In contrast to organismic theories, social constructionist approaches stress the primarily social as opposed to the biological nature of emotions (Harre 1986, 1991; Jackson 1993). From this perspective, 'emotions are not "inside" bodies, but rather actions we place in our world . . . feelings are *social* . . . constituted and sustained by group processes . . . irreducible to the bodily organism and to the particular individual who feels them' (McCarthy 1989: 57). More generally, social constructionists view human emotions as historical products and socially contingent phenomena (Stearns 1994; Stearns and Stearns 1988; Stearns and Haggarty 1991; Lutz 1988). Certainly, the naming of feeling, the situations in which they occur, the display rules associated with them, and their relationship to the self, are all endlessly elaborated across time and through culture. Yet in stressing these issues, social constructionists, like their organismic counterparts, fall foul of the temptation to overstretch their explanatory frames of reference (i.e. move to the other extreme of the organic-social spectrum). Indeed, a 'purely' constructionist perspective in the sociology of emotions, as Freund rightly argues: 'ignores biological process and presents a disembodied view of human emotions . . . The relationship between body and emotions are not resolved by ignoring the body's relevance or by viewing emotions simply as cognitive products' (1990: 455). 'Going beyond' the biological, in short, does not mean ignoring it altogether. Rather, it necessitates a more intricate model than organismic theorists or social constructionists propose of how social and cognitive influences 'join' physiological ones in the genesis of human emotions.

Hochschild, for example, develops an interactionist model, defining emotion as 'bodily co-operation with an image, a thought, a memory – a co-operation of which the individual is aware' (1979: 551). In doing so, she joins three theoretical currents. First, from Dewey (1922), Gerth and Mills (1964) and Goffman (1959), she explores what gets 'done' to emotions and how feelings are permeable to what gets done to them. Second, from Darwin (1955 [1895]) in the organismic tradition, she is able to posit a sense of what is there, impermeable, to be 'done to' (i.e. a biologically given sense, which in turn, is related to an orientation to action). Finally, through Freud's (1984 [1923]) work on the 'signal' function of human feelings, Hochschild is able to circle back from the organismic to the interactionist tradition, by tracing the way in which social factors influence what we expect and thus what these feelings actually 'signify' (Hochschild 1983: 222). From this starting point, Hochschild is able to develop her 'emotion management' perspective; one which enables her to inspect, through the sociological notion of 'The Managed Heart', the increasingly commoditised and commercialised relationship between emotional labour, feeling rules and ideology in advanced capitalist society (Williams 1998b).

These differing approaches to emotion, each in their own way, raise deeper philosophical and ontological questions concerning the problematic status of human embodiment as simultaneously both nature and culture. Emotions, as Denzin (1984) argues, are embodied experiences; ones which radiate through the body as a lived structure of on-going experience and centrally involve self-feelings which constitute the inner core of emotionality. For individuals to understand their own lived emotions, they must experience them socially and reflectively. It is here, according to Denzin, at the intersection between emotions as *embodied* experiences, their socially faceted nature, and their links with feelings of selfhood and personal identity, that a truly sociological perspective and understanding of emotions can most fruitfully be forged. Building on these insights, Burkitt (1997), in a more recent paper, has suggested that emotions are best seen as *complexes* rather than things; ones which are multi- rather than uni-dimensional in their composition. Emotions, he suggests, arise within social relationships, yet display a corporeal embodied aspect as well as a socio-cultural one; something which, in turn, is linked to techniques of the body (cf. Mauss 1978), learned within a social habitus (cf. Bourdieu 1991).

From this viewpoint – one which is not merely *about* the body but *from* the body – embodiment is neither reducible to representations of the body, to the body as an objectification of power, to the body as a physiological entity, nor to the body as an inalienable centre of individual consciousness (Csordas 1994a, 1994b). Rather, it becomes instead the existential basis of social and cultural life. Moreover, the interactive, relational character of embodied emotional experience offers a way of moving beyond microanalytic, subjective, internal or individualistic analyses, towards a more 'open-ended horizon' in which embodied agency can be understood not merely as individual but also as 'institution making' (Csordas 1994a: 14; Lyon and Barbalet 1994).

Emotions, in short, are most fruitfully seen as *embodied* existential modes of being; ones which involve an active engagement with the world and an intimate connection with both society and self, structure and agency, health and illness (Bendelow and Williams 1998). Not only do emotions underpin the phenomenological experience of our bodies in health and illness, they also provide the basis for social reciprocity and exchange (cf. the notion of 'deep sociality': Wentworth and Yardley 1994; and the 'link' between personal problems and broader public issues of social structure: Mills 1959). Indeed, to paraphrase Giddens's (1984) structuration theory, structure may fruitfully be seen as both the *medium* and *outcome* of the *emotionally embodied practices* it recursively organises. The emphasis here is on the active, emotionally expressive body as the basis of self, sociality, meaning, and order within the broader socio-cultural realms of everyday life and the 'ritualised' forms of interaction and exchange they involve.

Underpinning these arguments, of course, is a broader critique of the dualist legacies of the past; legacies which, as suggested above, have sought to divorce mind from body, nature from culture, and reason from emotion. Contra centuries of western thought, emotions and feelings are not 'intruders' into the rationalist (male) citadel, but inextricably enmeshed within its network; giving many subtle shades and textured nuances to cognitive decision-making processes (Damasio 1994). Seen in these terms, the irrational passion for dispassionate rationality is itself wholly unreasonable: one which not only serves ideological functions but drags attention away from the bodily basis of meaning, imagination and reason (Johnson 1987). It is this notion of the 'mindful' (Scheper-Hughes and Lock 1987), emotionally 'expressive' body (Freund 1990) as a lived reality, one which is active in the interactional contexts of power, conflict and social exchange which, I suggest, strikes at the very heart of these dualities (Williams and Bendelow 1998). Embodiment captures the essential ambiguity of human being as both nature and culture, and the transcendence of duality at the pre-objective level of on-going lived experience. Here, mind and body, reason and emotion, can only be arbitrarily separated by an act of conscious reflection and objectification.

Having sketched the outlines of these broader debates within the sociology of emotions, together with my own particular position within them, it is to fuller account of their relevance to the sociology of health and illness that we now turn. In doing so, I hope to further illustrate how emotion provides the 'missing link' between mind and body, experience and representation, structure and agency, macro and micro, public and private, and a host of other dichotomous ways of thinking.

Emotional 'capital' and the psychosocial pathways to disease

The relevance of emotions to the sociology of health and illness, as alluded to above, is axiomatic, spanning a diverse array of issues from the meaning and experience of pain and suffering (Bendelow 1993; Bendelow and Williams 1995a, 1995b), to the gendered division of emotional labour in health care (James 1989, 1992, 1993; Olesen and Bone 1997; Page and Meerabeau 1998; Smith 1992; Lawler 1991; Stacey 1988) and the proliferation of 'psy' and holistic therapies in contemporary western society (Williams and Bendelow 1996). In this particular chapter, however, I have chosen to concentrate instead on what is perhaps a less well developed, yet equally rich, topic of sociological investigation, namely the 'link' which emotions provide between social structure and health.

As Wilkinson (1996) has argued, the contemporary links between social structure and health draw attention to the fact that psychosocial, rather than material, factors are now the limiting component in the quality of life of developed western societies. Apparently regardless of the fact that health differences within societies remain so closely wedded to socio-economic status, once a country has passed a certain level of income – one associated with the 'epidemiological transition' from infectious to chronic degenerative diseases – its whole population can be 'more than twice as rich as another without being any healthier' (Wilkinson 1996: 3).

It is not so much the direct effects of absolute material living standards, as the indirect effects of 'social relativities'. As Wilkinson states

The indications that the links are psychosocial make these relationships as important for the real subjective quality of life among modern
populations as they are for their health ... Sources of social stress,
poor social networks, low self-esteem, high rates of depression,
anxiety, insecurity and loss of a sense of control, all have such a
fundamental impact on our experience of life that it is reasonable to
wonder whether the effects on the quality of life are not more important than their effects on the length of life.

(1996: 5–6)

To talk of psychosocial factors in the aetiology of disease does not, of
course, mean that the *basic* cause of these problems is psychological, or
that it can be dealt with in these terms. Rather, as Wilkinson rightly argues,
the point in differentiating psychosocial from material pathways is to
distinguish the social and economic problems affecting health 'indirectly'
through various forms of worry, stress, insecurity and vulnerability, from
those like environmental pollution, that affect health directly through
wholly material pathways, even if we are totally unaware or unconcerned
by them at the cognitive-emotional level (Wilkinson 1996: 184).

The upshot of these arguments is clear: having attained a basic minimum
standard of living for the vast majority of the population, psychosocial
rather than material factors become pre-eminent in the aetiology and social
patterning of contemporary western disease. This, in turn, places emotions
centre-stage, yet to date, as I have suggested, they remain a strangely
neglected topic and undertheorised aspect of the inequalities debate; particularly as the 'missing link' between structure and agency, mind and body,
biology and society.

How, then, are we to theorise this emotionally mediated micro–macro
link, and what empirical evidence is there to support these seemingly
abstract theoretical concepts and contentions? A first clue to these issues
is provided by Collins (1981, 1990), who argues, in classically Durkheimian style, that social order and solidarity ultimately rest on collective
moral sentiments and commitments which emerge in the course of 'interaction ritual' chains and emotional exchanges at the micro level. Conflict,
too, rests on an emotional foundation, involving as it does the mobilisation of sentiments of anger towards carriers of opposing social values and
interests. 'Power rituals', for instance, which mainly occur in large-scale
organisations, involve interactions structured in terms of 'order-givers' and
'order-takers'. Whilst order-givers derive positive 'emotional energy' from
these interactional exchanges, order-takers, on the other hand, frequently
experience a loss of emotional interest as a consequence of being neglected
and their wishes ignored. 'Status rituals', in contrast – which are somewhat independent of power-based rituals – involve interactions structured
along the lines of membership 'inclusion and exclusion', 'centrality or

periphery' of location, and the 'localism or cosmopolitanism' of one's network of interactional associates: divisions which, like power-based rituals,
increase or decrease emotional energy respectively (Collins 1981, 1990).

Underpinning these ideas lies Collins' suggestion that interaction
patterns, and the 'transient emotions' they involve, provide a micro foundation of long-term emotional resources or energies which in turn serve
as the basis for further interactions. It is these 'interaction ritual chains'
– chains which accumulate across time and space – that provide the macro
structures of social statitification. As Collins states:

> The IR [interaction ritual] chain model . . . proposes that individuals
> acquire or lose emotional energy in both power and status interac-
> tions. Order-givers gain EE [emotional energy], order-takers lose it;
> successful enactment of group membership raises EE, experiencing
> marginality or exclusion lowers it . . . Interaction rituals are connected
> in chains over time, with the results of the last interactions (in emotions
> and symbols) becoming inputs for the next interaction. Thus, EE tends
> to cumulate (either positively or negatively) over time.
>
> (1990: 39)

It is in this way that society 'gets inside' the individual's 'mindful' body.
Emotional energy ebbs and flows across a chain of interaction rituals
depending on the ups and downs of the individual's experiences of power
and status, operating both to 'stably reproduce social structure', and to
'energize the dynamics of conflict and change' (Collins 1990: 52).

Whilst the notion of 'emotional energy' is indeed useful, capturing as
it does the dynamic, animating–deanimating, aspect of emotional exchange
and social interaction, a more useful way of thinking sociologically about
these issues is perhaps through the Bourdieuesque concept of 'capital'. In
adopting this concept, Bourdieu (1984, 1990) has supplemented Marx's
discussion of economic capital with his own analysis of cultural, social
and symbolic capital, and the dynamic struggle for 'distinction': concepts
which, I have argued elsewhere, can usefully be applied to the class, health
and lifestyles debate (Williams 1995). Building on these Bourdieuesque
insights, 'emotional capital', I venture, is a concept which readily translates Collins's 'emotional energy' into a more thorough-going socio-
economic frame of reference. From this viewpoint, emotional exchange
involves an intricate 'balance sheet' of profits and losses, investments and
debts, including 'economies' of gratitude and resentment, and feelings of
pride and shame, which mesh more or less closely with broader patterns
of structured social (dis)advantage, power, status and prestige.

Another promising approach to these micro–macro links is provided by
Freund (1982, 1988, 1997, 1990), whose work on the emotionally 'expressive body' as a common ground for the sociology of emotions and health and

illness, offers an important theoretical bridge between hitherto disparate domains. A central part of understanding human emotions for Freund is to see them as existential 'modes of being' (Buytendijk 1950, 1962, 1974), involving a fusion of physical and psychic states which can be either 'pleasant' or 'unpleasant' in nature. The crucial issue for our purposes, however, is that – in keeping with notions emotional 'energy', 'capital' and 'exchange' raised above – these differing modes of emotional being are, in effect, different ways of feeling *empowered* or *disempowered*: feelings which are very much linked to people's material and psychosocial conditions of existence throughout their embodied biographies. It is here, at this nexus, that:

> 'External' social structural factors such as one's position in different systems of hierarchy or various forms of social control can influence the conditions of our existence, how we respond and apprehend these conditions and our sense of embodied self. These conditions can also affect our physical functioning.
>
> (Freund 1990: 461)

More precisely, a person's social position and status will determine the resources they have at their disposal in order to define and protect – through 'status shields' (cf. Hochschild 1983) and various other means – the boundaries of the self, and counter the potential for 'invalidation' by powerful and significant others. Being in an extremely powerless social status, in other words; 'increases the likelihood of experiencing "unpleasant" emotionality or emotional modes of being' (Freund 1990: 466). Less powerful people, Freund argues, face a 'structurally in built handicap' in managing social and emotional information; one which, in turn, may contribute to existential fear, anxiety and neuro-physiological perturbation of many different sorts. Since the body is a means of expressing meaning, including socio-cultural meaning, it is not unreasonable to suppose that:

> . . . people might somatically express the conditions of their existence. Pain, for instance, can express a sense of an existence that weighs heavily on one or a sense of powerlessness . . . Cultural factors can shape the language of the body.[3]
>
> (Freund 1990: 463)

In particular, the 'dramaturgical stress' (cf. Goffman 1959) of social relationships may engender, through the agency of an 'ontologically insecure self' (Laing 1965), a form of what Freund, borrowing from Kelly (1980), refers to as 'schizokinesis'; one in which a split occurs between what is shown and consciously experienced, as opposed to what occurs somatically. Here Freund poses two extremely important questions: first, 'how "deep" can the social construction of feelings go?', and second, 'can emotion work eliminate the responses of an unconsciously knowing body?' The implications of his argument seems to suggest that society affects physiological reactivity deep within the recesses of the human body although, as the concept of schizokinesis implies, the 'mind' may, consciously at least, be unaware of the 'body's' response. As continued emotional and other kinds of distress alter physiological reactivity, neurohormonally-related functions such as blood pressure may markedly increase in response to a psychosocial stressor but not be consciously experienced.[4]

Certainly, there is now plenty of evidence to support these contentions: from the 'physiological marks' of unremitting socio-economic stress to the biological effects (e.g. endocrine and immunological disorders) of status hierachies amongst baboons (Sapolsky 1991, 1993) and civil servants (Brunner 1996); and from the (un)anticipated consequences of unemployment, job insecurity, and a lack of control over one's working conditions (Mattison *et al.* 1990; Karasek and Theorell 1990; Marmot *et al.* 1991; Alfredsson *et al.* 1982), to the beneficial effects of social support, both at home and in the community, for health (Thoits 1995; Berkman 1995; Cohen and Syme 1985).

Key issues here include feelings of stress, hopelessness, depression, loss of a sense of 'coherence', and the dilemmas of insecurity and control. These, and many other factors have been shown to be associated with higher levels of mortality and morbidity. Karasek and Theorell (1990), for example, in the specific context of work, develop a two-fold model along the key dimensions of demand and control. When high demands are matched with high control, adverse health consequences are unlikely. In contrast, high demands and low control is, they suggest, associated with increased risk. In a similar vein, Siegrist and colleagues (1990) have developed a model which takes into account personal coping and adaptation to work demands. As they show, high effort and low reward (e.g. money, esteem, security etc.) leads to sustained distress and increased health risks (i.e. ischaemic heart disease).

These general findings have, in turn, been reinforced by research within the life-events paradigm which has documented, with ever increasing precision, the complex relationship between social factors, cognitive-emotional responses and the onset of a variety of physical and mental conditions. Brown and Harris (1978), for instance, in a classic sociological study, highlight the 'depressogenic' links between provoking agents (i.e. severe life events and long-term difficulties), vulnerability factors (e.g. death of mother before the age of 11, lack of a close confiding relationship, absence of outside employment, three or more children under the age of 15 at home), and the onset of clinical depression; a process which works, they suggest, through the ontological agency of 'chronically low self-esteem' and the transition from short-term to more generalised feelings of 'hopelessness'.

In their more recent work, Brown and Harris (1989) have usefully distinguished between what they see as two major sources of emotions: first, those arising from everyday activities of a largely routinised or taken-for-granted nature (e.g. feelings of self-worth and self-esteem emerging from social performances and interaction rituals of various kinds) and second, those arising from *plans* and *purposes*, motives and commitments (i.e. those linked to human intentionality). It is this latter, more complex, type of human emotionality which interests Brown and Harris most. As they stress, feelings typically occur at the juncture of plans, when an estimate of likely outcome is (radically) changed. It is here, at this precise nexus, that life-events are likely to have their greatest impact. In stressing these issues, we return, once again, to the problem of emotional capital – in this case, our investment in plans and purposes – raised above. In reality, of course, as Brown and Harris themselves readily acknowledge, these two types of emotion are inextricably interrelated: commitments and intentions, for example, invariably rest on tacit, taken-for-granted assumptions that certain core features of everyday life, including the ritualised conventions it contains, will continue (Brown and Harris 1989: 442).

Extending and developing these insights, Craig (1989) demonstrates the importance of goal-frustration, as opposed to the more usual loss or danger associated with severe events and long-term difficulties, in the onset of gastrointestinal disorders, contrasting the lowering of pain thresholds consequent upon emotional distress with changes in gut motility (i.e. abnormalities in motor activity of the bowel, causing the development of pain). Other studies, also within the life-events paradigm, have demonstrated the increased chances of conditions such as myocardial infarction in those experiencing accumulated work stress over a 10-year period (Neilson *et al.* 1989): a finding which appears to hold even after controlling for other possible confounding factors such as cigarette smoking and higher alcohol consumption. Perhaps a more subtle illustration of these, emotionally mediated, psychosocial processes of meaning construction, however, concerns Andrews and House's (1989) finding of a link between what they term 'conflict over speaking out' (CSO) events – i.e. situations which provide, on the one hand, a challenge to speak out, protest, or complain, and on the other, an unusual constraint upon such outspoken behaviour – and the development of functional dysphonia in women (i.e. a difficulty in vocal production which cannot be explained by way of structural lesions of the larynx or by any neurological lesion). In seeking to explicate this intriguing finding, the authors draw attention to the high rate of muscular tension these women experienced in the laryngeal region; a factor which, they suggest, may provide the intervening link between CSO events and functional dysphonia.[5]

Here we return, via these empirical examples, to the manner in which the emotionally expressive body translates broader structural and material conditions of existence, including conflict situations, into the recalcitrant language of disease and disorder.[6] The argument here is for a subtle and sophisticated form of socially 'pliable' biology rather than socio-biology; one which accords emotional modes of being a central role in linking the health and illness of the existential-phenomenologically embodied agent with wider structures of power and domination, civilisation and control in society. Freund summarises this position in the following terms:

> One's positions, and the roles that accompany them in various systems of social hierarchy, shape the conditions in which one lives. This position influences access to resources. It may also determine the forms of emotional-social control to which one is subject as well as the severity of the impact these controls have on the person ... Such a process may mean internalising the emotional definitions that others impose on what we are or 'should' be. The physiological aspects of such processes are of interest to those studying emotions. However, these physical aspects may also be seen as examples of ways in which controls are sedimented and fixed in the psycho-soma of the person. Physiological aspects of social activity can also act as a form of feedback that colours the tone of existence. This feedback can *indirectly* serve social control functions. For instance, conditions that create depression ... construct an emotional mode of being where the motivation to resist is blunted.
>
> (1990: 470)

It is here, at this existential nexus, that the 'mindful', emotionally 'expressive' body is located: one which is active in the context of power and status, conflict and control. This, in turn, raises broader questions concerning the relationship between emotions, health and 'distributive justice'; an issue to which I shall now turn in the next section of this chapter.

Emotions, health and 'distributive justice'

Talk of psychosocial pathways and subtly nuanced emotional responses suggests a complex, multi-factorial, picture of disease causation in contemporary western societies; one involving a considerable degree of individual variability which defies neat and tidy aetiological or epidemiological modelling. On the one hand, we have the 'immutable uncertainties' and 'fateful moments' of everyday life; events from which none of us are (wholly) immune. On the other hand, however, we must also confront the fact these very adversities, including the emotionally embodied responses they call forth, are socio-economically structured or 'patterned' in various ways. Seen in these terms, class structure and the broader political regime impinge on the health of the emotionally expressive body in two main ways:

First, through the impact they have on the incidence of life-events as such, and second, through the influence they exert on the availability of means and skills needed to cope with an event after it has occurred.

(Gerhardt 1979: 220)

Most of the class difference in female depression, for example, appears to be due to the fact that working-class women experience more provoking agents and vulnerability factors than their middle-class counterparts (Brown and Harris 1978). This, coupled with the notion of 'conveyor belts' to continuing adversity, serves to capture the dialectic, so central to the 'sociological imagination' (Mills 1959), between personal troubles and broader public issues of social structure.

To suggest that socio-economic factors now primarily affect health through indirect psychosocial rather than direct material routes, is not, therefore, to suggest that we concentrate on 'inner' rather than 'external', individual rather than political, issues. Quite the reverse. Far from being 'irrational', feelings of absurdity and alienation, entrapment and despair are often entirely realistic assessments of existing social circumstances. Here, 'inner' and 'outer' worlds meet, and it is from there that the sociologist must go on to build links with the wider cultural, economic and political system (Brown 1977: 11).

It is also not to suggest that these emotional problems and difficulties are solely confined to the structurally disadvantaged. Rather, as we have seen, they are more or less pervasive, albeit in varying degrees, across the social spectrum. Hochschild (1983), for example, has drawn attention to the detrimental consequences of emotion work – which, she claims, falls most heavily on the middle-classes – including feelings of 'burnout' and a loss of 'authenticity' (see also the earlier mentioned Whitehall studies on British civil servants (Marmot et al. 1978, 1991)). Here, the central issue becomes not simply the prevalence of emotional problems and difficulties per se – although these are, as we have seen, socially patterned in various ways – but the availability of skills and resources to 'meet' and to 'deal' with them satisfactorily.

Discussion of these issues, raises broader questions about the relationship between emotions, health and 'distributive justice'. As Wilkinson's (1996) work so clearly demonstrates, it is not the richest but the most egalitarian societies which have the best health: ones which foster, through more equitable forms of income distribution, a much needed sense of social cohesion in an increasingly 'atomised' age. Income distribution, in other words, alongside all the other factors considered above, is an important determinant of the 'psychosocial welfare' of a society, promoting not only more healthy societies, but also more egalitarian, internally cohesive, ones. This, in turn, tells us something very important about how the social fabric is affected by the amount of inequality in a society and its impact

on health. Recognition of this fact gives governments an important opportunity to take practical steps to improve, instead of side-step, these pressing
health-related matters:

> The importance of knowing that social cohesion is likely to be
> improved by narrower income differences is that it gives policy-makers
> a way of improving important aspects of life in our society . . . Because
> income distribution is powerfully affected by government policy,
> governments may be able to improve the psychosocial condition and
> morale of the whole population.
>
> (Wilkinson 1996: 184–5)

Emotions, health and distributive justice are therefore intimately related
in the developed western world. This, coupled with the earlier discussion
of 'emotional capital' and its broader links to key aspects of contemporary
social structure such as power, status and control, constitutes both a challenge and opportunity to governments concerned with the corrosive effects
of 'unhealthy societies' and the 'afflictions of inequality'.

Discussion and concluding remarks

A central aim of this chapter has been to discuss, albeit in an exploratory
fashion, the links between emotions, embodiment and health, using the
inequalities debate as a paradigmatic example. As I have argued, the fact
that socio-economic factors now primarily affect health through psychosocial rather than material pathways, places emotions centre-stage in the
social patterning of disease and disorder in advanced western societies. In
this sense, emotions, as existentially embodied modes of being-in-the-
world and an essential form of 'capital', provide the 'missing link' between
'personal troubles' and broader 'public issues' of social structure.

Underpinning these arguments, is a commitment to fundamentally
rethinking the 'biological' in non-reductionist terms. Biology is not fixed
or immutable. Rather, as biologically 'unfinished' creatures, human beings
are materially, socially and culturally 'completed', as well as 'depleted',
by society. In this respect, adapting Gerhardt's (1979) earlier reconstruction of the life-events approach, it may be useful to distinguish, analytically,
between what I shall here term 'psycho-neuro-immunological *adaptation*',
'psycho-social *coping*' and 'socio-political *praxis*'. In the first case, the
type of event experienced may be characterised as a disruptive 'change'
of some sort, for which psychoneuroimmunological 'arousal control'
and the restoration of 'homeostatic balance' is the most appropriate
adaptive response by the human organism. At the second, psycho-social
level of *coping*, the type of event experienced may loosely be referred
to as a 'loss' of some kind (e.g. a death, a cherished idea, an important

role etc.), and the appropriate response one of 'meaning construction'. Finally, at the broadest level of socio-political praxis, the type of event experienced may best be described as an on-going difficulty of some sort (e.g. housing or money problems), and the appropriate response one of 'project formation'. This, in turn, is linked to the wider economic and political structures of power, rights and privileges within society (Gerhardt 1979).

Different responses of the emotionally expressive body are, therefore, as Gerhardt (1979) points out, more or less successful, depending on the type of event experienced. In the case of long-term difficulties of a 'public' nature, for example, active changes in the individual's environment – rather than psycho-social coping via processes of meaning construction – may be the most appropriate response (Gerhardt 1989: 215). In contrast, disruptive changes involving no loss but considerable flexibility and endurance, may be most effectively overcome through adaptive 'psycho-neuroimmunological' processes of 'arousal control'.

After some eighteen years of radical right-wing policies, including the retrenchment of welfare state benefits and the championing of individual freedom and enterprise, we have, in the shape of the new Labour government, a pledge to tackle the inequalities issue head-on (Acheson 1998; DOH 1999). Whether or not this proves successful is, of course, open to considerable debate. The thrust of the arguments contained in this chapter suggest, however, that practical, tangible steps are indeed possible. Here we return again to broader questions regarding emotions, health and distributive justice, including problems of emotional capital, income distribution, social cohesion and control: issues which, I suggest, need to be at the forefront of future policy initiative within this area.

To conclude, a focus on the 'mindful', emotionally 'expressive' body provides, I suggest, a potentially very fruitful direction for future research within the sociology of health and illness. Whilst I have chosen to focus on the inequalities debate as illustrative of these issues, it is equally clear that emotions are central to a number of other issues within the sociology of health and illness, from human reproduction to the social organisation of health care, and from the ethical dilemmas of high-technology medicine to the growing popularity of holistic therapies and lay reskilling in a socially reflexive age. Previously banished to the margins of sociological thought and practice, emotions, in short, are critically re-configuring existing boundaries and re-embodying the research agendas of a discipline in transition.

References

Acheson, D. (1998) *Independent Inquiry into Irregularities in Health*, London: The Stationary Office.

Alfredsson, L., Karasek R. and Theorell T. (1982) 'Myocardial infarction risk and the psychosocial work environment', *Social Science and Medicine* 16: 463–7.

Andrews, H. and House, A. (1989) 'Functional dysfonia', in G. W. Brown and T. O. Harris (eds) *Life Events and Illness*, London: Unwin Hyman.

Barker, D. J. P. (1991) 'The foetal and infant origins of inequalities in health in Britain', *Journal of Public Health Medicine* 13: 64–8.

Bendelow, G. (1993) 'Pain perceptions, gender and emotion', *Sociology of Health and Illness* 15(3): 273–94.

Bendelow, G. and Williams, S. J. (1995a) 'Transcending the dualisms: towards a sociology of pain', *Sociology of Health and Illness* 17(2): 139–65.

—— (1995b) 'Pain and the mind–body dualism: a sociological approach', *Body and Society* 1(2): 83–103.

—— (1998) *Emotions in Social Life: Social Theories and Contemporary Issues*, London: Routledge.

Benton, T. (1991) 'Biology and social science: why the return of the repressed should be given a (cautious) welcome', *Sociology* 25(1): 1–29.

Berkman, L. F. (1995) 'The role of social relations in health promotion', *Psychosomatic Research* 57: 245–54.

Berkman, L. F. and Syme S. L. (1979) 'Social networks, host resistance, and mortality: a nine year follow-up of Almeda County residents,' *American Journal of Epidemiology* 109: 186–204.

Blane, D., Davey Smith, G. and Bartley, M. (1993) 'Social selection: what does it contribute to social class inequalities in health?', *Sociology of Health and Illness* 15(1): 1–15.

Bloor, M., Samphier, M. and Prior, L. (1987) 'Artefact explanations of inequalities in health: an analysis of evidence', *Sociology of Health and Illness* 9(3): 321–64.

Bourdieu, P. (1984) *Distinction: a Social Critique of the Judgement of Taste*, London: Routledge and Kegan Paul.

—— (1990) *The Logic of Practice*, Cambridge: Polity Press.

Brown, G. W. (1977) 'Depression: a sociological view', *Maudsley Gazette* (summer): 9–12.

Brown, G. W. and Harris T. O. (1978) *The Social Origins of Depression: a Study of Psychiatric Disorder in Women*, London: Tavistock.

—— (eds) (1989) *Life Events and Illness*, London: Unwin Hyman.

Brunner, E. (1996) 'The social and biological basis of cardiovascular disease in office workers', in E. Brunner, D. Blane and R. G. Wilkinson (eds) *Health and Social Organisation*, London: Routledge.

Burkitt, I. (1997) 'Social relationships and emotions', *Sociology* 31(1): 37–55.

Buytendijk F. J. J. (1950) 'The phenomenological approach to the problem of feelings and emtions' in M. C. Reymert (ed.) *Feelings and Emotions: the Mooseheart Symposium in Cooperation with the University of Chicago*, New York: McGraw-Hill Company Inc.

—— (1962) *Pain: Its Modes and Functions*, trans. Eda O'Shiel, Chicago: University of Chicago Press.

—— (1974) *Prolegomena to an Anthropological Physiology*, Pittsburgh: Duquesne University Press.

Cohen, L. and Syme, S. L. (eds) (1985) *Social Support and Health*, London: Academic Press Inc.

Collins, R. (1981) 'On the micro-foundations of macro-sociology', *American Journal of Sociology* 86: 984–1,014.

—— (1990) 'Stratification, emotional energy, and the transient emotions', in T. J. Kemper (ed.) *Research Agendas in the Sociology of Emotions*, New York: State University of New York Press.

Craig, T. (1989) 'Abdominal pain', in Brown G. W. and Harris T. O. (eds) *Life Events and Illness*, London: Unwin Hyman.

Csordas, T. J. (ed.) (1994a) *Embodiment and Experience: the Existential Ground of Culture and Self*, Cambridge: Cambridge University Press.

—— (1994b) 'Introduction: the body as representation and being-in-the-world', in T. J. Csordas (ed.) *Embodiment and Experience: the Existential Ground of Culture and Self*, Cambridge: Cambridge University Press.

Damasio, A. R. (1994) *Decartes' Error: Emotion, Reason and the Human Brain*, New York: Putnam.

Darwin, C. (1955)[1895] *The Expression of Emotions in Man and Animals*, New York: Philosophical Library.

Denzin, N. K. (1984) *On Understanding Emotion*, San Francisco: Jossey Bass.

Department of Health (DOH) (1999) *Saving Lives: Our Healthier Nation* (CM 4386), London: The Stationery Office.

Dewey J. (1922) *Human Nature and Conduct: an Introduction to Social Psychology*, New York: Holt.

DHSS (Black Report) *Inequalities in Health: Report of a Research Working Group*, London: Department of Health and Social Security

Featherstone, M., Hepworth, M. and Turner, B. S. (eds) (1991) *The Body: Social Process and Cultural Theory*, London: Sage.

Freud, S. (1984)[1923] *The Ego and the Id*, in S. Freud, *On Metapsychology*, Harmondsworth: Penguin.

Freund, P. (1982) *The Civilized Body: Social Control, Domination and Health*, Philadelphia, PA: Temple University Press.

—— (1988) 'Understanding socialized human nature', *Theory and Society* 17: 839–64.

—— (1990) 'The expressive body: a common ground for the sociology of emotions and health and illness', *Sociology of Health and Illness* 12(4): 452–77.

—— (1997) 'Social performances and their discontents: reflections on the bio-social psychology of role-playing', in G. Bendelow and S. J. Williams (eds) *Emotions in Social Life: Critical Themes and Contemporary Issues*, London: Routledge.

Gerhardt, U. (1979) 'Coping as social action: theoretical reconstruction of the life-events approach', *Sociology of Health and Illness* 1: 195–225.

Gerth, H. and Mills C. Wright (1964) *Character and Social Structure: the Psychology of Social Institutions*, New York: Harcourt, Brace and World.

Giddens, A. (1984) *The Constitution of Society*, Cambridge: Polity Press.

Goffman, E. (1959) *The Presentation of Everyday Life*, New York: Doubleday Anchor.

Grosz, E. (1994) *Volatile Bodies*, Bloomington and Indianapolis: Indiana University Press.

Harre, R. M. (ed.) (1986) *The Social Construction of Emotions*, New York: Basil Blackwell.

Haare, R. M. (1991) *Physical Being: A Theory of Corporeal Psychology*, Oxford: Blackwell.

Hochschild, A. (1979) 'Emotion work, feeling rules and social structure', *American Journal of Sociology* 85: 551–75.

—— (1983) *The Managed Heart: the Commercialisation of Human Feeling*, Berkeley, CA: University of California Press.

—— (1997) 'Emotions as a way of seeing: the case of love', in G. Bendelow and S. J. Williams (eds) *Emotions in Social Life: Critical Themes and Contemporary Issues*, London: Routledge.

Jackson, S. (1993) 'Even sociologists fall in love: an exploration of the sociology of emotions', *Sociology* 27(2): 201–20.

James, N. (1989) 'Emotional labour: skill and work in the social regulation of feelings', *The Sociological Review* 37: 15–42.

—— (1992) 'Care = organisation + physical labour + emotional labour', *Sociology of Health and Illness* 14(4): 488–509.

—— (1993) 'Divisions of emotional labour: the case of cancer and disclosure', in S. Fineman (ed.) *Emotion and Organizations*, London: Sage.

James, W. and Lange, C. (1922) *The Emotions*, Baltimore: Wilkins and Wilkins.

Johnson, M. (1987) *The Body in the Mind: the Bodily Basis of Meaning, Imagination and Reason*, Chicago: University of Chicago Press.

Karesek, R. and Theorell, T. (1990) *Healthy Work: Stress, Productivity and the Reconstruction of Working Life*, New York: Basic Books.

Kelly, D. (1980) *Anxiety and Emotions*, Springfield, IL: Charles C. Thomas Publishers.

Kemper, T. J. (1990) 'Themes and variations in the sociology of emotions', in T. J. Kemper (ed.) *Research Agendas in the Sociology of Emotions*, New York: State University of New York Press.

Laing, R. D. (1965) *The Divided Self*, Harmondsworth: Penguin.

Lawler, J. (1991) *Behind the Screens: Nursing, Somology and the Problem of the Body*, London: Churchill Livingstone.

Lutz, C. (1988) *Unnatural Emotions*, Chicago: University of Chicago Press.

Lynch, J. (1985) *The Language of the Heart: the Human Body in Dialogue*, New York: Basic Books.

Lyon, M. (1994) 'Emotion as mediator of somatic and social processes: the example of respiration', in W. M. Wentworth and J. Ryan (eds) *Social Perspectives on Emotion*, Vol. 2, Greenwich, CT: JAI Press Inc.

Lyon, M. and Barbalet, J. (1994) 'Society's body: emotion and the "somatization" of social theory', in T. J. Csordas (ed.) *Embodiment and Experience: the Existential Ground of Culture and Self*, Cambridge: Cambridge University Press.

McCarthy, E. Doyle (1989) 'Emotions are social things: an essay in the sociology of emotions', in D. D. Franks and E. Doyle McCarthy (eds) *The Sociology of Emotions: Original Essays and Research Papers*, Greenwich, CT: JAI Press Inc.

Marmot, M., Rose, G., Shipley, M. and Hamilton, P. J. S. (1978) 'Employment grade and coronary heart disease in British civil servants', *Journal of Epidemiology and Community Health* 32(4): 244–9.

Marmot, M., Davey Smith, G., Stansfield, S., Patel, C., North, F. and Head, J. (1991) 'Health inequalities among British civil servants: the Whitehall II study', *Lancet* 337: 1,387–93.

Mattison, R., Lingarde, F., Nilsson, J. A. and Theorell, T. (1990) 'Threat of unemployment and cardiovascular risk factors: longitudinal study of quality
of sleep and serum cholesterol concentrations in men threatened with redundancy', *British Medical Journal* 301: 461–66.

Mauss, M. (1978). *Sociology and Psychology*, London: Routledge.

Mills, C. Wright (1959) *The Sociological Imagination*, New York: Oxford
University Press.

Neilson, E., Brown, G. W. and Marmot, M. (1989) 'Myocardial infarction', in
Brown G. W. and Harris T. O. (eds) *Life Events and Illness*, London: Unwin
Hyman.

Oleson, V. and Bone, D. (1997) 'Emotional dynamics in changing institutional
contexts', in G. Bendelow and S. J. Williams (eds) *Emotions in Social Life:
Critical Themes and Contemporary Issues*, London: Routledge.

Page, S. and Meerabeau, L. (1998) 'Drama and dignity: nurses accounts of
cardiopulmonary resuscitation and death', in G. Bendelow and S. J. Williams
(eds) *Emotions in Social Life: Critical Themes and Contemporary Issues*,
London: Routledge.

Reich, W. (1949) *Character Analysis*, New York: Farrar, Straus and Giroux.

—— (1969)[1951] *The Sexual Revolution*, 4th revised edn, trans. T. P. Wolfe,
London: Vision Press Ltd.

—— (1983)[1942] *The Function of the Orgasm* trans. V. F. Carfagno, London:
Souvenir Press.

Sapolsky, R. M. (1991) 'Poverty's remains', *The Sciences* 31: 8–10.

—— (1993) 'Endocrinology alfresco: psychoendocrine studies of wild baboons',
Recent Progress in Hormone Research 48: 437–68.

Scheper-Hughes, N. and Lock, M. (1987) 'The mindful body: a prolegomenon to
future work in medical anthropology', *Medical Anthropology Quarterly* 1(1): 6–41.

Shilling, C. (1993) *The Body in Social Theory*, London: Sage.

Siegrist, J., Peter, R., Junge, A., Cremer, P. and Seidel, D. (1990) 'Low status,
high effort at work and ischaemic heart disease: prospective evidence from
blue-collar men', *Social Science and Medicine* 31: 1,127–34.

Smith, P. (1992) *The Emotional Labour of Nursing*, Basingstoke: Macmillan
Educational Books.

Stacey, M. (1988) *The Sociology of Health and Healing*, London: Routledge.

Stearns, P. N. (1994) *American Cool: Constructing a Twentieth Century American
Style*, New York: New York University Press.

Stearns, C. Z. and Stearns, P. N. (1988) *Emotions and Social Change*, New York:
Holmes and Meier.

Stearns, P. N. and Haggerty, T. (1991) 'The role of fear: transitions in American
emotional standards for children 1850–1950', *American Historical Review* 96:
63–94.

Thoits, P. (1995) 'Stress, coping, and social support processes: where are we?
What next?', *Journal of Health and Social Behaviour* (extra issue) 53–79.

Townsend, P. and Davidson, N. (1980) *The Black Report*, Harmondsworth:
Penguin.

Turner, B. S. (1992) *Regulating Bodies: Essays in Medical Sociology*, London:
Routledge.

—— (1996) *The Body and Society*, 2nd edn, London: Sage.

Wadsworth, M. E. J. (1991) *The Imprint of Time: Childhood History and Adult Life*, Oxford: Oxford University Press.

—— (1997) 'Health inequalities in the life course perspective', *Social Science and Medicine* 44(6): 859–70.

Wentworth, W. M. and Yardley, D. (1994) 'Deep sociality: a bioevolutionary perspective on the sociology of emotions', in W. M. Wentworth and J. Ryan (eds) *Social Perspectives on Emotion*, Greenwich, CT/London: JAI Press Inc.

West, P. (1991) 'Rethinking the health selection explanation for health inequalities', *Social Science Medicine* 32: 373–84.

Wilkinson, R. G. (1996) *Unhealthy Societies: the Afflictions of Inequality*, London: Routledge.

Williams, S. J. (1995) 'Theorising class, health and lifestyles: can Bourdieu help us?', *Sociology of Health and Illness* 17(5): 577–604.

—— (1998a) '"Capitalising" on emotions? Rethinking the inequalities debate', *Sociology* 32(1): 121–39.

—— (1998b) 'Arlie Russell Hochschild', in R. Stones (ed.) *Key Sociological Thinkers*, London: Macmillan.

Williams, S. J. and Bendelow, G. (1996) 'The emotional body', *Body and Society* 2(3): 125–39.

—— (1998) *The Lived Body: Sociological Times, Embodied Issues*, London: Routledge.

Chapter 16

Emotions and gender in US health care contexts

Implications for change and stasis in the division of labour

Virginia Olesen

Since the 1980s the sociology of emotions in mainstream sociology, anthropology and organisation studies has shifted from discussions on whether emotions are physiological ('wired in'), to debates on the extent to which emotions are socially constructed (Editorial 1988; Radley 1988). Perhaps most critical for medical sociology, recognition has grown that the emotions are experienced and expressed through a social body which is constituted in society and which contains society (Freund 1982; Scheper-Hughes and Lock 1987). Emotions are thus social, interactive and a reciprocal link between the individual and social life (Radley 1988: 5; Freund 1990):

> Bodily being and experience are always social, always a function of persons in relation. Emotion is thus an aspect of being in the world. Although it includes bodily components, emotion takes us beyond both individual and bodily domains and shows how the social is implicated in everyday life.
>
> (Lyon 1996: 71)

There are two implications here for medical sociology. First, is the part emotions play in health and illness, both mental and physical, a topic which has been well explored elsewhere (Charmaz 1980; Williams and Bendelow 1996). Second, the place of emotions in doing the work of health care which this chapter examines.

Recognition of how the social is implicated in everyday life points to consideration of material, normative and social structures which frame interactions and emotions: for instance, Lofland's classic paper on the conditions under which grief is expressed (1985) or Hochschild's (1983) influential concepts of materially based emotional labour and feeling rules. This chapter considers material, normative and social structures which frame interactions and emotions in the health care division of labour. It lodges that consideration in changes invoked by rationalising tendencies in currently troubled US health care contexts. This analysis of expectations for and expression of emotions in altering organisational settings pays particular attention to gender stratification, a key element in both the interactive and structural features of these contexts.[1] It picks up the challenge in Stacey's early, cogent criticism, 'The emotional component of human service has been ignored by classical theories but is critical to it' (1981: 174).

Within the many contexts in the complex US system multiple experiences and expression of emotions occur, ranging from providers disclosing bad news to patients (Fisher 1995) to offering emotional support to hospitalised or institutionalised patients (Foner 1994). The fiscal crisis in US health care with the attendant moves to greater rationalisation, managed care, curtailment of care and services has left few contexts or those working within them untouched. The nature and degree of alteration may differ and with it consequences for emotional behaviour in hospitals, clinics, hospices, long term care facilities. Moreover, the alteration may differ within types of contexts: for example, hospitals with dedicated AIDS units as against hospitals with scattered beds for AIDS patients.

Exploring the experience and enactment of emotions in changing care contexts which are highly stratified by gender raises new possibilities to examine again the old sociological question of the relationship between the micro and macro elements of social life (Gordon 1990: 147; Williams and Bendelow 1996: 43). Indeed, such exploration may help dissolve that binarism into issues that are at once more fluid and more vexed and less neatly contrasted than implied in the dualism, micro–macro. To do such an exploration one needs a concept which both recognises and blends micro–macro elements. This discussion will rely on emotional labour (Hochschild 1983), which allows for analysis of both the subjective aspects of social action as well as material and structural issues. This recognises and points to the integration of interacting individuals' selves, identities and emotional expressions with those of others in contexts which may or may not call for specific emotions. Out of such interactions emerge new meanings and structures which affirm or alter the social relationships in that context and become the characteristics of the next context.

Thus the chapter speaks to the confluence of two intriguing problems in the sociology of emotions and an enduring question in sociology: (1) the neglected problem of emotional expression in changing organisations (Gordon 1990: 149; Olesen and Bone 1998; Olesen 1997a); (2) the poorly understood problem of emotions in gendered social organisations (Hearn, 1994) and understanding of micro–macro issues in social life. It argues that this type of analysis in the sociology of health care can contribute to conceptual and theoretical issues in mainstream sociology, as has been done in other realms of the sociology of health, illness and health care (Charmaz and Olesen 1997). The chapter will take up emotions in changing organisations. It will then sketch current rationalisation in US health care contexts. This will provide the background for discussions of gender, occupational, emotional stratification and the relationship of emotion and gender. A section on 'deviant' emotions sets the ground for consideration of transformative aspects: the individual in the social. The chapter concludes with the implications for the sociology of emotions and the sociology of health care.

Emotions in changing organisations

The question of expectations for experience and expression of emotions in changing social organisations is part of an older puzzle regarding the relationship of social structure, rationality and emotional behaviour that goes back to Weber's (1978) formulations about bureaucracy. That older question seemed to suggest that organisations were without feelings and that rationality superseded or at least did not provide a place for emotionality. As scholars have argued, the Weberian formulation has been misinterpreted in ways which mistake Weber's concerns about bureaucracy with the nature of the organisation itself. They claim that Weber can be more properly interpreted as fully aware of and concerned with affectivity: 'The vital point is that not only does Weber allow for emotions within bureaucracy, but their rational calculation becomes an intrinsic part of their working' (Albrow 1992: 318).

There has been growing awareness that there is affectivity in social organisations, whilst recognising the tension between the rational proscriptions of bureaucracy and the orchestrated expression, or curtailing of emotional expression (Albrow 1992; Putnam and Mumby 1994; Ashforth and Humphrey 1995; Flam 1990; Garot 1995; Gibson 1994). This awareness, that rationality and emotionality intertwine in organisational settings, moves away from preformed ideas that rationality supersedes emotionality. It points to the fluidity of these elements and facilitates analysis of the simultaneous alterations of rationality and emotionality.

The substantial empirical literature analysing rationality and emotionality in customer service organisations and settings (Ashforth and Humphrey 1993; Hochschild 1983; Leidner 1993; Sutton 1991; Van Maanen and Kunda 1989) has not, for the most part, been paralleled in studies in the sociology of health care, with some notable exceptions (Strauss *et al.* 1982; James 1989, 1992; Foner 1994; Treweek 1996; Lupton 1996; Baker *et al.* 1996). However, earlier studies in medical sociology not focused on emotions nevertheless show glimpses of emotions embedded and articulated in a wide variety of settings. These contexts included the emergency room (Dingwall and Murray 1983; Roth 1986), the gynaecological examination (Emerson 1970), cancer clinics (Murcott 1981), paediatric clinics (Strong 1979; Silverman 1987), hospitals where children with polio were treated (Davis 1963), a burn unit (Fagerhaugh and Strauss 1977), an experimental research ward (Fox 1959) and the mental hospital (Caudill 1958).

These early studies saw, but did not foreground emotions in health care contexts nor did they relate them to issues in the division of labour.

Rationalisation in US health care contexts

A brief review of rationalising tendencies in the US health care system will facilitate understanding of the background against which emotions in health care organisations are enacted. Although pressures to make the health care system more efficient date to at least the 1920s, these increased in the 1980s and 1990s. In those later decades began the shift from fee-for-service to managed care. Rising costs of technology, costs of care not covered by patients' copayments (Passell 1997: 1), a growing belief 'that hospitals are not different from any other industry' (Goodrick *et al.* 1997: 39) and increasing demands for care from an ageing population were among the reasons for the pressures. These pressures, which have been widely documented (DeLew *et al.* 1992: 162; Pescosolido *et al.* 1997; Passell 1997) have touched all sectors: fee-for-service contexts, health maintenance organisations, general hospital care, and the new hospital chains run for profit by health care corporations (Gottlieb and Eichenwald 1997).

These strategies have made a major impact on US nursing which is mainly hospital based. Rationalising strategies in hospital settings call for the reduction of nursing staff and utilisation of other personnel (Campbell 1988; Fritz and Cheeseman 1994; Brannon 1994; Sovie 1995) or attempts to deploy fewer nurses more effectively (Zimmerman 1995; DeMoro 1996). One study of nursing, emotional care and downsizing, shows that 'emotional work becomes low priority when workloads are intensified' (Bone 1997: 151). As one respondent in this study commented:

> we have been able to accommodate it (budget cuts), where it's not fun, but it's doable ... all the fun parts that were there are barely there anymore. By fun parts, I mean the teaching, the educating, the emotional care. That's barely doable in many instances.

(For a theoretical examination of these changes and emotional expression in US nursing care, see Olesen and Bone 1998.)

These strategies coincide with and in part are the result of increased patient loads, alongside shortened hospital stays for all but the sickest patients. This has led to controversies, for instance, whether mastectomies should be done on an outpatient basis or whether new mothers should go home the day after giving birth.[2]

The rationalising processes have not only raised questions and worries about emotion in caring work. Job performance has also become part of the rationalisation scenario. Along with temporal speed-ups and workload increases, post-Taylorism managerial strategies call for industrially based performance evaluation techniques to improve service (Buerhaus 1994; Flery 1995; Kelly; 1995; Zonsius and Murphy 1995; Himali 1995). These attempts to 'customerise' the patient have in some places led to hotel corporations providing programmes to train hospital staff to be more courteous to 'guests' (patients) (Goodrick *et al.* 1977: 42). Customer or consumer satisfaction has become a favoured term in at least one major West Coast HMO.[3] This HMO routinely surveys customers (formerly known as patients) with elaborate mail questionnaires about their satisfaction with treatment received from physicians and nurse practitioners. At strategic locations in the HMO's hospitals and clinics postcards are also provided with which customers (patients) can express their satisfaction with a particular practitioner. In another sector of the health care industry, the for-profit hospital, one large chain pays managers' bonuses based on patient satisfaction surveys (Gottlieb and Eichenwald 1997: 10).[4]

Thus, US health care contexts exhibit two themes which relate to the question of emotions in these changing organisations: on the one hand the necessity for providers to be efficient, move patients along, cut costs, do more with less and on the other, the pressure to render emotionally satisfactory and satisfying care, treatment or cure (now known as service) in a realm where life's most poignant events occur.

What happens with emotional behaviour in these contextual crosscurrents which blur the distinction between patient and customer? The evidence, such as it is, is mixed: whereas in the early days of the hospice movement in the US free expression of emotions was usual (Munley 1983), later hospice studies suggest the routinisation of once freely enacted emotional behaviours as those institutions were changed to become profitable (Abel 1986). (For the situation in Britain see James and Field 1992.) Other studies of various contexts, intensive care units, and nursing homes, document situations where nurses or aides wished to express emotions, but the neutralising emphases of rationality and time cutting curtailed or even punished those enacting these feelings (Burfoot 1994; Diamond 1992; Foner 1994). For instance, a compassionate aide in a US nursing home was punished for her emotionality, while another aide, circumspectly cold and rational, was rewarded (Foner, 1995). Countering these findings, however, are those from a study of a dedicated AIDS ward where a 'free' emotional environment was deemed necessary to bring in patients who might go elsewhere in a competitive market (Kotarba *et al.* 1997). This suggests that expression of emotion in some health care settings, rather like that of the flight attendant on the aeroplane, is linked to the fiscal aims of the setting.[5]

These scattered studies indicate that it is tempting, but unwise, to assume that advancing rationalisation creates only either emotionless contexts or contexts where formulated emotional responses are demanded. It may well be that these countervailing themes exist simultaneously in a number of contexts, creating complex emotional environments for both the experience and expression of emotions.

Gender, occupational and emotional stratification

These altering contexts are, as has been amply documented, highly stratified by occupation and by gender. In most contexts white males usually occupy the prestigious, powerful and dominant positions of physicians and administrators. The remainder of both curers and carers (nurses, physical therapists) are largely female with the largest proportion of women of colour in the lower positions (nurses aides, maids, etc.: Butter *et al.* 1987; Olesen 1997b: 408). All of these occupations and their gendered attributes sort themselves into a pyramid with the most prestigious and well-paid males at the top, the least prestigious and least paid females at the bottom. How does that pyramid reflect the emotional stratification of caregiving occupations? It has been assumed that women, the lower status workers, do the emotional work. Emotional stratification was thought to reflect gender and occupational stratification, a view which implicitly subscribed to essentialist notions of gender (i.e. emotional capacity innate in men and women). This view undergirded the opinion that the increasing numbers of females moving into the higher roles especially those going into physician's roles in the caregiving system as is the case in the US, (Olesen 1997b: 413) would alter the emotional stratification. The evidence for this dubious prediction, which overlooks interactional and structural issues in emotional behaviour and incorrectly assumes them to be lodged in individuals, remains equivocal (Olesen 1997b: 413). Moreover, it does not take into account that both men and women in medical education experience socialisation which creates patients as objects and emphasises control of limited time (Baker *et al.* 1996: 174-179). In any case, newly arrived female physicians, like their male counterparts and other caregivers, such as nurse practitioners, are also affected by the rationalising trends noted earlier. They, too, have to do more with less.

What impact might these new scenarios of rationalisation have on various caregivers? One study of radical organisational change in non-HMO, for profit hospitals, documents that physicians are favoured over nurses in situations of organisational decline and instability; they are less apt to feel the dislocation of these processes, less prey to downsizing and deskilling (Leicht *et al.* 1995: 164). Judging from this evidence, albeit partial, it would seem unlikely that gender stratification in the rationalising contexts of the for-profit hospital will alter significantly. Thus emotional labour will continue to be expected from those upon whom the processes of rationalisation make the greatest impact.[6] It is not possible to go beyond this finding to other contexts and settings, but it points to the differential impact of rationalising on various gendered caregiving roles in structures undergoing change. That in turn raises the question of how gender and emotion are to be conceptualised.

Emotion and gender

Deeply imbedded and highly significant social and cultural elements influence gendered emotional experience and expression. These can be as obdurate as any presumed biological differences: nurturing, emotionally expressive females, and distanced, emotionally neutral males. Here, of course, lurks the problem of essentialism noted earlier: that is, certain emotional behaviours are seen as inherent in 'maleness' or 'femaleness'. This is difficult to dislodge because of interpretations within everyday interactions about gendered emotional behaviour. Many interactants in everyday life gloss the artful expression of emotion, usually not realising that the very expression of emotion is a social product, not a biologically imbedded one. Indeed, being accorded maleness or femaleness in everyday interactions rests in part on the 'correct' doing of emotion (West and Zimmerman 1987). For instance, Thoits' work has shown that men and women have different, but presumably gender appropriate, strategies for managing emotionally difficult situations (Thoits 1990).

This leads to the analysis of emotionality with regard to gendered expectations for interactants in specific contexts and how people 'do' emotions in those contexts.[7] As Hearn has argued emotions 'do not just happen "automatically", they have to be done' (1994: 149). Here a critical issue is the expression or doing of emotions which run counter to culturally or organisationally mandated gender expectations for emotionality. For instance, a study of men whose partners had experienced miscarriages shows the cultural and interactive pressures not to express emotions which counter normative rules for emotional expression. One man recalled his emotional experience:

> My mother came to the hospital just after we found that the baby was lost and I was upset ... I found it a trauma ... (Name of wife) had been in hospital and right through we were not sure if she was going to miscarry or not ... I had a bit of a weep, but mam snapped at me and said I was being selfish and had to pull myself together before I upset (wife).
>
> (Puddifoot and Johnson 1997: 539)

Although this grieving husband's emotional behaviour was culturally 'inappropriate' as his mother forcefully reminds him, this incident shows that, 'men's emotions, like emotions in general, do not have an unmediated existence' (Hearn 1994: 142). They are produced in contexts, in this case the highly charged venue of the hospital and, moreover, are dynamic. The sorrowing husband here shifts from a non-masculine emotional expression, weeping, to pulling himself together. This incident displays Radley's argument that 'emotion is a result of the interpretation of individual action and social system'. This view moves the problem away from seeing emotions as 'individualised' to a perspective which foregrounds the interactive and social elements in emotional behaviour (1988: 17).

'Deviant' emotions

Highlighting the element of context specific emotions underscores the utility of the concept of emotional 'deviance' (Thoits 1990) and the underlying norms to which the deviant expression points. However, it also problematises this concept. Questions must be raised about what becomes seen as deviant in specific contexts and by whom. Further, the dynamics of deviance in doing emotions may solidify or alter ideas of the appropriate gendered expression of emotions.

The issue of deviant emotional expression is useful for consideration of gender and emotion in changing health care contexts. The paths to and the contours of the altered emotional landscape may not be clear. Indeed, they may be marked with ambiguity, uncertainty and ambivalence (Weigert and Franks 1989), producing multiple and sometimes conflicting definitions of acceptable emotional behaviour. Deviance is fluid in such circumstances. The emergent feeling rules may not appear swiftly and clearly, but rather ambiguously and slowly, with emotions expressed uncertainly and perhaps even inconsistently. Thoits (1990: 187) has observed that 'with regard to time, emotions are sometimes slow to dissipate, so they may be carried over from one situation to another – appropriate in the first situation, but inappropriate in the next'. (Inappropriate emotions in the first situation also might well become appropriate emotions in the second.)

Practitioners enter and participate in contexts with well established emotional biographies which reflect both professional orientation and multiple emotional encounters in previous contexts. The possibility arises of 'emotional lag' (Olesen 1990; Olesen and Bone 1998). This refers to the situation where emergent emotional expectations run counter to a previously socialised emotional self with resultant emotional dissonance. Emotional lag might be seen when the practitioner struggles to produce the normative emotional responses called for in the new situation, while still feeling the older emotions. In the case of intensive care nurses prevented from expressing emotions, a type of numbing occurred (Burfoot 1994).

These situations of emotional lag may produce what Jaggar (1989: 160–1) has insightfully called 'outlaw emotions' (unconventional experience and expression of emotions). She argues that such emotions point to some underlying cultural or social constraints that obscure certain realities. As such, they 'should be attended to seriously and respectfully rather than condemned, ignored, discounted or suppressed' (Jaggar 1989: 163). Though both emotional lag and outlaw emotions refer to subjective issues, they are also framed by and indicate the interplay of the structural (normative demands for emotional expression), institutional (the nature of the rationalising organisation) and material (the economic themes at play on the health care context and system). In these elements, we see the confluence of micro and macro issues and the presence of the social in the individual.

The individual in the social

The individual also is *in* the social and *in* emotionality. Interaction involving emotion and emotion work contributes to the emergence of new meanings, new lines of action, new elements of structure eventuating in what Strauss *et al.* termed 'the negotiated order' (1963: 60). Or, as Collins (1981) has noted, every micro encounter takes place within a macro structure which has emerged from previous accumulations of micro encounters. Theoretically, this endless chain results from 'evocative transformations' (Couch 1992). Evocative transformations 'refers to those moments of emotionality in social interaction wherein sadness, jocularity and so forth emerge, sometimes initiated, but sometimes spontaneously' (Olesen 1997a: 213). In these transforming moments social relationships are created and corroded, thus altering structure. At a subjective level, participants shift views of themselves and others. Further, such evocative transformations can, as Fineman pointed out about sharing emotions, 'substantially redefine the emotional material and contribute to the emotional texture of the organisation' (1994: 217). The subjective, the social and the structural are intertwined and simultaneously altered in such moments. Much remains to be done in the exploration of emotional dynamics which lead to interactional and social transformations. In particular the part of gender and emotion merit examination.

Intertwined gender and occupational stratification systems found in health care contexts are, though not completely obdurate, nevertheless very slow to change. Reverby (1987) has amply demonstrated this in her analysis of American nursing.[8] These deeply imbedded systems are both sustained and subverted by the transformative aspects of emotionality and emotional labour. Ethnographic evidence from a study of American hospitals shows that certain staff members, most usually nurses, 'pick up the pieces' after a physician, interne, resident or technician has been callous, rude, uninformative or done even a simple, but painful, procedure without engaging in appropriate emotional labour:

I was following the resident who entered a woman's room, accompanied by five or six medical students, to do a cervical examination

> ... It [the examination] was done with scarcely an introduction, with little explanation or attention paid to her reactions. A nurse did hold the patient's hand. The resident did vaginal scraping, demonstrating to the students how to do this right. Then they all exited without a single word, only a passing nod from the resident. After they left, the patient burst into sobs, while the nurse consoled her.
>
> (Strauss *et al.* 1982, 264–5)

Here the very doing or not doing of emotional labour reaffirmed the gender and occupational arrangements.[9]

However, subversive possibilities in the emotional exist as well. Structural consequences can ensue from emotional subversiveness. Intensive care unit nurses in Burfoot's (1994) study were disaffected; organisational demands for neutral expression ran counter to their professional norms for emotional, supportive expressions. Acting on what Burfoot calls 'bootlegged emotions' (those feelings they felt, but were forbidden to) they eventually took collective action to change their situation and to reorganise care. The subversion here was not of the gender order, but of the organisational order. Strauss and his colleagues (1982: 275) have also pointed out that failure on a ward to do what they call sentimental work well can result in disruptions to the work order of the ward and indeed, the organisation and running of the ward.

In considering, then, the link between the individual and the social, analysts of emotional work need to look widely at how emotional labour is done and by whom. The actions of multiple participants in various contexts contribute to stasis and change. Although these changes have implicated the complete range of persons in roles offering cure or care or therapy, it is often difficult to know the emotional issues for practitioners other than physicians or nurses (physical therapists, social workers, technicians, aides) because medical sociology or in this case the sociology of health care, has usually focused on the primary players, physicians and nurses, to the neglect of those others. Exceptions are found in the research on aides' emotion work in nursing homes by Foner (1995), Diamond (1992) and on psychiatric attendants (Browner *et al.* 1987). Emotional work done by families or friends also merits attention (Strauss *et al.* 1982: 270).

In other words, a broader approach to contextualised emotional labour involving the culture of the context and all its players is required if the full dynamics of emotionality and the reciprocities between macro and micro issues are to be understood. By no means does this indicate that the analysis is only vertical – to and from doctor/nurse/aide/patient (see, for example, Cancian's (1997) discussion of caregivers' strategies to raise the value of nurturance). It is multi-directional, including the sometimes not so hidden emotional labour of caregivers managing their own and other providers' emotions as well as those of patients (Thoits, 1996). Research on physicians' management of emotions (DeCoster, 1997) and on nurses' responses to downsizing (Bone, 1997) moves in this direction. What is desirable here is a cultural analysis, whether the context is a burn unit, a drop-in clinic, a family planning clinic, a convalescent home for the elderly, or a unit for AIDS patients. This liberates the sociology of emotions from focus on individuals (Radley 1988) to explore the fluidities and rigidities of the gendered occupational stratification system and the emergence of feeling rules, selves, interactive forms and structures.

To look at culture in these complex situations it may be useful to examine the importance of organisational features which bear on caring work and by implication, emotional labour and expression. Recent evidence from studies on nursing of AIDS patients in different contexts provides such a lead. In a series of well designed and well executed comparative survey studies, Aiken and her colleagues (Aiken and Sloane 1997a; 1997b; Aiken *et al.* 1997a; 1997b) examined nurses' work in dedicated AIDS units, magnet hospitals with scattered beds for AIDS patients in different units, and scattered bed non-magnet hospitals.[10] They found that 'nurses on dedicated AIDS units and in magnet hospitals experience less job-related burnout or emotional exhaustion' (Aiken and Sloane 1997b: 218). They argue that nurse autonomy is critical and question the efficacy of 'the industrial model aggressively marketed by consulting firms to reduce professional autonomy and disciplinary identification' (p. 219). Although these important studies were not conceptualised to explore emotional work in these sites, the findings include patients' statements of satisfaction about ease of expressing feelings and nurse statements of satisfaction about time to spend with patients. They raise the question of cultural elements in the work site that shape emotion work. In this case, an important element was the professional autonomy of the nursing staff.

Sociology of emotions and the sociology of health care

How then do theories of emotion, organisation and gender, inform contemporary issues in the sociology of health care? At a very basic level they provide perspectives that help to avoid seeing and conceptualising such contexts as clinics, hospitals, etc., through 'medical' eyes. Taken in combination, and they are intertwined, they help steer the sociologist away from overly individualised or overly structuralised conceptions of care settings and to a firmer understanding of the complexities of agency and structure. They thus can lead to a more dynamic conceptualisation of the nature and functioning of formal contexts where care occurs. It is possible to see how contexts become stratified and altered through the emotional and gendered interactions that occur around health care. Given the extensive and as yet unclear changes underway in health care systems and contexts, at least in the case of the US, more recent thinking about the place of emotionality and rationality in organisations has much to offer the sociologist concerned with health care.

Work on emotions in rationalising gendered health care contexts, however, can enrich the sociology of emotions as well as the sociology of gender and gendered organisations. Downsizing and rationalising tendencies are major themes in organisational life in the late capitalist era: universities, clothing manufacturers, microchip producers, even the military. In these and many other realms, more is asked when less is available. The emotional issues in rationalising health care contexts could provide valuable leads to understanding those other contexts. In this sense rationalising health care contexts serve as exemplars of the interplay of gender, emotion and rationalisation. In many other areas, such as the law, education, business, the church, gendered differences in emotion – interactive and being done – are crucially and obdurately embedded in the occupational and gender stratification systems, with potential for insuring stability or posing disruption. Looking at differences in health care contexts and their relationship to institutional change will provide leads and concepts to see how these changes play out differentially in other areas.

Too often it is incorrectly assumed that the sociology of health, illness and health care is a discrete entity, separated from 'mainstream sociology'. In fact, when it is fully alive to the transformative aspects of emotions and the reciprocal play of the individual and the social, the analysis of emotional issues in the sociology of health care contexts opens new theoretical and empirical understanding of sociology's most enduring concerns, the problems of stasis and change.

Therein lies a crucial point to which the application of a cultural analysis could apply: the differentiation of health care contexts, their feeling rules, the gender composition of their interactants, the degree to which they are influenced or permeated by the new rationalisations (neutral emotions in the temporal speed up or pleasant emotions in the customer seeking ventures). In an era where transition is key we can examine different contexts, not assuming that the elements found in one will be found in all. Though this chapter has not touched on race and class, because almost nothing is known about these in the sociology of emotions, elements of those critical stratification systems are also part of these contexts and frame the feeling rules, emotional labour and new stages of emergent social structures.

In sum, the analysis of gender, emotions and altering health care contexts integrates the sociology of health, illness and health care and the discipline of sociology in ways which enlarge and expand theoretical possibilities within the parent discipline and attend to the enduring problem of a sociology of humane health care. A humane sociology of health and illness demands that the theoretical and empirical enterprise does not founder in thickets of abstractions or waves of objectified data, and hence risk losing sight of the interactive, affective, subjective and relational elements in these organisations. A major worry about managed care *qua* managed care, and the debates about managed care, is the concern that we lose sight of these interactive elements which lie at heart of the micro–macro nexus. A fully rounded sociology of humane care in formal organizations will take work seriously in the sociology of emotions and in so doing create a vibrant sociology contributing insights, concepts and theories for other parts of the sociological enterprise.

Acknowledgements

Debora Bone, with whom I earlier wrote on issues of emotional expression in changing American nursing (Olesen and Bone 1998), and who has pursued this question in her doctoral dissertation in sociology at the University of California, San Francisco (Bone 1997), did the important literature search on rationalisation in US nursing for which I am most appreciative.

References

Abel, E. K. (1986) 'The hospice movement: institutionalizing innovation', *International Journal of Health Services* 16: 71–85.

Aiken, L. H. and Sloane, D. M. (1997a) 'Effects of specialization and client differentiation on the status of nurses: the case of AIDS', *Journal of Health and Social Behavior* 38: 203–23.

—— (1997b) 'Effects of organizational innovations in AIDS care on burnout among urban hospital nurses', *Work and Occupations* 24: 453–77.

Aiken, L. H., Lake, E. T., Sochalski, J. and Sloane, D. M. (1997a) 'Design of an outcomes study of the organisation of hospital AIDS care', *Research in the Sociology of Health Care* 14: 3–26.

Aiken, L. H., Sloane, D. M. and Lake, E. T. (1997b) 'Satisfaction with inpatient acquired immunodeficiency syndrome care, a national comparison of dedicated and scattered bed units, *Medical Care* 35: 948–62.

Albrow, M. (1992) 'Sine ira et studio – or do organizations have feelings?', *Organization Studies* 13: 313–27.

Ashforth, B. E. and Humphrey, R. H. (1993) 'Emotional labor in service roles: the influence of identity', *Academy of Management Review* 18: 88–115.

—— (1995) 'Emotion in the workplace: a re-appraisal', *Human Relations* 48: 97–125.

Baker, P. S., Yoels, W. C. and Clair, J. M. (1996) 'Emotional expression during medical encounters: social dis-ease and the medical gaze', in V. James and J. Gabe (eds) *Health and the Sociology of Emotions*, Oxford: Blackwell Publishers, 173–99.

Bone, D. (1997) 'Feeling squeezed: dilemmas of emotion work in nursing under managed care'. Unpublished doctoral dissertation, Department of Social and Behavioral Sciences, School of Nursing, University of California, San Francisco.

Brannon, R. L. (1994) *Intensifying Care: The Hospital Industry, Professionalization, and the Reorganization of the Nursing Labor Process*, Amityville, NY: Baywood Publishing Co.

Browner, C. H., Ellis, K. A., Ford, T., Silsby, J., Tampoya, J. and Yee, C. (1987) 'Stress social support and health of psychiatric technicians in a state facility', *Mental Retardation* 25: 31–8.

Buerhaus, P. I. (1994) 'Economics of managed competition and consequences to nurses', *Nursing Economics* 12: 10–17 and 75–80, 106.

Burfoot, J. H. (1994) 'Outlaw emotions and the sensual dynamics of compassion: the case of emotion as instigator of social change', unpublished paper, Department of Sociology, Middlebury College.

Butler, J. (1990) *Gender Trouble*, New York: Routledge.

——— (1993) *Bodies That Matter: on the Discursive Limits of 'Sex'*, New York: Routledge.

Butter, I. H., Carpenter, E. S., Kay, B. J. and Simmons, R. (1987) 'Gender hierarchy in the health labor force', *International Journal of Health Services* 17: 133–49.

Campbell, M. (1988) 'Management as "ruling": A class phenomenon in nursing', *Studies in Political Economy* 27: 29–51.

Cancian, F. (1997) 'Emotional caring as paid work: caregivers' strategies for raising the value and quality of nurturance', unpublished paper, Department of Sociology, University of California, Irvine.

Caudill, W. (1958) *The Psychiatric Hospital as a Small Society*, Cambridge, MA: Harvard University Press.

Charmaz, K. (1980) 'The social construction of self-pity in the chronically ill', in N. K. Denzin (ed.) *Studies in Symbolic Interaction*, Vol. 3, Greenwich, CT: JAI Press, 123–46.

Charmaz, K. and Olesen, V. (1997) 'Ethnographic research in medical sociology, its foci and distinctive contribution', *Sociological Methods And Research* 25: 452–94.

Collins, R. (1981) 'On the microfoundations of macrosociology', *American Journal of Sociology* 6: 984–1,014.

Couch, C. J. (1992) 'Evocative transformations and social relationships', in N. K. Denzin (ed.) *Studies in Symbolic Interaction*, Vol. 13, Greenwich, CT: JAI Press, 141–54.

Davies, C. (1995) *Gender and the Professional Predicament in Nursing*, Milton Keynes: Open University Press.

Davis, F. (1963) *Passage Through Crisis*, Indianapolis, IN: Bobbs-Merrill.

DeCoster, A. V. (1997) 'Physician emotion management', unpublished paper, Department of Sociology, Louisiana State University.

DeLew, N., Greenberg, G. and Kinchen, K. (1992) 'A layman's guide to the US health care system', *Health Care Financing Review* 14: 151–69.

DeMoro, R. A. (1996) 'It's the reality that's scary in current health care trends', *California Nurse* 92: 3, 10.

Diamond, T. (1992) *Making Grey Gold: Narratives of Nursing Home Care*, Chicago: University of Chicago Press.

Dingwall, R. and Murray, T. (1983) 'Categorization in accident departments: "good" patients, "bad" patients and "children"', *Sociology of Health and Illness* 5: 127–48.

Editorial (1988) 'The social context of emotion: construction without deconstruction', *British Journal of Social Psychology* 27: 1–4.

Emerson, J. (1970) 'Behavior in private places: Sustaining definitions of reality in gynecological examinations', in H. P. Dreitzel (ed.) *Recent Sociology*, No. 2, *Patterns of Communicative Behavior*, New York: Macmillan, 10–15.

Fagerhaugh, S. and Strauss, A. L. (1977) *The Politics of Pain Management*, Menlo Park, CA: Addison-Wesley.

Fineman, S. (1994) 'An emotion agenda', in S. Fineman (ed.) *Emotions in Organizations*, London: Sage, 216–24.

Fisher, S. (1995) *Nursing Wounds: Nurse Practitioners, Doctors, Women Patients and the Negotiation of Meaning*, New Brunswick, NJ: Rutgers.

Flam, H. (1990) 'Emotional "man": II. Corporate actors as emotion-motivated emotional managers', *International Sociology* 5: 225–34.

Flery, D. L. (1995) *Redesigning Nursing Care Delivery: Transforming our Future*. Philadelphia: J. B. Lippincott.

Foner, N. (1994) *The Caregiving Dilemma: Work in an American Nursing Home*. Berkeley, CA: University of California Press.

—— (1995) 'The hidden injuries of bureaucracy: work in an American nursing home', *Human Organization*, 54: 229–37.

Fox, R. C. (1959) *Experiment Perilous: Physicians and Patients Facing the Unknown*. Glencoe, IL: The Free Press.

Freund, P. (1982) *The Civilized Body: Social Control, Domination and Health*. Philadelphia, PA: Temple University Press.

— (1990) 'The expressive body: a common ground for the sociology of emotions and illness', *Sociology of Health and Illness* 12: 452–77.

Fritz, D. J., and Cheeseman, S. (1994) 'Blueprint for integrating nurse extenders in critical care', *Nursing Economics* 12: 327–31.

Garot, R. (1995) 'Substantive rationality in a bureaucratic setting', unpublished paper, Department of Sociology, University of California, Los Angeles.

Gibson, D. (1994) 'The struggle for reason: the sociology of emotion in organizations', unpublished paper, Anderson Graduate School of Business, University of California, Los Angeles.

Goodrick, E., Meindl, J. R. and Flood, A. B. (1997) 'Business as usual: the adoption of managerial strategies by US hospitals', in J. J. Kronenfeld (ed.), *Research in the Sociology of Health Care*, Vol. 14, *The Evolving Health Care Delivery System: Necessary Changes for Providers of Care, Consumers and Patients*, Greenwich, CT: JAI Press, 27–50.

Gordon, S. L. (1990). 'Social structural effects on emotions', in T. D. Kemper (ed.) *Research Agendas in the Sociology of Emotions*. Albany: State University of New York, 145–79.

Gottlieb, M. and Eichenwald, K. (1997). 'A hospital chain's brass knuckles, and the backlash', *New York Times*, Sunday, 11 May, section 3, Business, pp. 1, 10–11.

Hearn, J. (1994) 'Emotions and the politics of difference', in Stephen Fineman (ed.) *Emotions in Organizations*, Thousand Oaks, CA: Sage, 142–66.

Himali, U. (1995) 'Managed care: does the promise meet the potential?', *The American Nurse* 1: 15–16.

Hochschild, A. R. (1983) *The Managed Heart: Commercialization of Human Feeling*, Berkeley, CA: University of California Press.

Jaggar, A. M. (1989) 'Love and knowledge: emotion in feminist epistemology', in A. M. Jaggar and S. R. Bordo (eds) *Gender/Body/Knowledge, Feminist Reconstructions of Being and Knowing*, New Brunswick, NJ: Rutgers University Press, 145–71.

James, N. (1989) 'Emotional labour: skill and work in the social regulation of feelings', *Sociological Review* 37: 15–42.

—— (1992) 'Care = organisation + physical labour', *Sociology of Health and Illness* 14: 488–509.

—— (1994) 'Divisions of emotional labour: disclosure and cancer', in S. Fineman (ed.) *Emotions in Organizations*, Thousand Oaks, CA: Sage, 94–117.

James, N. and Field, D. (1992) 'The routinization of charisma and bureaucratization', *Social Science and Medicine* 34: 1,363–75.

Kelly, K. (ed.) (1995) *Health Care Work Redesign*, Thousand Oaks, CA: Sage.

Kotarba, J. A., Ragsdale, D. and Morrow, J. R. Jr (1997) 'Everyday culture in a dedicated HIV–AIDS hospital unit', in J. J. Kronenfeld (ed.) *Research in the Sociology of Health Care Vol. 14. The Evolving Health Care Delivery System: Necessary Changes for Providers of Care, Consumers and Patients*, Greenwich, CT: JAI Press, 51–68.

Kramer, M. and Schmalenberg, C. (1988) 'Magnet hospitals: institutions of excellence', *Journal of Nursing Administration* 8: 13–24.

Leidner, R. (1993) *Fast Food, Fast Talk: Service Work and the Routinization of Life*, Berkeley, CA: University of California Press.

Leicht, K. T., Fennell, M. L. and Witkowski, K. M. (1995) 'The effects of hospital characteristics and radical organizational change on the relative standing of health care professions', *Journal of Health and Social Behavior*, 36: 151–68.

Lofland, L. H. (1985) 'The social shaping of emotion: the case of grief', *Symbolic Interaction* 8: 171–90.

Lupton, D. (1996) '"Your life in their hands": trust in the medical encounter', in V. James and J. Gabe (eds) *Health and the Sociology of the Emotions*, Oxford: Blackwell, 157–72.

Lyon, M. L. (1996) 'C. Wright Mills meets Prozac: the relevance of social emotion to the sociology of health and illness', in V. James and J. Gabe (eds) *Health and the Sociology of Emotions*, London: Basil Blackwell, 55–78.

Munley, A. (1983) *The Hospice Alternative: A New Context for Death and Dying*. New York: Basic Books.

Murcott, A. (1981) 'On the typification of "bad" patients', in P. Atkinson and C. Heath, (eds) *Medical Work, Realities and Routines*, London: Gower, 128–40.

O'Brien, M. (1994) 'The managed heart revisited: health and social control', *The Sociological Review* 42: 393–413.

Olesen, V. L. (1990) 'The neglected emotions: a challenge to medical sociology', *Medical Sociology News,* 16: 11–25.

—— (1997a) 'Evocative transformations: A neglected concept in the analysis of situated emotions', in D. E. Miller, M. A. Katovich and S. L. Saxton (eds) *Constructing Complexity: Symbolic Interaction and Social Forms*, Supplement 3, *Studies In Symbolic Interaction*, series editor, N. K. Denzin, Greenwich, CT: JAI Press, 213–20.

—— (1997b) 'Who cares? Women as informal and formal caregivers', in

S. B. Ruzek, V. L. Olesen, and A. E. Clarke (eds) *Women's Health, Complexities and Differences*, Columbus, OH: Ohio State University Press, 397–424.

Olesen, V. L. and Bone, D. (1998) 'Emotions in rationalizing organizations: conceptual notes from professional nursing in the US', in G. A. Bendelow and S. J. Williams (eds) *Emotions in Social Life: Critical Theories and Contemporary Issues*, London: Routledge, 313–29.

Passell, P. (1997) 'In medicine, government rises again', *New York Times Week in Review*, 7 November, pp. 1 and 4.

Pescosolido, B. A., Wright, E. R., McGrew, J., Mesche, D. J., Hohmann, A., Sullivan, W. P., Haugh, D., DeLiberty, R. and McDonald, E. C. (1997) 'The human and organizational markers of health care system change: Framing studies of hospital downsizing and closure', in J. J. Kronenfeld (ed.) *Research in the Sociology of Health Care*, Vol. 14, *The Evolving Health Care Delivery System: Necessary Changes for Providers of Care, Consumers, and Patients*, Greenwich, CT: JAI Press, 69–98.

Puddifoot, J. F. and Johnson, M. P. (1997) 'The legitimacy of grieving: the partner's experience at miscarriage', *Social Science and Medicine* 45: 837–45.

Putnam, L. L. and Mumby, D. K. (1994) 'Organisations, emotion and the myth of rationality', in S. Fineman (ed.) *Emotions in Organizations*, Thousand Oaks, CA: Sage, 36–57.

Radley, A. (1988) 'The social form of feeling', *British Journal of Social Psychology* 21: 5–18.

Reverby, S. (1987) *Ordered To Care: the Dilemma of American Nursing*, New York: Cambridge University Press.

Roth, J. (1986) 'Some contingencies of the moral evaluation and control of clients', in P. Conrad and R. Kern (eds) *The Sociology of Health and Illness*, New York: St Martin's Press, 322–33.

Scheper-Hughes, N. and Lock, M. (1987) 'The mindful body: a prolegomenon to future work in medical anthropology', *Medical Anthropology Quarterly*, new series: 16: 6–41.

Silverman, D. (1987) *Communication and Medical Practice: Social Relations in the Clinic*, Beverly Hills: Sage.

Sovie, M. D. (1995) 'Tailoring hospitals for managed care and integrated health systems', *Nursing Economics* 13: 72–83.

Stacey, M. (1981) 'The division of labor revisited or overcoming the two Adams', in P. Abrams, R. Deem, J. Finch and P. Rock (eds) *Practice and Progress: British Sociology 1950–1980*, London: Allen and Unwin, 172–204.

Stimson, G. and Webb, B. (1975) *Going to See the Doctor*, London: Routledge and Kegan Paul.

Strauss, A. L., Schatzman, L., Bucher, R., Erlich, D. and Sabshin, M. (1963) 'The hospital and its negotiated order', in E. Freidson (ed.) *The Hospital in Modern Society*, New York: The Free Press, 60–70.

Strauss, A. L., Fagerhaugh, S., Suczek, B. and Wiener, C. L. (1982) 'Sentimental work in the technological hospital', *Sociology of Health and Illness* 12: 254–78.

Strong, P. M. (1979) *The Ceremonial Order of the Clinic, Patients, Doctors and Medical Bureaucracies*, London: Routledge and Kegan Paul.

Sutton, R. I. (1991) 'Maintaining norms about expressed emotions', *Administrative Science Quarterly* 36: 245–68.

Thoits, P. A. (1990) 'Emotional deviance: research agendas', in T. D. Kemper (ed.) *Research Agendas in the Sociology of Emotions*, Albany, NY: State University of New York Press, 180–206.

—— (1996) 'Managing the emotions of others', *Symbolic Interaction* 19: 85–110.

Treweek, G. L. (1996) 'Emotion work in care assistant work', in V. James and J. Gabe (eds) *Health and the Sociology of Emotions*, Oxford: Blackwell Publishers, 115–32.

Van Maanen, J. and Kunda, G. (1989) '"Real feelings": emotional expression and organizational culture', in M. M. Staw and L. L. Cummings (eds) *Research in Organizational Behavior*, 2, Greenwich, CT: JAI Press, 43–103.

Weber, M. (1978) *Economy and Society*, trans. G. Roth and C. Wittich, Berkeley, CA: University of California Press.

Weigert, A. and Franks, D. D. (1989) 'Ambivalence: a touchstone of the modern temper', in D. D. Franks, and E. D. McCarthy (eds) *The Sociology of the Emotions, Original Essays and Research Papers*, Greenwich, CT: JAI Press, 205–27.

West, C. and Zimmerman, D. (1987) 'Doing gender', *Gender and Society* 1: 125–51.

Williams, S. J. and Bendelow, G. (1996) 'Emotion, health and illness', in V. James and J. Gabe, (eds) *Health and the Sociology of Emotions*, London: Basil Blackwell, 25–53.

Zimmerman, P. G. (1995) 'Replacement of nurses with unlicensed assistive personnel: the erosion of professional nursing and what we can do', *Journal of Emergency Nursing* 21: 208–12.

Zonsius, M. K., and Murphy, M. (1995) 'Use of total quality management sparks staff nurse participation in continuous quality improvement', *Nursing Clinics of North America* 30: 1–12.

Chapter 17

The ethics and politics of caring

Postmodern reflections

Nick Fox

Introduction

What does it mean to care? And what is the significance of being a care-giver or a recipient of care? Within the social sciences, 'care' is paradoxical. On one hand, it is based in intimate and human relations which value giving, love and concern. On the other, it is a set of practices – and theories about those practices – which are codified by the 'caring professions' as an occupation and the basis for disciplinary power and authority (Gardner 1992). As Thomas (1993: 649) also points out, care entails both the emotional 'caring about someone' and the more instrumental 'caring for a person'. 'Care' is a growth area for discourse at the present time, and careers in care professions and in research and academic life are being forged from the disciplinary work of care theorists: the fabrication of what I have called elsewhere (Fox 1995a) the *vigil* of care. These discourses on care are about power, intricately associated with 'knowledge', as it impinges on its subjects: those who are the recipients of this care-as-discipline.

Jacques Derrida, Jean François Lyotard, Hélène Cixous and Gilles Deleuze have variously recognised the centrality of language in the fabrication of reality. These and other writers, who may be called *postmodern*, are now making significant contributions to social theory, to our understanding of the relationship between power and knowledge; to explorations of the micro-politics of social control — in hospitals, schools, psychiatry and psychology; and to resistance to this power. The impact of post-modernism is, however, not simply upon social *theory*, it is also upon how that theory is translated into action. It is about acknowledging a commitment to difference, discontinuity and diversity rather than the concerns with identity and continuity in modernism (Haber 1994). It is about exploring the possibilities of resistance to discourse (Butler 1990; Deleuze and Guattari 1986; Critical Art Ensemble 1994). And these interests in difference and resistance have spawned an ethics which (perhaps paradoxically) offers possibilities for engagement with other people which counterposes the moral relativism of modernism (Bauman 1989, 1993b; Caputo 1993; Fox 1993; White 1991).

So it is from such a postmodern perspective that I shall seek in this chapter to explore the politics and ethics of *care-as-gift*, focusing on the celebration of difference which – unlike the *vigil* of care with its concern with power and control – is concerned with values of love, trust and giving, and which implicitly resists and rejects the *vigil*. While explicitly concerned with professional care, the argument extends to all 'care': in effect to human engagement with others more generally. The result is a 'nomadology' (to use Deleuze and Guattari's term): a manifesto for a subjectivity resisting and refusing discourse and growing through the *gifts* of those with whom it engages.

Within the framework of post-structuralism and postmodern social theory, both the *vigil* of care and *care-as-gift* are theorised through analysis of language, knowledge and power. Were the postulated opposition of the *vigil* of disciplinary care and *care-as-gift* to be couched in an essentialist or foundationalist framework, analysis would perhaps suggest how empowerment (individual or collective) could overcome institutional control, oppression or domination. A post-structuralist framework does not offer so straightforward a resolution, for the simple reason that from this perspective, there is no longer an essential subject. Subjectivity is an outcome of power/ knowledge: and both discourse (the *vigil*) and resistance to it (*care-as-gift*) operate in the same domain, namely that of language. This means that the mechanism of the vigil's disciplinary power is not situated outside the care setting – in policy or institutions or educational establishments (although these are often the places where discourses are codified) – but in the everyday practice of care, in the contact between carer and cared-for. But it is also within these contacts that the possibilities of resistance are to be found: documenting the vigil of care suggests how it may be resisted.

If care can be both discipline and gift, discourse and resistance to discourse, then in situations of care, there is always the potential for that which is positive, enabling and empowering to become (intentionally or unintentionally, explicitly or without being noted) a possessive, controlling discourse. To give an example: in a therapeutic setting, a person undergoing treatment may well invest trust and confidence in a therapist, reciprocating an investment on the part of the therapist to enable the patient to take control of her/his situation. These investments may enable the patient to grow and break free of the constraints of suffering and dependency. But if these investments become codified within discourses of professionalism, or as is sometimes the case in caring settings, within a repetition of a parent–child dependency (Parsons and Fox 1952; Forrester 1990; Fox 1993), then what was an empowering relationship becomes disempowerment, what might have enabled such growth becomes more to do with power and control.

So a 'nomadology' of care does not provide glib answers to issues of the ethics and politics of engagement with others. What it does offer is a perspective and a commitment to diversity, which fractures the understanding of what it means to be a carer, and a recipient of care.

The vigilance of the carer

Postmodernism is not the first perspective in social theory to point to the less attractive aspects of the practice of care. Materialist, feminist and liberal humanist analyses of health and welfare found a negative aspect to caring in the dominance arising from professional closure, patriarchy, capitalism or bureaucracy (Graham 1983; Lynch 1989; Stacey 1988; Ungerson 1987), or in 'unprofessional' labelling and stigmatisation of patients (de Swaan 1990; Goffman 1970). Those discourses which held up the loving care of familial relationships as an example for care services have been criticised for ignoring the politics of the domestic setting (Graham 1979; Dunlop 1986), while studies which examined care in terms of 'emotional labour' (Hochschild 1983; James 1989) also contributed to a pessimism about the progressiveness of 'care'.

What is significant in postmodern approaches is the association of power with knowledge, such that these negative aspects of care are seen not as anomalous, but as invested in the very character of the disciplines which formulate and codify 'care'. In English, the word 'discipline' means both a set of practices by which individuals become subjects of power, and, second, a professional or academic grouping. The connection between these meanings has been illustrated in post-structuralist writing (Foucault 1976, 1979; Goldstein 1984; Rose 1989), the common thread being the discourses by which knowledge both informs practice and supplies the authority for a group's claim to status and control. The association of power with knowledge suggests that in the context of care, the professionalisation of caring (creating a discipline) cannot but lead to a disciplining of care's clients. This construction of a discipline of power/knowledge entails a technology of surveillance, the *vigil* of care which is the continual subjection of care's clients, and increasingly, all aspects of the environment in which they live, to the vigilant scrutiny of carers, and the consequent fabrication and perpetuation of subjectivities as 'carer' and 'cared-for'.

Hence Gardner's (1992) argument concerning the paradox that as caring becomes a discipline it loses its grounding in love and giving. Reflecting on this paradox in relation to nursing, she concludes that 'the caring dimension of nursing helps to establish the independent practice area of nursing, and the growth in professionalism endows caring with a strength that did not exist when it was viewed as a "weak" form of occupational behaviour' (1992: 251).

Seen in this light, the organisation of care from Nightingale to the present-day is not only about caring *per se*, but is also the story of control and the fabrication of knowledge concerning 'care'. This emphasis is illustrated in the following advice to those who would enter the profession of nursing.

> When a candidate at interview is asked why she [*sic*] chose nursing the correct answer is no longer 'I want to help people'. If that is what she actually feels it would be more prudent to talk about social oblig-ations, nursing being a profession which involved relating to others, career mobility, academic and emotional gratification ... The value upon care remains high, but care is no longer 'tender' and 'loving', it is a specifiable commodity ... A nurse no longer has a vocation; she has a profession. She is no longer dedicated; she is professional. She is no longer moral; she is accountable.
>
> (Inglesby 1992: 54)

The theorising of care-as-discipline can be traced in countless discourses of professionals and academics, and the continual devising of new 'models' of care (for example, Brykczynska 1992; Lynaugh and Fagin 1988; Kershaw 1992; Salvage 1989). In an edited collection (Gray and Pratt 1991), we learn that nursing must adopt science as its framework, to achieve the goals of research, education and development of skills as scientific investigators as well as clinical expertise (1991: 4–8). Sims asserts the importance of devel-oping theory for successful nursing practice (1991: 51ff.), Anderson maps out an 'integrated health breakdown and intervention model' (1991: 108), while Cameron-Traub asserts the advantages for nursing theory of a catholic approach, encompassing 'alternative conceptualisations of nursing as meet-ing patients' needs, interactive processes of the nurse–patient dyad, outcomes for the patient, or influences on human–environment patterning' (1991: 37).

Such positions construct – in ways which compare with the similar fabrications of the medical gaze – not only the caring profession itself, but also its clients, and it is in this sense that it seems appropriate to typify a *vigil* of care. Patient-centredness, while offering a contrast with medicocentric practices, is also effective in extending the gaze of the carer. Thomas and Dolan (1993) argue that

> The nurse where appropriate, must be able to follow the client and be sufficiently skilled and adaptable to care in any environment, be it the ward, day care unit or community ... Nurses will play a more pro-active role in the maintenance of health and in providing primary, secondary and tertiary health education. Nurses of the 21st century will be actively involved in directing change and be adaptable to a changing world without fear of that change.
>
> (1993: 125, 129)

Access to, and observation of, the carers' client group and the activities of caring are essential for the formulation of theory; just as access to and observation of patients was crucial for the development of medical discourse (Foucault 1976). But technical skills and practical experience are not in themselves sufficient to construct the crucial body of knowledge claimed by a profession. Clients become the subjects of research and analysis, as 'occupations aspiring to professional status . . . emphasize relevant and appropriate research activities, attempt to construct a theoretical basis for their activities, identify concepts, principles and theories' (Shrock 1982: 104).

The *vigil* of care is the disciplinary technology which, through discourses of professionalism and theory, fabricates and inscribes those who receive care. It reminds us of the vigilance which Nightingale emphasised in her programme for the nursing profession, and the subsequent technologies which enabled her successors to mount their vigil over their patients and clients (Dunlop 1986). In the era of community care, Twinn (1991) can argue that the gaze of the health visitor should extend beyond individual advice giving, to the profiling of communities' health and to community development work (see also Bloor and McIntosh 1990 and Mayall and Foster 1989 for analyses of surveillance in community nursing). The *vigil* is both to do with practice and with theory, and is reflected in the discourses of carers (including lay and voluntary carers) whose work takes them far beyond the gaze of the clinic (Foucault 1976) or the dispensary (Armstrong 1983), into their clients' homes and private lives.

The ethical and political consequences of what may be reasonable or principled motives for generating such discourses, stems from the effects which the construction of disciplines of care have on those who are recipients of care. The centrality of the recipient of care as the subject which give caring disciplines their authority, cannot help but construct them within particular subjectivities. At the most basic level, caring professionals' establishment of a divide between themselves and those for whom they care – labelling them as clients or patients (Hugman 1991: 113ff.) creates a subjectivity for the cared-for which is then to be played out in the discursive gaze of the vigil. The construction and strengthening of disciplinary markers of knowledge shift the balance of power away from clients and patients towards health professionals, as discourses such as those outlined here identify and achieve a distinctive 'care-as-discipline'.

Resisting the vigil: the gift of care

Sociological analyses of care which uncritically identify it as a 'good thing' are too simplistic. But so too is an analysis which implicates caring as a disciplinary procedure pure and simple. Caring has a dual character: on the one hand, it has the potential to subject the cared-for within discourses of the *vigil*. On the other, and differently constituted, it can supply the possibility of resistance to discourse on the part of the person who is in need of care, to assist her to resist this disciplining.

In counterposing these two versions of care, I am comparing the disciplinary *vigil* with a very different form of engagement, which I typify as the *gift* of care. This latter concept draws on the work of the feminist post-structuralist Cixous, who has theorised two realms, those of the 'Gift' and the 'Proper' (Cixous 1986). Cixous contrasts *gift* relationships (which she chooses to formulate as feminine, but might be more widely understood as responsive to difference) with the masculine realm of the *proper*: of property, propriety, possession, identity and dominance. The characteristics of gift relationships would seem particularly apposite for relations entailing care, and might include *generosity, trust, confidence, love, commitment, delight* and *esteem*.

Few of these words are to be found in articulations of the disciplinary *vigil* of professional care. Indeed, some suggest relations which could be seen as *un-professional* and inappropriate to the highly theorised, formalised care documented in textbooks, in which the carer/cared-for distinction is so strong and so impenetrable. Care in the realm of the *proper* is a possessive controlling relationship which constantly requires its subject to behave in certain ways, to be defined as 'patient' or 'client', and to repeat the patterns of those who have been the objects of 'care' before.

The force and value of this distinction between the *gift* and the *proper* rests in the possibility that things could be different. It offers the potential for an ethics and politics of engagement based on a celebration of difference, not of identity (Haber 1994). The *proper* is a possessive relationship, constantly requiring of its object that it behaves in certain ways, that it is defined (as 'patient', 'nurse, 'carer'), and repeats the patterns of those who have been the objects of its discourse previously. Substituting *gift* relationships changes everything: we engage with others now as others, not as those with whom we might wish to identify. Definition is replaced with metaphor and allusion, analysis and theory with poetics and expression, professional care by love and the celebration of difference.

The notion of the gift is not new in sociology. The Durkheimian ethnographer Mauss (1990) wrote a classic monograph in the 1920s (reprinted 1990) on the role of the gift in various societies, and the significance of a gift as a form of social bonding based in obligation and reciprocity has been addressed by Hochschild (1983: 80–2). But let me be clear what I mean when I speak of a *gift*, because it is possible to have *proper* gifts! What Mauss and Hochschild describe in talking of 'gift economies' based in reciprocity are *proper* relationships, and in the realm of the *proper*, a gift is threatening because it establishes an inequality, a difference, an imbalance in power. The act of giving becomes an act of aggression, an exposure of the Other (Moi 1985: 112).

Gifts may also serve other purposes. In recent work on the care offered by volunteers (Fox 1999), I found that voluntary caring was rarely undertaken for altruistic reasons, but for reasons of career progression, brushing up skills, or simply to get out of the house and do something to fill the day. These volunteers gained much from their interactions with those for whom they cared, often to the point where one wondered what the recipient got back! In contrast, the *gift* is not given with any expectation of reciprocity; in the realm of the gift, those who give do not expect gratefulness or even an acknowledgement of their effort. The true *gift* is one which one does not even realise one is giving (Derrida 1992).

So we must be very cautious about these distinctions. Similarly, we must not under-estimate the impact (and difficulty) of replacing the *proper* in our disciplines of the academy and the caring professions. Substituting such relations with those based on *gifts* is about replacing a modernist responsibility to act with a responsibility to otherness (White 1991). Despite the attractions for professionalising groups of the *vigil* some nursing theorists have (perhaps paradoxically) addressed this different kind of engagement. Thus, Parse (1987) has developed a perspective on health as 'human becoming' and similarly Brykczynska speaks of a *gift*-like care as actualisation, a sharing of a moment of joy, of being truly present alongside an other:

> True caring involves growth, mutual growth of carer and recipient of care; and it is this ability to grow, to change, to progress from pain to disintegration to purpose and equilibrium that gives the caring phenomena [*sic*] its impetus and rationale.
>
> (Brykczynska 1992: 237)

Yet even here it is necessary to ask what constitutes purpose and equilibrium, and by whom these are defined? There is no guarantee that *acting* in the world will lead to a facilitation of becoming, even within such a perspective. To think more about what such a commitment to becoming might look like, I want to turn to the work of Deleuze and Guattari and their 'nomadology'.

Care and nomadic subjectivity

In their political philosophy of resistance, Deleuze and Guattari (1986, 1988) provide us with an anti-icon for a postmodern ethos: the *nomad*. Nomadology is the response of the dispossessed to those who wield power through their discourses on the human condition (the lawyer, the priest, the doctor or care professional).

The nomad does not put down roots, or manipulate her environment to suit her needs and wishes. She does not seek control, she takes what is on offer, assimilates it, and moves on. She refuses to acknowledge the forces which would territorialise her, the rationalism which values the stable, the static and the instrumentalism of matching actions to goals (Deleuze and Guattari 1986). Civilisation, norms, taste, social distinctions mean nothing to her: she is at one with her environment, yet never part of it. She is a warrior without a strategy (Deleuze and Guattari 1986; Plant 1993). The nomad is a refusenik, rejecting the 'territorialisations' of her subjectivity which discourse seeks to impose. Her silence is eloquence, her passivity is an act of resistance, her politics of non-engagement in the political and legal apparatus of the state has the authority of Gandhi or Christ.

It is hard to be a nomad; in fact there *are* no nomads, there is only nomadism, it is a process, not an identity. Nomadism is about becoming other, and one never finally becomes other, rather, we lurch from one identity to another. Deleuze and Guattari see nomadism as 'rhizomatic', a growth which is branching and diversifying, refusing to follow a single line of development 'form a rhizome, increase your territory by deterritorialization, extend the line of flight to the point where it becomes an abstract machine covering the entire plane of consistency' (Deleuze and Guattari 1988: 11).

The arena in which nomadism is played out is the philosophical surface which Deleuze and Guattari (1984, 1988) call the *Body-without-Organs* (BwO). The BwO is not like a physical Body-with-Organs or 'organism', it is constructed socially, exists in, and is patterned by, the intertextualities of discourse and resistance to discourse. It is the BwO which Foucault describes when he documents the constructions of the body by medicine and other disciplines, and the self-disciplining of subjectivity in an 'aesthetics of existence' (Foucault 1986) involving the most intimate aspects of life – of what amounts to the 'care of the self'. In this view, civilisation relentlessly writes this body, transforming it into a cultural object (Butler 1990: 129–30). But unlike Foucault's pessimistic view of a subjectivity entirely inscribed by discourse, Deleuze and Guattari see the possibilities for resistance. To be a nomad is always to be engaged in a battle for the BwO

> you are forever attaining it, it is a limit . . . But you're already on it, scurrying like a vermin, groping like a blind person, or running like a lunatic: desert travels and nomad of the steppes. On it we sleep, live our waking lives, fight – fight and are fought – seek our place, experience untold happiness and fabulous defeats: on it we penetrate and are penetrated: on it we love.
>
> (Deleuze and Guattari 1988: 150)

This brings us back neatly to the *gift,* because central to this theme of resistance, to the 'becoming' of the subject, is the contribution of the other to that process. In a social world of power relations, the other may be significant in the quest for nomadic subjectivity. If such a subjectivity is about possibility, then those around us may be very important in enabling us to achieve those potentials. Where we are limited or constrained – as, for instance, recipients of care may be by physical or psychological factors – this support may be of particular value. In the final section, I want to look more closely at what it means to base our caring in a relationship of giving, and how we may challenge our own assumptions about those around us.

Nomadology for carers and recipients of care

The fabrication of the human body is so insistent that it seems hard to question its facticity. Since the Enlightenment, the discourses of biological science have created an organism by which we envision the body and its interior (Deleuze and Guattari 1984; Foucault 1976). Since these early days of anatomy and physiology, new sciences have refined that vision. Where once the limits of the body were defined by anatomy, now we are delimited through genetics and immunology (Haraway 1991; Hogle 1995; Levin and Solomon 1990), and perhaps less significantly, through the social sciences applied to biomedicine.

But postmodern perspectives indicate that there is not a single 'truth' out there concerning the way the body really is: the body is a contested realm, on which the discourses of the medical, the social, the legal, the theological collide. Every datum from that materiality, every datum from the internal world of sensation and pain, are refracted through the lens of language as we process it into 'experience' of ourselves and our bodies. The anti-realism of postmodernism recognises world-in-language as the only world we inhabit, that it is not a mirror or duplicate, but the only world: the world within which we live out our lives, love, grieve, suffer and die (Cupitt 1994: 47).

We can see just such a challenge to the facticity of the human body in the virtualisation of 'reality' in cyber-culture. The 'cyberpunk' writer William Gibson (author of the novel *Neuromancer*) explores a future in which humans are downloaded into computers, and carry on a non-corporeal existence in cyberspace: we are challenged to reflect on our relations with such 'constructs', and on their humanity (Bukatman 1993). In a different realm, performance artists Stellarc and Orlan challenge the limits of our embodiment. Stellarc has begun to explore the philosophical challenges of the cyborg in a series of performances, including the construction of an artificial third arm, and the control of this and other parts of his body by strangers via the Internet. Orlan's performance art entails changing her appearance through plastic surgery – some of which is conventional, while the creation of lumps on her temples challenge norms of human physiognomy and beauty. What they have in common is a questioning of the limits of the body, and of what it means to be human and to live in relationship with other 'humans'. They are interested, as are the cyberpunk writers, in developing the post-human, who is free from the constraints of the body. In these ways, cyber-culture is testing the limits of embodied humanity, as constituted in the traditional discourses of the body.

Reading the work of Oliver Sacks (1986, 1995), we realise that just as the body is not a fixed entity, nor are 'health' or 'illness'. His studies shed light on our assumptions about what it is to be human, to be 'healthy' and 'normal'. In some circumstances, what Sacks assumed to be deviation in his neurologically-different patients, he later realised to be a heightening, while the 'cured' patient seemed to have lost precisely what had originally made them who they were. In other cases, Sacks' patients refused the treatment offered. An artist who had lost his colour sight, chose not to have it restored, as he had developed a distinctive monochrome style of painting. A person diagnosed as having Tourette's syndrome chose to have medication during the week, but at weekends to revert to his 'witty ticcy' self. An 86-year-old woman with neurosyphilis appreciated the 'friskiness' that the disease gave her. One wonders how many other 'cures' diminish the people who are their subjects – with no acknowledgement of their right to otherness?

Nomadology questions the privileged status of 'health', and opens the possibility for what is both a radically different conception of human potential, and a recognition of our responsibility to otherness. I have called this alternative, *arche-health* (Fox 1993). *Arche-health* is a becoming, a deterritorialising of the BwO, a resistance to discourse, a generosity towards otherness, a nomadic subjectivity. It is not intended to suggest a natural, essential or in any way prior kind of health, upon which the other healths are superimposed, it is not supposed to be a rival concept, indeed the reason for using this rather strange term is its homage to Derrida's notion of *arche-writing*, which is not writing but that which supplied the possibility of writing, that is, the system of difference upon which language is based: *differance* – that which differs and is deferred. Similarly, *arche-health*:

- Is the *becoming* of the organism which made it possible for the first time to speak of health or illness.
- Can never become the object of scientific investigation, without falling back into discourse on health/illness. It is not the outcome of deconstruction of these discourses, it *is* deconstruction: difference and becoming.
- Is multiple in its effects. As difference, it is meaningless to speak of its unity or its division.

Parse *et al.* (1985), in theorising 'health as human becoming', addresses many of the same reflections, and her view is that such a becoming 'is the process of reaching beyond self towards the not-yet . . . The possibles arise from the multi-dimensional experiences and the context of situations, and are opportunities from which alternatives are chosen' (1985: 12). Elsewhere, Parse argues that health is an unfolding, a lived experience which 'cannot be qualified by terms such as good, bad, more or less . . . it is not the opposite of disease or a state that man [*sic*] has, but rather is a continuously changing process' (Parse 1987: 160).

The path to *arche-health* is not an easy one, as we are all territorialised in discourses on the body, health and illness. For those who receive care, we can see the double burden, not only of a dependency, but of the fabrication of a self which is dependent, as a 'patient'. My research in Thailand and Australia, in which I spoke to old people about being recipients of care, demonstrated just that: people spoke of the agony of having to ask for help, of 'being a burden', and of how they learnt never to complain and delay their requests for assistance as long as they could (Fox 1999). Here is the relevance of nomadology for those who care, and for those who receive care: of breaking down that subjectivity, to offer the potential for becoming other, replacing the *proper* by the *gift* in caring and healing relationships. If this is simple to say, then it seems that it is far harder in practice.

Exploring care and the relationships between carers and those who receive care, I have been struck by the extent to which *proper* relations impinge on an area which – intuitively – one might expect to reflect the *gift* (Fox 1995a, 1995b, 1999). We can see the ease with which a gift relationship becomes one of possession and repetition in Bond's (1991) study of the rationalisation and formalising of informal caring by family or friends as part of 'care in the community'. Arrangements under the UK Care in the Community provisions supplies the possibility of financially rewarding informal carers, and providing training to ensure standards of care are achieved. Bond argues that this professionalisation of informal care leads to a loss of the 'caring-about' element of the relationship through four processes: the implementation of expert knowledge, the legitimation of care through medical judgements of health and illness, the individual-isation of behaviour and its consequent de-politicisation (1991: 11–12). We see the substitution of the *vigil* for the *gift*, replacing the investments of love, involvement and generosity which carers supply in caring with a relation of possession, in which the recipient of care is the property of the carer, upon whom the carer 'does' care. In place of the trust, confidence and esteem on the part of the recipient of care towards the carer, invest-ments which make care synonymous with the relationship, the recipient of care enters into a relation of negative dependency.

While rationalisation may be a response to economic or political con-texts, it can also be a response to the ontological threat of the caring relationship. To be in need of care can challenge many psychological and emotional aspects of our sense-of-self at the deepest level, as can the requirement to provide care to another. De Swaan's (1990) study of a cancer ward suggests the difficulties of contemplating a caring relationship based on generosity. Here, as de Swaan describes it, is a libidinal economy in which – while the anger and fear of patients may be distressingly manifest – the anxieties of staff caring for people who are dying are displaced or translated into medical terms. Patients' bodies are cared for, while their emotions go untended; staff do not discuss their upset with colleagues. Doctors and nurses learn not to become attached to seriously ill and dying people: the investment of care, affection and generosity by a member of staff in a patient goes 'unrewarded' when the next day the patient is dead (de Swaan 1990: 42–7). Yet sometimes, even at the level of physical caring, there are possibilities for a *gift*, enabling patients to 'become'.

> To patients it means much when doctors and nurses know how to handle their wounds competently and without fear. The nurse patiently washing a dilapidated patient, changing his clothes, is also the only one who dares touch him without disgust or fear, who quietly and competently handles the body which so torments and frightens the patient . . . [and who] knows how to deal skilfully with the wounds and lumps, in doing so liberating the patients for the moment from their isolation.
>
> (1990: 48)

This extract suggests how one is to understand the force of the *gift*: it is constituted in an open-endedness. It is the moment of 'becoming other', of nomadism which breaks through and beyond discourse, even a discourse on liberation or empowerment (for example, Malin and Teasdale 1991), which tells the other *how* to be more free or more sexy or more something else, and of course in doing so, closes down the possibilities, making the other an appendage of the discourse, inscribed with the power of the word. It does not say what something is, or is not: it allows, for a moment at least, a thing to become multiple, to be both something and another thing and another. Bunting offers as an example of such opening-up

> a family working with a child with special health needs. As the family members work with the child and with one another, each moves beyond the self and the present reality to the possibles that unfold . . . The family's health is the movement towards and the expression of these possibles as they are chosen and lived.
>
> (Bunting 1993: 14)

So, if we are to have a 'manifesto' of the *gift*, it may have to be limiting, rather than all-encompassing (a 'grand' narrative). It might go something like this:

- *If you have to take sides, be on the side of the nomad thought.* The wandering nomad broken free (for however short a time) from discourse. From such a position comes the reflection that acting is to be judged in terms of its consequences, not by any overarching discourse of good or truth.
- *If you must have values, celebrate difference and otherness.* Structures and systems force us into sameness. Recognise the undecidability and openness of the world, its capacity always to become other.
- *If you must desire anything, desire in a spirit of generosity, not for mastery.* Do not try to possess the object of your desire (the Other): make it possible that your relationship is a gift requiring no response or repetition. Accept the gifts which others may make available to you, and take pleasure in them for their own sake.

Conclusion

I suggested earlier that care was paradoxical, and I have outlined the conflicts between the two irreconcilable elements of care, as a *vigil* and as a *gift*. In concluding, I would suggest that this paradox has faced carers as they have sought to valorise their activities. I can illustrate this by reference to James's (1989) writing on emotional labour in a hospice. Emotional labour, she found, was an important contribution to a 'guiding ideology' of 'total care', defined as 'the social, spiritual, emotional and physical care [which] encompasses elements of care which are usually obscured in medical settings . . . and require management and attention in the same way that physical symptoms do' (1989: 20). Staff saw emotional labour as integral to their jobs, but when under pressure, it was emotional labour which tended to get lost among apparently more pressing demands, usually for physical labour (1989: 32–5). James suggests that

> the contradictions of emotion at work, and of emotional labourers in the public domain, are those which arise because 'emotion' is held to contrast with 'rational', because 'emotion' sits uneasily with work-place values of timetabling, predictability and efficiency . . . because emotions belong at home, they are women's work and unskilled.
>
> (1989: 37)

If this is the case, then the efforts by carers to increase the status of their work, to develop the very discourses of 'total care' mentioned by James in her study are understandable and reasonable ways to attempt to maximise the kind of caring which will give support and love to those for whom they care. That is why I commented at the outset that something which has the potential to be empowering can so easily become controlling: a *gift* of care becomes codified and turns into a further element of the disciplinary *vigil* of care.

Perhaps it is necessary to reflect on these conflicting relations of care in terms of ethical engagement with others. Modernism and humanism have, in their pursuit of rationality, relativised moral codes (Bauman 1989; Caputo 1993), yet White (1991) argues that the underlying and unacknowledged ethics of modernism is a *will to mastery*. This can be seen in the emphasis in modern medicine upon the heroic, where the attempt to succeed has sometimes come to be held in greater esteem than any possible benefits of action (Knowles 1977; Fox 1994). At the root of any such claim to justify intervention is the *responsibility to act* (White 1991); theories and codes of professional conduct underpin such active engagement – potentially regardless of outcome or impact.

Along with other postmodern writers (Bauman 1993b; Haber 1994), White goes on to connect postmodern concerns with *difference* with an ethics distinct from that of modernism, based in a *responsibility to otherness*. This is the rejection of a will to mastery, and the substitution of this *proper*, identity-seeking discourse with a *gift* relation, in which that which is other, different and diverse is celebrated. It is a responsibility to be taken seriously, not a casual relativism. White (1991) suggests that the 'mood' of such an engagement based in a *gift* might be one of 'grieving delight'. Quietly allowing the recognition of mortality and limitations of human affairs into everyday life, this mood would

> come alive in the spacing between the self and otherness. The delight with the appearance of the other brings with it the urge to draw it closer. But that urge must realise its limits, beyond which the drawing nearer becomes a gesture of grasping. And that realisation will be palpable only when we are sensitive to the appearance of the particular other as testimony of finitude. Then delight will be paired with a sense of grief or mourning at the fragility and momentary quality of the appearance of the other.
>
> (White 1991: 90)

Grief sensitises us to injustice, while the element of delight deepens the concern with fostering difference: love and difference.

An ethos of a responsibility to otherness requires a radically different conception of human potential or its failing, and of what constitutes the 'care' which engages with this potential. The objective of care in this perspective is to do with becoming and possibilities, about resistance to discourse, and a generosity towards otherness. It is a process which offers promise, rather than fulfilling it, offers possibility in place of certainty, multiplicity in place of repetition, difference in place of identity. It is the *gift* which expects no recognition.

Love and difference: the promise of postmodernism for the engagements which we call 'caring' concerns the reintroduction of the emotional, the non-rationalistic into those interactions. To use Bauman's (1993a) term, it is a *re-enchantment* following the dis-enchantment of modernity with its emphasis on the secular and the rational. Needless to say, this cuts against the grain of modernist disciplines which have based their authority on the knowledge generated by their *gaze* and their *vigil*. Basing care in a relationship of a *gift* necessarily evens out the power balance between client and practitioner, teacher and student, all such engagements become (to subvert Tuckett *et al.*'s (1985) phrase) *meetings between novices*. It forces us to reflect upon what it is to be human, and to engage with other human beings. Care grounded in an ethics and politics of love and difference means there is no longer a simple recipe for a caring which enables; no formula can provide the answer. The celebration of difference entails an abandonment of tried and tested formulae, for any such formula would offer nothing other than a new discourse on 'how to do caring'. But we can point to the kinds of activities within caring which constitute the vigil, and reflect that there is always the possibility of resistance, that anything we do is potentially a *gift*, that things can be different, and take it from there.

References

Anderson, B. M. (1991) 'Mapping the terrain of the discipline, in G. Gray and R. Pratt (eds) *Towards a Discipline of Nursing*, Melbourne: Churchill Livingstone.

Armstrong D. (1983) *The Political Anatomy of the Body*, Cambridge: Cambridge University Press.

Bauman, Z. (1989) *Modernity and the Holocaust*, Cambridge: Polity Press.

—— (1993a) *Intimations of Postmodernity*, London: Routledge.

—— (1993b) *Postmodern Ethics*, Oxford: Blackwell.

Bloor, M. and McIntosh, J. (1990) 'Surveillance and concealment', in S. Cunningham-Burley and N. McKeganey (eds) *Readings in Medical Sociology*, London: Routledge.

Bond, J. (1991) 'The politics of care-giving: the professionalization of informal care', paper presented at the British Sociological Association conference, Manchester.

Brykczynska, G. (1992) 'Caring: a dying art?', in M. Jolley and G. Brykczynska (eds) *Nursing Care: the Challenge to Change*, London: Edward Arnold.

Bukatman, S. (1993) 'Gibson's typewriter', in M. Derv (ed.) *Flame Wars: The Discourse of Cyberculture*, Durham, NC: Duke University Press.

Bunting, S. (1993) *Rosemarie Parse: Theory of Health as Human Becoming*, Newbury Park, CA: Sage.

Butler, J. (1990) *Gender Trouble*, London: Routledge.

Cameron-Traub, E. (1991) 'An evolving discipline', in G. Gray and R. Pratt (eds) *Towards a Discipline of Nursing*, Melbourne: Churchill Livingstone.

Caputo, J. D. (1993) *Against Ethics*, Bloomington, IN: Indiana University Press.

Cixous, H. (1986) 'Sorties', in H. Cixous and C. Clement (eds) *The Newly Born Woman*, Manchester: Manchester University Press.

Critical Art Ensemble (1994) *The Electronic Disturbance*, London: Semiotexte.

Cupitt, D. (1994) *After All: Religion without Alienation*, London: SCM Press.

Deleuze, G. and Guattari, F. (1984) *Anti-Oedipus: Capitalism and Schizophrenia*, London: Athlone.

—— (1986) *Nomadology: The War Machine*, New York: Semiotext(e).

—— (1988) *A Thousand Plateaus*, London: Athlone.

Derrida, J. (1992) *Given Time. 1: Counterfeit Money*, Chicago: Chicago University Press.

de Swaan, A. (1990) *The Management of Normality*, London: Routledge.

Dunlop, M. J. (1986) 'Is a science of caring possible?', *Journal of Advanced Nursing* 11: 661–70.

Forrester, J. (1990) *The Seductions of Psychoanalysis*, Cambridge: Cambridge University Press.

Foucault M. (1976) *Birth of the Clinic*, London: Tavistock.

—— (1979) *Discipline and Punish*, Harmondsworth: Peregrine.

—— (1986) *The Care of the Self*, New York: Random House.

Fox N. J. (1993) *Postmodernism, Sociology and Health*, Buckingham: Open University Press.

—— (1994) 'Anaesthetists, the discourse on patient fitness and the organisation of surgery', *Sociology of Health & Illness* 16: 1–18.

—— (1995a) 'Postmodern perspectives on care: the vigil and the gift', *Critical Social Policy* 15: 107–25.

—— (1995b) 'Professional models of school absence associated with home responsibilities', *British Journal of Sociology of Education* 16: 221–42.

—— (1999) *Beyond Health: Postmodernism and Embodiment*, London: Free Association Books.

Gardner, K. (1992) 'The historical conflict between caring and professionalisation: a dilemma for nursing', in D. A. Gaut (ed.) *The Presence of Caring*, New York: National League for Nursing Press.

Goffman, E. (1970) *Stigma*, Harmondsworth: Penguin.

Goldstein, J. (1984) 'Foucault among the sociologists', *History and Theory* 15: 170–92.

Graham, H. (1979) 'Prevention and health: every mother's business', in Harris, C. (ed.) *The Sociology of Family*, Keele: Keele University Press.

—— (1983) 'Caring: a labour of love', in J. Finch and D. Groves (eds) *A Labour of Love: Women, Work and Caring*, London: Routledge and Kegan Paul.

Gray, G. and Pratt, R. (eds) (1991) *Towards a Discipline of Nursing*, Melbourne: Churchill Livingstone.

Haber, H. (1994) *Beyond Postmodern Politics: Lyotard, Rorty, Foucault*, New York: Routledge.

Haraway, D. (1991) *Simians, Cyborgs and Women*, London: Free Association Books.

Hochschild, A. R. (1983) *A Managed Heart*, Berkeley: University of California Press.

Hogle, L. F. (1995) 'Tales from the crypt: technology meets organism in the living cadaver', in C. H. Gray (ed.) *The Cyborg Handbook*, London: Routledge.

Hugman, R. (1991) *Power in Caring Professions*, Basingstoke: Macmillan.

Inglesby, E. (1992) 'Values and philosophy of nursing: the dynamic of change', in M. Jolley and G. Brykczynska (eds) *Nursing Care: the Challenge to Change*, London: Edward Arnold.

James, N. (1989) 'Emotional labour: skill and work in the social regulation of feelings', *Sociological Review* 37: 15–42.

Kershaw, B. 'Nursing models', in M. Jolley and G. Brykczynska (1992) (eds) *Nursing Care: the Challenge to Change*, London: Edward Arnold.

Kleinman A. (1988) *The Illness Narratives*, New York: Basic Books.

Knowles, J. (1977) *Doing Better and Feeling Worse*, New York: Norton.

Levin, D. M. and Solomon, G. F. (1990) 'The discursive formation of the body in the history of medicine', *Journal of Medical Philosophy* 15: 515–37.

Lynaugh, J. and Fagin, C. (1988) 'Nursing comes of age', *Image* 20: 184–90.

Lynch, K. (1989) 'Solidary labour: its nature and marginalisation', *Sociological Review* 37: 1–14.

Malin, N. and Teasdale, K. (1991) 'Caring versus empowerment: considerations for nursing practice', *Journal of Advanced Nursing* 16: 657–62.

Mauss, M. (1990) *The Gift: the Form and Reason for Exchange in Archaic Societies*, London: Routledge.

Mayall, B. and Foster, M. C. (1989) *Child Health Care*, Oxford: Heinemann.

Moi, T. (1985) *Sexual Textual Politics*, London: Methuen.

Parse, R. (1987) *Nursing Science: Major Paradigms, Theories and Critiques*, Philadelphia: W. B. Saunders.

Parse, R., Coyne, A. B. and Smith, M. J. (1985) *Nursing Research: Qualitative Methods*, Bowie, Maryland: Brady.

Parsons, T. and Fox, R. (1952) 'Illness, therapy and the modern American family', *Journal of Social Issues* 8: 31–44.

Plant, S. (1993) 'Nomads and revolutionaries', *Journal of the British Society for Phenomenology* 24: 88–101.

Rose, N. (1989) *Governing the Soul*, London: Routledge.

Sacks, O. (1986) *The Man Who Thought his Wife was a Hat*, London: Picador.

—— (1995) *An Anthropologist on Mars: Seven Paradoxical Tales*, London: Picador.

Salvage, J. (1989) 'Selling ourselves', *Nursing Times* 85: 24.

Shrock, R. A. (1982) 'Is health visiting a profession?', *Health Visitor* 55: 104–6.

Sims, S. E. R. (1991) 'The nature and relevance of theory for practice', in G. Gray and R. Pratt (eds) *Towards a Discipline of Nursing*, Melbourne: Churchill Livingstone.

Stacey, M. (1988) *The Sociology of Health and Healing*, London: Unwin Hyman.

Thomas, C. (1993) 'Deconstructing concepts of care', *Sociology* 27: 649–70.

Thomas, J. and Dolan, B. (1993) 'The changing face of nursing 2000 and beyond' in B. Dolan (ed.) *Project 2000: Reflection and Celebration*, London: Scutari.

Tuckett, D., Boulton, M., Olson, C. and Williams, A. (1985) *Meetings between Experts*, London: Tavistock.

Twinn, S. F. (1991) 'Conflicting paradigms of health visiting: a continuing debate for professional practice', *Journal of Advanced Nursing* 16: 966–73.

Ungerson, C. (1987) *Policy is Personal: Sex, Gender and Informal Care*, London: Tavistock.

White, S. (1991) *Political Theory and Postmodernism*, Cambridge: Cambridge University Press.

Notes

Introduction

1 See, for example, Straus (1957), Gold (1977), Stacey and Homans (1978), Strong (1979), Clarke (1981), Claus (1983) Scambler (1987), Gerhardt (1989), Turner (1992, 1996), Annandale (1998), Williams *et al.* (1998).

2 Claus (1983), in fact, goes further back to the social aspects of health and disease studied in disciplines like social medicine, public health and anthropology since the eighteenth century – cf. Foucault's (1973, 1977) contention that sociology is merely a branch of social medicine. Modern European medical sociology, in this respect, bears the hallmarks of its antecedent or 'pre-modern' phase.

3 Medical sociology is now the largest single grouping of the British Sociological Association (BSA) with similarly 'healthy' status in both America and Europe.

4 Whilst intimations of postmodern social theorising are beginning to occur within the sociology of health and illness (Fox 1993), to date this has remained a muted theme rather than a paradigmatic force. Medical sociology, in short, seems to have 'weathered the postmodern storm' without too much turbulence.

5 Kemper, for example, traces the beginnings of American sociological interest in emotions back to the 'watershed year' of 1975, arguing that, by the brink of the 1980s, the sociology of emotions was truly 'poised for developmental take-off' (1990: 4). Landmark texts here include Hochschild's *The Managed Heart* (1983) and, more recently, *The Second Shift* (1990); Denzin's (1984) *On Understanding Emotion*; together with a variety of edited collections including Franks and McCarthy's (1989) *The Sociology of Emotions*, Kemper's (1990) *Research Agendas in the Sociology of Emotions*, and two recent British texts, Fineman's (1993) *Emotion in Organizations* and James and Gabe's (1996) *Health and the Sociology of Emotions*. To this, we may add other, more populist texts, such as Goleman's (1996) number one bestseller: *Emotional Intelligence: Why it Can Matter More Than IQ.*

6 Broadly speaking, approaches to emotions can be divided into the organismic (i.e. biological) at one end of the spectrum, and the social constructionist (i.e. cultural) at the other, with 'interactionist' (i.e. biological and social) approaches, as the name implies, somewhere in between.

2 Gender, postmodernism and health

1 Modernist feminism as conceived by Ebert, is a very broad perspective which includes radical, liberal and cultural feminists.

2 It would of course be rash to draw any firm conclusions from this, particularly given that changes in the age structure (not considered here) can induce changes in the male/female differential. But looking at age-standardised rates to account for this, Tickle (1996) finds an overall improvement of 17 per cent for women and 18 per cent for men over the period 1982 to 1992 in the UK.

3   A place for race? Medical sociology and the critique of racial ideology

1 See Banks (1996) and Smith (1996) for useful critiques of the concept of ethnicity along these lines.
2 A historical overview of the emergence of both these modes of thinking is provided by Stocking (1968) in a detailed analysis which remains unsurpassed.
3 See Marmot (1989) for an explicit argument of this sort.
4 See Foucault (1970), Dumont (1986), Habermas (1987), Taylor (1989) and Hannaford (1996) for accounts of the emergence of these ideas.
5 This, of course, is an over-simplification. Medieval societies certainly did produce egalitarian counter-ideologies. However, these shared a worldview in which the human order was not disengaged from the hierarchical order of the cosmos (see Taylor 1989).
6 It should perhaps be pointed out that this inference from Gilroy's work is one that he himself would probably not share.
7 Sheldon and Parker do comment that 'it would be foolish to suggest that all use of race or ethnicity as a ... research tool is misplaced' (1992: 109), although, on the basis of their preceding arguments, it is unclear how one might proceed in this respect. Despite my opposition to their approach, I nevertheless concur with their critique of the essentialism in much of the research literature.
8 Though see Bentley (1987), Williams (1991) and Smaje (1997a).
9 It is this aspect of his writing that Williams (1995) has developed in his discussion of health and lifestyles in relation to class.
10 One of the problems with respect to the latter point is the crude racial/ethnic categories often employed in research and social surveys. Although this in turn partly stems from the lack of adequate theory about the interactions between race, health and other social factors, I regard this failing as largely methodological, and reject the tendency to read legitimate critique of crude racial/ethnic categories in research as if it were a theoretical critique of race and ethnicity, thereby elevating methodology to ontology. See Smaje (1995a) for an overview of these arguments.
11 See Smaje (1995a) for an overview of the British evidence. See also Nazroo (1997) for the most detailed and up-to-date findings.

5   Childhood bodies: social construction and translation

1 The literature on the body is widely known among medical sociologists. The sociology of childhood emerged in the 1980s exemplified in writings by Jenks (1982), James and Prout (1990) and Qvortrup et al. (1994). Its trends and analyses are discussed in James et al. (1998).

6   'Flexible' bodies: science and a new culture of health in the US

1 The issue of causal or other relationships we have in the cultural and economic realms is discussed further in *Flexible Bodies*. The important role of the media (TV, film, advertisements) is taken up there at length also.
2 All names of people interviewed are pseudonyms. *Flexible Bodies'* appendix contains information about their age and occupation.
3 Parker and Slaughter (1990: 32ff.) describe what they aptly call 'management-by-stress in the automobile industry, which is often associated with an overriding fear of job loss: 'The goal is to stretch the system like a rubber band on the point of breaking. Breakdowns in the system are thus made inevitable but are in fact welcomed, because they show where the weak points are, weak points that can then be immediately corrected' (p. 33).
4 In Orange County, California (1992 population 2.48 million), an area of the US where I am now doing research on corporate human resource management, a great number of institutions offer credit for continuing education courses at the post-secondary level. *Not counting* the University of California and California State University, and omitting religiously affiliated schools and vocational schools, there are over forty such institutions.
5 According to Jameson, postmodern forms reveal the 'cultural logic' of late capitalism (1984: 57). They are a 'figuration of . . . the whole world system of present-day multinational capitalism' (p. 79). They are an approach to a representation of a new reality, a peculiar new form of realism, a kind of mimesis of reality (p. 88). For Harvey these forms are also mimetic, 'In the last instance' they are produced by the experience of time-space compression, itself the product of processes in flexible accumulation (1989: 344).
6 Michel Callon suggested this in conversations with me.

7   'Recombinant bodies': narrative, metaphor and the gene

1 Haraway (1989) argues that 'fiction is inescapably implicated in a dialectic of the true (natural) and the counterfeit (artifactual) . . . [both] rooted in an epistemology that appeals to experience' (p. 4) and linked through processes of scientific and extra-scientific story-telling.
2 See for example: Martin (1994); Butler (1993); Bordo (1993); Grosz (1994); Waldby (1996).
3 Michael Crichton and Robin Cook (both medical doctors by training) are prominent examples of that authorial crossover, although their fictional works could not be described as exactly celebratory of science. Crichton's *Jurassic Park* and *The Lost World*, for example, provide a significant critique of the epistemic economies of recombinant genetic science, yet this critique is articulated through an alternative scientific perspective (chaos theory) embodied in the character of Ian Malcolm.
4 There is, however, a marginal sub-genre of such texts which provide critiques of science and medicine (e.g. Elkington 1985; Piller and Yamamoto 1988; Garrett 1994). These texts appear infrequently, rarely in numbers greater than two or three at any one time (quite often there are none at all).
5 Elsewhere (Steinberg 1997), for example, I have discussed the constitution of the gene as monad in machine within both professional and popular literatures on preimplantation diagnosis (genetic biopsy on embryos produced through *in vitro* fertilisation).

6 Foucault (1977). See also Steinberg (1996b and 1997) for further discussion of genes as 'docile' bodies in the Foucauldian sense.

7 Yanchinski's discussion of using genetically engineered *E. coli* to produce human growth hormone provides an edifying illustration of the inter-embeddedness of commercial and medicalised logics in her bio-industrial utopia: 'Human growth hormone is constantly in demand for treating dwarfism, and currently most of it comes from the brains of human cadavers. Unlimited supplies of this scarce material would not only ensure that all dwarfs received treatment, but would also enable doctors to consider treating "short stature" children who are simply undersized for their age and help heal bone fractures. New material, new niches' (1985: 102).

8 As Yanchinski puts it: '[Genetically manipulated] bacteria and yeasts are highly specialized and overbred, the aristocrats of the microbe world, and they thrive only in the highly artificial environment of the fermenter. Change the temperature by a degree or two, or the acidity by a fraction, or delay adding a food component, and they react badly, often reverting back to the wild type or simply dying' (p. 20).

In addition to the class discourse through which it is science that confers 'aristocratic' identity to the gene, there is also a colonial subtext embedded in the evolutionary notion of 'wild types', those primitive entities to which the cultured gene reverts without the civilising accoutrements of the laboratory hot house.

9 Yanchinski reiterates an early conceptualisation, in the history of genetic science, that 'RNA was the "factory foreman" who directed the manufacture of proteins by transcribing the *blueprint* laid down by the "boss" DNA' (p. 27).

10 Yanchinski writes: 'Clever chemical engineers . . . incorporated the bench-top chemistry into a range of "gene machines" which busy scientists not so skilled in chemistry could buy to make gene fragments' (p. 49).

11 The fourth biotechnology era can be said to have begun with the advent of genetic engineering in the early 1970s. The tremendous impact of this technology, which involves inserting foreign genes into microbial cells, thus converting the host into a protein-making factory, will only be truly felt in twenty years' time (Yanchinski 1985: 15).

12 Weiss (1987) examines efficiency as a class ideal and industrial logic underpinning eugenic politics as articulated through the philosophy of William Schallmayer.

13 Weiss further argues that the logic of efficiency 'formed the common bond which united those race hygienists who accepted ideologies of Aryan supremacy and those non-racist eugenicists, like Schallmayer, who vehemently rejected them (p. 6).

14 Of 'immobilized cell technology', Yanchinski writes: 'But most exciting of all is the thought of . . . cells, instead of floating suspended in their own food [but rather] fixed to a solid support – in a tall steel column say, through which flowed a fine stream bearing all the food nutrients the cells need. If the column were cheap enough, it could even be thrown away when the cells were past further use' (p. 24).

15 Jones writes: '[S]ome biologists believe that it is worth looking for treasure in the depths of the molecular forest – after all, no-one has any idea what could be hidden there (1993: 125).

16 Patricia Hill Collins (1990) uses the term 'controlling myths' to describe the dominant cultural mythologies invested in commonsense constructions of African American maleness and femaleness. In particular, she locates these

mythologies within the specific history of European colonial exploitation of the African continent and the enslavement of African peoples.

17 The notion of 'nonsense DNA' imputes 'meaninglessness' as an essential property of these sequences (rather than, for example, a reflection of the limitations of the science/scientist).

18 See, for example, Strobel (1991) for a discussion of the ways in which imperial conquest in India was, in part, rationalised through references to Indian women's status as index of its putatively lesser civilisation.

19 A similarly disturbing and suggestively anti-Semitic reference is taken up in the visual 'gag' deployed to critique Lamark's genetic experiments (cutting off the tails of mice to test his hypothesis that genetic traits are acquired environmentally). The figure of Lamark tossing amputated mouse tails into a 'tail pail' laments 'This is the twentieth generation and – damn it – still they've all got tails!' The wifely figure of a woman in the background replies 'But Jews have been doing the same thing for years'. The textual juxtaposition of Jews and tails and the veiled reference to ritual circumcision recuperates racialised mythologies of difference/deviance, embodied, in part, through mutilation. See, for example, Gilman (1991) for further discussion of the Jew as deviance embodied, and the role of circumcision in that corporealisation.

8   The politics of 'disabled' bodies

1 We are not sure that it is possible or meaningful to identify a group of 'disability theorists'. In using the term we have in mind a heterogeneous group of writers and researchers. Some of these are themselves self-identified as disabled and politically involved in various cultural and political movements of disabled people. Others are not disabled – or have not declared themselves to be so – but are sympathetic to the aims and strategies of the movement. It is also important to recognise that the movements of disabled people in Britain and elsewhere, notably the USA, vary in terms of the languages they use, the theoretical analyses they develop and the political strategies they adopt.

11   The ritual of health promotion

1 A critical theory of health, however, must explore the 'continuity' or complex articulations of any one axis with other crucial axes which organise meaning and experience as well as other domains of experience which are in some ways continuous with health. Each axis is an analytical focus and therefore a momentary restriction of complexity, a way of addressing certain questions about health discourse as well as the relation of health to other discourses.

2 The depth and complexity – historical, cultural, experiential – of this symbolic-dispositional opposition extend far beyond the one structural contradiction I am discussing in this essay. Rieff (1966) argues that 'control and release' are constituent symbolic properties of every culture. Throughout the history of western culture, oppositions that share certain properties with the one I am discussing have been interpreted from various perspectives: for example, the Apollonian and Dionysian, mind/body dualism, and the Freudian psychic structure.

3 Again, the issues are more complicated than I have space to discuss here. Ambivalence is not only a matter of the internalised co-presence of opposing mandates, a question of more or less of the one or the other. Each side of the contradiction, articulated with meanings, values and ideologies associated with but not confined to them, are also sites of ambivalence. The plurality of meanings attached to control and discipline on the one hand, and release,

desire, and pleasure on the other, are integral to physical and psychological life. Though structured in domination, these sets are also the symbolic frames through which deeply felt longings, not simply the products of domination, are experienced and expressed. Both work and self-control and consumption and pleasure are the sources of and means to personal and collective practices that are creative, transformative and emancipatory. The cultural force and breadth of these polarities also account, I am arguing, for their ritualisation.

4 I have purposely restricted my discussion to 'middle-class' approaches to health promotion. Ethnicity, class, gender, age, sexual orientation, and other demographic and subcultural factors complicate the theoretical perspective I have advanced here, so will specific political and economic circumstances, including a range of other factors influencing the ideological success of economic reordering or the level of suspicion of government or of other institutions that sponsor health promotion messages. My claim, however, is that, at least in the United States and probably in other advanced capitalist cultures, the axis of health promotion discourse I have identified is a structuring feature of varied subcultural discourses, all the more to the extent that they are also middle class. Recent work on 'lay epidemiology' is noteworthy for its theoretical advances on how 'people assimilate official information in a creative and active way, within the contexts of everyday life, and against the backdrop of personal and shared experiences' (Bury 1994: 29; Davison *et al.* 1991, 1992; see also Backett 1992; Lupton 1995).

13 Health care and consumption

1 Unfortunately there is insufficient space to consider the changing relationship between the health service provided by the state and market and health care provided by households and voluntary organisations.

15 Emotions, social structure and health: re-thinking the class inequalities debate

1 This chapter is a revised version of an article which previously appeared in *Sociology* (Williams 1998a).

2 Organismic theorists include Darwin (1955[1885]), for whom emotion is an 'archaic remnant' of instinctual bodily gesture, Freud (1984[1923]) who saw emotions in 'dammed up' libidinal and 'signal function' terms (e.g. anxiety as the model for all other emotions) and James and Lange (1922), for whom emotion was the brain's conscious reaction to instinctual visceral change.

3 Lynch (1985) makes a similar point in his book '*The Language of the Heart: the Human Body in Dialogue*'.

4 See also Lyon's (1994) account of the relationship between emotions and respiration.

5 For other methodologically rigorous and empirically convincing examples of this life-events and illness link – including anxiety, schizophrenia, appendicitis, menstrual disorders, and multiple sclerosis – see Brown and Harris (1989).

6 Perhaps the first person to systematically explore this link was the 'sexual radical' Reich (1983[1942], 1969[1951], 1949), whose work on 'character armour' and its translation into 'muscular tension' and rigid bodily posture has now been transformed, via contemporary discourses on stress, from a psychotherapeutic insight into conventionalised wisdom within popular culture.

16   Emotions and gender in US health care contexts: implications for change and stasis in the division of labour

1 The changing US health care system is a theoretically attractive case for analysis because of the rapidity of alterations in all sectors of the system. For example, movement away from fee-for-service and new emphases on cost accounting practices and procedures which have focused on care. These have an impact on all providers in the structures involved. Intriguing changes in other westernised, bureaucratised health care systems such as the United Kingdom and Canada merit future comparative analysis. They represent different structural elements and different emphases on fee-for-service.

2 These strategies have also generated a fresh set of caregiving and emotional problems for families, friends and support groups who pick up care when the patient leaves the hospital early or is not admitted (Olesen 1997b: 405; Pescosolido *et al.* 1997: 78–9). Thus emotional issues in rationalising health care organisations often extend beyond the organisation's caregiving staff and the formal boundaries of the organisation or context.

3 An HMO (health maintenance organisation) is a group practice which also owns hospitals. It enrolls members whose employers pay dues or who pay dues themselves and who receive care. Depending on the type of contract the individual member has, he or she pays nothing or a very modest co-payment, e.g. $5.00 for a physician visit or procedure. Members can choose a physician or are assigned to a doctor. Though HMOs are not-for-profit, they, too, are under pressure to cut costs (Passell 1977).

4 Some worry that such an emphasis on customer satisfaction may, for instance, in the case of nurses, lead to an emphasis on production of customer/patient loyalty to the detriment of care (Goodrick *et al.* 1997: 46).

5 Is nurses' emotional labour utilised to manipulate and control patient emotions in order to realise administrative health agendas? O'Brien (1994) found this to be the case in a study of British nurses. However, another British study of a residential home for the elderly argues that the care assistants themselves utilised emotional work, that is their own emotions (not those prescribed or proscribed), to control residents and assure smooth delivery of care (Treweek 1996).

6 An additional problem is the emotional impact of downsizing on remaining staff and their ability to express emotions (Pescosolido *et al.* 1997: 83).

7 Gender *qua* gender is, as Butler (1990, 1993) and other postmodernists have pointed out, unstable and continually performed and created, sometimes subversively (e.g., gender bending displays of clothing, hair style, mannerisms which explode the very meaning of 'sex' and the 'materiality' of the body itself). How emotionality might be part of such subversive performances in health care contexts such as the hospital or clinic raises the issue of the interplay between the instability of gender and the obduracy of occupational stratification and the attendant sentimental order.

8 Davies (1995) has examined this issue in British nursing.

9 James' (1994: 114) research has analysed differential and deferential divisions of emotional labour in a British context where patients were told of their cancer diagnosis. Her findings show continued dominance of high status roles, mostly male roles, in this process. In this difficult situation lower status persons often served as 'status shields' (Hochschild 1983: 14–75). 'Status shields' refer to persons in lower status roles who deflect, absorb and shield higher status individuals from emotional problems, for example, the secretary who fends for the supervisor. In James's study the very doing of emotional labour reaffirmed both the gender and occupational stratification arrangements.

10 A magnet hospital is one of 41 US hospitals which the American Nurses Association designated in 1982 as hospitals with reputations for excellent patient care and known as good places for nurses to work (Kramer and Schmalenberg 1988). Scattered bed hospitals are magnet and non-magnet hospitals, where AIDS patients are found throughout the hospital wards. The dedicated AIDS unit in non-magnet hospitals, by contrast, cares only for AIDS patients.

Index

UNIVERSITY OF
PAISLEY LIBRARY